IDEOLOGY
ON A
FRONTIER

Recent titles in
Contributions in Intercultural and Comparative Studies
Series Editor: Ann M. Pescatello

Power and Pawn: The Female in Iberian Families, Societies,
and Cultures
Ann M. Pescatello

Tegotomono: Music for the Japanese Koto
Bonnie C. Wade

Historical Archaeology: A Structural Approach in an
African Culture
Peter R. Schmidt

Sacred Words: A Study of Navajo Religion and Prayer
Sam D. Gill

Liberalism in an Illiberal Age: New Culture Liberals in
Republican China, 1919-1937
Eugene Lubot

Revolution and Counterrevolution: Mozambique's War of
Independence, 1964-1974
Thomas H. Henriksen

Flying Dragons, Flowing Streams: Music in the Life
of San Francisco's Chinese
Ronald Riddle

Communicating with Quotes: The Igbo Case
Joyce Penfield

Language, Science, and Action: Korzybski's General Semantics—
A Study in Comparative Intellectual History
Ross Evans Paulson

The Justice of the Western Consular Courts in
Nineteenth-Century Japan
Richard T. Chang

Performance Practice: Ethnomusicological Perspectives
Gerard Béhague, editor

IDEOLOGY ON A FRONTIER

The Theological Foundation of Afrikaner Nationalism, 1652-1910

J. Alton Templin

Contributions in Intercultural and Comparative Studies, Number 11

GREENWOOD PRESS
Westport, Connecticut • London, England

Library of Congress Cataloging in Publication Data

Templin, J. Alton.
  Ideology on a frontier.

  (Contributions in intercultural and comparative
studies, ISSN 0147-1031 ; no. 11)
  Bibliography: p.
  Includes index.
  1. Afrikaners—Ethnic identity.   2. Afrikaners—
History.   3. South Africa—History.   4. Theology,
Doctrinal—South Africa—History.   5. Nationalism—
Religious aspects—Christianity.   I. Title.   II. Series.
DT888.T32   1984   968'.0043936   83-10884
ISBN 0-313-24104-X

Library of Congress Catalog Card Number: 83-10884
ISBN: 0-313-24104-X
ISSN: 0147-1031

First published in 1984

Greenwood Press
A division of Congressional Information Service, Inc
88 Post Road West
Westport, Connecticut 06881

Printed in the United States of America
10 9 8 7 6 5 4 3 2 1

Copyright Acknowledgments

Grateful acknowledgment is given for permission to reprint from the article published by
Gordon Allport in *The Crane Review* (Fall 1959) entitled "Religion and Prejudice," and other
copyrighted materials from *The Crane Review*, copyright 1959 by Crane Theological School,
Tufts University, Medford, Massachusetts.

We are also indebted to *The Iliff Review* for permission to reprint portions of the article "Implications for a Social Concern in the Theology of Calvin," Fall issue, 1969, vol. 26, no. 3; and
for portions adapted with permission from the American Society of Church History from an
article entitled "God and the Covenant in the South African Wilderness," which appeared in
Church History 37 (September 1968): 281-297.

Ad quattuor e praeceptoribus eximiis meis:

Floyd L. Sampson
Martin Rist
William H. Bernhardt
George Huntston Williams

From the very beginning of its history two national concepts have dominated Jewish life—the concepts of the Chosen
People and the Promised Land. . . . From the ancient Hebrews
nationalism everywhere took over these two concepts: the first
of a unique and exclusive relationship, God or History having
selected one people as pre-eminently called upon to serve a
Cause, often the greatest and ultimate Cause; and, second, the
concept of a part of this earth being singled out by destiny and
mystery to be owned forever by the one people. (Hans Kohn,
Zion and the Jewish National Idea, p. 179.)

An African nationalist of South Africa recently stated:

We are fighting against nobody. Our energies and forces
are directed against a set-up, against a conception and a
myth. (This myth—others call it racial superiority, others call
it *Herrenvolkism*, others, white leadership with justice, or
white supremacy.) We are fighting against the Calvinistic
doctrine that a certain nation was specially chosen by God to
lead, guide, and protect other nations. (Philip Kgosama,
quoted in Jack Mendelssohn, *God, Allah and Ju Ju*, pp. 27-28.)

The nation justifies its existence and aspirations and tries
to prove its worth by raising the appeal of a special assignment, purpose, calling or destiny. . . . The concept of a special
destiny leads to the growth of a historical legend and of a
national ideology; the conception of a calling gives form to the
nation and with it a feeling of uniqueness, assurance and self-
esteem. Each nation acquires an ideology of special destiny
that is inseparable from its national historical legend; the
Afrikaner people is no exception. (F. A. van Jaarsveld, *The
Afrikaner's Interpretation of South African History*, p. 5.)

Contents

List of Maps

Preface

One of the phenomena currently receiving careful historical consideration is nationalism. National ideologies, however, are based on varying factors depending on geography, historical development, and cultural considerations. Furthermore, one of the dimensions of most homogeneous national constructions is a theological justification—a concern which is considered ultimate. The analysis of one aspect of Afrikaner nationalism presented in this book seeks to make a contribution to cultural understanding by isolating one specific theological concept from the cultural milieu in which it is deeply imbedded. This study is a theological history because the Afrikaners saw themselves in terms more glorious than many other nationalisms. Their "cause" was God's cause, and their nation was an elect people, called out from others in the area for a unique task, at once political, racial, and theological. This organizing concept functioned as an ideology based on theological words rather than as a purely theological construction.

Afrikaner self-consciousness was not always expressed by the actors in the historical situation but was an interpretation read back into history from a later generation. Evidence contemporary with the events and supporting the growing theological self-consciousness is scant. Various tendencies, however, are sifted from political and sociological data. The sources used include records of the Dutch East India Company and of the Reformed churches of the Netherlands and of South Africa; narratives of travelers through South Africa in the eighteenth century; papers of the South African and British archives relative to South Africa; diaries; letters in newspapers of the period; tracts; speeches of Afrikaner leaders; and histories of the period, which give a special nationalistic interpretation to their South African history.

Two sections of this study have been printed in earlier versions. Portions of Chapter III are adapted with permission from the American Society of Church History from an article entitled "God and the Covenant in the South African Wilderness," which appeared in *Church History* 37 (September, 1968):   281-297.   A section of Chapter X was used in an article, "Implications for a Social Concern in the Theology of Calvin," which appeared in *The Iliff Review*, XXVI, no. 3, (Fall, 1969), pp. 33-44. This is used with the permission of The Iliff School of Theology and the editor of *The Iliff Review*. In addition, the material in Chapter X, footnote 34, is quoted with permission of the editor of *The Crane Review*, from an article by Gordon Allport which appeared in Vol. II, (1959), pp. 8-9. Portions of Chapters VI and VII have been presented as lectures to the African History section of the Rocky Mountain Social Science Association meeting in Lubbock, Texas; the American Academy of Religion meeting in Chicago; and the American Society of Church History meeting in New Orleans.

I should like to express appreciation for the contributions of the three mentors most critically involved in this study.   George Huntston Williams of Harvard University first called attention to the theological dimension within Afrikaner nationalism and helped to sharpen the focus of the study on the doctrine of election as the basis of the ideology. He contributed invaluably to the precise formulation of the systematic analysis in Chapter IX. The late Gordon W. Allport was concerned that the dynamics of social and psychological factors have their rightful place.   He was especially helpful with respect to the sections dealing with racial strife and conflict between Afrikaners and British and contributed suggestions embodied in Chapter X.   Robert I. Rotberg, now of the Massachusetts Institute of Technology, from his knowledge of African history, made many suggestions which helped to clarify the complex African tribal background. He also made many suggestions that helped to place the study in its precise historical framework in which the theological dimension of the culture is allowed to have its rightful dominant role.   All three men read various sections during the preparation, and for their concern and efforts on my behalf, I express my sincere gratitude.

Research in the Republic of South Africa was made possible by three study and travel grants.   These were from: the Joint Committee on African Studies of the Social Science Research Council and the American Council of Learned Societies; the Research Associates Program of the Graduate School of International Studies, The University or Denver; and the Alumni Association of The Iliff School of Theology.   To each of these organizations, I express my sincere appreciation.   For hospitable courtesy and special help during my stay in the Republic of South Africa, I should like to acknowledge indebtedness to: F. A. van Jaarsveld of the Rand Afrikaans University (Johannesburg); Albert Geyser of the Department of Theology of the University of the Witwatersrand (Johannesburg); C. F. J. Muller, D. W. Krüger, and M. Boucher, all of the University of South Africa (Pretoria); the Rev. Bouke Spoelstra of the Sunnyside Gereformeerde Kerk of Pretoria; C. F. Rex, archivist of the Hervormde Kerk Archives (Pretoria); the staff of the Afrikaans section of the Library of the University of the Witwatersrand (Johannesburg); the staff of the Afrikaans section of the Johannesburg Public Library; S. du Toit, of the University of Potchefstroom; T. N. Hanekom and Pieter A. Verhoef of the University of Stellenbosch; the staff of the Jagger Library of the University of Cape Town; librarians of the University of Natal (Pietermaritzburg); the archivist of the State Archives (Pretoria); and the archivist of the Nederduits Gereformeerde Kerk (Cape Town). Finally, I am indebted to the Rev. Fred van Wyk, the Rev. W. B. de Villiers, and the Rev. Beyers Naudé of the Christian Institute of South Africa (Johannesburg) for arranging contacts for me with many of the above-named individuals. All contributed immeasurably to the success of my research in their country.

Many people helped in the preparation of this study. To all of them I express my sincere thanks: Priscilla Kirchbaum and Patricia Batsel, research librarians, assisted with many aspects of research, and located books and documents in many places; Eleanor Gage, Margaret Manion and Karen Bornstein typed many portions; Maurya Horgan and Paul Kobelski efficiently prepared the final copy. Finally, to my wife, Dorothy, who has lived with my South African studies for many years, I express appreciation for constant interest and encouragement in my endeavors. My children, Kayla, Revae, and Bryce, are just beginning to think historically and do not know whether they contributed anything substantial to the study.

J. A. T.

IDEOLOGY ON A FRONTIER

Introduction

In our time Africa has come alive, with new interest being developed in all sections of the continent, especially the area south of the equator. Much of this burgeoning interest is centered in the emergence from colonialism to independence of nations of Africans, such as Angola, Mozambique, Zimbabwe, Namibia, and others. The Republic of South Africa, by contrast, was founded as one of the major white Christian settlements in African and has a unique history and theology. The Dutch Boers (farmers) in a previous century were the ancestors of the present Afrikaners who in the nineteenth and early twentieth centuries developed a strong nationalist spirit. The Afrikaners' ideology, closely associating nationalism with a theological motif, plays an increasingly significant role in South Africa today.

Leaders of many developing societies form certain justifications or objectives for their culture. Some assume that theological goals are irrelevant—as in contemporary Russian communist theory—and seek to deny all theological influence. More likely, however, a culture has as one or more of its basic elements certain theological ideas or justifications, whether explicit or implicit. These may or may not become the basis of their emerging ideology.

In the Judaeo-Christian tradition, several different options have been chosen, drawn from some section of either the Old Testament or the New Testament. The Wilderness or Paradise motif has been widely used at various times in history.[1] Closely related to this has been the concept of a Promised Land to which God is leading His people.[2] Often an emphasis on freedom from oppression has led certain leaders to recall the similarities between their situation and that of Moses and the Exodus.[3] Others have seen themselves as reenacting the Joshua and conquest motif. The Radical Reformers of Münster (1534) based their expectations of God's immediate

triumph over wrong on their close and literal reading of the Book of Revelation.[4] Less militaristic Reformers such as the Dutch Mennonites sought
to justify their culture as a restitution of the early church based on a close
reading of the Book of Acts.[5] The Disciples of Christ in the United States
followed a similar restitution theme when their leader stated as a guiding
maxim: "Where the Bible [New Testament] speaks we speak, and where the
Bible is silent we are silent."[6] English and American Shakers based their
communal doctrines on the biblical record: "All that believed were together, and had all things in common; and sold their possessions and goods;
and parted them to all men as every man had need" (Acts 2:45).[7]

One such motif with a long and significant history is the chosen people
or elect people concept. An example of this is the Deuteronomic emphasis
of the Jews as God's chosen people,[8] now much modified in contemporary
Zionist theory.[9] The Christian doctrine of election has its origin in a
modification of the concept of a chosen people, developed by the Apostle
Paul and the early church and used by Augustine and Reformers such as
Luther, Calvin, and Zwingli.[10] This idea of election has received serious
scholarly attention throughout the centuries. H. H. Rowley wrote concerning *The Biblical Doctrine of Election,* Krister Stendahl analyzed the idea of
election in the Gospels, and Cyril Eastwood surveyed the doctrine from
biblical times to the later Middle Ages.[11] Most recently William Haller
studied this concept as it was developed into an extensive legend in Eliza-
bethan England following the appearance of John Foxe's *Actes and Monu-
mentes (The Book of Martyrs, 1554, 1559, 1563, 1572)* and the theological
interpretations derived therefrom.[12] John Calvin spelled out the doctrine
more completely in *The Institutes,* as well as in *De Aeterna Dei Predestinatione,* as he coordinated the concept with his doctrine of the Providence of
God.[13]

When theological motifs are adopted by a culture, they are also
adapted and transformed for various existential reasons, political, sociological, or cultural. Resulting developments are often as much aberrations
from as logical deductions from the beginning presuppositions. Concepts
often become so twisted that they are almost unrecognizable and would be
repudiated by the originator. The example, Adolf Hitler's emphasis on the
Aryan "race" as a super-race with authority to obliterate non-Aryans is an
aberration of the concept of one people chosen by God or by destiny.[14] In
any society the full-blown cultural complex cannot be completely understood until the underlying theological motifs and aberrations have been
explored.[15] The theological ideas adopted in a given culture and the modifications that develop help us to understand the ultimate concerns that
shaped the developing society.[16]

By the term *ideology* in the title of this book, we mean a set of "sche-
matic images of the social order."[17] Thus defined, "the function of the
ideology is to make an autonomous politics possible by providing the
authoritative concepts that render it meaningful, the suasive images by

means of which it can be sensibly grasped."[18] This term is not meant to be judgmental, as though it refers only to misguided interpretation, although this may indeed be one of the outcomes. Whether the elements woven together into an ideology are interpreted accurately or are patterned after wishful thinking is not the issue. What is at stake is the assumption that all societies, or subgroups within societies, are organized around ideologies. Some of the more familiar are Americanism, or a master Aryan race, or Christian nationalism as in South Africa. Furthermore, in this study we shall see how the ideological development in South Africa was one possible response to many strains and challenges that confronted the loyal Boers.[19] This study seeks to be analytic rather than to form premature evaluation. After a study of the development of that ideology, or as I more often refer to it as folk theology, I analyze the completed ideology in the last two chapters.

In seeking to understand themselves and their challenges, the Afrikaners took a decidedly religious or theological direction. Even this interpretation is one dimension of ideology as Geertz summarizes it: "A religion is a system of symbols which acts to establish powerful pervasive and long-lasting moods and motivations in men by formulating conceptions of a general order of existence and clothing these conceptions with such an aura of factuality that the moods and motivations seem uniquely realistic."[20]

Each of the elements of this definition will be found in the developing society of South Africa, although these specific words will not necessarily be employed. Furthermore, Geertz provides theoretical formulation for the function of religion in this, as in all other societies:

> On the one hand, it objectivizes moral and aesthetic preferences by depicting them as the imposed conditions of life implicit in a world with a particular structure, as mere common sense given the unalterable shape of reality. On the other, it supports these received beliefs about the world's body by invoking deeply felt moral and aesthetic sentiments as experiential evidence for their truth.[21]

This results in a certain circularity of reasoning, as we shall see. Assumptions such as these will be elaborated more fully in this study, using terms such as *ultimate concern* (Tillich), *predestination* or *elect people* (Calvin), or *theological history* (George Williams).

The theological interpretations developed by the Afrikaners were an outgrowth of, and indirectly related to, the wide influence of the Reformed faith. The Boers who developed the most extensive white European society on the African continent were continually sustained and encouraged by strong adherence to the tenets of their religious faith. As we undertake such a study of the ideological background of South Africa, we must analyze the use of Reformed theological terms and note the function of theological ideas in the society.

When we look to this European settlement in South Africa, we encounter another modified version of the idea of one people chosen by God for furthering His will and preserving His culture in a hostile environment. The Dutch who were the original settlers in South Africa, and whose descendants still form the most numerous section of Europeans in that land, were citizens of a proud nation and evaluated their history with theological assumptions. Their victory over the Spanish after eighty years made a deep impression on their ideology, and they referred to this triumph many times in later years. The princes of Orange were later considered God's chosen agents in history, and, by inference, the Dutch Protestants held a high place in God's favor. In Deuteronomic terms, the Dutch later assumed that prosperity was evidence of God's approval, while adversity was evidence of the wrath of God sent to backsliders.[22]

The Dutch were members of the Calvinistic Dutch Reformed church. This denomination was one of the major Reformed groups, along with the Huguenots and the German Reformed, participating in the Synod of Dort (1618-1619), where the idea of divine election was made a cardinal doctrine of the faith.[23] Thereafter the Reformed peoples adhered to the decrees of the Synod of Dort more than to the earlier Heidelberg Catechism and the Belgic Confession as the creedal statements of their faith. The Dutch in the far-flung reaches of the commercial empire of the Dutch East India Company took with them the assumption that their "divinely" chosen princes of Orange and their Reformed doctrine of divine election were closely related. As the Dutch burghers in South Africa began to develop their culture in their newly-adopted homeland, various other factors entered to shape and to modify their original concepts. They were confronted in turn by three major challenges to which they reacted at various times in their development. First, they confronted the elements of nature —arid regions and steep mountains ranges—and the limitations of economic resources and equally limited outlets for their produce. Second, they confronted many African tribes, some with only rudimentary social development and others highly organized competitors for land and livestock. Third, they confronted the "foreign" and even "repressive" encroachment of the British Empire.

Two adjectives, hence two indications of sources of tradition, are often used to characterize the Afrikaners' self-understanding: *Calvinistic* and *biblical*. This culture at the southern tip of Africa was at first composed of Dutch East India Company personnel and early immigrants from the Netherlands, augmented in time by religious refugees—Huguenots from France and German Reformed from the Holy Roman Empire. In the development of the frontier society of South Africa, certain biblical episodes were elaborately developed and made to apply directly to pioneer life. Cultural election and divine election were amalgamated into one basic assumption about the correctness of the policies of the loyal Dutch burghers, whether opposing the Dutch East India Company's rule in Cape Town or building a nation in the Traansvaal. The Rev. Coenraad Spoelstra stated in a sermon in 1897: "Brothers and Sisters, there are repeated instances of the noteworthy similarities which exist between Israel's history and the history of our land and people."[24] This one biblical and Calvinistic doctrine is singled out for special study as it wove its way through the Dutch and the British periods in South African history, down to the outbreak of the Boer War (1899) and on to the formation of the Union of South Africa (1910). This is the doctrine of the elect people.

The thesis of this study is that because the concept of the elect people is one of the theological elements underlying the total development of Afrikaner culture, this culture cannot be completely understood until this motif is recognized and analyzed. We attempt to show that the reaction of the Afrikaners in the various cultural crises was colored by a prior assumption that they could discern God's will and were in some sense chosen by God to maintain His culture in the face of all odds. In turn, their successful reaction in times of crisis strengthened their prior assumption, and the concept became completely circular. The modifications in the theological idea thus introduced formed not only the basis of the growing Afrikaner nationalism of the late nineteenth century but also the basis of the Wars of Independence (1880-1881, 1899-1902). These theological ideas had no small influence in the formation of the Union of South Africa in 1910, the doctrine of *apartheid* following the election of 1948, and even of the republic in 1961.

When we consider the elaboration of the doctrine of the elect people, we must recognize at least two possible ways this could have developed. The theological doctrine might have been placed before the people as a norm and the systematic exposition evolved from it. This is similar to the situation that existed, for example, in early New England where the theological framework was presupposed from the beginning. In New England there was an attempt to establish a holy commonwealth based on theological doctrines, an educated ministry, and well-trained governmental leaders. At a very early stage of New England history, a university was established to maintain the high level of cultural development.

The development in South Africa, however, forms a sharp contrast to this example. This settlement was not based on any aspect of systematic theology. What theological concepts they derived were much more rooted in the culture on the frontier and the popular piety of the people. The original settlers went to South Africa not for religious but for economic reasons. There was provision for religious leadership at the inception of the settlement, but with the moving frontier these provisions quickly became inadequate. There was practically no educated leadership, theological or otherwise, on the frontier for two centuries. The first attempt at higher education came two hundred years after the first settlers arrived.

This was the organization of a Board of Examiners in 1858, the forerunner of the University of Cape Town (1873). The first theological seminary was organized at Stellenbosch in 1859 to counteract European influence. Before this every person had to travel the long, arduous distance to Europe for an education. The theological development in South Africa was so different from other Calvinistic settlements as to make comparison difficult.

The concept of an elect people in South Africa was not the result of a carefully constructed theological formula; rather, the concept "blundered into being" from a particular cultural matrix.[25] The roots of the idea of a particular people selected by God for a particular destiny were deeply imbedded in the cultural development of the nation even before the ideas were enunciated, certainly before any attempt was made to systematize them.

This analysis is presented as a study in theological history. By this we mean a study of a particular theological motif as it was manifest in or adapted to historical situations. No attempt is made to be complete with respect to the total political history, the institutional church, race relations during the period, or British imperial policies. Rather, each of these aspects of the cultural history is drawn on only to establish the thesis that the underlying theological assumptions cut across and influenced all aspects of this developing culture.

To substantiate this thesis, we survey various developments in South African society that exemplify theological assumptions. Often these assumptions were not explicitly stated because the basic presuppositions were not systematized or verbalized by the participants in the historical drama. On many occasions theological ideas were read back into previous history. This practice gives us more understanding about the period in which they were written than the era about which they were writing. The Bible was often used, but selectively. Theological terminology was used, especially in times of crisis, to instill loyalty and a sense of common purpose among the faithful followers. We may assume that similar theological ideas were held by many Afrikaners in times of peace even though they were not stated. We may also assume that the leaders who used biblical and theological ideas to justify their cause either spoke for a large portion of their followers or were so convincing in their "exegesis" that their followers gladly joined in the cause.

The challenges of the South African frontier caused unique modifications in the doctrine of the elect people. These permutations appear in several aspects of the culture: Afrikaners believed they must maintain a scriptural framework for their government and for their personal lives; they assumed that cultural advancement was a sign of God's approval; they sought freedom from Dutch, or more usually from British, domination; they fought to maintain their language whether Dutch or Afrikaans; they assumed they were superior to Africans educationally and culturally, and hence more surely were chosen; and they integrated the theological ideology into their total culture. Afrikaner leaders saw themselves as a special people led as the pastoral children of Abraham in search of prosperity and religious peace or as the followers of a new Moses or Joshua going to a promised land. They had made their covenant with God, and they believed implicitly that He was to be their God in a special way, and they were a special people in His sight. This interpretation soon ceased to be strictly theological and entered the realm more properly called legend, or even rationalization, as the leaders attempted to justify their position in the last half of the nineteenth century. With this understanding of themselves and the theological interpretation of their own cultural destiny, they conquered the wilderness while they oppressed the Africans; they exploited the land while they opposed social reforms inspired by European intellectual developments; they became more orthodox in their theology while they reacted against various new theological and philosophical ideas of the eighteenth and nineteenth centuries. In many ways the Afrikaner society retained its seventeenth-century character until after the Boer War. The theological and scriptural doctrine of an elect people afforded a means whereby the Afrikaners could both create a new society and react against a foreign influence.

The Afrikaners' understanding of, and use of, the Calvinistic doctrine of election was scarcely what the Genevan Reformer had envisaged or what the leaders at Dort had attempted to make specific. Rather, their interpretation of themselves as elect or chosen was always a permutation, an adaptation of the original doctrine, taken from the invisible realm of high theology, transformed radically, and returned to the ethnic context of Old Testament narrative.

The study is presented chronologically. Chapter I sketches the beginnings of the settlement and of the institutional church; shows the change in the Afrikaners' concept of their destiny that developed as settlers migrated farther into the interior; and analyzes the reaction the Boers developed in the face of a strong and organized foe, the Bantu tribes. This chapter concerns what may be called the Dutch period of South African history. Beginning with Chapter II, the added complication of British influence must be considered. The first thirty years of British occupation convinced the Boers that their basic ideology was being challenged to the core by British ideas. In Chapters III and IV, we go with the Boers on their Great Trek, their futile attempt to escape British influence. Chapters V, VI, and VII illustrate the growing theological nationalism of the Afrikaners as they slowly came to realize that they must come to terms with British authorities. The concluding section of Chapter VII, the Boer War, illustrates the frantic and intensified effort to recapture something that could not be retrieved. Chapter VIII sketches briefly the settlement following the Boer War that led to the Union in 1910. Various interpretations appear from time to time, but a comprehensive theological analysis of full-blown Afrikaner nationalism appears as Chapter IX. A critique from a larger perspective forms Chapter X.

Historical materials of a political, social, or cultural nature are introduced only when they bear directly on a theological interpretation or are necessary to elucidate the context of events. This study is not meant to be a complete history; rather, historical events are used only to indicate how the ideology was based on theological terms and how it was modified by the existential situation.

During three centuries of Afrikaner civilization, there were many vicissitudes, many challenges, many turning points. The major one was the Anglo-Boer War (1899-1902). Before this war, Afrikaner society was in the process of development and adaptation. The war so solidified much of the tradition and many ideas the people had about their society that the history following the year 1900 was built on the foundation thus developed. After the year 1900, the struggling nations moved quickly, though not inevitably, into a Union of South Africa, and more recently have assumed the status of a republic (1961). Because the sociotheological developments in the culture were solidified in the South Africa Act of 1909, and the subsequent Union in 1910, this date is taken as the *terminus ad quem* for this study. By this date the frontier period was over. The *terminus a quo* is April 6, 1652, the date of the landing of Jan van Riebeeck and his three ships on the shores of Table Bay, where Cape Town was later developed.

NOTES

1. George H. Williams, *Wilderness and Paradise in Christian Thought* (New York: Harper & Row, 1962).

2. God "revealed" this to Joseph Smith: "With one heart and with one mind gather up your riches that he may purchase an inheritance which shall hereafter be appointed unto you. It shall be called the New Jerusalem, a land of peace, a city of refuge, a place of safety for the Saints of the Most High God." *Doctrine and Covenants,* section 45. A compendium of the *Book of Mormon* lists many similar references: Verla Birrell, *The Book of Mormon Guide Book* (Salt Lake City: Birrell Book Company, 1948), pp. 8-15. Cf. Thomas F. O'Dea, *The Mormons* (Chicago: University of Chicago Press, 1957), pp. 76-97; Fawn Brodie, *No Man Knows My History* (New York: Alfred D. Knopf, 1946), pp. 98-114; Ray B. West, *Kingdom of the Saints: The Story of Brigham Young and the Mormons* (New York: Viking, 1957).

3. "Let my people go" was the emphasis of the Rev. Dr. Martin Luther King, Jr., at his Boston civil rights rally in April 1965. Cf. Albert Luthuli, *Let My People Go* (New York: McGraw-Hill, 1962).

4. John Horsh, "The Rise and Fall of the Anabaptists of Münster," *Mennonite Quarterly Review,* IX (1935), pp. 92-103, 129-144.

5. Franklin Hamlin Littell, *The Anabaptist View of the Church* (Boston: Star King Press, 1958).

6. This phrase was first adopted at the Christian Association of Washington Pa. , organized August 17, 1809; Winfred Ernest Garrison and Alfred T. de Groot, *The Disciples of Christ, a History* (St. Louis: Christian Board of Publication, 1948), p. 140. Alfred T. de Groot has recently summarized the idea of restitution of the true faith of Christianity's founder throughout twenty centuries in his *The Restoration Principle* (St. Louis: Bethany Press, 1960).

7. Ernest Deming Andrews, *The People Called Shakers: A Search for the Perfect Society* (New York: Oxford University Press, 1953); Marguerite Fellows Melcher, *The Shaker Adventure* (Princeton: Princeton University Press, 1941); Charles Nordhoff, *Communistic Societies of the United States* (London: J. Murray, 1875).

8. Deuteronomy 7:6-13; Genesis 12:1-3, 17:1-8.

9. Hans Kohn, *Zion and the Jewish National Idea* (New York: D. van Nostrand Co., 1963).

10. Romans 8:30-33; I Cor. 1:27-28; Col. 3:12; Acts 13:17.

11. Harold Henry Rowley, *The Biblical Doctrine of Election* (London: Lutterworth Press, 1950); Krister Stendahl, "The Called and the Chosen," in *The Root of the Vine: Essays in Biblical Theology,* ed. Anton Fridrickson

(Westminster: Dacre Press, 1953), pp. 63-80; Cyril Eastwood, *The Royal Priesthood of the Faithful* (London: Epworth Press, 1963).

12. William Haller, *The Elect Nation: The Meaning and Relevance of Foxe's Book of Martyrs* (New York: Harper and Row, 1963).

13. Predestination or election is the subject treated in *The Institutes* III:XXI-XXIV. The most complete statement of the doctrine, both in exposition and in defense of the doctrine against theological opponents, may be found in *De Aeterna Dei Predestinatione* (1552), translated as *Concerning the Eternal Predestination of God*, trans. J. K. S. Reid (London: Clark & Co. Ltd., 1961).

14. Note, for example, his glorification of the Aryan "race" in *Mein Kampf*.

15. C. C. Richardson called attention to the necessity of looking to deeper levels of understanding. In his inaugural lecture at Union Theological Seminary (1949), he stated the enlarged problem of the church historian: "If he tries to write sacred history in its fullest sense, . . . he has to tell the story against the background of ultimate meanings. He has to realize that he stands on the bounds between symbol and fact, between myth and history, because the events with which he deals are transformed by the holy," in *Union Seminary Quarterly Review*, V (1949), p. 3; quoted by George H. Williams in Arnold Nash, ed., *Protestant Thought in the Twentieth Century* (New York: Macmillan, 1951), p. 173.

16. In his attempt to broaden the basis of theology of culture beyond the confines of systematic theology, Paul Tillich has stated, "Religion is the substance of culture and culture the form of religion." *The Protestant Era*, trans. James Luther Adams (Chicago: Phoenix Books, University of Chicago Press, 1957), p. 57. See also Paul Tillich, "Über die Idee einer Theologie der Kultur" (Vortrag, gehalten in der Berliner Abteilung der Kant-Gesellschaft am 16 April, 1919), in *Religions Philosophie der Kultur* (Berlin: Reuter and Reinhard, 1920).

17. Clifford Geertz, *The Interpretation of Cultures* (New York: Basic Books, Inc., 1973), p. 218.

18. *Ibid.*

19. *Ibid.*, pp. 201-217. Following this anthropologist's further analysis of ideology, we note that he assumes that they are of two types. First, he summarizes the interest theory, or the attempt to gain advantage of power. Second, he refers to the strain theory, or the social attempt to bring stability and understanding out of "sociopsychological disequilibrium" (p. 201). The many situations assumed to be disequilibrium, although not always consciously analyzed as such, are summarized in their chronological context. We shall note many instances in which "the power of ideology to knit a social group or class together" (p. 205) is exemplified in the developing Afrikaner culture. Furthermore, ideologies may be of many types, all reflected in South Africa, such as "projections of unacknowledged fears, disguises for ulterior motives, phatic expressions of group solidarity"

(p. 220). They are also "maps of problematic social reality and matrices for the creation of collective conscience" (p. 220).

20. *Ibid.*, p. 90.

21. *Ibid.*

22. This concept was presented, for example, by Arnoldus Rotterdam, *Gods Weg met Nederland* (1762). Similar tracts of this period are analyzed by Pieter Geyl, *Het stadhouderschap in de Partijliteratuur onder De Wit* (Published by Mededeling der Kon. Ned. Akademie van Wetenschappen, 1947). Summarized in Pieter Geyl, *Use and Abuse of History* (New Haven: Yale University Press, 1955), pp. 6, 13.

23. To be sure, election was not unknown in Reformed thought before 1618, but the Synod of Dort so emphasized this doctrine that it became the leading section of the decrees. Thereafter election played a much more influential role than it had in the earlier Heidelberg Catechism. The decrees of Dort are printed in Philip Schaff, *The Creeds of Christendom* (New York: Harpers Brothers, 1877, 1919), III, 550-597. The Heidelberg Catechism is printed in the same work, pp. 307-355, and the Belgic Confession is on pp. 383-436.

24. "Br. & Z. er is meermalen gewezen op de merkwaardige overeenkomst, die er bestaat, tusschen Israëls historie en de geschiedenis van ons land en volk." Coenrad Spoelstra, ed., *Het Kerkelijk en Godsdienstig leven der Boeren na den Grooten Trek* (Kampen: J. H. Kok, 1915), p. 386.

25. This term was suggested by the late Professor Gordon Allport.

I.

A Historical Introduction: The Dutch in South Africa, 1652-1795

THE DUTCH COLONY 1652-1707

The settlement of a colony at the southern end of the African continent was almost an accident and was thought unwise until long after it was an established fact. The United Dutch East India Company, organized in 1602 as part of the vast commercial empire of the Netherlands, sailed its ships around the tip of the continent without any serious thought of stopping.[1] The destination was the East Indies where they would obtain spices and return to home port.[2] It was quite by accident that in March 1647 a merchant ship, the *Haarlem*, was wrecked in a storm, although the crew was able to reach land where they were marooned for approximately one year.[3] Waiting on the shores of South Africa to be rescued by another ship, the crew tilled some of the land and bartered with the friendly African Khoikhoi, sometimes called Hottentots. One of the crewmen of the ship that rescued them, however, surgeon Jan van Riebeeck, evaluated the situation differently. He looked at these Africans as a "brutal lot, a people living without conscience."[4] Many settlers of later years, especially after they had associations with various African groups, came to share a similar condescending viewpoint.

This accident of a shipwreck gave a strong impetus leading to the decision to construct a small settlement in South Africa for the use of ships of the Dutch East India Company. A refreshment stop in South Africa had long been considered desirable and would be a welcome respite in the midst of a long journey. The trip from Amsterdam to Batavia (Jakarta in contemporary Java) took approximately nine months.[5] The men who spent so much time on board ship suffered continually from scurvy and dysentery. Two men who had been shipwrecked drew up an elaborate plan and suggested to the "Herren XVII"[6] of the Dutch East India Company that the southern tip of the continent be made a refreshment station where ships going out to the East or returning could procure fruit, water, fresh meat, butter, cheese, and milk.[7] A few men could be stationed at the refreshment settlement to till the land and to supply ships.[8]

Favorably impressed, the XVII made plans to proceed and chose Jan van Riebeeck as leader of the expedition. In addition to economic benefits, they were certain that their enterprise was blessed by God. Indeed, they believed it was God's will that this garden be planted to alleviate sickness and, as an afterthought, to further the Christian cause.[9] "God grant you wisdom and understanding . . . that God's holy Name may be magnified, the Church of Christ be built up, and likewise the private honor and reputation of yourselves."[10] The settlers believed they had a mandate to further the Reformed faith, the "true" Christian cause. This mandate with the temporal and eternal concerns intertwined was summarized by Jan van Riebeeck as he wrote just before he sailed on his economic and history-making venture. He concluded "That the natives or their children are able to learn the Dutch language is important and a very good thing, but of greater moment is the furtherance of our Reformed Christian religion."[11]

The expedition with both economic motives and theological justifications set sail from Amsterdam on December 24, 1651, with three ships, the *Dromedaris,* the *Rieger,* and the *Goede Hoope.* Jan van Riebeeck was confident that God's providence was guiding him and guarding him:

> (December 30) Not being able to reach the English coast we used this favourable wind and sailed outward along the channel, west and west by north, in the hope that the Almighty would let us keep this favourable wind until we were beyond the peril of enemies.
> (December 31) . . . had grave fears of her capsizing. From this the Almighty has preserved us on this occasion.
> (January 5) Hardly an hour after we had tacked about, the Lord God made the rough weather subside and gave us a favourable wind.[12]

After more than three months, the ships came within sight of what became a new land for European commerce and religion. The landing of the body of Company servants at Table Bay on April 6, 1652, established the white European Christian civilization at the point known as *Kaap de Goede Hoope.*

This "temporary" stay of Jan van Riebeeck lasted ten years, and his establishment of the colony at Table Bay was much more substantial than he could have imagined at the outset. These few people developed an image of themselves during these ten years as they undertook three major objectives: to carve a homeland out of the wilderness by building, farming, and exploring; to develop a favorable relationship with the Africans; and to organize certain religious activities, a church organization, and strengthened religious leadership.

While the settlers were constructing their crude huts in the vicinity of what became Cape Town, they had their first experience with the Africans in the immediate area, people they called *Ottenots* or *Hottentots*. A more precise name, however, which does not imply a centuries-long ridicule and condescension, is *Khoikhoi*. This means simply "men of men" and is the name by which they refer to themselves. For this reason, it is accepted by modern students of these indigenous peoples.[13] The Khoikhoi were yellow- or brown-skinned and not Negroid. Their language included the well-known clicks, which distinguished them from those who spoke the many Bantu languages. Unknown to the earliest settlers, the Khoikhoi were not one unified group but were organized, however, in different geographical regions within the area the settlers would soon occupy.[14] These African people were dependent for their livings on herds of sheep and cattle. Consequently they wandered from place to place depending on the conditions of pasture. The Dutch wanted to obtain cattle for food for themselves and to supply the needs of the ships. The Khoikhoi, however, were not always eager to part with their best cattle, and this difference became the basis of some of the earliest conflicts between the Africans and the new settlers.

Among the colonists two opposing ideas arose immediately with respect to the newly encountered people, and both attitudes continue to this day. Constant tension existed between the optimism of the distant Company officials and the more realistic and practical view of the actual settlers. Company officials insisted that van Riebeeck should treat the Khoikhoi with respect, should not harm them, and should forget petty grievances. Only then could their goodwill be won and the major concern of the Company—cattle and profit—be fulfilled.[15] Commander van Riebeeck held a less optimistic attitude, indicated by the prayer he offered immediately on arriving at his new settlement.[16] His earliest experiences tended to authenticate his assumptions concerning "wild, brutal men," and on the third day at the South African port, he issued a proclamation forbidding contact with the Khoikhoi except for barter of animals, reflecting that "these uncivilized people are little to be trusted."[17] The XVII, counseling moderation, conceived of other ways to control the situation. Because "the natives cannot refrain from stealing," they should be hindered by physical means.[18] Commissioner Rykloff van Goens, on an inspecting trip in 1657, proposed a canal to separate the peninsula where the Europeans lived from the mainland where the Khoikhoi lived, but this was found not feasible. Ultimately five protective watch-houses were constructed with realistic names.[19] The "barbarians" were taken by surprise with the stronger protections and were "almost completely deprived of the means of stealing and carrying off the cattle."[20]

The Khoikhoi soon realized that they were gradually being excluded from the land which they had held for many generations. Furthermore, their ancient custom of herding cattle over the whole region was compromised by the growing settlement, the fences, and new crops. They banded together to harass the settlers in what is called the First Hottentot War (1659-1660). They stole the settlers' cattle and disrupted their farms, suffering few losses themselves. Another defensive boundary composed of a thick hedge and guard houses between the warring groups was suggested. Company officials in the Netherlands, on hearing of the problems, expressed their pessimistic opinion: "We fear that this unfortunate blow . . . will shake the Cape Colony which has already cost the Company so much expense. . . . We never entertained any high idea of the Cape scheme."[21] A temporary truce was finally concluded April 6, 1660.[22] Slightly over a decade later, another War was waged because the Khoikhoi saw their land being gradually absorbed by the settlers. Both groups used the Wars for excuses for plunder and thievery. Conflicts such as these laid the foundation for the permanent suspicion and distrust that the settlers held with respect to these and other Africans.

All Europeans living at the Cape were originally servants of the Company. In 1657, however, some of the more venturesome servants obtained permission to work for themselves as *vrij burghers*. These "free burghers" would be encouraged to work harder through incentives of "free enterprise" if they owned their own land rather than remaining employees of the Company. The XVII hoped their enterprise would decrease the need to depend on the Company. Burghers were allowed to settle on plots of approximately twenty-eight acres each, although the amounts of land would be augmented extensively in the next decades. The original objective was to have this new class of workers engage in farming and tilling the land for the good of the Company and its employees. Almost immediately, however, the burghers found that it was more profitable to raise the needed cattle and sheep for supplying the meat for the ships or to follow their own trades. During the decade van Riebeeck was at the Cape, 195 *vrijbrieven* (letters of freedom) were issued, largely to farmers but also to "free" fishermen, woodcutters, lime burners, brick makers, bakers, masons, tailors, hunters, a brewer, a miller, and a keeper of the tap house.[23]

The Company controlled all prices, usually lower than the burghers would have hoped. Although the free farmers gradually came to believe they were being exploited, they developed a sense of group consciousness. Soon they were given the right of representation on the governing council.[24] They found trade with the Khoikhoi profitable, but that was again prohibited by an edict in 1658. They were resentful that some of the free colonists had monopolies on products such as milk, cheese, and cattle, while others had no such advantage and were more vulnerable to attack and robbery from Africans now that they were living farther and farther outside the fort.[25]

The growing group consciousness of the free burghers resulted in more antagonism against Company officials. Further initiative on the part of the free burghers culminated in a long petition presented to Company officials in 1658.[26] The tone of the document reflects a self-conscious group of individuals who thought they should have more rights concerning with whom they could trade, the quality of animals they would receive from the Company, prices that were established, and protection from the Khoikhoi. This reflected not so much a misunderstanding of the original agreement as an attempt on the part of the burghers to enhance their position with relation to Company rules. Van Riebeeck's reply to the free burghers was very clear: "Till as you are told, as free men; or you will lose your freedom and till for the Company."[27] The XVII interpreted the petition in terms of unwarranted assumptions on the part of the settlers and sent their reply to the Cape. They saw only "sedition and rebellion" and wanted only to maintain a Company outpost according to the original plan.[28] It seemed to the XVII that the free burghers were developing a permanent settlement instead. This antagonism between the free burghers and Company officials intensified while the growing group consciousness of the burghers was augmented.

Another innovation was undertaken by the struggling settlement in 1658. Company officials captured a Portuguese ship with one hundred seventy slaves from Angola and landed them in South Africa. Most of them were young boys and girls kept in a special slave compound and taught the Dutch language in a special school.[29] Soon other slaves came from Angola and from the East Indies colonies of the Dutch East India Company. Slavery continued to be expanded from a few hundred in the 1650s to over 25,000 in 1795 when the Company disbanded. Indeed, during the eighteenth century, the slave population grew in approximately equal numbers as compared with the burghers themselves.[30] The slaves were most numerous at first among the Company employees in the Cape Town area. Over the years, however, the ratio shifted until during most of the eighteenth century there were many times more slaves in the vast frontier regions than in the limited Cape settlement. They became a population mixed with Khoikhoi, white, and Asian peoples and are one of the groups forming what is now known as the Cape Colored population. This importation of slaves was not an unmixed blessing. The idea that certain labor was for slaves and beneath the dignity of the white settlers reinforced their assumptions about racial superiority, later to be continued among colored or other African peoples long after slavery as an institution had disappeared.[31]

The development of specifically religious organizations in the new settlement came only slowly. During the first century of the settlement, the theological presuppositions underlying the culture were more implied than stated. The Dutch had confidence that they had a special mandate from God to possess the land and that God was protecting their faith as well as testing it. For example, a severe illness in 1656 was interpreted as God's punishment for wrongdoing, and the people were admonished to

improve their spiritual life.[32] Very much a part of the greater Netherlands, these settlers "knew" that God was on the side of the freedom lovers
against the Portuguese, the French, and the English. In South Africa, they
were urged to pray to God that He would bless their righteous cause.[33]
Had not God proved His concern for them in their recently completed
eighty-year war for their own freedom (the Netherlands versus Spain, 1568-
1648)?

The Dutch East India Company provided for religious leadership in
colonies and on ship. Each ship had either a chaplain or a *Zieckentrooster*,
and many of the latter worked in the new areas in the East Indies or later
in South Africa.   The *Zieckentrooster* (Dutch) or *Sieckentrooster* (Afrikaans) had a specific function, which was outlined in several articles in the
Kerkorde of the Classis of Amsterdam (1643), which governed the church in
all areas of the Dutch East India Company.[34] These leaders were not fully
ordained ministers and were not considered such. They were forbidden to
preach their own ideas or to perform the sacraments of the church. The
"sick visitor" led in worship services and above all was a teacher of children
and a visitor among the sick. They taught the catechism and the Bible and
knew the tunes of all Psalms in order to sing them rather than to read
them.[35]

It was the "sick visitor," Willem Barents Wylant, arriving with van
Riebeeck and the first expedition, who first provided religious leadership in
the settlement in South Africa. Until the first fully ordained minister was
appointed at the Cape in 1665, Wylant was the major religious influence,
apart from ordained chaplains who baptized and celebrated the Eucharist
while their ships were in port. It seems certain that religion did not play a
decisive role in this earliest decade of South African white civilization
partly because the religious leadership was very official, completely controlled from Amsterdam, and intertwined with Company policy. In addition, many settlers concluded that their stay in the settlement was only
temporary, and they deemed permanent religious institutions unnecessary.

Before the first religious organization was officially established in
1665, the Cape colony had many problems all its own, each of which contributed to making the history complex and the religious imagery unique.
The colony was beset with problems with respect to economics, their major
objective for the whole settlement; tensions between the Company and the
free burghers; frustrations in conquering the land through building, exploration, and farming; and confusion with respect to the Khoikhoi and later
with the imported slaves. In the midst of these problems, the theological
questions were placed. In the frontier situation, the people had so many
more pressing concerns that they gave their religious development scant
attention. In later generations as they began to develop their theological
imagery, they were already conditioned by social, economic, racial, and
geographical concerns, which must be understood as the foundation for the
theological permutations of South African society.

The first church was organized at Cape Town. The first fully ordained minister assigned to the Cape colony was Johan van Arkle, arriving in August 1665.[36] Up to this date there was no *Kerkraad* (church council), so all decisions were handled through the political *Raad*. The religious concepts and the political organization were closely intertwined, for half the members of the Kerkraad were to be chosen by the government, and no legal meeting could be held unless the government officials were present.[37] The decision to organize a church was closely related to the rebuilding of the fort using more permanent materials. The first church building was begun January 2, 1666.

In orthodox Reformed theological tradition, baptism had always played a significant role, for theoretically this is a sacrament that moves one from heathenism into membership in the Body of Christ. The Heidelberg Catechism states specifically: "They [infants] are also by baptism, as a sign of the Covenant, to be ingrafted into the Christian Church, and distinguished from the children of unbelievers, as was done in the Old Testament by circumcision, in place of which in the New Testament baptism is appointed."[38] To be baptized is "to be renewed by the Holy Ghost, and sanctified to be members of Christ, but so we may more and more die unto sin, and lead holy and unblameable lives."[39] Two standard implications of this concept of baptism appeared at the beginning of the South African settlement. First, baptism was considered indispensable in the development of individuals as faithful Christians; and second, the profession of Christianity through baptism placed all equal in the sight of God. In theory, this held true for the first period of South African history, but it was radically modified as the culture developed. Richard Elphick and Robert Shell have tabulated the slave children and adults baptized between 1665 and 1795. Of 2,012 baptisms recorded, less than 10 per cent were of adult slaves, leaving over 90 per cent of this number baptized children. During the same one and one-third century, those who were allowed their freedom were only a negligible portion of the baptized slave Christians.[40] Almost immediately stronger cultural concerns forced theological theory into the background.

Gradually settlers equated civilization with their homeland, and Khoikhoi who learned civilized ways were partly changed from "native" to "European"; at least, this wording appears in the records. Not only were children of Dutch settlers baptized by ministers, but also Africans who learned the rudiments of the Dutch language were baptized and brought into the Christian covenant. Eva was the most well-known example of a Khoikhoi who not only was baptized as a Christian but also married a Dutch settler. About her it was said that "Eva had a Dutch heart inside her and would never forget the Dutch but would always try to be of service to us whenever she could."[41] That Eva returned to her former ways is proof that however much it was hoped that baptism could help to change culture, such radical change was not so simple.

Despite the difficulty of changing culturally ingrained ways of life, some considered the relation between white and nonwhite not so much a question of race as of culture. For example, a Bengalese slave was given permission to marry a local free burgher in July 1658 because she had been bought out of slavery by her future husband and because "Maria not only understands Dutch perfectly but speaks it clearly and already has a fair knowledge of Christ according to the Reformed religion, the [Council] has decided to grant the young people their fair request."[42]

Illegitimate children of slave women were accorded the privilege of baptism,[43] and it was assumed that they would be educated by the father as Christians.[44] The problem of baptism of children when neither parent was a Christian caused further concern. The decision finally came from the Classis, or the church governing body, of Amsterdam that even they should be welcomed if their parents or guardians promised to educate them in the Christian faith.[45] Baptism and conversion to the Christian faith, however, were soon subverted from theological concepts to merely utilitarian ends. The Christian faith was used, for example, as a civilizing or "taming" influence, meant to make Africans amenable to the wishes of the white settlers.[46]

More significant than the theology and the religious concern, the earliest education at the Cape was planned to benefit both African and European children. The first school at the Cape, an aspect of Christian nurture, was begun in 1658, taught by the Zieckentrooster.[47] The school was "for the Company's servants and free men . . . and where all the Company's slave children may learn betimes to know and worship their creator."[48] This lofty view of the function of education, however, did not sufficiently permeate the culture to cause any lasting effect in this early period.

In addition to the problems concerning religion and education in the settled areas, another complication developed as settlers moved eastward. Many were too far away to attend one of the few established churches regularly, and the few ministers there were could not serve many of the outlying regions. Educational opportunities were either sporadic or nonexistent. The simple literalism of the Old Testament stories was the only substitute for organized religion or education on the frontier. Because of the situation in which they found themselves, these pioneers developed popular theology parallel to the official religion, and this was to increase greatly in the century yet ahead. For these reasons, the religious organization in the new settlement did not necessarily lead to a meaningful and significant religious development; just the opposite was often the case. Penalties were established for those who were unfaithful in daily prayer and attendance, in order that God's blessing might rest again on the settlement. Holy Communion, although an important requirement in the Reformed faith, was referred to as a "Holy Duty" and was only sparsely attended.[49]

The idea of a colony in place of or in addition to a refreshment station for the Company was officially considered as the Cape settlement slowly expanded. By 1679 enough free burghers with their families had pushed the thirty miles to the southeast so that a definite turning point came in the conception of the South African experiment. A new town was established on the expanding frontier, which had not been part of the refreshment settlement. This was Stellenbosch, named after the governor, Simon van der Stel (the bos, "woods" or "forest" of Stel). A church was organized there in 1687.[50] The idea of the Company and its servants' dominating all Europeans living in Southern Africa was a theory that was not workable even in this early period. As the settlers continued to move east and north during the next century, the Company controls became more tenuous and even nonexistent on much of the frontier.

The events that followed Louis XIV's 1685 revocation of the Edict of Nantes in French territories led to another source of settlers in South Africa. Many of the French Huguenots who fled France for their faith and their lives went to the Netherlands, and some of those decided to make the trip to South Africa. As their first ship landed at Cape Town, April 13, 1688, they began to enlarge the cultural outlook of the Dutch who were there.[51] During the next few years, approximately 150 French refugees came.[52] As part of the Reformed faith, they did not bring new religious forms; rather, they intensified what they found. The French left their homeland, as contrasted to the Dutch in South Africa, not for economic gain but for religious freedom. Protestants of the Netherlands were strongly related to Dutch nationalism. On the contrary, however, the Protestantism of the Huguenots forced them to leave their nation behind. Their religious faith and French nationalism could not support each other. The religious faith of the Huguenots was thereby strengthened as it was forced to stand by itself, without a nation or a geographical area to call its own.

The French settlers congregated in a valley a few miles east of Stellenbosch they named *Franschehoek*, using a Dutch spelling. They brought vines for grapes and developed a rich South African wine, still produced today. They formed a church with a French-speaking minister, although soon the minister was required to know both French and Dutch. Originally there were separate schools for children using the two languages, but these were finally integrated so the French-speaking children could learn Dutch "in order to unite our nation by this means."[53] Gradually the French language and French customs declined, and all became members of the developing South African society. The strong national ties that were expressed in the French language did not die soon. In 1702 the government decreed that only enough education was to be given in French to enable the children to learn Dutch, but not enough time had passed to permit such a step.[54] Petitions were circulated to the effect that the older people could not understand Dutch, and the rule was partially suspended. In 1706 instructions were given that French was not to be used in official communications.[55]

The French language was used by an ever-dwindling number throughout the eighteenth century, and by the end of the Dutch period when South Africa came under British authority, there seemed to be no more French spoken in the Cape Colony.[56] French family names, however, some modified to reflect a Dutch spelling, exist to this day in great numbers.[57]

In October 1885, two centuries after the revocation of the Edict of Nantes, a special commemoration was held in South Africa during which time the great contribution of the Huguenots was recalled. The Rev. Andrew Murray, Jr., speaking on the occasion, reminded his hearers that the devotion to religious duty that forced the Huguenots from France and finally to South Africa was the same spirit that brought incentive to their education, their government, and their general welfare in their adopted land. Another speaker alluded to the Huguenot emblem of the burning bush and suggested that the same God who was with Moses and with the Huguenots was even now with them.[58] The strengthening of the faith attributed to the Huguenots two hundred years before was considered another proof of God's special favor to South Africa in 1885. It was stated that since the Huguenots fought for freedom against the Roman Catholic oppression in France, they in turn strengthened the faith of the descendants of the Dutch who earlier had fought the oppressive Roman Catholic government of Spain. In South Africa, it was asserted, both the Dutch patriots and the French Huguenots had been freedom fighters in God's (Protestant) cause.

The French assimilation into the Dutch settlement, not yet accomplished in 1700, was aided by an outside threat against which both groups rose as a body. Simon van der Stel had completed a long and successful administration as governor of South Africa (1679-1699) when he was succeeded by his son, Willem Adriaan van der Stel (1699-1707). The Company policy forbade officials of the Company to engage in private trading or farming. Rather, the officials were charged with administering the policies for the good of the Company alone. Soon after the younger van der Stel arrived, however, he established extensive land holdings and sought to gain a large percentage of the profit available at the Cape. Records were so camouflaged that it was difficult to determine the extent to which he carried out his extralegal activities. He granted land to servants and then "bought" it for himself, thus blurring the transactions reported to the XVII, which the latter scrutinized carefully. It is estimated that he controlled one-third of the land around the Cape, and his holdings around the farm *Vergelegen* grew to 20,000 acres.[59] Indeed, the governor and his close associates hoped that soon "no free burghers would be required at the Cape . . . and that there was a chance for them, the four or five or them, to provide the Company and the Cape with everything."[60]

The farming community realized the seriousness of the situation and discussed it often.[61] In 1705 they drew up a memorial, which they sent directly to Company officials in the Far East. To circumvent the normal channels of communication and to go directly to the leaders was as unprecedented as it was dangerous. This document spelled out in great detail the illegal business of the governor and stated the settlers' grievances clearly.[62] The Company quickly acted and on October 30, 1706, recalled four officials: the governor, Willem Adriaan van der Stel; the second in command, Samuel Elsevier; the minister of Cape Town, Petrus Kalden; and the landdrost (magistrate) of Stellenbosch, Johannes Starrenburg.[63] These officials had played a large part in the growing drama, documented in the diary of Adam Tas, one of the younger free burghers.

The economic necessity that drove the colonists to rise as a body to oppose the governor was sufficient to forge the disparate nationalities into a unified group to throw off the "intolerable yoke."[64] Leo Fouché has pointed out that of sixty-three signatories of the memorial, thirty-one have French names.[65] The outgoing governor referred to this group of settlers who had now attained a unified concept of their own destiny as "boors," "ignorant boors," or "insolent rascals of boors."[66] Thus the name *Boer* came to refer not only to farmers but to designate a new people.

In 1707 the XVII discouraged further emigration from the Netherlands to the Cape of Good Hope, closing a significant period in the history of the Boer nation. In its first half-century, there was an embryonic development of national self-consciousness, although this had not yet been elaborated with theological or biblical justification. French refugees had been assimilated, a successful revolt had been organized, and a name for the new group—the Boers—was suggested. Over the next century, the settlement was enlarged through the natural birth rate and by settlers from other European countries. The theological concepts of the moving frontier were modified as the Boers expanded their land holdings and extended their influence farther into the interior of the continent. A half-century of immigration had ended; the century of the *veeboer-pionier* (cattle-raising pioneer) had begun.

DEVELOPMENTS ON THE EASTERN FRONTIER, 1707-1779

The outpost of the Company established at Cape Town remained an economic and military necessity during the eighteenth century but had decreasing importance for the settlement as a whole. The Company officials early began to realize that because their subjects and the frontier farmers were not living peacefully together, they must be aggressive if they wished to maintain their monopoly.[67] Various means were used to limit the colonists to an area that the Company could easily control. They issued warnings, drew boundary lines beyond which settlers could not go, and required new grazing land to be registered at Cape Town. All this was to no avail, however, and an increasing number of frontiersmen trekked to new areas out of range of the jurisdiction of the Cape Town government.[68]

The real significance for purposes of this study, concerning the cultural development during the eighteenth century therefore was not in the Cape Town settlement but on the rapidly advancing frontier. In 1707 the South African settlement was largely confined to an area extending hardly fifty miles north and east of Cape Town. Seventy years later there were Afrikaners as far away as Kamiesberg, three hundred miles north from Cape Town; the Great Fish River, five hundred miles east; and the Sneuwbergen region at the northeastern corner of the settlement near present Graaff-Reinet, approximately five hundred miles from the settled region. During the intervening three or more generations, significant changes took place in the total culture of the frontier cattlemen. They ceased being farmers and devoted their time to the pursuit of grazing. Furthermore, they severed their connecting ties with European civilization, which could be made with people from ships visiting at Cape Town; they lost much of their refinement as to culture, education, and religion; and they had an experience among other Africans—the San, or Bushmen—virtually unknown to those who remained at Cape Town. The frontiersmen gradually gave up their loyalty to Europe; Africa was their home—they were Afrikaners.

By the time the settlers had been in South Africa for a half century, they had formed a working relation with the first African people they met, the Khoikhoi. The Khoikhoi depended on herding for a livelihood, but an increasing number of European settlers did also. Among all the different groups of the Khoikhoi, the continuing spread of the white population took increasing amounts of the best land the Africans had been using. Various skirmishes between the peoples resulted in victory for the newcomers, and decreasing strength for the Africans because they were not strongly organized into tribal units. Gradually the Khoikhoi found that they could maintain their way of life if they took care of the settlers' cattle and became servants for the herdsmen.[69]

Another problem that developed hastened the breakup of whatever loose organization the Khoikhoi possessed. In 1713 a widespread smallpox epidemic caused many deaths among slaves, Europeans, and, especially, the Khoikhoi. This last group lost such great numbers that their tribal organization was virtually lost. They quickly consented to live and travel with the Boers to herd the cattle, to take responsibility for the children, and to become domestic servants. The most enterprising gradually learned the Dutch language as well. The Khoikhoi ceased to speak their own language and gradually spoke only Dutch. They adopted many of the cultural traits of their overlords, even the Dutch Reformed faith. They were usually loyal to their Boer masters in the face of sporadic attacks on the frontier. This use of African servants was common in all areas of the eastern sections of the colony, and the Khoikhoi grew to become more numerous than the growing number of slaves.[70] Consequently this relationship between Boer and Khoikhoi was to have a significant influence in the developing attitudes of the frontier Boers.

As the frontiersmen continued their movement away from the settled areas, the policy with respect to land was changed. Previously a farmer had a small tract of freehold and often some grazing land in addition. He had no security on the latter but usually had no difficulty in maintaining his rights. The Company maintained the fiction that all land was theirs and the settlers were ultimately responsible to the Company. In 1714 this monopoly was relaxed and the development of loan farms (leenings plaatse) began.[71] The number of recorded loan farms grew enormously over a twenty-year period. In 1716, there were none; in 1720, 15; in 1725, 50; and in 1735, 122.[72]

Following the good grazing lands for their cattle and assisted by their Khoikhoi servants, the trekboers moved relentlessly eastward. They crossed the Vier en Twintig Rivier in 1716 and settled along the southern coast as far as the Breed River to the area known as Clanwilliam by 1732.[73] A third group went directly east to the site of the present town of Robertson and to the Nex River by 1720. Within the twenty-three years since Adriaan van der Stel had been removed from office, the Cape Colony had doubled in area, while immigration was practically stopped. In the twenty years from 1730 to 1750, settlements reached Calvinia 200 miles to the north and the Mossel Bay 250 miles to the east, to double the total area again in these twenty years.[75] (See map I.)

By 1745 the Cape government, attempting to extend its influence into the frontier, organized an administrative center at Swellendam, named for Governor Swellengrebel and his wife, whose family name was ten Damme.[76] This was not far enough into the eastern district, however, to have meaningful effect. The pioneers continued to push onward, and for the twenty years after 1750 the Company officials gave evidence of little concern.[77] Settlements are reported at the following places: along the coast at the Gamtoos River, 1765;[78] in the central plains in the vicinity of Prince Albert and Willowmere, 1760;[79] to the north to Kamiesberg and Kubiskow, 1760;[80] and to the extreme northeast, the Camdeboo region north of present Graaff-Reinet, 1768;[81] Somerset East, 1771;[82] and north of the Sneeuwbergen, 1771.[83] The eastern boundary was set in 1770 at the Gamtoos River,[84] in 1775 at the Bushman's River, and in 1780 at the Great Fish River.[85]

By 1778 a number of families living at the extreme northeastern border of the colony petitioned the governor to have a church and a court of law established in the eastern section. Governor Joachim, Baron van Plettenberg, had been in the Cape colony several years and knew something of their problems.[86] He sensed that more control on, or at least knowledge of, the eastern frontier was a major need. Consequently he visited the area in that same year and established a beacon at the northernmost point in the

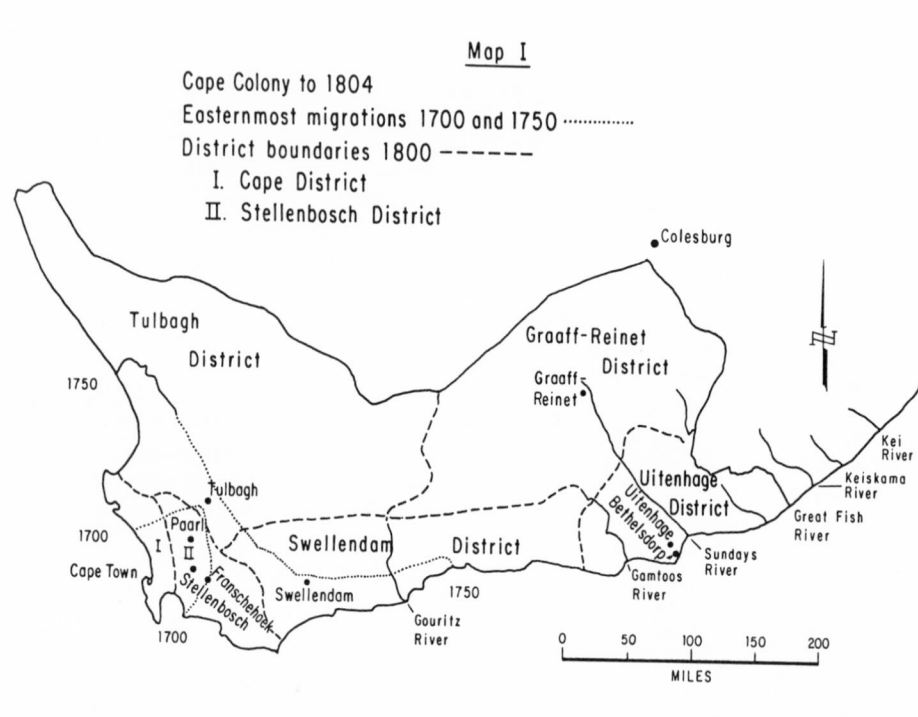

Map I

Cape Colony to 1804
Easternmost migrations 1700 and 1750 ....
District boundaries 1800 ------
   I. Cape District
   II. Stellenbosch District

• Colesburg

Tulbagh
  District

Graaff-Reinet
   District

1750

Graaff-
Reinet •

Kei
River

• Tulbagh

Uitenhage
District

Keiskama
River

1700

I

II
Paarl

Swellendam

District

Uitenhage
Bethelsdorp •

Great Fish
River

Cape Town

Stellenbosch
Franschehoek

Sundays
River

1700

• Swellendam

1750

Gamtoos
River

Gouritz
River

0   50   100   150   200

MILES

colony. Further developments were to come shortly when Graaff-Reinet became a Landdrosdy (an established government outpost) in 1786, with a church established there in 1792.[87]

The external forces of the frontier not only shaped the direction of cultural changes but molded and solidified the way of life of these people. The strongest fears of the government were substantiated in time as the frontiersmen grew disrespectful of law. As succeeding generations lived on the undeveloped frontier among the forces of nature and the hostile tribes, they grew away from their heritage of European civilization. They lived on lands that had never been procured legally; some people were but unsettled wanderers. Lichtenstein indicates some of the difficulties in the frontier areas.

> These people were of the poorest class in the colony, who call themselves wandering men, because they have no fixed habitation, but move about with their flocks from place to place. . . . They often render themselves liable to punishment by atrocities toward the savages, and disobedience to the government. . . . They are almost sunk to the situation of savages.[88]

The settlers had been in close contact with the Khoikhoi almost as long as they had been in South Africa. As they moved farther out from the Cape peninsula, however, they encountered another type of African. The settlers named them Bushmen—*Bosjesmans* (from *Bosje,* a bush). Many writers of the period use this derogatory term, and this name is maintained in direct quotations from the period. A more common name used by scholars, however, is *San*—the name given them by the Khoikhoi and probably also derogatory.[89] The early settlers believed the Khoikhoi and the San were quite different peoples because the former herded animals, while the latter had no settlements but lived exclusively by hunting. Some scholars prefer the name *hunter-gatherers* rather than San because the latter term implies a type of homogeneity or cultural similarity that they did not possess.[90] The term *San* is used in this study despite its imprecision.

Europeans thought the San lived and acted more like wild animals than human beings and treated them accordingly. These small and wiry people did not keep animals of their own, nor did they farm. They ate whatever they could find—trapped elephants, hippopotami, insects, and roots.[91] They lived in huts or holes in the hills, which seemed to Europeans to be only one step removed from the habits of animals. Full-grown adults stood slightly over four feet and often looked like walking skeletons.[92] It is little wonder these little people considered it a worthwhile risk to amplify their diets with cattle in their region, and thus they were driven to plunder the Boers' herds. These San hunters were a constant threat in all parts of the eastern colony, and they remained a force to be attacked throughout the century until they were almost completely exterminated. One count during a ten-year period amounted to 2,504 San killed and 669 taken prisoner.[93]

Dr. Lichtenstein, an outside observer, with as much scientific objectivity as we possess from this period, suggested after careful observations: "I must allow the validity of their claims to be classed among rational creatures, I cannot forbear however saying that a Bosjesman, certainly in his mein and all his gestures, has more resemblance to an ape than to a man."[94] If it so appeared to him, how much more did it appear so to the settlers who bore the brunt of the unorganized, but often efficient, raids on their cattle. Indeed, it was probably such observations by a less qualified but more personally involved individual that led to the practice of referring to the San as "baboons."[95]

The negative attitude the frontiersmen took toward the San was based on their experiences. The San were represented as "ferocious monsters and cannibals,"[96] and they caused settlers to retreat from some areas where they had settled on the eastern frontier. Finally, the government told settlers to "put in execution such measures in the matter, as you shall find to be necessay for the extirpation of the said rapacious tribes."[97] Adriaan van Jaarsveld, the frontier fighter, decided that this meant that in San country one should "follow the Bushmen on the trail and shoot them dead."[98] To carry out their policy, they used trickery of all sorts. For example, he reported in 1775 that he shot some hippopotami and left them as bait. When the San came to devour the meat, the commando leader reported that they "overthrew the robbers there; where on searching, we found one hundred and twenty-two dead, and five escaped."[99] Another frontiersman spoke of shooting San as casually as if he shot pheasants or tigers. Sparrman reported on one occasion that some of these people were taken slaves, but the others "were hunted and exterminated as wild animals whose customs and disposition they had adopted."[100] There were many commandos or hunting expeditions against the San, who were no match for the mounted riflemen when their own weapons were only bows and arrows. Thousands were killed.[101]

In addition to the rapid geographical expansion and the problems related to the San, however, another development must be considered in the same period. Because the XVII discouraged further emigration from the Netherlands to the Cape of Good Hope after 1707, newcomers were usually of different nationalities and did not have strong loyalties to the Netherlands or to the Company officials in Cape Town. It has been estimated that in 1700 there were 1,300 white inhabitants in South Africa, and in 1778 there were 10,000.[102] Part of this growth can be explained by the natural birth rate, but there was in addition a growing number of Germans who settled during this period—Germans in the service of the Dutch East India Company discharged at the Cape. Many of them married Dutch wives and soon lost their language in favor of the developing Cape Dutch, and their culture added its part to the evolution of the Boers in the eighteenth century. H.T. Colenbrander has compiled the following figures on immigration into South Africa over a century:[103]

	1718-1777	1778-1807	Total
Men from the Netherlands	204	125	329
Women from the Netherlands	156	67	223
Men from German areas	508	218	726
Women from German areas	36	50	86

This immigration of Germans began in the previous century and gained momentum in the eighteenth century. Werner Schmidt-Pretoria estimates that by 1806 the national background of the South African settlement was as follows:[104]

50 per cent from the Netherlands
27 per cent from the Empire (German)
17 per cent from France
 6 per cent all others

The rapid increase of the number of German men helps to explain the impatience the settlers had with the Netherlands-controlled Cape Town government.   As was the case of the language of the French Huguenot settlers, spoken German also gradually disappeared. Because the larger number of mothers were Dutch the children were taught not German but rather Dutch and became members of the mothers' Dutch Reformed congregations. As the seventeenth-century French refugees were assimilated into the predominant Cape Dutch culture, so the eighteenth-century German settlers gradually merged their identity into the new Afrikaner culture.

This assimilation was not always smooth. The Germans were not completely comfortable within the Reformed churches, although they did join as members and had their children baptized. In 1730 their satisfactory arrangement was disturbed when a Danish book on theology became known at the Cape. Written by Hector Godfried Masius, it was devoted to showing the differences between Calvinism and Lutheranism. The Lutherans at the Cape became concerned when they read, for example: "Whether God has condemned the larger part of mankind to damnation (The Lutherans say 'no'—the Calvinists say 'yes'); whether God predetermined or willed that Adam should fall (the Lutherans say 'no'—the Calvinists say 'yes')."[105] Further questions concerned baptism and the real presence in the Eucharist. Some Cape Town Lutherans continued to contemplate establishing a Lutheran church.

In 1740 a Danish missionary who visited the Cape continued the agitation. He saw there were many Lutherans with no minister and reported to his Danish officials, who made inquiries of the Dutch. The XVII in turn wrote to the Cape government for a count of the Lutherans at the Cape. The report in 1741 indicated that of 509 Lutherans at the Cape, 399 were Company servants, 92 were free burghers, and 18 were women.[106] Other pleas and petitions were submitted, and finally their persistence was rewarded. A Lutheran layman, Martin Melck, who came as a soldier in 1746 and became a burgher in 1750, developing an extensive wine acreage, allowed one of his buildings to be used by the Lutherans for religious services between 1770 and 1780.[107] Following a petition in March 1780 the XVII appointed the Rev. Andreas Lutgerus Kelver from the Lutheran church in Rotterdam as minister at the Cape. He arrived at his new post in November 1780.[108] A third protestant national and religious group was thus established at the Cape.

The earlier French immigrants had fewer theological differences and were absorbed into the Dutch Reformed congregations. The Cape authorities had difficulty accepting the separate German organizations, however, for in the close relation between church and state existing under the establishment, any other church appeared to be in effect a foreign power and generated much suspicion.

Expansion across the frontier wilderness had many far-reaching effects on the mental outlook and the theological interpretations of the Boer frontiersmen. In South Africa all settlers were several months by slow sea travel from European ports; the eastern settlers, in addition, were several weeks separated from Cape Town and were even more isolated. Out of range of the regular governmental influence of the settled area, they took political matters into their own hands. They also developed their own simple pioneer piety. Cultural restraints were relaxed so that some frontiersmen indulged in miscegenation with the Africans, especially Khoikhoi, while others developed a strong group consciousness of racial exclusiveness, making miscegenation less common, even anathema.[109] Living insecurely because of the threat of attack by the San, the Boers developed their own means of dealing with surprise attacks. They became self-sufficient individualists. Culturally this period of the expansion on the frontier became for the white frontiersmen almost the "Dark Ages" of South Africa.[110] The other side is just as true, however, as it was suggested that "in the long quietude of the eighteenth century the Boer race was formed."[111]

Two aspects of this development during the eighteenth century concerned institutional religion and attempts at education. There were only three churches organized in or near Cape Town for many decades until the fourth, Roodezand (Tulbagh, 1743), and the fifth, Zwartland (Malmesbury, 1745), were formed. These last two were the result of the visit and report of Baron Gustaaf Willem van Imhoff in 1743. He stated that many people "were so ignorant and indifferent that they cared little or nothing for religion and thus were more like an assemblage of blind heathens than a colony of Europeans and Christians."[112] Their situation seemed to belie the Company's official policy: "Religion is one point concerning which the supervision and the responsibility of the authorities is not any less committed than other things."[113] This was policy without effective means of implementation. Even with the establishment of two new churches, the opportunities for spiritual care for all people on the expanding frontier were inadequate.

As the pioneers moved eastward, it became more and more difficult to continue regular attendance at their churches because of the great distances. Baptism and the Holy Communion were the two most important rites of the church, and these were the two times the people hoped to be present at the church. "It is a common occurrence that remote farmers do not bring their children in for baptism until they are a couple of years old. More than once has it happened that several children have been brought into town for baptism at the same time."[114] The time of the quarterly Holy Communion became a combination of many things: a religious service, a visit to a common market place, and a chance to visit and have a social gathering.[115]

As the frontier moved farther from Cape Town, the practice of popular piety increased. By the latter half of the eighteenth century, many people on the frontier had never heard a sermon by a trained minister; their religious understanding came either from their fathers or their often inept school "meesters." This practice continued the outward forms of the religious life, but over time many untheological and situational interpretations were read into the faith.[116]

As the people gathered in their homes or in the homes of their neighbors, their group consciousness became more assured. The often-repeated sermons or Psalms came to be their own, to have a special meaning to them. As they were wanderers in the wilderness, it was natural that they should seek out those passages that reflected wilderness situations such as those of Moses and his wanderings or of Abraham and his family and flocks. Since they were looking for their own Promised Land, they gave some of their geographical features biblical names. Near Cape Town they found the valley of Jehosaphat,[117] and a hill was named the Tower of Babel.[118] Slaves were given biblical names—Adam, Amos, Moses.[119] When Boers met one another on the plains, a topic of conversation was undoubtedly a discussion of the relation between the experiences they had recently encountered and the biblical experiences with which they were familiar. God helped them find pasture around the hill or led them to overcome their problems of drought or attack by the San.[120]

Although these religious services in the pioneers' homes often included the Khoikhoi, there was little consistent attempt to convert these Africans to the faith, with all its implications. In fact, there was no economic necessity for conversion since the Khoikhoi were already loyal to and dependent on the Boers. Consequently there was almost a total lack of interest in the spiritual nature of either Khoikhoi or the San.[121] Many concerns seemed more pressing than the religious development of the people. While Christians were "preening themselves on their Christianity" and believing that all others were "merely crafty heathen, whose only intention was to destroy the Christians," it is little wonder that the settlers' religious responsibilities to the indigenous peoples were seldom considered.[122]

During the long frontier years, many insecurities and hardships constantly plagued the settlers, but they remained confident that they would not have survived at all but for the protecting hand of God. They gradually came to believe that they were special people in the sight of God. They had maintained their faith among all difficulties, and God would surely continue to be their guide. In face of wild beasts they would call on the Lord, and God was on their side as they attacked "wild men."[123]   For example, one military leader wrote this report:

> I found such an immense assemblage of robbers, that we had not the courage to attack them; but reflecting that we have the promise in our favor, that they have the threats against them, and that the Lord does what seems good in his eyes, we advanced upon them, and they were put to flight by the powerful hand of the Ruler of Heaven and earth, and seventeen of them killed there.[124]

The Boers assumed that God would do what was right in His eyes, and they not only hoped but sincerely expected that God's decision would be whatever they had already conceived to be right. They seemed assured that God would confirm their group-centered wishes. "The Lord will do what is good in his sight, therefore, may He give you courage to contend against our enemies, for the insolence of the heathen is striving to get the upper hand more every day. Oh! who shall live if God will [sic] otherwise."[125]

Despite this growth of popular piety, the frontiersmen wanted reinforcement for their faith; in short, they wanted a church in the interior of the colony. They had sought a church in Swellendam in 1751 and again in 1758, without success.[126]   Finally, in 1778 when Governor van Plettenberg visited the interior, the settlers petitioned him to organize a church in the Camdeboo region.   In their petition, the settlers gave a summary of the religious life at this distant corner of the colony, with the statement that many young people in their religious faith were growing up like "ignorant cattle."[127]   Van Plettenberg accepted their petition and sent his request on to the XVII in the Netherlands.[128]   It was more than a decade later, in 1792, that this church was finally organized in Graaff-Reinet, near the northeastern-most settlements.

Another of the determining factors of the frontier culture was the lack of adequate educational opportunities.   In 1743 "the state of education was deplorable and the majority of the teachers incompetent."[129]   This was true, but it was not the whole story.   Schools were organized at each of the three churches and later at the five churches in the settled area in and around Cape Town, but in this period there was no church, and hence no school, on the frontier. What meager education the children received was from parents who were only slightly educated or from traveling "meesters." These itinerant schoolmasters were sometimes well educated but often ineffective because of laziness or drunkenness. Some were discharged from the Company for inefficiency, some deserted their ships, some were very "peculiar characters."[130] They lived with the family and received food and a room in exchange for teaching the rudiments of reading, writing, the catechism, the Bible, and some arithmetic.[131] Their main objective was to prepare the children and youth for church membership—to read the Bible and the catechism. Although these wandering teachers were part of the South African frontier for over a hundred years, until the latter part of the nineteenth century in the Orange Free State and the Transvaal,[132] they did little to form the basis of the developing culture. "Among them are few indeed capable of infusing into the minds of African colonists any taste for European civilization."[133]

Education on the frontier continued in a haphazard fashion and was not considered the most basic aspect of the culture. The practical pursuits of the moment took precedence, for "when a young planter can drive a wagon and exercise a whip his education is nearly completed."[134] The education of a girl was similar.[135] Education in religion was mediocre and in no way could be termed theological. Whenever theological terminology was used, it was for an ulterior and untheological reason. Mentzel observed:

> As soon as they are taken out of school, they generally forget everything about the Christian religion in which they have received some instructions from such teachers as they had; and since they neither attend church nor receive Communion, they cannot be considered as part of the Christian congregation except insofar as they have been baptized.[136]

The education that was available, inadequate as it was, contributed to the developing image of the individualists but gave virtually no directive to the culture. The Bible was the basic textbook, and according to Afrikaner understanding its stories were being reenacted in the South African situation. Examples were often called to mind for various extrinsic motivations, depending on the situation. Thus the pioneers used religious ideas to justify conclusions arrived at for personal or group-centered, short-term objectives.

Beyond the concerns of religion and education as aspects of the development of the culture, there were external factors as well. Two groups of Africans played a part in helping to form the group consciousness of the frontier Boer: the Khoikhoi and the San. The former had been associated with the settlers since the landing of van Riebeeck, and many had become friendly with the settlers. The smallpox epidemic of 1713 had depleted great numbers of the Khoikhoi, shattering their group organization and

making their transition to a servile people much easier. Now as the frontiersmen trekked over the land, they were accompanied by one or more
Khoikhoi servants and sometimes by whole families. Technically these
were not slaves, but the mentality of the Boers seldom allowed for a sharp
distinction.

A growing portion of the Khoikhoi were racially mixed with the whites.
Those who were not servants lived together in their own groups, and were
called Bastaards or Gricquas, and still later Cape Colored. These people
came to be ostracized by the whites. A French traveler reported a visit to
one such family in 1783, where their true feelings were expressed. A
European man had married a Khoikhoi woman and then left his wife and
children so he could marry a European woman. He then disowned all his
children by the African wife. One of the children was asked, since she was
a daughter of a European, why she should choose to live among the Khoikhoi. She replied:

> It is true, I am the daughter of a white man, but my mother is
> a Hottentot. Thus allied by birth to two different races, I had
> to choose with which of them I would live. You know *the pro-
> found contempt which the whites entertain for the blacks, and
> even for those of a mixed breed* like myself. To settle among
> them was to expose myself to daily disgrace and affronts, or to
> be reduced to live alone, solitary and unhappy.[137]

The attitude toward Khoikhoi on the frontier had changed radically during
the eighteenth century. The Khoikhoi were necessay for helping the Boer
in many ways, but at the same time the European attitude toward them was
condescending.

During the frontier period it was common for Europeans to refer to
themselves as Christians and to the Africans as heathens.[138] In the early
years, so few Africans were Christian that the statement was basically
true. The resulting implications, however, were great and far-reaching.
Through such superficial use of the term *Christian*, it came to mean, first,
"civilized man or woman" and later "European." The difference between
peoples was so great that no one questioned this terminology. The theological terms lost their religious connotation when it was possible that a
person from Europe could be called a Christian although his life had little
connection with a religious faith.[139] The misunderstanding so constructed
continued even after a large number of Khoikhoi became part of the church
through various missionary agencies. The twentieth century white South
African assumption that they must preserve white civilization against
overwhelming numbers of black second-class citizens is one logical outcome of this misinterpreted theological attitude developed in the
eighteenth century.

This concept of the inherent shortcomings of the indigenous peoples was carried one step further. Africans were to be subservient to Europeans; hence anything that helped them to have more status in their own eyes or in the eyes of the community was a challenge to the Christian Europeans. This is exemplified in a conversation in 1800:

> I spoke to Susanna's master, who was a Deacon, and reputed one of the best-intentioned members of the reformed church, but he persisted in refusing to have his slave baptized. He said, that it was not so much the loss of his right to sell her that determined him to object against it, but his apprehension lest her pride should grow insupportable by her admission among the Christians.[140]

This attempt to keep the Africans "in their place" was carried further, for it was thought that "a Hottentot had better be exempted from taxes, the imposition of which might have been considered a tacit acknowledgement of his right to citizenship."[141]

It was even suggested that the blood of Europeans was different from that of Africans. The settlers were only slightly removed from the European culture in which the blood of nobility was thought to be different from that of the commoners. The South Africans carried this one step further as they assumed that their blood was different from African; "black blood," compared with "Christian blood," was a type all its own. We note the striking contrast: "The children of Hottentot women, in whose veins *Christian blood* often flowed, were educated in Christianity; they learnt to sing psalms, and to read."[142] "It is true, a great many of the whites have so much pride, as to hinder, as far as lies in their power, the blacks or their offspring from mixing their *blood*."[143] Toward the end of the century, it was true that "whether the individual was baptized or not, *black blood* by this time had definitely become a social handicap."[144]

Boer aversion to miscegenation thus became solidified. It was beneath a white person's dignity to marry a person of an "inferior" race, but sexual relations outside marriage did not cause undue concern. For the white person, it was considered a "source of amusement."[145] Miscegenation usually involved white men and African women, but it also occurred between white women and African men. In all cases the punishment was more severe for the African person involved.[146] Outward conformity to the religious faith was thus more important than questions of morality. It was more of a disgrace to refrain from the rite of baptism than to be involved in sexual promiscuity.[147]

The popular piety of the frontiersmen had reinforced their group consciousness not only with respect to their own primitive culture but in contrast to the African groups with whom they had close contacts. This piety was sharply challenged by a missionary movement, unfamiliar with, and even disagreeing with, the most elementary assumptions of the Afrikaner faith: white superiority. The earliest Zieckentroosters sought to teach the Khoikhoi the Dutch language, to read the Bible, and to learn Christian doctrine. They achieved little success and baptized only a few people. For almost a century no concentrated missionary work among the Africans was conducted by any of the Dutch ministers or settlers. It was thus a new idea that greeted the settlers when in July 1737 the Rev. Georg Schmidt, a German sent as a German missionary from Zinzendorf's settlement at Herrnhut, arrived in South Africa.[148]

Schmidt immediately began to work among the Khoikhoi on the eastern frontier, setting up a tent and then building a cabin as a center for his work. A few Africans came because of curiosity, and some were genuinely interested. They were taught how to plant crops, how to build more substantial houses, and other rudiments of civilization. Schmidt also taught about the religious faith—how all are sinners and need saving grace. He taught that Christ died for all, including Khoikhoi. Some Africans seemed to be learning the basic elements of the faith and came to pray often. Finally the missionary baptized five persons by immersion, but their faith was not unwavering. Schmidt reported in 1741: "With my people it seems very bad. They have lived for a long time quarreling with each other about external things, about land and cattle, and they cannot yet settle down. I have often warned them and said, 'If you want to learn to know the Savior and to live together as brothers and sisters you must not continue this strife among each other.' They are a very queer people."[149]

This incident of a missionary from outside the Afrikaner culture illustrates two aspects of the developing group consciousness of the settlers. First, they adhered strongly to the external rules of their official church as to baptism and ordination. This was to be expected, however, in almost all parts of the Christian world in the eighteenth century. In addition to this there was a second motivation operative in South Africa: the condescending attitude toward the Khoikhoi. The settlers had not expended time to educate many Africans and had come to believe that their proper station in life was one of servitude. A person such as Georg Schmidt, whose theology denied the basic concept of the Boers, was a threat to them. Schmidt insisted that all were sinners in the sight of God and that none was more privileged than another. In addition, he taught Khoikhoi that they could be more self-sufficient and need not rely completely on the European colonists. Had this type of education continued for a long period of time, the Khoikhoi could conceivably have risen to a point where they could live independent of the Europeans and might have become equal in many ways. Georg Schmidt represented a challenge to the growing group consciousness in the Cape colony and was subjected to public pressure to force him to cease his labors.

A greater problem was being envisioned, however, by the so-called Christian Europeans living in South Africa. Schmidt had baptized Khoikhoi by immersion, was irregularly ordained by a non-Dutch group, and was a stranger in a strictly Reformed settlement. As he was preparing to leave South Africa, charges against him were summed up as follows:

> You have sneaked into another house and have given no justification or answer for your teaching. Now you do not want to be under the orders of the established church here, but you want to make division. . . . It is a great arrogance that you have followed the order of your church. Here no one may baptize for we are Reformed.[150]

Georg Schmidt left the Cape in March 1744, but some fruits of his labors remained among the converted Khoikhoi for many years.

As soon as the Afrikaners came into contact with different types of people, it became evident that they had developed an exclusiveness that had religious, cultural, and racial implications. In relation with both the Khoikhoi and the San, the most obvious difference was skin color. This difference gradually became synonymous with lack of culture. After the transfer of attitude from culture to color, the condescending assumption with respect to the latter could remain even after the cultural level of the Africans might be raised considerably. Two Afrikaner writers recently admitted this background of the whole idea of *apartheid*: "There existed amongst the farmer-pioneers an unwritten common code of behavior toward the non-whites. The development and crystallization of the pioneer's color morality went hand in hand with the gradual emergence in the eighteenth century of a Boer-Afrikaner type."[151]

Between 1707 and 1779, the white culture of South Africa was radically modified. From a narrow strip along the mountains at Cape Town, it now extended six hundred miles into the interior. A cleavage developed between the western, more settled frontier, and the moving eastern frontier. Another contrast was more important, however. A difference had been forged between two races of humanity, the white European and the black African. The Europeans, with a longer history of education, civilization, and "Christianity" to draw from, were, in their own eyes, chosen by God to protect and control the "benighted heathen." God gave the white race a great destiny in South Africa, and their deep, untheological popular piety gave them determination to carry through the work of God with whatever means might be necessay to advance and to protect His cause. Thus the developments of the eighteenth century were decisive in the formation of the theological self-consciousness of the Afrikaner nation.

TENSION AT CAPE TOWN AND THE FIRST CONTACT
WITH BANTU TRIBES, 1779-1795

The tensions around Cape Town continued through the century between Company officials and those in the vicinity who considered themselves independent South African burghers. These conflicts were brought sharply to a focus with the arrest early in 1779 of Carel Hendrik Buytendag, one of the free burghers near Cape Town. He was charged with drunkenness and was sent to Batavia in the East Indies. Approximately four hundred burghers, known as the Patriots, in and around Cape Town banded together to compose a petition on May 7, 1779.[152] Their complaints were directed to the company officials in the Netherlands and included not only the demand that their compatriot be brought back to the Cape Colony but summarized many other grievances.

The sharpest criticism concerned William Cornelis Boers, the independent fiscal (attorney general) at Cape Town. He was a loyal employee of the Company and understood the purpose of the settlement in narrow Company terms. He considered himself responsible to his superiors for all aspects of life at this establishment and was surprised that the burghers wanted "an exclusive right to enter into negotiations at Cape Town."[153] The burghers asked for better prices for wine and cattle, permission to trade directly with the Netherlands or the East Indies (rather than channel all goods through the Company officials), the return of Buytendag, and limits as to who could keep shops in the colony because they believed they were challenged by liberated Chinese or East Indian former prisoners who were establishing businesses. They requested that no one should be allowed to settle there except former employees of the Company. Furthermore, they wanted representation on the Judicial Board and their own nominations for certain offices.

Interwoven in the petition were reflections of the growing attitude of the white settlers with respect to the Africans in their midst. Under part III of the petition, the fourth article raised objections not only to the arrest of Buytendag but by whom the arrest was made. "In the future no burgher should be apprehended with violence and with Caffres, taken to prison, or criminally arrested, unless he is found to be a criminal and flagrantly delinquent; much less should a burgher be dragged from his house. . . . A burgher should be arrested by no one but burghers."[154]

Article 6 of the same section gives another insight into the grievances. The burghers asked that they "be allowed to punish their slaves themselves, short, however, of tyranny."[155] The punishments meted out by Company officials were not considered harsh enough. As an afterthought, article 36 suggested that more churches ought to be built in the interior.[156]

The Patriot movement at Cape Town represented not only political and economic ideas and reflected racial attitudes but presupposed a theological analysis as well. An anonymous pamphlet wrote about the *Voice of the People*—the *Volkstem* of later writings.[157] This will of the people was considered the highest good; rulers must be concerned about the general good of all. Should the people see something amiss in their society, it was their right and duty to do whatever they could about it, even if it meant opposing their constituted authorities.

> It is clear, truly, that whenever a people sees its burgher society falling from within, weakened from without, and placed in greatest danger, all characterized by an unhappy anxiety, where each is hurt more or less, in the end a total ruin must follow; I say, the people then have the right to stand up against their authorities, and as original and fellow citizens themselves, to make such arrangements as they shall find are needed.[158]

The Volkstem idea was presented more directly in a letter a few years later:

> We see through this election . . . a possible concealed leading of God Almighty, now made known, and we must look to the participating *Volkstem* as legal, called to support and uphold our Fatherland, and its brave and oppressed inhabitants. . . . It is an indisputable truth that all civilized people of the earth received especially this right of nature directly from God the Almighty, that whenever the certainty of their persons and dearest possessions are threatened and undermined, by forms and under pretexts of appearing to be right, they rally to the defense and protection from all such iniquities. For such purpose the *Volkstem* was established.[159]

Another anonymous tract at Cape Town elaborated the theological assumption that God himself gave them the ability to work for just laws for all. To work for the good of all was to fulfill God's plan; the official who does otherwise opposes God's plan, and the assembled people have the right to challenge him. Burghers must be ready to give their all—even their blood—for the general good, for God gave them all land as free burghers, and they must not fail God.[160] This emphasis on the Volkstem used in eighteenth-century Cape Town later became important in South Africa's concept of its destiny. A century later Paul Kruger, the Transvaal leader in the 1880s and 1890s, said that the voice of God is heard through the voice of the people.[161]

The burgher leaders were acting from this theological perspective when they took their petition to Amsterdam and presented it to the XVII on October 9, 1779. Little was accomplished, even when the grievances were presented again in 1784. Undoubtedly there would have been intense group feeling at Cape Town against the government's restrictions even had the problem of Buytendag not arisen, but the arrest and the petition gave outward evidence of this bitterness. During the eighteenth century, the burghers continued to shift their loyalties from the Company and gave allegiance instead to their own Volkstaat (or the state made up of their own group members). They began to call South Africa "het Vaderland,"[162] replacing the Netherlands. In 1784 one of the inhabitants wrote a letter in which he referred to his friends as "us Afrikaners."[163]

Active resistance to the Company exemplified by the Patriot movement ended by 1788, after having achieved very few of the demands. It would be only ten more years before the Dutch East India Company would be dissolved in bankruptcy, and complaints of the South African settlers would be directed not against the Company but against the mighty British Empire.

While the Patriots were making their economic and political demands at Cape Town and in the Netherlands, the eastern frontiersmen's concerns were focused in the opposite direction. Their major problem concerned a more formidable foe on the eastern frontier, the Kaffir, or more properly, the Bantu. Various names were used for this new opponent continually met on the eastern side of the Great Fish River late in the eighteenth century, especially following 1779. The settlers usually called their opponents Caffres, now written Kaffirs. This term was used when early Muslims had contact with the East African tribes; it is the Arabic word for "pagan," or "unbeliever."[164] The Portuguese who landed on the eastern coast of Africa a century before the Dutch used the same word. When the Dutch borrowed the term, they may have done so knowing the root meaning, but more likely they did not know the origin of the word. Because of its religious association and its pejorative connotation, this term is avoided in this study except in quotations. The more precise designation for these Africans is the Bantu, a linguistic term used collectively for a large number of tribes who inhabit the southern half of Africa. Among the more common groups among the Bantu in southern Africa are the Tswana, the Xhosa, the Sotho, the Zulu, the Swazi, the Mpondo, and the Ndebele.

The new foe of the Boers was a much more serious threat than either the San or the Khoikhoi had been because the Bantu way of life was in more ways similar to that of the Boers. They had a social organization around the tribal leader or chief; they used land for permanent settlements to farm and more often to raise cattle; they had a group loyalty that could be directed and organized for military puposes; and they had their own religious organization.

The Boers' eastward migration was stopped when they were confronted by great numbers of Xhosas at the Great Fish River in 1779. This tribe was part of the larger grouping known as the Nguni people who occupied all the territory between the coast and the Drakensberg, including the Pondo tribe and the great Zulu and Swazi settlements. They had all been migrating southward along the coast for several centuries. The Xhosa were heavily settled in the region of the Great Fish River by the beginning of the eighteenth century.[165] Ultimately they proved too numerous to displace, and the Boer migration would be forced to take another route—straight north across the Orange River.

Prior to this meeting of the different peoples in 1779, however, there had been contacts of various types. Hunters and explorers who went far in advance of the colonists had made earlier reports. On one such trip as early as 1736, a hunting party was attacked by these newly discovered Africans along the Great Fish River.[166] In reaction to the reports sent to the Cape, the officials formulated the policy forbidding all contact and all trade with these Africans.[167] The reaction seems not to have been based on racial considerations; rather it was concerned with the settlers' self-preservation. Although hunters, and later settled pioneers themselves, had conflicts with the Bantu, they found that they could barter cattle from the Bantu for trinkets and began to develop an extensive business. The officials uncovered one such extensive, although illicit, trading business in February 1770 and reacted accordingly.[168]

The Company, however, could not control such illegal and harmful bartering between the Africans and the Europeans. In a move of desperation, the officials extended the eastern boundary in 1775 to the Fish River in the north and the Bushmen's River in the South.[169] Five years later they concluded the eastward movement as they placed the boundary at the Great Fish River all the way to the ocean. All attempts to prevent trading contacts proved unworkable, and what the Company had most feared came to pass in 1779: the first Kaffir war.

The skirmishes with the various Bantu groups continued intermittently for a hundred years, and it is an arbitrary distinction to give certain dates and numbers to each of the nine wars. The Company commanded the Boers to stay on the west side of the Great Fish River, but the Boers disregarded the order. For example, Willem Prinsloo had attacked beyond the river, killing Africans and stealing cattle. Likewise, there were Bantu living on the west side of the same river. The Boers tried to barter as many cattle as possible for little in return. Because the two groups were competing for the same commodities (land and cattle) the conflict was sharp. The Boers soon found to their own harm, however, that the Bantu could not be attacked a few at a time as had been the case with the San or Khoikhoi. The Bantu fought back with an organized force. In retaliation a commando was formed with Adriaan van Jaarsveld as leader. He reported that his victory was gained through trickery.[170] Seemingly anything was fair when dealing with the Xhosa, and it hardly seemed a crime to kill them in such a manner. This first "Kaffir" War ended in July 1781, but a permanent peace was not established.

This first skirmish alerted Company officials to the need of a government outpost on the frontier. The landdrosdy of Graaff-Reinet was organized December 13, 1785, named for the Governor Cornelis Jacob van der Graaff and his wife, whose maiden name was Reinet. The first church on the frontier was also organized there in 1792. When asked why he was not successful in establishing order, the newly appointed landdrost complained that "every one tended to do as he liked," and he lamented the "corruption" that was rapidly spreading in the district.[171] He reported a "rebellious cabal living in Agter de Bruyntjes Hoogte"[172] and much unrest on the frontier from leaders such as Adriaan van Jaarsveld who had ceased to be commander after the arrival of the landdrost. Unruly white men living outside the law contributed as much to the second "Kaffir" war as did the Africans. Boer families were forced from their homes late in 1793, and another disturbance began. In the midst of this conflict a new landdrost was appointed to Graaff-Reinet, H. C. D. Maynier, who became in the eyes of the Boers one of the greatest "villains," or at least an opponent of "true" Boers' ideas.[173]

The new landdrost decided to come to agreeable terms with his opponents. Although Maynier had lived long on the frontier among his Boer compatriots, he was a responsible government official. He released the captive Bantu women and children and sent them home with presents and with the suggestions that they invite their chiefs to discuss a settlement. On November 8, 1783, Maynier and A. A. Faure, landdrost of Swellendam, negotiated a peace with the Bantu, thus recognizing that the Bantu had some human rights. These officials had thus challenged the Boers' basic prejudices, and the Boers' hope for massive retaliation was swept away. The challenge this caused on the frontier gives insight into the self-image of the Boers at the end of the eighteenth century.

When Maynier came to the eastern frontier, he knew something of the situation existing there. Many of the farmers had not paid rent for as much as ten years and did not intend to do so now.[174] Maynier also knew about the covetousness and the warlike tendencies of the frontiersmen, for he had letters to the effect, which he presented at his defense in 1802.[175] He was also convinced that it was the Boers who had been responsible for the Bantu attack of 1793.[176] Since much of the fighting was done by Khoikhoi servants who often risked more than the Boers, Maynier considered it equitable to share the booty with them in proportion to their service. This act earned him the further reputation that "he preferred the Heathens before the Christians." He was not successful as he sought peace and tranquility on the frontier, for the "more I fulfilled in this regard ... the more enemies and adversaries I created to myself among those who saw their scheme thereby threatened."[177] The basic dishonesty, self-serving activities, and lack of good faith among the Boers were unmasked.[178]

The disgruntled Boers took the law into their own hands. In February 1795 a few of their representaives, terming themselves the Volkstem, appeared before Maynier and ordered him to leave within a few hours.[179] The report concerning this action, filed at Cape Town, contained eleven propositions. The general tone of the statement was that they wanted to be independent, they refused leadership from Cape authorities, they recognized no civil rights of the Khoikhoi servants, and they rejected the Herrnhut missionaries who had been among them teaching the Christian religion, and hence equality, to those Africans who wished to listen.[180]   When government officials asked the rebels why Maynier was expelled, they replied that "it was all due to Maynier's conduct of the war against the Kafirs; that he had made peace before the stolen cattle had been recaptured, as a result of which the Boers were plunged into 'poverty and misery.'"[181]

The burghers for the time being had succeeded in their plan to rid themselves of a challenge to their narrow and self-centered concept of life and elected their own landdrost.   Final submission to the authorized government came in February 1797 and George McCartney, the new governor of Cape colony, sent a Mr. Bresler back to be a firm but considerate landdrost of Graaff-Reinet. Although the rebellion was ended, the grievances, only partially real and partly a product of constructed legend, in later years continued to arise.

Little over one year later, another rebellion was organized. In November 1798, Adriaan van Jaarsveld, the veteran commando leader against the San and one of the men who worked for the rebellion of 1795, was arrested for forgery.[182]   When Bresler served notice of such action, he was greeted with the reply from van Jaarsveld: "Sir, I apprehend this will occasion a motion among the people."[183]   The lawbreaker was to be sent to Cape Town for a fair trial. Hardly had the party begun the trip, however, when a large number of Boers, led by Marthinus Prinsloo, stopped the caravan and forcibly freed van Jaarsveld.[184]   Repeated negotiation by the government finally brought surrender.[185]   Van Jaarsveld, Marthinus Prinsloo, and sixteen others were tried. The first two were sentenced to death in Cape Town.[186]   Van Jaarsveld died in prison, and Prinsloo was held in captivity until 1803.

It is not so much the details of the insurrection which are important to us as the underlying suspicion and fears of the Boers, which provide insight into their view of themselves vis-à-vis governmental authority, whether Dutch or British. The suspicion of the Boers against the government was closely linked with their already deep-seated assumption of the lower nature of the Africans. In both areas Afrikaners attempted to maintain the status quo—God's given pattern of life. The suspicions of the Boers, when related to their insecurity and uncertainties, caused them to fluctuate between a bigoted self-confidence and a fear that was near panic. The unifying concept of the "voice of the people," the Volkstem, was used often.[187]   They reasoned that they "were to fight for honor, on pain of being considered as traitors to *their country*."[188] The country for which they rallied their strength, however, was not that represented by the Cape government but the country being developed in the minds of the Boers—the Afrikaner group spirit.

This was more than a political concern. It was the cause of God and was related, they thought, to the spirit of the French Revolution. During his trial in 1800, some of Prinsloo's papers were found revealing this idea:

> Zwellendam is with us and the men leapt for joy when they heard the patriotism was resumed, and the *Lord* is really arrived again at the Cape with the men that left the Cape with him, even as far as the Cape the people are in an insurrection, the Lord was respected by the French in the Revolution and necessitated to take his refuge to the Cape.[189]

That these self-styled patriots, organized as the Volkstem, were true to the cause of the French Revolution is highly questionable. They knew little of the details of the revolution but rather used the terminology in their own particular way.[190] Lichtenstein, a scientific observer in South Africa, was probably accurate when he evaluated the mind of the Boer in 1803: "It is not very easy to make a farmer, and, above all, an African one, listen to reason; or to convince him of any thing, when he has a directly contrary idea in his head."[191] Their long tradition of popular homespun piety led them to equate what they considered important with what God willed. Then in their circular logic, they used this religious terminology to justify their narrow and self-centered half-truths.

While the insurrections were being brought to their ignominious end, the conflicts on the frontier were becoming more severe. The peace settlement of 1793 had included the promise that to alleviate tensions, the Bantu on the west side of the Great Fish River would leave the Boer territory and the Boers would cease trade with the Bantu. Neither promise was kept. In March 1799 the Bantu swept across the Fish River and gained control of land along the Bosjesman, Gamtoos, and Zondags rivers.[192] The murder of some of the Boer families caused others to flee so rapidly that the landdrost was unable to raise any type of defense as he had done in the past.[193] The conflict, entitled the Third Kaffir War, was almost a rout through July and August 1799.[194] A new problem appeared in this war: the Khoikhoi were becoming more discouraged with their servile status, and in retaliation some deserted their Boer masters to join the invading Bantu, resulting in further panic among the Boers.

As a result of the reverses on the frontier, the Cape government called into service again a man who had no small influence over the Khoikhoi. Maynier had been living quietly on his farm in Stellenbosch after being rejected at Graaff-Reinet in 1795. In August 1799 he was summoned to return to his post in the east for a short time to attempt reconciliation with the Khoikhoi.[195] He was partially successful as he won many Africans back to loyalty to their former masters, but his success laid the basis for further conflict related to governmental policy, which was interpreted as "interference with Boer ideas."[196] The concessions he negotiated with the Khoikhoi were at the direction of the Cape government but were in keeping with his own ideas as expressed several years earlier.[197] The main thrust of the agreement was the recognition of the civil rights of the Khoikhoi as individuals. The terms of the peace were that the "government should protect them against the ill treatment of the Boors" and "when they served the Boors that they should be well-paid and well-treated."[198] This was accomplished by establishing a register of all Khoikhoi working for Boers, including the names of the servant and the Boer farmer, ages, and terms of service. There were also certain restrictions on punishments allowed.[199] The Khoikhoi renewed their confidence in the British government because they saw it in contrast to the wanton treatment by Boers without effective governmental control.

Maynier returned home after having accomplished the task for which he was sent to the frontier. He was no longer actively challenging the self-concept of the frontier Boer, but the Boers' own historian, George McCall Theal, added a very biased evaluation of Maynier's appointment and of his career. He stated that "it was one of the most injudicious appointments ever made in South Africa, for no one could have been more out of sympathy with the colonists than Maynier was."[200]

The insurrections against governmental authority and the wars against a cohesive Bantu population were the raw materials from which further ideological concepts or expressions of group consciousness would be formed. The German visitor, Martin K. H. Lichtenstein, gave a good summary of the state of the society already showing evidences of these influences.

> The total seclusion of the colonists from general intercourse with the world, and with civilized life, their confinement to the little circle of their own families, and easy manner in which the first necessities of our nature are satisfied, are very disadvantageous to them under any point of view . . . . Selfishness, lawlessness, hardiness, intolerance, and a thirst for revenge, are the reigning vices in their character, which will perhaps hardly be thought atoned for by a disposition to be easily satisfied, by a spirit of economy yet united with unbounded hospitality, a firm adherence to truth, and a *great respect for religion*. What is most to be depreciated in the character among them, is the harshness with which they treat their slaves and Hottentots, and in others, the bitterness and irreconcilable animosity with which they carry on their differences with one another.[201]

Three aspects of this statement are significant: the condescending attitude he noticed with respect to the Africans on the frontier, the use of religion extrinsically, almost as if it should justify the preconceived attitudes of the frontiersmen, and the isolation of the Boers from any civilizing influences which could shape their culture in a different direction.

One evidence that some were seeking meaning and understanding was the speculation late in the eighteenth century concerning the origin of the Africans. Barrow speculated that they probably came overland from the region of the Nile or from Arabia.[202] Lichtenstein argued from the stand-point of culture that the Africans, if they were from the Near East, mi-grated many centuries ago, for they had lost almost all traces of a culture which they might have brought with them.[203] Sir George Cory suggested that a Semitic origin was a possibility because the Bantu practiced circum-cision.[204] If these thoughts were entertained by casual travelers to South Africa, we may assume that the settlers had read their Bibles and already speculated on similar thoughts. Many Boers had already concluded that the Africans were an inferior people. Could not this conclusion be justified on theological or religious grounds? Indeed, one of the Boers, among the agitators at Swellendam, related this logic to his simple Bible study. The attitude was reported by Governor J. W. Janssens in 1803:

> Instruction! Instruction! is what they lack above all else; they call themselves men and Christians, the Kaffirs and Hottentots heathen, and for this reason they believe that they are permit-ted everything. A brother of Thomas Ferreira who pretends to have some literature, has made the discovery that the Hotten-tots are the descendants of the accursed race of Ham, and consequently are condemned by God Almighty to servitude and ill-treatment.[205]

This concept of the Africans as the children of Ham did not, however, play a significant part in the literature of the eighteenth and nineteenth cen-turies. Other biblical references would be applied to the Africans in the next few decades.

The sharp challenge that came to the Boers late in the eighteenth century forced them to find new images which could be applied to their experiences. Their intepretations of these new challenges reflected their self-consciousness now being openly expressed, whereas it had been only implicit for many decades. Their inadequate reactions were but attempts to bring order and meaning and a coherent world view to their deprived cultural setting. Because they had already equated Christianity with culture and had related themselves to both as opposed to uncultured heathen, their feelings of superiority on the frontier were more real than any official or enlightened theological interpretation so seldom heard in the newly settled areas. Consequently, an effective guide, such as the church, for the developing culture in this remote part of the world did not exist. The cultural ideology that developed instead used some theological terminology, although this matured outside the institutional church and often in spite of the church. This process of formulation was rapidly expanded in the extended period of British administration in South Africa, which began in 1795.

NOTES

1. Representative studies of the great commercial interests of the Company are: Clive Day, *The Dutch in Java* (New York: 1904); Albert Hyma, *The Dutch in the Far East* (Ann Arbor: George Walker, 1942); E. S. de-Klerck, *History of the Netherlands East Indies* (2 vols., Rotterdam: 1938); George Masselman, *The Cradle of Colonialism* (New Haven: Yale University Press, 1963); Pieter van Dam, *Beschryvinge van de Oostindische Compagnie* (4 vols., The Hague: Nijhoff, 1937).

2. Kristof Glaman, *Dutch-Asiatic Trade, 1620-1740* (The Hague: Nijhoff, 1958), pp. 13-14. The major products brought to the Netherlands were: spices (nutmeg, cloves, cinnamon), pepper, sugar, tea and coffee, saltpeter, metal (lead, copper, tin, iron, zinc), and textiles (silk and cotton and others). At different periods different products were more in demand, but throughout the period textiles and pepper each averaged approximately one-third of the cargo, with one-third of the space reserved for all other commodities.

3. Jan van Riebeeck, *Journal* (3 vols., Cape Town: A. A. Balkema, 1952-1959), April 7, 1652.

4. T. S. van Rooyen and J. F. Eloff, *'n Historiese Oorsig oor die Inbesitname van Gronde in Suid-Afrika*, quoted in N. J. Rhoodie and H. J. Venter, *Die Apartheidsgedagte* (Cape Town: H. A. U. M., 1960), p. 42.

5. Glaman, *Dutch-Asiatic Trade*, p. 25.

6. The Seventeen, the ruling trustees of the D. E. I. Co. This Company and its trustees had been given broad powers by the Netherlands government, including the right to build forts, appoint civil and military officers, and maintain troops. South Africa became in time one of their outposts on this basis; it was not a colony of the Netherlands.

7. The plan included the following: "By making a fort and a garden adequate to the requirements of the crews of the Company's passing vessels in the Table Valley, and protecting the whole with a garrison of 60 or 70 soldiers and sailors, and likewise providing the establishment with a proper staff of experienced gardeners, a great deal of produce could be raised. . . . The soil is very good in the valley, and during the dry season the water can be used for irrigation as required. Everything will grow there. . . . It is also beyond doubt that all kinds of fruit trees will thrive there, as orange, lime, apple, citron, shaddock, pear, plum, cherry, gooseberry, and currant, which could be kept on board for a long time. . . . From all this it is plain how necessary the said fort or garden at the Cape has become, as it is well known how difficult it will be for the sailors to reach home without intermediate refreshment; and the company's ships would be liable to great peril from severe illness. The Cape would be most convenient for all ships going to and coming from India, especially if the officers were ordered whenever practicable not to pass, but to touch at the Cape for refreshment." H. C. V. Leibbrandt, ed., *Letters and Documents Received, Part I, Precis of the Cape Archives* (Cape Town: W. A. Rickards & Sons, 1898), pp. 2-8.

8. "If it be asked by whom the garden is to be cultivated, we reply that if 3 or 4 gardeners from Holland are stationed there, enough men will be found among the sailors and soldiers to dig and delve, whilst from Batavia some Chinese, who are an industrious people may be introduced, who are well versed in gardening, and of whom there are always a sufficient number in irons." Leibbrandt, *Letters*, p. 8.

9. "Living on good terms with them [African natives], some of their children may afterwards be employed as servants, and educated in the Christian religion, by which means, if Almighty God blesses the work, as He has done at Tayouan and Formosa, many souls will be brought to the Christian Reformed Religion and to God." Leibbrandt, *Letters*, p. 14.

10. *Ibid.*, p. 16. Letter, July 26, 1649, signed in Amsterdam by Leendert Jansz and N. Proot.

11. Leibbrandt, *Letters*, p. 16.

12. Riebeeck, *Journal*; see appropriate dates, 1651-1652.

13. See "Orthography of Africa's Tribal Names," *Africa* 6 (1933), p. 479. This is referred to and discussed by Monica Wilson in Monica Wilson and Leonard Thompson, eds., *The Oxford History of South Africa* (2 vols., New York and Oxford: Oxford University Press, 1969), I, x, 40-47.

14. Richard Elphick, *Kraal and Castle: Khoikhoi and the Founding of White South Africa* (New Haven: Yale University Press, 1977). This study gives many details concerning several groups who came into contact with the settlers. Especially see the map on p. 50 and the chart on p. 53 giving several of the major groups.

15. April 1, 1652: "and whereas such a new undertaking, especially as regards the natives of that country, who are very brutal, should be proceeded with much prudence, and it will be necessary to be thoroughly on our guard, and in a state of thorough defence, and likewise to give them no cause for dissatisfaction, but on the contrary to do everything to show them all friendship and amiability, in order by affectionate intercourse to make them inclined to associate with us, and provide us with cattle of all sorts, and further to minimize whatever inconvenience we might otherwise suffer from them in our agricultural pursuits, etc., to be undertaken for the refreshment of the Company's ships, at present the chief object of the Directors," Leibbrandt, *Letters*, II, 352, April 1, 1652.

16. Van Riebeeck prayed: Translation: "O merciful, gracious God and heavenly Father, since it is by your divine majesty and love that we are called to direct the affairs of the D. E. I. Company here at the Cape of Good Hope . . . in order to make such resolutions whereby the most service of the said Company may be furthered, justice may be maintained, and among *these wild brutal men*, may it be that *your true Reformed doctrines*, in the course of time, may be propagated and extended, to the honor and praise of your Holy Name. . . . So we pray that you, with your Heavenly wisdom . . . will so enlighten our hearts . . . that we will make no other resolutions than those which will go to magnify and honor your Holy Name." Willem Jacobus van der Merwe, *The Development of Missionary Attitudes*

in the Dutch Reformed Church in South Africa (Cape Town: Nasionale Pers, 1936), p. 242. Italics added.

17. Riebeeck, *Journal,* April 8, 1652.

18. *Ibid.,* October 18, 1656.

19. The watchhouses were: Keert de Koe (Turn the Cow), August 9, 1659; Houdt den Bul (Hold the Bull), September 1, 1659; Kijckuijt (Look Out), August 9 1659; Koornhoop (Corn Pile), July 17, 1657; and Duinhoop (Sand Heap), February 7, 1654. The dates given indicate the place they are first entered in the discussion in Riebeeck, *Journal.*

20. Leibbrandt, *Letters,* II, 244.

21. *Ibid.,* I, 242.

22. Riebeeck, *Journal,* April 6, 1660.

23. *Ibid.* A statistical survey related to the development of this group of free burgers can be found in Gerrit Schutte, "Company and Colonists at the Cape," in Richard Elphick and Hermann Giliomee, *The Shaping of South African Society, 1652-1820* (Cape Town: Longmans, 1979), pp. 187-192.

24. Leibbrandt, *Letters,* April 6, 1657.

25. *Ibid.,* May 4, 18, 1658.

26. For the complete petition and the reply by van Riebeeck, see his *Journal,* December 23, 1658, pp. 391-401.

27. *Ibid.*

28. Leibbrandt, *Letters,* April 6, 1660. Further tension was expected, as the XVII urged the settlers at the Cape not to consider building a larger colony or town: "From your letters we have remarked that you are gradually tending towards the building of a town there, and the enlarging of the colony; but as we look upon it here, this idea should be abandoned, and you should get along with the men and the freemen whom you have with you at present, without extending yourselves any farther." Signed by C. de Graeff, in *ibid.,* August 23, 1661.

29. *Ibid.,* March 1658.

30. James C. Armstrong, "The Slaves, 1652-1795," in Elphick and Giliomee, *Shaping of South African Society,* p.75. See the informative chart on p. 91.

31. "The large-scale use of cheap non-white labor is one of the most far-reaching developments in the history of relations with the colored in South Africa." N. J. Rhoodie, and Herman J. Venter, *Die Apartheidsgedagte: 'n sosio-historiese uiteensetting van sy ontstaan en ontwikkeling* (Cape Town: H. A. U. M. 1960), p. 44. English trans., *Apartheid: A Sociohistorical*

Exposition of the Origin and Development of the Apartheid Idea (Cape Town: H.A.U.M., 1960).

32. Riebeeck, *Journal,* June 26, 1656.

33. *Ibid.,* April 28-29, 1656.

34. "(73) The office of sick-visitor is first of all to instruct the sick from God's Holy Word, to encourage them and strengthen them at certain times and according to ability; in addition, second, to sing from God's Holy Word a few chapters or also to inspire the people by reading a good sermon from the Decades of Bullinger, or Ursinus' *Catechism,* or another book written by a teacher of the true Christian Reformed religion; to begin and end his own work with prayer before and after meals; and fourth, to use every special opportunity to instruct people from God's holy word, instructing the ignorant in the basis of the faith, to admonish the sinner concerning mercy and repentance of sin by holding up the punishments of God, to warn those from their ruin, especially those who curse, misuse the name of God, and indulge in all manner of undisciplined words and works; and also to give to the faithful or discouraged, that in which to trust and to strengthen them; and this shall all be done without presuming on his own, under any pretext, to do that which is right only of the minister."
"(75) The sick visitor shall also visit the persons condemned to death by the authorities, by remaining with them in order to use the opportunity to teach them from God's Holy Word.
"(78) The office of the sick visitor in the hospital is, in the morning and evening to read a chapter of God's word, and to sing a verse; finally to visit the sick twice a day."
"Die Kerkorde van 1643" was the basis of the Reformed church in all areas of the Dutch commercial empire. The order concerning the Zieckentrooster is printed in Coenraad Spoelstra, *Bouwstoffen voor de Geschiedenis der Nederduitsch-Gereformeerde Kerken in Zuid-Afrika* (2 vols., Cape Town and Amsterdam: 1906), II, 594-595.

35. "Ze Moesten de voisen [wijsen] van alle Psalmen kennen" ("They must know the tunes of all Psalms"). C. A. L. van Troostenburg de Bruyn, *De Hervormde Kerk in Nederlandsch Oost Indie* (Arnheim: H. A. Tjeenk Willink, 1884), p. 338.

36. Spoelstra, *Bouwstoffen,* II, p. 40.

37. John M'Carter, *The Dutch Reformed Church in South Africa* (Edinburgh: W. & C. Inglis, 1869), p. 7.

38. *The Heidelberg Catechism,* ques. 74.

39. *Ibid.,* ques. 70.

40. Elphick and Giliomee, *Shaping of South African Society,* p. 121.

41. Riebeeck, *Journal,* November 8, 1658. Eva was a child taken into the home of Jan van Riebeeck, taught the Dutch language, baptized into the Christian faith, trained as an interpreter for the Dutch, and on June 2, 1664, she married Pieter van Meerhoff, a settler from Copenhagen. There

"appeared before the Council, Pieter van Meerhoff, of Copenhagen, surgeon's assistant, aged 28 years, and the Hottentot interpreter Eva, aged 18
years, who having engaged themselves in marriage to each other, desired
that they might be duly united in the holy state of matrimony.

"The Council, therefore, not having been able to learn anything but
that they were both free persons—who, according to their own statements,
have not contracted any other similar engagement—have thought fit to
consent to the reasonable request of these persons;—because through this
alliance of the said Hottentot interpreter Eva—who has long since had
herself baptized, and has begun to acquire a taste for our knowledge of our
religion—with such a good, sober, and respectable man, these native tribes
will become more and more attached to us." *Journal,* April 12, 1664, in
D. Moodie, ed., *The Record: A Series of Official Papers Relative to the
Condition and Treatment of the Native Tribes of South Africa* (Cape Town:
Robertson, 1838-1841), p. 280. Since Eva was eighteen years old at the
time, she could have been only six or seven when van Riebeeck first arrived
at the Cape.

Children born to the couple were baptized as Christians. The interpretation of Christian baptism as a civilizing and life-changing sacrament was
stated in these words: "This day departed this life, a certain female Hottentot, named Eva, long taken from the African brood in her tender child-
hood by the Hon. van Riebeeck, and educated in his house as well as
brought to the knowledge of the Christian faith, and being thus *transformed
from a female Hottentot almost into a Netherland woman.*" Leibbrandt,
Journal, July 29, 1674. Italics added.

42. Riebeeck, *Journal,* July 6, 1658.

43. "Peter Cassier . . . preached an edifying sermon, after which 12
children were baptized. Only one, however, was found to be of Netherland
Christian parents, the rest were all of the female slaves of the Company,
mostly illegitimate and born from time to time." Leibbrandt, *Precis,
Journal,* September 16, 1663.

44. "The baptized slave children of the Company and the burghers, especially those descended from European or Christian fathers, should be
educated and in time brought to the true knowledge of God, as the sick
comforter had already done. . . . On which may God Almighty grant His
grace and blessing." Leibbrandt, *Precis, Journal,* November 30, 1663.

"Company slaves were to be forced to attend prayers; children, the
progeny of Europeans and slaves, of whom 12 were then at school, were to
be taught, and particular care to be taken that they were not alienated, so
as to remain in constant slavery, but that they might in due time enjoy the
freedom to which, in the right of the father, they were born." Isbrand
Goske, commissioner, subsequently governor, left this memorandum behind,
February 23, 1671. Moodie, *Record,* p. 309.

45. "It has been a matter of dispute whether the children of unbelieving
parents should be admitted to baptism, and that, after reference to the
classis in Holland, the question was decided in the affirmative; provided the
person with whom they live, whether the owner or not, obliges himself to
educate them in the Christian religion; this being chiefly founded upon the
example of the Patriarch Abraham, in whose faith all who were in his house
were circumcised; and the observance has accordingly *been long followed*

here; even with those belonging to the Company, which has established schools for the purpose, where, as soon as they come to the proper age, they are instructed in the Christian religion. You may therefore take this regulation for your guidance, and if you proceed in that holy work, there, as is done here, you will do well and act the part of a Christian." Dispatch from Batavia, January 1664. Moodie, *Record,* p. 273. Italics added.

46. That "these native tribes will become more and more attended to us." Moodie, *Record,* April 12, 1664, p. 280.

47. "Arrangements were started for establishing a school for the Company's male and female slaves. . . . The sick comforter, Pieter van der Stael of Rotterdam, has been entrusted with the task of giving them instruction in the morning and afternoon, besides his duties of visiting the sick, particularly because he reads Dutch well and correctly. To encourage the slaves to attend and to hear or learn the Christian prayers, it is ordered that after school every one is to receive a small glass of brandy and two inches of tobacco." Riebeeck, *Journal,* April 17, 1658.
   "In the same way the baptized slave children of the Company and the burghers, especially those descended from European or Christian fathers, should be educated and in time brought to the true knowledge of God, as the sick comforter has already done." Signed by Z. Wagenaer, in Leibbrandt, *Precis, Journal,* November 30, 1663.

48. Leibbrandt, *Precis, Journal,* September 24, 1666. Likewise, in the year 1663, "Ernestus Back, who had been industrious in teaching and catechising children, both Dutch and black." *Ibid.,* November 30, 1663.
   "D. Engelgraef of Amsterdam had arrived in 1663 as a soldier. During life he had been a quiet and useful young man, and for that reason we had afterwards employed him as a schoolmaster for the Cape white and black children." Wagenaer to the XVII, Leibbrandt, *Precis, Journal,* September 13, 1666.

49. Riebeeck, *Journal,* September 6, 1665.

50. J. du Plessis, "Grepe uit de Geskiedenis van Stellenbosch," in *Stellenbosch* (Stellenbosch: Horters, 1929).

51. There are two studies concerned specifically with the French refugees at the Cape: Colin Graham Botha, *The French Refugees at the Cape* (Cape Town: Cape Times, 1919), and Manfred Nathan, *The Huguenots in South Africa* (Johannesburg: Central News Agency, 1939).

52. Botha, *French Refugees,* p. 155. See also G. Elmore Reaman, *The Trail of the Huguenots in Europe, the United States, South Africa and Canada* (London: Frederick Miller, 1964), pp. 108-109.

53. Leibbrandt, *Letters,* December 17, 1690.

54. The local government promised to carry out this policy so that "by the use of Dutch in the church and school there, the French tongue will fall into disuse amongst the inhabitants of that community, and afterwards, in course of time, die out; and this will the more readily take place inasmuch

as there are no French schools." Letter to the Chamber XVII in Amsterdam, March 20, 1702, in Botha, *French Refugees,* p. 159.

55. Petition dated June 24, 1703, in Nathan, *Huguenots,* p. 115.

56. In 1723 it was stated, "there are some 25 or 26 old people in the district who do not understand Dutch very well." Botha, *French Refugees,* p. 14.
    In 1724 the Bible was publicly read in French for the last time. In 1739 there was another prohibition of French in worship services, indicating that previous prohibitions had not been entirely successful. In 1752 Abbée de la Caille, an astronomer, visited the Cape and mentioned the gradual extinction of French among the children of Huguenots. In 1780 the French traveler, LeVaillant, recorded that he found only one man who understood French. Nathan, *Huguenots,* pp. 118, 120.

57. Examples of French names respelled in Dutch fashion: Jourdan becomes Jordaan; Retif becomes Retief; de Clercq becomes de Klerk; Rousseau becomes Rossouw; du Pre becomes du Preez. George McCall Theal, *History and Ethnology of Africa South of the Zambezi before 1795* (3 vols., London: Swan Sonnenschein & Co., 1910), III, 440-444. Other significant family names dating from the seventeenth century that retained their French spelling are: Malan, de Villiers, du Toit, Marais, and Joubert. See the complete listing by families of all French refugees who settled in South Africa in Botha, *French Refugees,* pp. 59-96.

58. Summarized in Nathan, *Huguenots,* pp. 132-133.

59. *Ibid.,* p. 96.   The 400 farmers' land totaled perhaps 40,000 acres; hence the few Company officials controlled approximately one-third of the Cape farming land.

60. Leo Fouché, ed. *Het Dagboek van Adam Tas,* 1705-1706, trans. A. C. Patterson (London: Longmans, Green and Co., 1914), p. 96 (hereafter cited as *Tas Diary*).

61. The colonists quickly saw that the advantage belonged to the official leaders: "But Lord! Our great ones, how they do know to tip the ball from one to other!" *Tas Diary,* August 14, 1705. This conspiracy against the governor is analyzed in detail in the diary of Adam Tas, one of the opponents of the governor.

62. The complete *Memorial* is to be found in Leibbrandt, *Precis of the Cape Archives,* IV, pp. 52-65. Further details concerning this Van der Stel affair are summarized by Gerrit Schutte in Elphick and Giliomee, *Shaping of South African Society,* pp. 192-196.

63. Nathan, *Huguenots,* p. 104.

64. Fouché, *Tas Diary,* p. 361.

65. *Ibid.,* p. 381. See also Leo Fouché, *Die evolutie van die Trekboer* (Pretoria: 1910), and Leo Fouché, "Foundation of the Cape Colony, 1652-

1708," *The Cambridge History of the British Empire*, VIII, *South Africa* (Cambridge: Cambridge University Press, 1936).

66. "Dit heb ik reeds weg, en dit hebben de Boeren mij gebakken." (Trans.: "I have already lost, and the Boers have baked me"—colloquially "have cooked my goose." Fouché, *Tas Diary*, p. 362.

67. "The Commissioners have to proceed inland to collect the burgher returns; and . . . abuses occur among most of the burghers or farmers of this government in estimating and returning their annual crops, still standing or lying in the fields, or already gathered . . . stating just what they like, and withholding a large portion; and as in this way they have defrauded the Company out of its lawful right of tithes to the very great extent, notwithstanding all their lands have hitherto been granted to them gratis, but principally under the servitude contained in all the title deeds, that they shall annually deliver to the Company the tithes of their harvest gathered." Leibbrandt, *Journal*, December 19, 1708.

68. "Many servants of the Company have deserted and fled with other offenders and Englishmen and other foreigners towards the wilderness and mountains, leading a thievish and godless life. Every attempt to apprehend them hitherto a failure. The probability of their repentance and disgust with the life led by them, considered; . . . the Council decides to clear this Colony of all such pernicious people, from whom only evil can be expected, by pardoning them, and publishing a general amnesty to all, excepting incendiaries, murderers, burglars, cattle thieves and highwaymen. Within two months after date they are to report themselves at the Castle. Should they fail to do so and be captured afterwards, they are to be punished as fugitives and deserters, vagrants and disturbers of the public peace." Leibbrandt, *Journal*, June 18, 1709.

69. Richard Elphick, "The Khoisan to c. 1770" in Elphick and Giliomee, *Shaping of South African Society*, pp. 18-21.

70. The Boers provided only food and shelter for the Khoikhoi and in return received help to expand their grazing activities. Travelers who wrote about this period were Andrew Sparrman, O. F. Mentzel, John Barrow, François le Vaillant, and Henry Lichtenstein.

71. C. Graham Botha's discussion of "Early Land Tenure" in *Collected Works* (3 vols., Cape Town: C. Struik, 1962), II, chap. VI, pp. 81-100.

72. A. J. H. Van der Walt, *Die Ausdehnung der Kolonie am Kap der Guten Hofnung, 1700-79; Eine historisch-ökonomische Untersuchung uber das Werden und Wesen des Pionierlebens im 18 Jahrhundert* (Berlin: Ebering, 1928), p. 36.

73. Botha, *Collected Works*, I, 109. A recent statistical and sociological study of the eastward movement may be found in Leonard Guelke, "The White Settlers, 1652-1780" in Elphick and Giliomee, *Shaping of South African Society*, pp. 41-71.

74. Van der Walt, *Ausdehnung*, p. 65.

75. Botha, *Collected Works*, I, 110.

76. Martin Karl Heinrich Lichtenstein, *Travels in Southern Africa*, 2 vols., trans. Anne Plumptre (Cape Town: Van Riebeeck Society Publications), vol. X (1928), vol. XI (1930), X, 200.

77. Van der Walt, *Ausdehnung*, p. 70.

78. *Ibid.*, p. 70.

79. Botha, *Collected Works*, I, 111.

80. Van der Walt, *Ausdehnung*, p. 69.

81. *Ibid.*

82. S. F. N. Gie, "The Cape Colony under Company Rule, 1708-1795," *Cambridge History of the British Empire*, VIII, 148.

83. *Ibid.*

84. Botha, *Collected Works*, I, 111.

85. Van der Walt, *Ausdehnung*, p. 75.

86. C. F. J. Muller, *Five Hundred Years: A History of South Africa* (Pretoria and Cape Town: Academia, 1969), pp. 60-61.

87. Botha, *Collected Works*, I, 196-197.

88. Henry Lichtenstein, *Travels in Southern Africa in the Years 1803-1806* (2 vols., Cape Town: Van Riebeeck Publications, 1928), II, 63.

89. Wilson and Thompson, *Oxford History of South Africa*, I, 40-47.

90. Elphick and Giliomee, *Shaping of South African Society*, p. 4.

91. Sparrman, Andrew, *A Voyage to the Cape of Good Hope* (London: R. Morrison, 1789), p. 143. Lichtenstein, a medical student from Germany, took care to check on this type of information. See Lichtenstein, *Travels*, II, 54. Authoritative studies of the Bushmen are I. Schapera, *The Khoisan Peoples of South Africa: Bushmen and Khoikhois* (London: Routledge, 1930), pp. 75-220, and George W. Stow, *The Native Races of South Africa* (London: Swan Sonnenschein, 1905), pp. 1-231.

92. "These Bushmen live between the highest-mountains, in the loneliest most arid regions, in the direst poverty, often suffering the sharpest hunger for days on end and are sometimes compelled to fill their bellies with the most execrable food, so that they look like skeletons encased in leather. Having no cattle and often lacking even edible roots and other wild fruits, they are forced to steal and in desperation have to risk their lives to fill their stomachs. They, therefore, do not easily let an opportunity pass to stalk, attack and overwhelm the tame Khoikhois, to drive off and steal

some of their cattle." Mentzel, *Geographical and Topographical Description of the Cape of Good Hope*, Van Riebeeck Society Publication, XXV, 260-261.

93. George Cory, *The Rise of South Africa* (5 vols., London: Longmans & Green, 1910), I, 19.

94. Lichtenstein, *Travels*, XI, 281.

95. This is a custom still remembered by many Bushmen visited as recently as 1936. See I. D. MacCrone, *Race Attitudes in South Africa* (London: Oxford University Press, 1937), p. 122.

96. Le Vaillant, *Travels*, I, 150.

97. Moodie, *Record*, III, 80.

98. "Dusdanig dat een ieder in zy contry de Bosjesmans op de spoor te vervolg en dood te schieten." Quoted in MacCrone, *Race Attitudes*, p. 123.

99. Moodie, *Record*, III, 44.

100. "Als wilde Tiere, deren Sitten und Gemütsart sie angenommen haben, jagten und ausrotteten." Quoted in van der Walt, *Ausdehnung*, p. 46.

101. Typical commando raids are reported for August, September, and November 1774, as follows: "a skirmish began with the Bushmen, 16 were shot in their kraal, and 6 taken prisoners. . . . Found a kraal, in which 9 were killed; . . . Kraal, in which 30 were killed . . . Van Rensburg found a kraal, in which 8 were killed and 1 taken; . . . he found a small kraal, in which 4 bushmen were shot, 2 were taken, and 2 escaped; . . . 13 were shot and 1 taken; and then another small kraal, in which 9 were shot and 7 taken . . . 11 were shot and 14 taken." Moodie, *Record*, III, 36.

102. S. F. N. Gie, "The Cape Colony Under Company Rule," *Cambridge History*, Vol. VIII, *South Africa*, p. 154. We note a slight difference in pagination between the almost identical editions of 1936 and 1963.

103. H. T. Colenbrander, *De Afkomst der Boeren* (Het Algemeen Nederlandsch Verbond, 1902), p. 113.

104. Werner Schmidt-Pretoria, *Der Kulturanteil des Deutschtums am Aufbau des Burenvolkes* (Hanover: Hahnsche, 1938), p. 268.

105. J. Hoge, "Die Geskiendenis van die Lutherse Kerk aan die Kaap," *Argief Jaarboek vir Suid Afrikaanse Geskiendenis*, I (1938), part 2, pp. 26-28.

106. *Uitgaande Brief* July 14, 1741; quoted in *ibid.*, p. 30.

107. "Somewhat farther to the right lies Elsenberg, a farm celebrated for its fertility. It formerly belonged to a man by name of Martin Milch . . . a native of Memel, who, although he could neither read nor write, grew

so rich that he was able to build the Lutheran chapel at the Cape Town, entirely at his own expense." Lichtenstein, *Travels*, II, 125.

108. J. Hoge, "Geskiedenis van die Lutherse Kerk," p. 80.

109. See the discussion in Lichtenstein, *Travels*, II, 303.

110. Ernst G. Malherbe, *Education in South Africa, 1652-1922* (Cape Town: Juta and Co., 1925), p. 19.

111. Cornelius W. de Kiewiet, *A History of South Africa, Social and Economic* (London: Oxford University Press, 1960), p. 17.

112. Van Imhoff, March 15, 1743, quoted in MacCrone, *Race Attitudes*, p. 98.

113. Van der Walt, *Ausdehnung*, p. 97.

114. Mentzel, *Description of Cape of Good Hope*, Part I, 149.

115. "Once a quarter the Holy Communion was celebrated, when the farmers came in their wagons from far and wide. The square in front of the church was a lively scene of people and wagons and here the sale and bartering of goods went on. The farmers generally arrived in the village the Tuesday night before the celebration as on the Friday afternoon a preparatory service was held. . . . Those who could attended this quarterly service regularly, others only once a year. The visit was the occasion to bring produce to the market and to lay in a stock of groceries and other household requirements." Botha, "Social Life in the Cape Colony," *Collected Works*, I, 202.

116. A traveler in the eastern portion of the colony at the end of the eighteenth century summarized the practice that had been continued by a large portion of the pioneers for two or three generations. "Much time was also passed in the services of devotion . . . at which I regularly attended. . . . The day was begun regularly with a psalm being sung, and a chapter from the Bible being read. Not only the children, but all the slaves and Khoikhois, were required to attend. Among the latter, almost all the women had learnt the favourite psalms by heart, and joined in singing them with their sharp and shrill tones. [In the evening] a table was set out, at which all the Christians seated themselves; the slaves and Khoikhois squatting, as in the morning, round the room. The father then read some extracts from his old sermons, which was followed by the whole company singing a psalm. The ceremony was concluded by the evening blessing. Besides this, on the Sunday morning a solemn service was performed; at which a long sermon was read . . . there were no other books in the house but the sermons and a Bible." Lichtenstein, *Travels*, II, 447.

117. *Ibid.*, II, 121.

118. Andres Sparrman, *A Voyage to the Cape of Good Hope* (London: R. Morrison, 1789), p. 51. Historical developments of the nineteenth century in the Transvaal produced other examples: Land of Goshen, the town of Bethlehem, and the River Nyl.

119. Botha, *Collected Works,* I, 296.

120. An aged grazier spoke "about the lives of . . . the Old Testament heroes or . . . compare a storm on the lofty inland plains with that grand description of the one given in the twenty-ninth psalm. On subjects like this the grazier could talk freely enough, because they came within the range of his experience. He was living under such skies as those under which Abraham lived, his occupation was the same, he understood the imagery of the Hebrew writers more perfectly than anyone in Europe would understand it, for it spoke to him of his daily life. He had heard the continuous roll of thunder which was as the voice of the Lord upon many waters, and had seen the affrighted antelopes drop their young as they fled before the storm, when the great trees came down with a crash, and the lightening divided like flames of fire. He knew, too, of skies like brass and of earth like iron, of little clouds seemingly no larger than a man's hand presaging a deluge of rain, and of swarms of locusts before whose track was the garden of the Lord, while behind was a naked desert." Malherbe, *Education in South Africa,* pp. 47-48.

121. Along the road the traveler spoke with an African companion about religion. "He asserted that I was the first that had ever spoken to him on that subject. . . . He knew very well, that the white people assembled together in churches, but had never thought of enquiring for what purpose. . . . Upon the whole, his mind was perfectly capable of being illuminated; but as making proselytes neither advantages the Dutch in capital nor interest, this poor soul was neglected, with many others of his country." Sparrman, *Voyage to Cape of Good Hope,* p. 55.

122. MacCrone, *Race Attitudes,* p. 130.

123. A lion was attacking. "I called softly to the mother not to be alarmed, and, invoking the name of the Lord, fired the piece." Lichtenstein, *Travels,* II, 225.

124. Report of Field Sergeant Carel van der Merwe to the landdrost of Stellenbosch, September 3, 1779, in Moodie, *Record,* III, 82: "Although the victory does not depend on numbers, the Lord has often employed the arms of war to subdue his enemies, as was done by the great illustrious King David, and is recorded for us in 2nd Samuel; and as the rule is laid down for us, in God's holy word, to seek human aid in time of need (Joshua 10 and 11), so do not turn away from us, but come and help to defeat the great kraal, and let us be strong and fight for the name of the Lord our God." Andries P. Burger to the Field Corporal, December 30, 1776, Moodie, *Record,* III, 62.

125. Andries P. Burger to A. P. Burger, December 30, 1776, Moodie, *Record,* III, 62.

126. Van der Walt, *Ausdehnung,* p. 97.

127. "Having long reflected upon this matter, we have thought it fit to lay our desires before you with all humility, as it is perhaps possible that, on consideration of our prayers, you may favor us with a clergyman and a Landdrost, not that we wish, from any ground of discontent, to separate

from Stellenbosch, but solely on account of the great distance of that place; for how many are there here in the country who have already departed from the commands of their God, and to our great injury, became disobedient to Him, and to those who, by His will, are established in authority. As they live so far distant, they think our correctors do not see it, and how can they become aware of our misdeeds? Under this feeling they commit wilful insubordination from which we apprehend serious oppression, unless God, through your means and power, should be mercifully pleased to prevent it.

"But alas! It is no great matter of wonder that things go on so ill in some parts of this country; for, as before said, we have been hitherto without teachers and clergy, so that many fine young people are growing up like the *ignorant cattle*, without any opportunity of learning in their youth the first principles, from which they may not depart when old." Moodie *Record*, III, 74-75. Italics added.

128. The statement, dated March 1, 1779, in which van Plettenberg summarized much of the same material, is printed in Moodie, *Record*, III, 78.

129. E. G. Pells, *300 Years of Education in South Africa* (Cape Town: Juta and Co., 1954), p. 17.

130. Malherbe, *Education in South Africa*, p. 37.

131. Botha, "Social Life in the Cape Colony," *Collected Works*, I, 179.

132. Malherbe, *Education in South Africa*, p. 37.

133. Lichtenstein, *Travels*, II, 96-97.

134. Le Vaillant, *Travels*, I, 66.

135. When girls "have become moderately efficient in reading and writing, their schooling is at an end; thereafter their education is domestic, and under their mother's eye. Idleness is not encouraged; some sewing or knitting must fill up every leisure hour." Mentzel, *Description of Cape of Good Hope*, Part II, 108-109.

136. O. F. Mentzel, *A Geographical-Topographical Description of the Cape of Good Hope*, trans. H. J. Mandelbrote (Cape Town: Van Riebeeck Society Publications, 1925), XXV, 119.

137. Le Vaillant, *Travels*, II, 45. Italics added.

138. In an official meeting at Stellenbosch, March 28, 1774, it was stated "that there might be thus employed about 100 Europeans, or Christians, and 150 Bastards and other Khoikhois, and thus in all 250." Moodie, *Record*, III, 22.

In 1803 we read: "Our whole company now consisted, besides the Landdrost and myself, of six Christians, . . . of twelve Khoikhois, and five slaves, in all 25 persons." Lichtenstein, *Travels*, II, 254.

An expedition undertaken in 1761 and 1762 consisted of "a company of 17 Christians and 68 bastard Khoikhois." Instructions drawn up by Gov. Ryk

Tulbagh and the Council. Mentzel, *Description of Cape of Good Hope*, Part III, 128.

139. "Their colonists' harsh rough manners have led them to acts of revenge which are a disgrace to Christians, to persons who derive their origin from cultivated and civilized nations." Lichtenstein, *Travels*, II, 64-65.

140. September 15, 1801. *Transactions of the Missionary Society*, I, 491, quoted in MacCrone, *Race Attitudes*, p. 129n.

141. Lichtenstein, *Travels*, XI, 303.

142. *Ibid.* Italics added.

143. Sparrman, *Voyage to the Cape of Good Hope*, I, 385. Italics added.

144. McCrone, *Race Attitudes*, p. 131n.

145. "Boys who, through force or circumstances, have to remain at home during these impressionable years between 16 and 21 more often than not commit some folly, and get entangled with a handsome slave-girl belonging to the household. These affairs are not regarded as very serious. The girl is sternly rebuked for her wantonness. . . . It does not hurt the boy's prospects; his escapade is a *source of amusement*, and he is dubbed a young fellow who has shown the stuff he is made of." Mentzel, *Description of Cape of Good Hope*, Part II, 109-110. Italics added.

146. A daughter "had, by some accident or other, already been delivered of a black child, the father of which, as a reward for his kindness, had been advanced from the condition of slave to that of prisoner for life . . . and the daughter to that of wife of her father's bailiff." Sparrman, *Voyage to the Cape of Good Hope*, p. 46.

147. "The domestic life of many was of a very slovenly kind, and the worse cases were those of Ehrenkroon and Hans Dietlof, the former of whom lived with a Bastard woman and the latter with a female Hottentot, while the case of Frederik Zeelen revealed a worse mess, he having two brothers-in-law, named Smit . . . who were not even baptized." J. W. Cloppenburg, *Annotatien en Remarques*, I, chapter 7, quoted in MacCrone, *Race Attitudes*, p. 117.

148. Karl Müller, *200 Jahre Brüdermission* (Herrnhut: Missions-Buchhandlung, 1931), p. 173.   Cf. J. D. Schreuder, "Die opvoedkundige bedrywighede van die Morawiese Broederkerk onder die Kleurlinge in Suid-Afrika, 1737-1743 (en) 1792-1950; 'n historieskritiese studie," (D. Ed. thesis, University of Potchefstroom, 1951).

149. Müller, *200 Jahre Brüdermission*, p. 175.

150. *Ibid.*, p. 180. They justified this attitude on the basis of a decree by the Dutch East India Company of 1642: "In prescribed lands no other service of religion shall be allowed, much less taught or propagated, whether privately or public, than the Reformed Christian faith which is taught in the churches of the United Netherlands." Whoever teaches another religion

shall "be banned from the land, or be punished." Quoted in C. van Gelderen, *Kerk en sending in Suid-Afrika* (Amsterdam: van Battenburg, 1923), p. 60.

151. N. J. Rhoodie and H. J. Venter, *Apartheid: A Socio-Historical Exposition of the Origin and Development of the Apartheid Idea* (Cape Town: H. A. U. M., 1960), p. 54.

152. The petition is printed in full in Coenraad Beyers, *Die Kaapse Patriotte* (Cape Town: Juta and Kie, 1929), pp. 8-38.

153. *Ibid.,* p. 40.

154. *Ibid.,* pp. 26-27.

155. *Ibid.,* p. 27.

156. Article 36 of the memorial in *ibid.,* p. 36.

157. These primary sources are printed in Beyers, *Die Kaapse Patriotte,* pp. 203-213; and Bylaag B, pp. 214-216.

158. *Ibid.,* p. 151. "It is for the people themselves that the Will of the People is to be conducted, so that all will become one will, the object of which shall be the general good for the total society. It follows from this that the welfare of the people is the highest law, that the reality of the authority consists in maintaining the rights of the subjects, and for the common good, the concern of the rules must be more concerned with the whole than a section of the people." Beyers, *Die Kaapse Patriotte,* p. 149f.

159. *Ibid.,* p. 220. Letter by Marthinus Adrianus Bergh, December 14, 1784.

160. "We have found that nothing is more true, nothing that the reading of the Holy Scriptures teaches is more true, that the Almighty has put this law on each man as the basic law of all obligations. Namely that he, following his best knowledge, shall further his own well-being with that of his assembled compatriots that as much may be accomplished as possible.

"Out of these general obligations, given to each man by the Almighty creator, flows these two laws, that each man follows the way wherein he works to the well-being of all, and especially to the well-being of the Burgher community, where he is a member—as far as is possible for him. . . .

"We have considered it an honor to offer goods and blood for the general interest, whether you agree with our objectives or not. It is our obligation out of force of the two mentioned basic laws we are impelled as one to get into the work in order to further the general good, and there to use the means which God and nature put into our hands as free burghers, of a colony of the freely constituted United Netherlands." Beyers, *Die Kaapse Patriotte,* pp. 214-215.

161. "Ik sta heir voor uw aangezicht, geroepen door het Volk; in die stem van het Volk heb ik behoord die stem van God, den Konig der volken, en ik gehoorsaam." (Trans. "I stand here before your face, called by the people; in the voice of the people I have heard the voice of God, the King of the people, and I am obedient.") Coenraad Beyers, "Die Groot Trek met

betrekking tot ons Natsiegroei," *Argief-Jaarboek vir Suid-Afrikaanse Geskiendenis*, IV (1941), Part I, p. 9.

162. *Ibid.*, p. 165.

163. *Ibid.*, p. 231.

164. Edgar Prestage, "The Portuguese in South Africa," *Cambridge History of the British Empire*, VIII, *South Africa*, p. 86. See also Lichtenstein, *Travels*, X, 297n.

165. An excellent survey of the many tribes living in the areas soon to be occupied and/or annexed by the white governments—whether British or Boer—is given in J. D. Omer-Cooper, *The Zulu Aftermath: A Nineteenth Century Revolution in Bantu Africa* (London: Longman Group, 1966). This reference to Xhosa migrations is cited on pp. 21 and 22.

166. Rhoodie and Venter, *Apartheid*, p. 51.

167. Moodie, *Record*, III, 5-6. December 8, 1739.

168. "But it must be concluded, beyond doubt, that such covetous conduct is chiefly practiced in order to enable them more conveniently to carry on an illicit traffic in the bartering of cattle, whether with the Hottentots residing thereabouts, or with the so-called Kafirs, as—among other appearances noticed by the said Commission—sufficiently appears from their having found a beaten wagon road leading out of the Swellendam District to the residence of the Kaffirs; and this all, notwithstanding that the said cattle barter has been from time to time prohibited, on pain of bodily and capital punishment, especially by the proclamation still in force, of the 8th December 1739." Report by a commission of a trip to the east to investigate complaints in 1770, in Moodie, *Record*, III, 5-6.

169. Moodie, *Record*, II, 49.

170. Van Jaarsveld reported concerning the expulsion of the Bantu on July 20, 1781: "Kaffirs again moved in among us. . . . I therefore, assembled a strong Commando, and began to expel the Kaffirs on the 23rd day of May last. . . . They were among Bantu and seemed to be overpowered and as I quickly saw that if we allowed the Kafirs to make the first attack, it could not be otherwise than that many must fall on my side, I hastily collected all the tobacco the men had with them, and having cut it into small bits, I went about twelve paces in front, and threw it to the Kafirs, calling to them to pick it up; they ran out from amongst us, and forgot their plan. I then gave the word to fire, when the said three Captains and all their fencible men were overthrown and slain, and part of their cattle, to the number of 800, taken." Moodie, *Record*, II, 110-112. This statement is duplicated in Jeffreys, *Kaapse Archiefstukken*, IV (1781), 539.

171. J. S. Marais, *Maynier and the First Boer Republic* (Cape Town: Maskew Miller, 1944), p. 14. Further discussion of this frontier development can be found in Hermann Giliomee, "The 'Patriotic' Movement in

Graaff-Reinet, 1795-1799," in Elphick and Giliomee, *Shaping of South African Society*, pp. 338-342.

172. Marais, *Maynier and the First Boer Republic*, p. 87n.

173. *Ibid.*, p. 34.

174. *Ibid.*, p. 1n.

175. Maynier's complete defense is given in George McCall Theal, *Records of the Cape Colony* (35 vols., London: Wm. Clowes and Sons, 1905), IV, 283-329.

176. Marais, *Maynier*, p. 56.

177. Theal, *Records*, IV, 286.

178. Cf. Bresler to General Craig, December 27, 1796, in Theal, *Records*, I, 497.

179. Theal, *Records*, IV, 287.

180. Memorandum on the condition of the colony—the Graaff-Reinet rebellion. Theal, *Records*, I, 172.

181. Marais, *Maynier*, p. 61.

182. Theal, *Records*, II, 349, Van Jaarsveld was arrested for attempting to forge his financial reports. He had a tax-return receipt that indicated he had paid to 1791 but attempted to change the final number to a "4" to avoid paying taxes for 1792-1794.

183. *Ibid.*, II, 389.

184. *Ibid.*, p. 390.

185. *Ibid.*, p. 425, May 14, 1799.

186. *Ibid.*, III, 295.

187. *Ibid.*, II, 392; cf. *ibid.*, p. 221.

188. *Ibid.*, III, 221.

189. The trial was held in August 1800.   *Ibid.*, pp. 234-235.   Italics added.

190. Marais, *Maynier*, p. 89.

191. Lichtenstein, *Travels*, XI, 13.

192. *Ibid.*, II, 459; IV, 291; II, 451.

193. *Ibid.*, II, 461; II, 446.

194. *Ibid.*, II, 451; II, 461.

195. *Ibid.*, IV, 290.

196. Maynier stated his case: "From the month of December 1799 till the month of July 1801 however, I succeeded extremely well. I appeased the savages and furious Hottentots. I engaged the most part of them to re-enter into the service of the Christians. I succeeded happily in my repeated negotiations with both nations of the Caffres. I brought it about that Ghyka placed more confidence in the Government, and greater mistrust in Buis, so much so that he expelled the latter from his country, and I should certainly have succeeded entirely had the Boers united instead of interfering with me." *Ibid.*, IV, 326.

197. Dundas reported to Younge in February 1800: "[It is] Maynier to whom goes honor of settlement . . . he did not hesitate at my desire to go to the kraals of the Caffres and Hottentots to communicate to them my arrival in the country with a view, as he informed them, to remove every grievance and to do justice to all descriptions of men, and through the exertions of this gentleman with his perfect knowledge of their habits, dispositions and propensities of the savages with whom he had to treat there was not much difficulty in bringing them to submit themselves to such conditions as I was willing to prescribe." Theal, *Records*, III, 53.

198. Theal, *Records*, IV, 326.

199. Instructions to Maynier, February 20, 1880, Theal, *Records*, III, 53.

200. About Maynier Theal said: "It was one of the most injudicious appointments ever made in South Africa, for no one could have been more out of sympathy with the colonists than Maynier was. It seems almost impossible that any man living on the frontier of the Cape Colony could really have held the views concerning the simplicity and honesty of barbarians enunciated by the French philosophers whose influence was then at its greatest height, yet he seems to have been sincere in professing them." Theal, *Records*, III, 216.

201. Lichtenstein, *Travels*, I, 463-464. Italics added.

202. Barrow, *Travels*, I, 238-239.

203. Lichtenstein, *Travels*, I, 302.

204. George E. Cory, *The Rise of South Africa* (5 vols., London: Longmans, 1910-1930), I, 22.

205. Reply of landdrost of Stellenbosch to the Fiscal, April 2, 1812. Quoted in MacCrone, *Race Attitudes*, p. 130n.

II.

The Afrikaners Challenged
by Britain, 1795–1835

The last decade of the eighteenth century and the first three decades of the nineteenth century comprised a period of major crisis and transformation in the culture of the South African Boers. In a real sense they were transitional years for many reasons.[1] These changes involved economic, political, religious, and legal developments. Some of the decisive modifications of this period were the bankruptcy of the commercial Dutch East India Company, the parent of the South African settlement; the European wars in which Britain and France involved the Dutch and ultimately the Dutch possessions; the occupation of South Africa by the British; the influence of a strong British missionary movement; the British migration into South Africa; Anglicizing activities among the Boers, including the establishment of English as the official language of the strife-torn colony; the official recognition of the Khoikhoi as individuals with specific rights; and the abolition of slavery throughout the British Empire. Not all of these cultural changes were recognized as major challenges at the time, however, but as Boer mythology was developed in later years, many events of this period took on increasing significance. Ultimately the Boers' self-image was twisted and strained at many points.

In addition to these many changes brought largely by British influence, there were other problems for the Boers. These were related to the Bantu civilization with which they were coming into closer contact. There were not any consistent policies with respect to these interrelations, which was part of the problem. The wars we have already noted were caused because the white settlers were encroaching on land the Bantu had been using for generations. The Africans welcomed some settlers to use the land as they did, but private ownership, which the Afrikaners insisted on, was not understood by the Bantu. More probably it was a blatant affront to Bantu traditions. There were unscrupulous white freebooters who had preceded any orderly development of the government. There were plans for driving large numbers of Xhosa off their land, either to give it to white settlers or to make it a neutral zone. Driving out such a large number of Bantu proved to be impossible, however, and opportunists on both sides took advantage of neutral land by settling on it themselves. These complex government policies proceeded alongside all the other cultural changes, and together they resulted in a very turbulent period, especially for the eastern frontiersmen who had experienced only limited government interference heretofore.

As a background for an understanding of the period, we must sketch the major political events by means of which South Africa passed from Dutch dependency to become a part of the British Empire. During the eighteenth century, Dutch sea power and economic advantage steadily declined, while that of the British expanded. The change at Cape Town did not come, however, as a result of direct conflict between the Dutch and the British. The third force was Revolutionary France under the leadership of Napoleon Bonaparte. In 1793 the French declared war on the Netherlands, which capitulated in the next year to become part of the Batavian Republic, a puppet government controlled by France. The stadtholder, William V, fled from the Netherlands to England and formed a government in exile. The British proceeded to take over all Dutch possessions in the East Indies and South Africa and formed a protectorate on the authority of their exiled Dutch ally.

When British warships dropped anchor at Cape Town on September 16, 1795, the South African leaders were unaware of all the complications of European politics, and some South Africans were even sympathetic with France. All inhabitants, however, were required to take an oath of allegiance to King George III of England, and gradually most of the population did so. Many gave allegiance with the expectation that the British control would be only temporary. The British, however, went to great lengths to develop and maintain their authority at the Cape where there were almost no British colonists because South Africa played a role in their colonial plans. The region was strategic because British imperial plans focused on India. Britain knew that its major rival was France and dared not allow France to control the settlement. The Cape European population at the time was approximately 15,000, hardly any of them British; and there were almost 17,000 slaves scattered over an area twice the size of England.[2] In addition there were countless Africans grouped in many tribes.

The Dutch East India Company completed its historic role and passed into bankruptcy in 1798.[3] When the treaty of Amiens was signed in March 1802, Britain turned the South African settlement not back to the Company but to the Netherlands government, the Batavian Republic. The New South African government, headed by Commissioner General Jacob Abraham de Mist, proved to be a sharp contrast to the commercial government maintained by the Dutch East India Company. De Mist was an enlightened governmental leader, experienced in administration and sympathetic with the revolutionary policies in France. He had been a member of the National Assembly in the Netherlands, which replaced the Staats-General in 1795.[4] He began far-reaching governmental reforms, which if continued could have developed South Africa into a modern nation. He sought education reforms, religious development, and economic stability. Attempting to develop more control on the frontiers, in 1804 he declared the area of Uitenhage a separate Drosdy (government center) on the eastern frontier, and a few months later a sixth government outpost was established at Tulbagh, along the coast north of the Cape.[5]

De Mist concluded that the most important problem was the relation between the settlers and the Africans, which had never been effectively regulated by laws. The Dutch leader suggested policies for which the British were strongly criticized throughout the remainder of the century when he advocated equal and just treatment for the Africans. After an exploration trip into the interior, one of his associates wrote in 1803 that the Khoikhoi "must be pardoned for their rebellious conduct. . . . Special effort must be made to become acquainted with the names of the colonists, who, by God-forsaken ill-treatment, have driven these people to despair and vengeance."[6] De Mist even questioned the advisability of continuing slavery because it was inhumane and was no longer of any necessity.[7]

Such an enlightened vision of the needs of the struggling colony might well have been developed into reality by the Dutch leader had he remained a sufficient time in the Cape Colony. In 1806, however, war broke out again, and the British again occupied Cape Town. As part of the peace settlement in August 1814, the British returned the East Indies to the Netherlands but were allowed to retain the Cape as a permanent colony. This British imperial authority remained in South Africa until the formation of the Union of South Africa as part of the British Commonwealth in 1910 and to a certain extent even into the early decades of the twentieth century. Major directions for developing a thriving and well-organized Cape Colony were suggested, but these would be only partially achieved by British administrators, and only in face of extreme difficulty, rebellion, and war.

At the beginning of British influence, an equally significant development was taking place within the Reformed church at the Cape. The Rev. Helperus Ritzema van Lier, a young but well-trained minister, arrived from the Netherlands in September 1786. A contemporary biographer concluded that he was "the best teacher the Cape Church ever had."[8] Van Lier became the third minister at the Cape Church, joining Petrus Serrurier who had been there since 1760 and Christian Fleck who arrived in 1781. Van Lier and Serrurier were born in the Netherlands and received their theological training there.[9] Although Fleck was born in South Africa, he also studied at Leiden and became a leader in education at Cape Town, organizing a school which later grew into part of the University of Cape Town.

Van Lier was probably the most important leader the church had during the latter part of the century from his arrival in 1786 until his death in 1793 at the age of twenty-nine.[10]   He attempted to make the religious faith at the Cape a vital and decisive influence at the heart of the society. Had he lived a long life, his work would undoubtedly have had great influence, for even in a short time he set a high standard. His preaching was evangelical and biblically based. His theology was based on the assertion, "I hope I never forget that I must not preach concerning myself, but Christ the crucified" (Cf. I Cor. 1:23).[11]   He also insisted, following Reformed thought, that all are by nature sinners and need the benefit of the blood of Christ.[12]   Equally significant was the doctrine of God's sovereignty, not only as creator of heaven and earth but also as sovereign over the affairs of humanity.[13]   He gleaned the truths of the Christian faith from both the New Testament and the Old, rather than emphasizing the latter alone, for which Calvinism is often criticized.[14]

The Christian faith was not a decisive influence in the Christian community to which these men ministered. Undoubtedly the comment of van Lier in 1789 reflected a large segment of the population surrounding Cape Town, where there had always been more cultural and religious advantages than among the inland settlers. He said that "many despise the revealed religious faith and exhibit not one of the signs of godliness."[15] Van Lier's theological concern was not limited to the European community as had often been the case with early ministers. When he had been in Africa only two years, he became active in bringing the Christian message to Africans and slaves.[16] He was broad-minded enough to realize that this work with the indigenous people was not outside the church but a legitimate part of its concern. In 1789 he expressed his deep concern in a sermon: "the Gospel must be brought to every one who can bear the name of man—to the most ungodly heathen and the most barbaric nations, to the simplest and the most ignorant."[17] As a result of this concern, he established a school for slaves, one of the "most fruitful undertakings" in which he was engaged at the Cape.[18] He realized along with de Mist that both the educational and the religious institutions as a whole should be strengthened if they were to add their part to the developing society.[19] With this broad concern it is not surprising that he was mentioned favorably as one of the Dutch Reformed ministers who welcomed the first Moravian missionaries when they were allowed to return in 1792.[20]

Another Dutch Reformed minister sympathetic to the returning Moravian missionaries was working in South Africa. He was the Rev. Michael Christiaan Vos, born in Cape Town, and like all others of the period educated in the Netherlands. He returned to South Africa in 1794, the year after van Lier's death, remaining there until his retirement in 1819. He helped to deepen the Christian spirit while at Cape Town and continued his work among the slave population. He welcomed the four missionaries of the new London Missionary Society as they arrived in 1799,[21] and even assisted the missionary leader, J.T. van der Kemp, to ordain the English missionaries, John Edmonds and William Edwards.[22]   Vos attempted to convince the population both in the Cape Town area and in Graaff-Reinet that political order is as much a part of the religious life as is piety.[23]   In his concern for the African people, he was worthy successor of van Lier.[24]

Attempts to apply the Christian faith to social questions of the day brought the ministers into conflict with the population. Vos' insistence that he preach to Africans as well as to white Europeans brought prejudice against him. Two other trained and deeply devoted Dutch Reformed ministers were even more forcibly excluded from the communities where they attempted to have some intrinisic effect on the lives of their people. The minister in Graaff-Reinet during the uprising of 1795 was Johan Heinrich von Manger, who came to the Cape in 1792 and worked for a short time with van Lier.   He was expelled from Graaff-Reinet along with the land-drost, Maynier.[25]   Another who met resistance was Hendrik Willem Ballot who came to South Africa in 1798 and became minister at Graaff-Reinet. He was expelled in 1799 during the van Jaarsveld uprising.[26]

It is interesting to compare the Boers' attitudes with their actions. Although they begged for more educational leadership, such leaders were not welcome unless they reinforced the presuppositions of the Boers' superiority over the Africans and Boers' insistence on their own rights in the face of the law and order of the central government.   Consequently attempts to deepen the religious influence in South Africa became direct threats to the Boers' concept of their own society. In spite of this attitude there was no lack of "exterior marks of devotion among the laity."[27] Indeed, "in the country the boors [sic] carry their devotion to an excess of inconvenience that looks like hypocrisy."[28]   Concerning the Boers at Graaff-Reinet a missionary reported in 1811 that "they stood more in need of instruction than even the heathens themselves; hundreds of them, when I came here, did not know even the name of Christ, and thence necessarily could feel no interest in the doctrine of the gospel; nor had they the smallest notion of the sinfulness of their nature."[29]   As a result, these few enlightened and trained theological leaders did not represent a cross-section of their society; they were shining exceptions. Whereas they undoubtedly had some influence in Cape Town, they had very little on the frontier. More mundane concerns motivated those who were far from the city.   There were no theological leaders, almost no churches, and the semiliterate fathers of the settlements furthered their own simple gospel of biblical literalism and cultural exclusiveness. It is in this light that we must see the problems that the newly arriving missionaries faced.

During the political turmoil at the turn of the century and during the de Mist interregnum, another complicating factor in South African religion and politics was developing: foreign missionaries. European missionaries, sent by both Moravian and the London Missionary societies, arrived to work among the African tribes. The Moravians had established a mission station at Sergeant River (Baviaan's Kloof) in 1737 but the leader, Georg Schmidt, was forced to leave in 1743. Several of Schmidt's converts continued to practice the faith for many years, but gradually this influence ceased. Throughout most of the remainder of the century, the only religious influence in the colony came from the Dutch Reformed ministers and, following 1780, the Lutheran church at Cape Town. Little was done to further Christianity among the colonists living in the interior and almost nothing on behalf of the Africans.

Although they had been expelled a half-century before, the Moravian interest in missions continued. In 1791 they received permission from the XVII to return to the Cape Colony, with the stipulation that they should not work in any area where there was a Dutch Reformed church.[30] With this understanding three missionaries arrived in South Africa late in 1792.[31] They began their work at the site formerly occupied by Georg Schmidt, fifty miles east of Cape Town.[32] Early in January 1793 they began to rebuild, using stones taken from the remains of Schmidt's house.[33] The missionaries then began to gather Khoikhoi around their settlement. From the first they taught not only the Christian message but, in addition, methods of raising vegetables and of building permanent homes. Africans began to build huts in the vicinity of the mission until within a few years as many as six hundred had settled there.[34] Soon other Moravian missionaries came to South Africa with similar objectives, continuing to teach Africans the rudiments of culture.[35] Genadendal was established in 1792, and by 1813 there were as many as 1,157 Khoikhoi related to it.[36] The success of the venture led to the formation of the second Moravian settlement at Groene Kloof (Mamre) in 1808. By 1814 there were eight Moravian missionaries at work in South Africa.[37]

Shortly after the reestablishment of the Moravian mission at Baviaan's Kloof, the second missionary society began its work in South Africa. The London Missionary Society, organized in 1795, sent its first four missionaries to South Africa in 1799. This group became more important in future history, and their influence was greater because they had more missionaries and more settlements. The first leaders of this group were Johannes Theodorus van der Kemp, the son of a Dutch Lutheran minister, and his companion, Johannes Jacobus Kicherer.[38] They were assisted by two Englishmen who arrived with them March 1799.[39] On Algoa Bay van der Kemp organized the settlement he named Bethelsdorp (from Genesis 35:2-3), near present Port Elizabeth. As this became the major settlement of the London Missionary Society, van der Kemp and his successors bore the brunt of the most forceful criticism of the colonists.

Because these missionaries were sent from London, the Boers assumed that they had a close relationship with government officials and were sent to carry out the political policies. Theal expressed the Boers' opinion:

> In 1799 the first agents of the London Missionary Society
> arrived in South Africa. Unfortunately, almost from the day of

their landing, some of them took a more prominent part in politics than in elevating the heathen, and as they advocated social equality between barbarians and civilized people, they were speedily at feud with the colonists.[40]

The individual who became the focal point of this criticism was the Rev. Dr. John Philip. During his thirty-year service (1819-1850) in South Africa, he became, in the eyes of the Boers, the prime example of a "meddling politician" tampering with the *status quo*.[41]

London Missionary Society stations grew not only in influence but in numbers as well. From the establishment of Bethelsdorp in 1802, the organization expanded until in 1818 they included approximately one thousand Khoikhoi. Within two decades the London Society established twelve other stations, most of them on the northern or eastern borders of the colony.[42] By 1820 when John Philip became the superintendent of the missions, thirty-eight missionaries had been sent by the society, of whom many remained.[43]

These missionaries soon found that not all European inhabitants at the Cape were as cordial as the few Dutch Reformed ministers they first met; in fact, they found outright hostility. One of them reported soon after arriving in South Africa that

> some peasants came to our host . . . to inquire whether it was really a fact, that Moravians were come to teach the Hottentots. The report spread like wildfire in the country, and we were considered almost as a new species. . . . The peasants in general are not very willing to help us, for they disapprove altogether of our being here.[44]

Some Boers carried their hatred a step further and threatened violence. Some plotted to destroy Baviaan's Kloof,[45] and others suggested the missionaries should be shot.[46] At one point the commanding general at the Cape decreed "that no inhabitant should in any shape molest the Herrn-hüters on pain of incurring the heaviest displeasure of the government."[47]

The reaction of the Boers was not based so much on the actual work of the mission station as it was on fears of the implications arising therefrom. Any work among the Africans making them self-sufficient or raising their cultural standards led to apprehension and fear among the colonists. The Boers had already come to believe that the Africans in their midst were second-class citizens, if citizens at all; they were children unable to learn, needing protection. Any work of the missionaries was a direct challenge to the privileged status of the Boers if it gave any advantage to the African. Insofar as the authorities wished equal justice for all, there was indeed protection for the Khoikhoi if the Boers were exploiting or persecuting them. Boers assumed instead that the government and other institutions should be overwhelmingly partial to them.

The Boers' major concern was for an inexpensive labor supply. There were many charges that the missionaries were seeking to undermine the Boers' way of life by inducing their servants to leave the farms. The missionaries found it hard to work between the "ignorance of the Hottentot and the anxiety of the Boer to retain his service."[48] Some farmers misinterpreted the lack of governmental control as license to continue their oppression.[49] Closely related to the charge of subverting laborers was a second concern: the fear that the missionary stations were encouraging idleness and vice. A pro-Boer account, based on half-truth and rumor, gave a gloomy summary of Bethelsdorp in 1812:

> Laziness and idleness, and consequently dirt and filth, grow there in perfection . . . frequently the other Hottentots are drawn away from the service of the farmers and seduced to increase the number of idle and lazy. . . . There are many Hottentots at Bethelsdorp who have had a considerable part in plundering, robbing, setting fire to places, and even murdering the inhabitants.[50]

With semiofficial reports such as these in circulation, it is clear why prejudice against the missionaries continued. Some Khoikhoi undoubtedly took advantage of the missionary institutions, but to judge the total organization by the shortcomings of a few is misleading.

Criticisms against education for Africans took two forms. First, and partially justified, the colonists complained that the Africans had educational advantages on the frontier which the Europeans did not have.[51] To be sure, the educational institutions for the European children were inadequate, but this criticism was only part of the reaction. The second aspect of the reaction against education for Khoikhoi questioned their ability to profit from their advantages. One government official stated "that reading and writing should not form any part of their instruction but a knowledge of all the mechanical arts, except that of gunsmith, should be encouraged."[52] Another stated that "the Hottentots were much better pleased with leading an indolent life in van der Kemp's school than with gaining their bread by labor," implying that they should be working rather than learning.[53] Van der Kemp, they thought, stood not only against Boer but against the government as well.[54]

The implications of eventual equality arising from British educational activities was an implicit challenge to the Boers' way of life. The relation between the Boers and their servants was changing. Some previously benign, passive servants were gaining confidence in themselves through education, religious training, and regular pay for employment. The already strained attitude of the Boers was further challenged when both van der

Kemp and James Read married women who were neither white nor European. The former married a "woman of Madagascar extraction," and Read married a young Khoikhoi woman he had baptized shortly before.[55] The colonists interpreted these as the logical outcome of the deluded and misguided theory of the missionaries who dared to consider an African the equal of a European. To the skeptical, concern for the African led to intermarriage.

The place of Christian missions in the South African society was viewed in a variety of ways. The Boers saw the Khoikhoi only as a source of labor, with few rights and little potential for development.[56] The government, when it supported the mission work, was concerned first that the Khoikhoi should become model subjects; religion was a "taming" influence.[57] The missionaries saw in each Khoikhoi a potential child of God who could learn if given a chance to be taught. The relation between the European and the Khoikhoi would undoubtedly improve if more "Christians" in the Cape Colony took their faith more seriously. For example, "one of their [Boer] women, the wife of a farmer, of a respectable family, is the first fruits of Christ's victory." Her conversion was complete and was "signalized by her conduct towards our Hottentots: She received them with affection at her house and at her table; and sat down at their feet to hear the word of life."[58] The reaction against the British government and against the missionaries was based on different conceptions of the role of law in modern society and an assumption that the two races were unequal.

The general suspicions and criticisms of the missionaries were brought clearly into focus by the actions of one of their members. The Rev. James Read charged that the Boers were mistreating their Khoikhoi servants.[59] This accusation stirred controversy in England and led ultimately to several changes at the Cape. The deputy colonial secretary asked the landdrost of Uitenhage, where Bethelsdorp was situated, to investigate. Read was asked to substantiate his claims.[60] One of Read's letters is typical of many of the period. He prepared "two papers containing many acts of barbarity . . . where no justice had ever been administered . . . which is undoubtedly the cause of the continuance of the inhumanity committed against the poor people [Khoikhoi]."[61] Soon both Read and van der Kemp were called to Cape Town in April 1811 for further investigation of the charges. Van der Kemp was ill and remained in Cape Town, where he died December 15, 1811,[62] while Read returned to his work.

This charge of cruelty led to strengthening and expanding the law courts. The governor issued a proclamation in May 1811 establishing circuit courts for justice in the eastern Drosdies of Tulbagh, Swellendam, Graaff-Reinet, Uitenhage, and George, especially the last three. The first circuit court made its visits between October 1811 and February 1812 before the full impact of the challenge of Read had its effect. The circuit court reported favorably concerning the work of the religious leaders and urged that clergymen be appointed in the eastern region as a "civilizing" influence.[63]   A year later the second circuit court had quite a different effect on the attitude of the Boers. This court, which traveled through the eastern areas between September 1812 and January 1813, proved to be an overt challenge to the Boers' way of life when it assumed that "the maintenance of equal right and equal protection of all classes of society forms the basis of His Majesty's government."[64]   This was distasteful for the Boers of the frontier, but in Uitenhage the problem was carried one step further.   There, following the charges of the missionaries such as James Read, testimony was taken from Africans that implicated white men— hence the name *Black Circuit*.   The Boers of the eastern frontier now realized that equal justice for all people would include the Khoikhoi and the San, whom they did not wish to consider their equals. This Black Circuit of 1812 became a symbol of British repression of Boers in favor of Africans.

Shortly after the infamous Black Circuit, a minor rebellion at Slagters' Nek, in the Drosdy of Graaff-Reinet, became another symbol of Afrikaner reaction.[65]   The situation was not provoked in this case by the missionary charges but by an application of British justice.   In April 1813 a Khoikhoi servant complained of harsh treatment by his master, Frederick Cornelius Bezuidenhout. Wages were withheld and the African's cattle were confiscated. The landdrost asked that the accused make his appearance at court to answer to the charges. Bezuidenhout answered, "I cannot possibly leave home."[66]   A few months later, after another request to appear, he answered, "I cannot endure riding so far" (about seventy miles).[67]   A third letter came from the accused in May 1814 stating that the charges were all lies.[68]   Furthermore, the authorities discovered that the Khoikhoi had not received his stolen cattle back but rather was beaten when he returned home.[69]   The landdrost of the Graaff-Reinet believed that "such stubborn opposition to all lawful authority should be punished in a very exemplary manner."[70]

Not to be defeated by delay, in October 1816 the landdrost of Graaff-Reinet authorized a small group of law enforcement officials to proceed to the accused and to bring him by force.[71]   When the officers arrived, the accused resisted arrest and fled to the hills where he had concealed ammunition in a cave.   Several shots were fired, one of which mortally wounded Bezuidenhout.   The white accomplice and the Khoikhoi servant who had been forced to accompany the Boer rebel as a hostage immediately surrendered to British authorities.[72]   News of the "martyrdom" of Bezuidenhout spread rapidly among the disaffected Boers.   Many were anxious to take the law into their own hands.   In less than a month the landdrost of Graaff-Reinet issued official warning against certain inhabitants who had begun to organize to avenge the death of their "hero" and to drive British authority from the eastern frontier.[73]

Governor John Cradock authorized martial law if necessary after the plea was not heeded and after fifteen insurgents were arrested.[74]   Many more rebels were captured, and in the skirmishes accompanying the arrest

Johannes Bezuidenhout was killed trying to avenge the death of his brother.[75] The special court called to try the rebels continued from December 1815 until January of the next year[76] and heard the cases of forty-seven men.[77] The sentences decreed execution of six men[78] and banishment or imprisonment of thirty-two.[79] The remaining nine were released without charge. Governor Charles Somerset later pardoned one man, but the five remaining were executed on a nearby farm in March 1816.[80] These five in addition to the two Bezuidenhout brothers became martyrs for the cause of Afrikaner reaction against British authority.

The alleged reason for the insurrection was to avenge the death of Bezuidenhout. Officials who wrote a comprehensive analysis for the government, however, assumed that this was only one aspect of a larger reaction.[81] They noted the similarity between this rebellion and those of 1795 and 1799, which had affected the same portion of the eastern frontier. Indeed one of the rebels executed in 1816 was Hendrik Prinsloo, son of Marthinus Prinsloo, an earlier rebel who was arrested with van Jaarsveld in 1799, imprisoned, and pardoned in 1803 by de Mist. There was "dissatisfaction with certain measures of the government, amongst others, with the present existing laws connected with the possession and obtaining of lands."[82] Most of the rebels, however, were not landowners but rather wandered with their cattle from pasture to pasture.

> Their dissatisfaction must be sought in nothing but malice and a wrong imagination to which must be added that most of them, having grown up in an almost savage state and without education, have with difficulty been able to accustom themselves to any discipline or subordination, and could thus easily have been seduced to set themselves against everything that might stand in the way of giving a free rein to their passions.[83]

This revolt had a supposedly religious basis. The insurgents had been bound together under Johannes Bezuidenhout by an oath of allegiance to their cause, not unlike the Volkstem of the previous generation. The oath "was considered sacred to them" and had the force of a religious dedication.[84] Contrary to the laws of the nation, the insurgents had close associations with the neighboring Bantu, courting their favor and hoping for their help in overthrowing British authority to establish a separate nation on the frontier. In later history this incident at Slagters' Nek was used to augment nationalistic opposition to all British policies.[85]

Slowly but methodically the legislation concerning the Africans was being modified by the proclamations of the government and by the actions of its military leaders as well. The Boers believed the Africans were to be "kept in their place," which meant they would do the work of whites but would have no rights of their own, no set wages, no rights in the law courts, and no right to own property; they were beneath such dignity. Whenever this concept of the African seemed to be modified, it brought forth a stream of protests from the Boers who saw their ideas challenged. By the time the British had controlled the Cape for only one decade, the direction of their policies became very clear and very distasteful to the discontented Boers, especially on the eastern frontier.

The beginning for this constructive policy with respect to Khoikhoi came in 1809 when the governor issued his proclamation concerning their status.[86] This proclamation, in sixteen sections, was directed toward regularizing the conditions of hire between Khoikhoi and settlers and contained provisions requiring Khoikhoi to produce proof of a regularly constituted home or be considered vagabonds. To change one's place of abode required a certificate—a pass—issued by the landdrost or other official in the district. This was the first of many so-called pass laws, which continue to the present day. The Africans could be required to show the pass at any time. In addition to the restrictions imposed on Khoikhoi, there were reciprocal requirements for the farmers who hired such workers. Employers, without restrictions in the past, now were required to prepare a contract, including the hiring agreement, the length of service, and details concerning wages and terms of payment. The farmers who neglected such contract would find that the law supported the African laborer. No longer could the terms of contract be extended by bribery, by detaining wife or children, or by threats. Heavy fines were established for the Boers who chose to neglect the law.

For the first one hundred years of the European settlement in South Africa, it was assumed, and in 1770 reinforced by law, that adherence to the Christian faith made a slave eligible for emancipation. The profit motive entered so strongly into the society, however, that the intent of this concept was subverted. Boers feared that to let one's slaves hear the Christian message would mean a loss of valuable laborers through required emancipation of baptized Christians. Consequently, in practice, it became common to deny the subjected peoples any instruction in the Christian faith to ensure continued service of the slave or Khoikhoi.

In October 1812 Governor John Cradock issued a proclamation pertaining to Christianizing of slaves:

> Whereas by a resolution taken by the Governor in Council at Batavia, dated the 10th of April 1770, it is enacted and prescribed that slaves who have been catechized and confirmed in the Christian religion shall not be sold, and whereas by experience it has appeared that a Law intended for the promotion of Christianity and true religion has not been attended with the desired, but rather the contrary, effect; his excellency hereby enacts and ordains that the said clause of the Batavian law of 1770 be repealed and of no effect; and it is hereby repealed and annulled.[87]

This proclamation at first reading seems to imply a negative concept of the Africans, but it actually indicated the government's growing concern for the plight of the slaves. It was an effective method for separating the religious from the economic question so that the latter could no longer dictate policies with respect to religion. Now one need not prohibit a worker from hearing the Christian message to retain his or her services as a laborer.

This was closely followed by another change in policy that ultimately had far-reaching effects on the Cape. Leaders of Britain and the United Netherlands agreed that the Cape would remain British territory, and they embodied their objectives in the Convention of London (1814). This included Britain's promise to prohibit further slave trade.[88] Consequently, from this date there was no way for new slaves to be brought into the Cape Colony, while the expanding colony needed more laborers. The colonists turned to a greater use of Khoikhoi, who were still plentiful. The latter were, however, partially protected by the law of 1809 and could not be exploited as the farmers might have wished. The labor situation continued difficult. Boers argued that the British law courts and the "pro-British" missionaries were robbing them of needed laborers. More important, however, the Boers now saw that the British policies were changing their relation to the slaves and other Africans by changing the Africans' image of themselves. The Boers' later anti-British reaction had its roots in real concerns, both economic and social, reinforced by their ideas of religious exclusiveness.

British policies concerned not only Khoikhoi and slaves, but their most trying challenges came as they sought to construct a workable policy toward the Bantu. The Bantu resented continued encroachment on their long-held lands. Since the settlers had first met this strong and well-organized force, there were breaches of agreements on both sides. Early in 1811 news was relayed to Cape Town concerning many raids by Bantus against the colonists on this eastern frontier. The skirmishes came to be called the Fourth Kaffir War.[89] Governor Cradock, fearing defeat for the settlers and hence decline in economic advantage, decided to apply a portion of an earlier recommendation when he issued his order:

> It has fallen to my lot . . . to free the territories of His Majesty from the incursions of the Caffre nations or any other tribes that may molest His Majesty's subjects. . . . It will be my desire that you take the most effectual measures to clear His Majesty's territories of the Kaffer nation, . . . and that they may be repelled permanently within their own borders.[90]

A successful commando drove the Bantu from the territory they had held for some time, the so-called Zuurveld between the Sundays River on the west and the Fish River on the east.[91] More positive action, however, was necessary. In July 1812 the governor established two more government outposts at Grahamstown, named after a military leader of the period, and Cradock, both on the easter frontier. The policy of geographical segregation between the two peoples was attempted once more, reinforced by military posts, but was effective only for a short time.

During the so-called Fifth Kaffir War of 1819, a change in policy was introduced when Governor Charles Somerset went one step further than his predecessors. He suggested that they stabilize the frontier by giving the Africans some incentive for maintaining order. Consequently, rather than maintain order by force alone, they sought to maintain stability by treating the Bantu leaders with the dignity of partners in a political agreement. The Bantu surrendered in September 1819, and the new plan was introduced.[92] The land between the Great Fish River and the Keiskamma River would become a neutralized buffer zone.[93] The idea was well conceived but unworkable without a larger population and more effective governmental control among both peoples. Even the white settlers did not honor their government's request.

A larger white population was clearly needed if the eastern frontier were to be stabilized. Consequently officials conceived a plan to include British settlers who would come from Europe at governmental expense. Begun in 1820, this plan involved the Albany settlers.[94] The new development was an attempt to form a settled area as a protection against incursions by Xhosa cattle thieves and to stabilize the European areas as well. It was not long, however, before many of the new settlers began to sympathize with the Boers when they became frustrated at the inefficient policies of Governor Somerset.   One disillusioned Albany settler was Thomas Phillips who wrote, after only two years in South Africa, "We now experience that the Caffre is not to be trusted, and all our feelings to treat them leniently have vanished."[95]   For at least this one individual, the experience with the Africans had an effect similar to that among the Boers who had lived there for many generations.

In the midst of the problems in which the Albany settlers found themselves, another Anglicizing move was made. In July 1822 the governor issued a proclamation requiring the exclusive use of the English language. He was probably premature when he suggested that "the language of the *parent country* should be more universally diffused" because those who considered Britain their parent country were still a small minority; thousands in the interior could speak little if any English.[96] Nevertheless, after January 1, 1825, all documents from public offices, and after January 1, 1827, all judicial acts and proceedings, were to be issued in English. The policy of requiring Dutch and forbidding the French language a century earlier was successful only because the small number of French settlers was absorbed into the Dutch majority. The governor could not foresee, however, that the proclamation of 1822 would have quite different results. This attempted suppression of the language of the majority would ultimately become one aspect of the growing Boer nationalism and of the solidifying of a new language: Afrikaans.

A further suggestion at this time had religious significance. To expand his Anglicizing activity, Governor Somerset suggested that ministers should be brought from the Church of Scotland "whose religious tenets are precisely similar to those of the Reformed Church of this country."[97] These Scottish ministers must, however, receive training in the Dutch language.[98] Among the many ministers who came under this plan, no names are more widely revered than those of Scottish-born Andrew Murray and his two South African-born sons, Andrew, Jr., the minister, and John, the theological professor.

The antagonism between Boers and missionaries resulting from the Black Circuit was still fresh when Dr. John Philip arrived in South Africa in 1819 to become superintendent of all the London Missionary establishments. He took an active interest in the plight of the Khoikhoi not only as heathen in need of salvation but as oppressed people in need of justice. Philip used his influence among interested and influential persons in London to force needed changes in the government in the Cape colony. He knew of the interest in philanthropy, abolition of slavery, and humanitarian activities in England, led by William Wilberforce, Thomas Buxton, and others. In 1826 he made a return trip to London and presented his story directly to this group. He documented the problem with his two-volume *Researches in South Africa* (1828) and convinced enough leaders so that in July 1828 the Advisory Council of the Cape government passed the celebrated Ordinance No. 50, embodying many of Philip's major concerns.[99] This ordinance was "for improving the condition of Khoikhoi and other free persons of color at the Cape of Good Hope."[100]

This law of 1828 ensured that Africans were persons with civil rights and human rights. The new law removed the passes of the 1809 proclamation. Khoikhoi could not be restrained under the charge of being vagabonds but were entitled to a fair trial as any other citizen of South Africa and they were now allowed to own land. Because some Khoikhoi could not read the contracts they had signed in the past, they had been exploited. Now to guard against this, the maximum agreement for Khoikhoi labor was one month, with certain exceptions.

Hardly had the shock of this law been felt when in August 1833 Britain abolished slavery in all parts of the Empire. In South Africa the law was to become effective December 1, 1834.[101] The amount of money the British Parliament allowed as compensation for the farmers was considered woefully inadequate.[102] The slaves were concentrated in the western portion of the colony, while Khoikhoi were the laborers more often used in the east. Both the "Hottentot" law of 1828, and the emancipation of the slaves presented a serious challenge to the Boers.

One more situation caused complications in the relations between the races and the nationalities. The forays between the Bantu and the settlers continued until in December 1834 the situation had deteriorated enough to be called the Sixth Kaffir War. Newly arrived Governor Benjamin D'Urban was sent to the Cape to implement details concerning the abolition of slavery and to attempt to stabilize the eastern frontier district. The neutral belt of land declared in 1819 had been violated. There were both Africans and Europeans in the area. Ultimately, by a treaty of May 11, 1835, British authority was extended beyond the Keiskamma River to the Kei River.[103] The British thought it necessary to expel all Africans from what would become Queen Adelaide Province. Africans were too numerous, however, so in a treaty declared September 1, 1836, Africans living in the area were allowed to remain and were declared subjects of Britain.[104]

This was the first time a large number of Africans had been taken into the British Commonwealth, and the decree superseded the policy of complete segregation. The government now assumed the task of civilizing Africans as a means for stabilizing the frontier. This has been called "civilization by mingling" (or infiltration) by Monica Wilson.[105] Such a move might have caused resentment among the Boers, but they were also encouraged when some of the land in the newly acquired territory was opened to settlement by Europeans. The land-hungry European settlers, both Boer and British, accepted the opportunity, but the Bantu, equally land hungry, were not satisfied. Governor D'Urban had overstepped his authority in annexing territory and in bringing many more subjects under British rule. He suspected that his policies might be questioned in London; indeed they were strongly challenged and ultimately reversed.

D'Urban was followed by Baron Charles J. Glenelg, the colonial secretary closely associated with the unpopular withdrawal in South Africa. He sent a representative to the eastern frontier to prepare for the retreat of all troops and settlers back to the Fish River. The new province of Queen Adelaide was abandoned late in 1836.[106] Such reversal of policy was based not on racial but on economic considerations. The authorities did not object because there were Africans under British authority, but they knew that the expenses to maintain the new area would increase significantly.

There were similar developments on the eastern frontier for a half-century yet. (See Map II.) Queen Adelaide Province was bounded on the west by the Keiskamma River and on the east by the Kei River. By 1847 the government had extended its influence again to the Kei and by 1858 to the Mbashe River. Two more developments would extend their authority over all the land to the Mtatha River in 1878. Inland along the Drakensberg, the area known first as Nomansland and developed in the 1860s as Griqualand East was annexed in 1879. Finally all land was annexed to the Mtamvuna River in 1894.[107] Thus the administrative expansion along the southeast coast would meet the administrative developments, which extended from Durban south to the Mtamvuna River. The area east of the Kei River was heavily settled by Xhosa tribes—the present Transkei—and farther to the northeast, much of the Pondo tribe would be incorporated as well. Because of the extensive Bantu developments east of the Kei River,

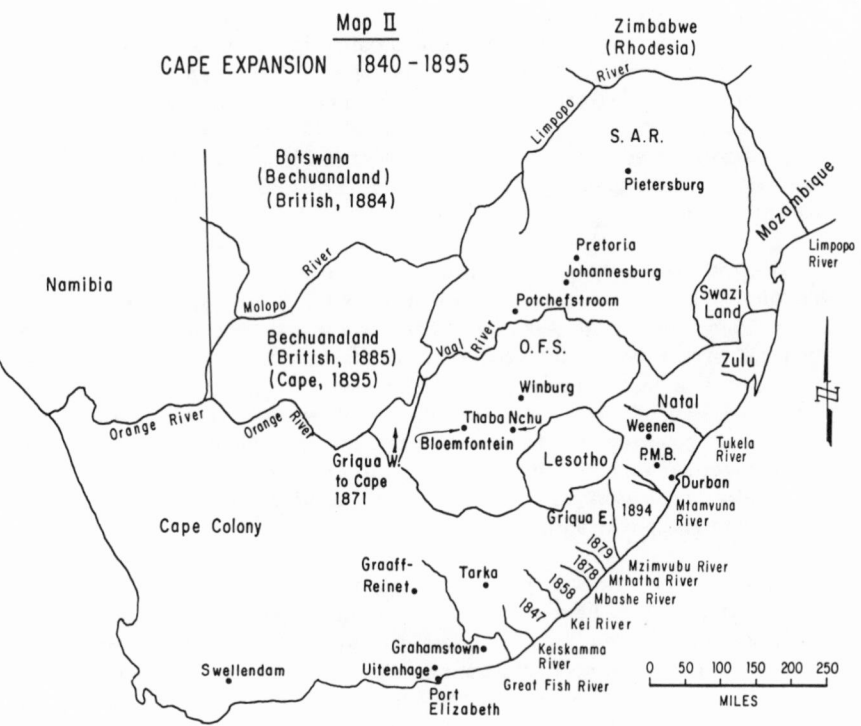

Map II

CAPE EXPANSION   1840 - 1895

Zimbabwe
(Rhodesia)

S. A. R.

Pietersburg

Botswana
(Bechuanaland)
(British, 1884)

Limpopo   River

Mozambique

Limpopo
River

Namibia

River

Molopo

Pretoria
Johannesburg

Potchefstroom

Swazi
Land

Bechuanaland
(British, 1885)
(Cape, 1895)

Vaal   River

O. F. S.

Zulu

Winburg

Natal

Orange   River   Orange   River

Thaba Nchu
Bloemfontein

Weenen
P.M.B.

Tukela
River

Griqua W.
to Cape
1871

Lesotho

Durban

Cape Colony

Griqua E.   1894

Mtamvuna
River

1879

1878

Mzimvubu River

Graaff-
Reinet

Tarka

1858

Mthatha River
Mbashe River

1847

Kei River

Swellendam

Grahamstown
Uitenhage

Keiskamma
River

Port
Elizabeth

Great Fish River

0   50   100 150 200 250

MILES

there would be a limited number of white settlers. Because there was not strong tribal organization, however, these Africans were not able to maintain their own nations but were incorporated piecemeal into the expanding Cape Colony. These regions, however, did not play a large part in the development of the Afrikaner ideology. During this half-century, many of the Boers had gone on their Great Trek and were developing in different areas, in the future Orange Free State, the South African Republic, and Natal.

We have already noted the isolation of the frontier Boers from European culture and even from that of Cape Town. By 1779 the eastern-most frontiersmen were over five hundred miles from the Cape and almost as far from the nearest church. They took with them their Bibles, however, and certain orthodox theological books and a collection of sermons, all of which they used extensively. As each succeeding generation came to adulthood, however, they grew farther from the rudimentary culture of the more enlightened section of South Africa. On the frontier, opportunities with respect to both education and religion were lacking. There was no trained minister on the eastern frontier until 1792 at Graaff-Reinet, and even he had little permeating influence.

As the British pushed eastward during the first part of the nineteenth century, the isolated frontiersmen became aware of how different they were from other South Africans. There were differences not only in the concept of the law and of the relation to the Africans, but differences appeared also in the religious faith and even in the dress of the simple eastern Boer. The conservatism of the latter was very marked. More important, however, as the differences became evident Boers tended to draw together to maintain their separate traditions. John Murray, the theological professor, later gave an analysis of conservative Doppers, a significant group of traditionalists on the frontier.[108]

The origin of the word *Dopper* is unknown. There are four possibilities. First, the word may have arisen from the cut of their hair; they supposedly used an upturned *dop* ("bowl") to cut it evenly.[109] Second, the word may have arisen from *domper* ("to extinguish"); those who maintained their old ways were backward and narrow and extinguished all new ideas.[110] A third possibility is from the word *dope* ("Anabaptist"), whom the Doppers paralleled in their strict separation from this world and all worldly pleasures.[111] The fourth suggestion is that the root is *dorper* or "village dweller". This term was used earlier in the Netherlands for this type of cultural difference, the unsophisticated, unrefined, and simple believers.[112] While we cannot be certain how the word came into common use in South Africa, we do know that it denoted a basically different approach to life as a whole and pointed to a deep cleavage between the total culture of the frontier area in contrast to the settled portion of the nation. At first the term was used only for reproach, but later it became a proud title of the Doppers who opposed change in politics, in social concepts, as well as in their religious interpretations.

The later schism in the Transvaal in 1859 brought the Dopper denomination into being, but the spirit had a long history before that date.[113] It is probably not an overstatement to assume this characteristic extended well back into the eighteenth century long before the British arrived at Cape Town. As such, the Dopper spirit was not so much an anti-British reaction as it was an antimodern outlook.[114] By the 1820s there was a self-conscious grouping that could be referred to as the Dopper people.

Theological ideas of the Doppers included many additions to the previous conservatism on the frontier. They were strongly opposed to any equality with the Africans and assumed their own superiority as a people.[115] Closely related to this, they held the idea that they were specially chosen by God to further His culture in Africa.[116] To be certain that they maintained God's pure word, they rejected evangelical songs, which were introduced into the South African church early in the nineteenth century. Nothing but the Psalms were orthodox, all others were "man-made." This attitude gave rise to the conflict over singing in Cradock, Graaff-Reinet, and Colesburg, although Graaff-Reinet ultimately accepted evangelical songs and voted against the Doppers' limited concept of hymnology.[117] The Doppers' strong reliance on the sovereignty of God led them to a stern individualism in all aspects of life. They needed no intermediate power; all were responsible directly to God. As a consequence, they continually rejected governmental authority for the sake of freedom.[118] They rejected the British philanthropic concept concerning the Africans, and they rebelled against liberal nineteenth-century laws concerning equality. The British came to epitomize all laws and customs which the Doppers feared.[119] The isolation on the frontier, the pious use of the Bible, and the challenge from modern European ideas contributed to form a unique people, the Doppers. Through their circular reasoning, what they believed God required of them they sought to maintain against all odds, even if it meant flight or war.

This forty-year period since 1795 represented a relentless challenge by the British government—later called "Pharoah" by Andries Pretorius—against God's chosen people: the Afrikaners. The Boers' self-satisfied and introverted concept of themselves was incompatible with the new government and the new style of life. Insofar as the Boers believed their cause was righteous and blessed by God, these incidents became a religious challenge. Their fear of equality with the Africans and their opposition to British policies of repression also assumed a theological dimension. In the face of these many pressures, the Boers were driven to reaction. They could have rebelled and instigated a civil war, or they could have given up their ideals and become assimilated into the British culture of South Africa. A third way, however, was chosen. They began their Great Trek, the attempt to leave British jurisdiction behind and build a nation where Boer ideals could be supreme. Some Afrikaner *veeboers* (cattle farmers) had migrated north of the Orange River early in the century, but the major migration known as the Great Trek intensified in 1835 and continued for several years.

NOTES

1. William M. Freund has used this term in "The Cape under the Transitional Governments, 1795-1814," in Elphick and Giliomee, *Shaping of South African Society*. It is a summary of more extensive work he has done on this Batavian period.

2. A census taken in 1795 gives many interesting details of the period:

Census of South Africa, 1795

	Cape Province	Stellen-bosch	Swellendam	Graaff-Reinet	Total
Europeans					
Men	1,294	1,309	848	808	4,359
Women	1,057	880	337	596	2,870
Boys	1,265	1,207	581	910	3,963
Girls	1,341	1,258	477	761	3,837
Total	**4,957**	**4,654**	**2,243**	**3,075**	**14,929**
Slaves					
Men	6,068	4,300	818	369	11,555
Women	2,981	1,690	403	210	5,284
Total	**9,049**	**5,990**	**1,221**	**579**	**16,839**
Other					
Bullocks	8,681	22,220	14,490	26,273	71,664
Sheep	12,967	118,318	65,052	222,480	418,817

This census shows that the slave population tended to be centered mainly in the western part of the settlement. The farther one went east, the more cattle and sheep there were *per capita,* which indicates increasing landholdings as well. While there were fewer slaves to the east, the difference was the increasing use of Khoikhoi as servants, not counted in this census. All statistics from Theal, *Records,* I, 296.

3. "We can . . . take our departure from the Great Company without rancor or resentment. Its government ended as a fiasco, but we should remember that we owe to the Netherlands East India Company the establishment of white South Africa—and that its neglect of its own administrative duties, its denial of all rights for the colonists outside the Company, these assisted in the development of their independence and self-sufficiency." S. F. N. Gie, *Geskiedenis van Suid Afrika* (2 vols., Stellenbosch: 1924-1928), I, 252, quoted in Malherbe, *Education in South Africa,* p. 45.

4. S. F. N. Gie, ed., *The Memorandum of Commissary J. A. de Mist, Containing Recommendations for the Form and Administration of Government at the Cape of Good Hope* (Cape Town: Van Riebeeck Society Publications, 1920), III. See A. H. Murray, *The Political Philosophy of J. A. de Mist—A Study of Political Pluralism* (Cape Town: H. A. U. M., 1963).

5. Eric A. Walker, *A History of Southern Africa* (London: Longmans-Green, 3d ed., 1957), p. 135.

6. W. Blommaert and J. A. Wiid, eds., *Die Joernaal van Dirk Gysbert van Reenen, 1803* (Cape Town: Van Riebeeck Society Publications, vol. XVIII, 1937), p. 109.

7. Gie, *Memorandum of de Mist,* p. 251.

8. M. C. Vos, *Merkwaardig Verhall, 1784,* quoted in T. N. Hanekom, *Helperus Ritzema van Lier: Die lewensbeeld van 'n Kaapse Predikant uit de 18de Eeu* (Cape Town: N. G. Kerk Uitgewer, 1959), p. 313.

9. Serrurier at Leiden, Van Lier, M.A., and Ph.D. at Groningen. S. P. Engelbrecht, *Die Kaapse Predikante van die Sewentiende en Agtiende Eeuw* (Cape Town: H. A. U. M., 1952), pp. 77-78; 82-84; 88-90.

10. Hanekom, *van Lier,* pp. 91-92, Engelbrecht, *Kaapse Predikante,* pp. 88-90.

11. Hanekom, *van Lier,* p. 136.

12. *Ibid.,* p. 140.

13. *Ibid.,* p. 142.

14. *Ibid.,* p. 148.

15. *Ibid.,* p. 157.

16. *Ibid.,* p. 173.

17. "Of set purpose does Jesus use the expression *to all creatures* [Matthew 28:19]—in order to teach us that the Gospel must be brought to every one who can bear the name of man—to the most ungodly heathen and the most barbaric nations, to the simplest and the most ignorant. No exception may be made. Jesus has anticipated all excuses. His gospel must be proclaimed to every human being, however savage, ignorant, degraded or sinful he be. No one can be too ignorant or too sinful for the Gospel to be offered to him; no one is so virtuous as not to need the Gospel. No man, whatever profession of virtue or innocence he may make, can do without the gospel; to no man, however, guilty and depraved he be, may the Gospel be refused." Van Lier's sermon, May 17, 1789, quoted in J. du Plessis, *A History of Christian Missions in South Africa* (London: Longmans, Green & Co., 1911), p. 63.

18. Hanekom, *van Lier,* p. 174.

19. *Ibid.,* p. 185.

20. *Ibid.,* p. 209. Cf. *Periodical Accounts Relating to the Missions of the Church of the United Brethren Established among the Heathens* (London: United Brethren Society, 1790-1796), I, 165.

21. Engelbrecht, *Kaapse Predikante*, p. 95.

22. *Ibid.*

23. "Mr. Vos, . . . left us with his friends. We were thankful for his visit, and glad to become acquainted with this worthy servant of Christ. By such visits may prejudices against us wear off." *Periodical Accounts*, II (1797–1800), March 22, 1800.

24. du Plessis, *Christian Missions*, p. 422. "The Director Vos . . . not only labors here with zeal at the instruction of heathen and Christians, by his preaching, catechising, pastoral visitation, etc.; but several other friends of religion, encouraged thereto by him, are also doing their utmost to acquaint the heathen in their own homes and in those of their neighbors with the way of salvation."

25. Engelbrecht, *Kaapse Predikante*, p. 91.

26. *Ibid.*, p. 98.

27. Barrow, *Travels*, II, 147.

28. *Ibid.*

29. Letter from Mr. Kicherer at Graaff-Reinet, October 30, 1811, quoted in *Transactions of the London Missionary Society* (1812), pp. 430–431.

30. Hanekom, *van Lier*, p. 308.

31. They were Hendrik Marsveld, David Schwinn, and Johann Christian Kühnel, arriving in South Africa in 1792. *Periodical Accounts*, I, 165.

32. *Periodical Accounts*, I, 165.

33. *Ibid.*, I, 244.

34. Barrow, *Travels*, I, 308–309.

35. *Ibid.*, p. 311.

36. du Plessis, *Christian Missions*, p. 88.

37. *Ibid.*

38. *Ibid.*, p. 451.

39. They were John Edmond and William Edwards. *Transactions of the London Missionary Society*, I, 94.

40. Theal, *History of South Africa* (one-volume edition, 1894), pp. 126–128.

41. John Philip came to South Africa in 1819, becoming superintendent the next year. He remained until his death in 1850. His understanding of the situation in South Africa is contained in his two-volume *Researches in South Africa,* 1828. W. M. Macmillan used Philip's papers to write two volumes: *Bantu, Boer and Briton* (London: Faber and Gwyer, 1929; rev. Oxford: Clarendon Press, 1963), and *The Cape Colour Question* (London: Faber and Gwyer, 1927). The major primary sources were the papers of Dr. John Philip. These papers were subsequently destroyed by fire in 1931 when the Library of the University of the Witwatersrand, Johannesburg, burned. Fortunately both volumes carry extensive quotations from the primary sources. In John S. Galbraith, *Reluctant Empire: British Policy on the South African Frontier, 1834-1854* (Berkeley: University of California Press, 1963), the primary sources are British documents, both from South African archives and from Britain. Macmillan attempted to tell the story about Dr. Philip and to counteract the intense criticism against him from pro-Boer historians. Galbraith attempted to sketch British policy on the frontier. With these divergent purposes duly recognized, there is remarkable agreement between the two in their treatment of the frontier problems from the first period of British influence to the beginning of the Great Trek.

42. A complete list of the stations is given in Richard Lovett, *The History of the London Missionary Society* (London: Henry Frowde, 1899), I, 537-538. A map appears on p. 481.

43. A complete list of the missionaries is given in Lovett, *History,* I, 798.

44. *Periodical Accounts,* I, 272, a diary of missionaries recently arrived in South Africa. A manifesto of a group of farmers carried this clarification: "Those Hottentots who were born on a farmer's estate must live there, and serve the farmer till they are 25 years old, before they receive wages.
  "The Hottentots must live among the farmers and not assemble together as at Baviaan's Kloof.
  "All Bushmen, or wild Hottentots caught by us, must remain slaves for life.
  "Item, the Moravians were never meant to be employed among the Hottentots of this country, but among the Bushmen." From *Periodical Accounts,* quoted in J. S. Raum, "The Development of the Coloured Community in Genadendal under the Influence of the Missionaries of the Unitas Fratrum, 1792-1892" (Master's thesis, University of Cape Town, 1953), p. 75. Further information of a similar nature can be seen in J. D. Schreuder, "Die Opvoedkundige bedrywighede van die Morawiese Broederkerk onder die Kleurlinge in Suid-Afrika, 1737-1743 en 1792-1950: 'n histories-kritiese studie" (D. Ed. thesis, University of Potchefstroom, 1951).

45. du Plessis, *Christian Missions,* p. 423.

46. *Ibid.* A similar incident was reported by Lady Barnard, *South Africa a Century Ago: Letters from the Cape, 1797-1801* (London: S. Elder and Co., 1910), p. 170. The date was May 8, 1798.

47. Barrow, *Travels,* I, 311-312.

48. Theal, *Records,* VII, 172-174.

49. *Periodical Accounts,* I, 299.

50. Theal's quotation of an 1812 report by a Commission of Circuit for the eastern district, quoted in J. A. I. Agar-Hamilton, *Native Policy of the Voortrekkers* (Cape Town: Maskew Miller, 1928), p. 92.

51. One Boer responded: "What, are the Hottentots to be made wise, when so many Christian children run about and learn nothing. Only wait a little and your place shall be destroyed, for I would have you to know that we are now the governors." *Periodical Accounts,* II, 27. Another said: "We will not permit any Moravians to live here and instruct the Hottentots; for as there are many Christians who receive no instruction, it is not proper that the Hottentots should be taught; but they must remain in the same state they were before." John Holmes, *Historical Sketches of the Mission of the United Brethren for Propagating the Gospel among the Heathen from Their Commencement to the Present Time* (Dublin: R. Napper, 1818), p. 402.

52. Theal, *Records,* VII, 110.

53. Lichtenstein, *Travels in South Africa,* I, 291.

54. Lovett, *History of the London Missionary Society,* I, 291. He comments further about Governor Janssens who "seemed prejudiced against our teaching the Hottentots to write, considering them not to be sufficiently civilized to make use of it. This prejudice we supposed had been much strengthened by the Christians."

55. du Plessis, *Christian Missions,* p. 126.

56. Barrow summarized it well: "The cause of the farmer's hatred to these people is their having taught the Hottentots the use of their liberty, and the value of their labor, of which they had long been kept in ignorance." Barrow, *Travels,* I, 312.

57. "The object of government in promoting settlements of the Hottentot tribes has always been to improve their moral as well as religious habits, to lead them from a wandering to an industrious course, and to prove to them from the comfort which they would enjoy in the peaceable possession of their own cottages, gardens, and agriculture, the advantages of that system which their Christian teachers, with so much charity and perseverance endeavor to inculcate." Theal, *Records,* X, 177.

58. "The rage and hatred of the Christians, as they call themselves, of this country in general, seems rather to be increased than to subside; it was long intolerable to them to see the mercies of God conferred on the heathen; but to see its almighty power glorified among their own race, drives them almost to madness." *Transactions of the London Society,* I, 281.

59. Theal, *Records,* VII, 375.

60. *Ibid.,* VII, 128.

61. "On the 8th of this month I was summoned to appear before Major Cuyler, the Landdrost [of Uitenhage] to give information of some acts of cruelty and murder mentioned in a letter of mine written to England dated August 30th, 1808. I have given the Major an account of the persons who informed me, and shall with the greatest cheerfulness give every further information in my power, if it should be your Lordship's desire. I have likewise given to Major Cuyler two papers containing many acts of barbarity since I have been in this country, and where no justice has ever been adminstered, not even the least notice taken of them, which is undoubtedly the cause of the continuance of the inhumanity committed against the poor people in question. It has pleased God in his providence, my lord, to cast me and my fellow labourers in such a situation as enables me to become better acquainted with the sufferings of this people than any other person whatever. The poor Hottentot in vain turns his eye to any to whom he dare unbosom himself. He has sought perhaps for redress at the hazard of his life, at last he finds a friend in the Missionary, whom he begins to experience is more or less concerned for his temporal as well as his spiritual welfare; then, but not without some degree of fear, he tells his pitiable story, and a heart of stone must bleed to hear the father relate the slavery of his child, the child the loss of his father, the tender husband of his wife, and wife the loss of her husband, the survivor forced into endless bondage and the orphans worse than slaves. I hope that the time is near and their cries will be heard, and their complaints impartially attended to, and effectual means adopted to deliver them from their oppressions. . . . From the reports of the Major's conduct toward the Hottentots bringing their complaints before him I am sorry to say that I can not look on him as an impartial person to examine the grievances of this class of afflicted people. Another idea of the utmost importance which I have to suggest is the rooted dread that reigns in the minds of the Hottentots in these distant districts to give information against any Boer, as he considers himself endangering his life by exposing himself to the resentment of all the connections of those against whom he is called to bear witness. The truth will never be brought to light till effectual means are taken to protect and encourage those who are able to give information. . . . Nothing would be gratifying to me as to be honored with an interview with your Lordship, in order to state my ideas on the subject which it is almost impossible to do in its full extent by letter." October 19, 1810, Theal, *Records*, VIII, 128-30.

62. Lovett, *History of the London Missionary Society*, I, 511.

63. "It is well known that some years ago the greatest part of Graaff-Reinet had the character of uncivilization and unmorality. This however at present seems to alter. Such a prejudice was even entertained against Hottentots and slaves that it was considered degrading to allow them as heathens access to the church. . . . The churches being built here [in the east] . . . lays the foundation for villages, and therefore considered as well in a religious and moral as in a political point of view, tends to the increase of *gradual civilization*, and as a spur to industry and agriculture." Theal, *Records*, VIII, 297-298. Italics added.

64. Theal, *Records of the Cape Colony*, IX, 56.

65. H. V. C. Leibbrandt, ed., *The Rebellion of 1815, Generally Known as Slachters' Nek* (Cape Town: J. C. Juta, 1902). The extensive primary

sources are conveniently grouped together in this collection. Further details concerning this rebellion can be found in Hermann Giliomee, "The Slagtersnek Rebellion of 1815," in Elphick and Giliomee, *Shaping of South African Society*, pp. 348-351.

66. Leibbrandt, *Rebellions*, p. 891.

67. *Ibid.*, p. 892.

68. *Ibid.*

69. *Ibid.*, p. 895.

70. *Ibid.*, p. 900.

71. *Ibid.*, p. 897.

72. *Ibid.*, p. 903.

73. *Ibid.*, p. 789.

74. *Ibid.*, p. 789.

75. *Ibid.*, pp. 802, 858.

76. *Ibid.*, pp. 801, 811, 858.

77. *Ibid.*, p. 29-30.

78. *Ibid.*, p. 19.

79. *Ibid.*, p. 20.

80. *Ibid.*, p. 822.

81. September 21, 1816, *ibid.*, pp. 858-868. "What happened to Fr. Bezuidenhout was merely seized as a pretext, and as a favorable opportunity to carry out the criminal intentions which possibly they had cherished for a long while." *Ibid.*, p. 86.

82. *Ibid.*, p. 860.

83. *Ibid.*, p. 861.

84. *Ibid.*, p. 863.

85. For example, in 1899 we read of "the murderous tragedy of Slachters' Nek. . . . It was at Slachters' Nek that the first blood-stained beacon was erected which makes the boundary between Boer and Briton in South Africa, and the eyes of posterity still glance back shudderingly through the long vista of years at that tragedy of horror." *A Century of Wrong*, issued by F. W. Reitz (London: "Review of Reviews' Office, 1900), p. 6.

86. Theal, *Records*, VII, 211-216.

87. *Ibid.*, VIII, 500.

88. Article VIII of the London Convention reads: "[The British promise] to bring about the total abolition of the trade in slaves . . . and having . . . issued a decree dated the fifteenth of June, 1814, wherein it is enjoined that no ships or vessels whatsoever destined for trade in slaves, be cleared out or equipped in any of the harbors or places of His Dominions. . . . [His Majesty] does hereby . . . prohibit all His subjects . . . from taking any share whatsoever in such inhuman traffick." Theal, *Records*, VIII, 500.

89. See the list of cattle stolen and colonists murdered in Theal, *Records*, VIII, 26-29, 49. Fifty or more farms were abandoned. *Ibid.*, VIII, 49-54, 73-74, 90-91.

90. Theal, *Records*, VIII, 159-161.

91. Cradock reported to London March, 1812, "It affords me great satisfaction to be enabled to announce to your Lordship that the whole of the Kaffir tribes have been expelled from His Majesty's territories." Theal, *Records*, VIII, 353.

92. Theal, *Records*, XII, 193-194, 321.

93. *Ibid.*, XII, 343-344.

94. The British settlers came to the Cape in twenty-four ships, leaving the British isles in January 1820, and arriving in May and June 1820. Most of the approximately 3,500 newcomers were victims of poverty and lack of employment then widespread in Britain following the Napoleonic wars. The plan was to settle them in the area known as Albany to increase the population of the eastern frontier, to help maintain order, and to prevent further incursions by the Bantu. Several problems immediately arose. Most of the settlers were not farmers and were not able to make a decent home for themselves or their families in the wilderness. The area in which they landed was not suitable for farming, and expansion of cattle grazing was not possible when each farmer had only 100 acres. In addition, crop failure plagued them for three years. The consequence was that many of the settlers quickly migrated to the towns to return to their trades as artisans. Those who stayed on the land became owners of increasing herds, and the population was not as densely settled as the government had hoped. Finally, the appearance of more cattle in their neighborhood tempted the Bantu to make raids again, and the ultimate purpose of the settlement was frustrated. This is carefully analyzed and documented in two studies: Isobel Eirlys Edwards, *The 1820 Settlers in South Africa* (London: Longmans, Green & Co., 1934), and H. E. Hockly, *The Story of the British Settlers in South Africa* (Cape Town: Juta & Co., 1948). An interesting collection of letters covering almost ten years, written by Thomas Phillips, one of the 1820 settlers, is Arthur Keppel-Jones, ed., *Phillips, 1820 Settler* (Pietermaritzburg: Shuter and Shooter, 1960).

95. Phillips' letter dated July 15, 1821; Keppel-Jones, *Phillips*, pp. 102-103.

96. Theal, *Records*, XII, 452. Italics added.

97. *Ibid.*, XII, 452.

98. The entire proclamation is printed in *ibid.*, XII, 452-453.

99. John Philip, *Researches in South Africa* (2 vols., London: Duncan, 1828).

100.   G. W. Eybers, *Select Constitutional Documents Illustrating South African History, 1795-1910* (London: George Routledge and Son, 1918), pp. 26-28. Cf. Harry Gailey, "John Phillips' Role in Hottentot Emancipation," *Journal of African History* III (1962), 419-433.

101.   Eybers, *Documents,* p. 38.

102.   There were 39,021 slaves in South Africa in 1834 for which the owners were paid 3,041,290 pounds. Eybers, *Select Constitutional Documents,* p. 38.

103.   Galbraith, *Reluctant Empire,* p. 113.

104.   *Ibid.,* p. 117.

105.   Monica Wilson, "Cooperation and Conflict: The Eastern Cape Frontier," in Wilson and Thompson, *Oxford History of South Africa,* I, pp. 260-268.

106.   Galbraith, *Reluctant Empire,* p. 133.

107.   Monica Wilson, "Fragmentation and Pressure on Land," in Wilson and Thompson, *Oxford History of South Africa,* I, p. 252.

108.   "In the early part of the 19th century the ward of Rhenosterberg, between Graaff-Reinet and what was afterwards Colesburg, was inhabited by a number of large families—almost clans—nearly connected by inter-marriages. . . . The prominent family names were Van der Walt, Kruger, Venter, and Coetzee. To return to our account of the Doppers. The Van der Walts and other families who moved northward settled in Rhenoster-berg (now Middleburg district) and along the Cow River (now Philips Town district). Gradually they developed the peculiarities which have won for them their distinguishing epithet. Living in secluded districts, clinging to old fashions and habits, inter-marrying only among near neighbors and relatives, a clannish spirit was formed separating them not merely from the English settlers of later date, but even from their own fellow countrymen." John Murray, "Some Characteristics of Our Fellow Colonists," *Cape Monthly Magazine,* XV (July-December, 1877), p. 373, quoted in Barend Roedolph Krüger, *Die Ontstaan van die Gereformeerde Kerk in Suid-Afrika* (Pretoria: V. en R. Drukkery, 1957), p. 72.

109.   Krüger, *Ontstaan,* p. 67.

110.   *Ibid.,* pp. 67-68.

111.   *Ibid.,* p. 68.

112.   *Ibid.*

113.   See Chapter V.

114.   He [the Dopper] rested on decrees. . . . There was an innate feel-ing that everything new must of necessity be erroneous." B. Spoelstra, *Die "Doppers" in Suid-Afrika, 1760-1899* (Cape Town: Nasionale Boekhandel, 1963), p. 28.

115.   Krüger, *Ontstaan,* p. 70.

116.   *Ibid.,* p. 75. John Murray evaluated their concept: "Their convic-tion that they are a select class, a peculiar people, that have kept the deposit of their faith pure, gives them a self-assertion which others feel." Spoelstra, *Doppers,* p. 26. "They sought to establish the pure light from God's word without error." Dr. Oculis, *The Doppers,* p. 18, quoted in Krüger, *Ontstaan,* pp. 75, 77.

117.   Krüger, *Ontstaan,* pp. 78-105. Cf. S. P. Engelbrecht, *Geskiedenis van die Nederduits Hervormde Kerk van Afrika* (Pretoria: J. H. de Bussy, 1936), pp. 141-42.

118.   Spoelstra, *Doppers,* p. 25; Krüger, *Ontstaan,* p. 66.

119.   "The Doppers saw a danger for their national well-being in the British missionaries, officials, soldiers and settlers. This arose not only because of political considerations, but it also was a challenge to their religious ideology. Actually they feared the Boers would be denationalized [would lose their identity]. Thus from the beginning the unifying attitude among the Boers was that they were in heart and soul anti-British. They were afraid of all that was strange and unknown and they drew into their shells. First they withdrew deeper into the interior—to Tarka, Oli-fantshoek, Hantam and so to the Great Orange River and beyond, planning never to return. The Doppers were concerned about nothing else beyond themselves and their own families." Dr. Oculis, *The Doppers,* p. 16, quoted in Krüger, *Ontstaan,* pp. 65-66. L. P. Vorster added his comment: "So close are the concerns of our church and our nation, that if the Afrikaner nations should be Anglicized, the Gereforemeerde Kerk, as a church, would not be able to remain." Quoted in Krüger, *Ontstaan,* p. 66.

III.
The Great Trek: I: Natal, 1835–1843

The last decade of the eighteenth century and the first three decades of the nineteenth century was a period of rapid transition in the culture—economic, political, religious, and legal—of the South African Boers. These rapid developments challenged the self-sufficient Boers' way of life, previously relatively free from government interference, especially on the eastern frontier. This isolation had allowed them free rein with respect to cattle and sheep, land, and African servants. As a reaction the Boers began to systematize concepts of themselves around biblical events they believed reflected their own situation. At least one Boer assumed the "children of Ham" were to be controlled, while British governmental restrictions were "oppression" led by "Pharaoh."[1] The Boers' self-image was twisted and strained at many points. Their culture and God-given uniqueness, they thought, would be weakened, if not destroyed, if the Africans were considered equals. Their loyalty to God would be subverted; it would be blasphemy to accommodate themselves to the new developing order of society. The resulting interpretations set the stage for what became the central event in Afrikaner nationalist history, the Great Trek.

Not all of these cultural changes were recognized as major challenges at the time. As Boer mythology developed in later years, the significance of many events of this period was magnified, and the oppressed Boers increasingly envisaged themselves as chosen by God to maintain their own way of life.[2] They sought relief this time not by revolt but by abandoning their homes and settling in new areas. They would renew their covenant in blood, if necessary, and ultimately would construct a new nation of God's elect beyond the boundaries of British authority.

The reasons given for the migration of farmers in this mass exodus, now called the Great Trek, are a composite of various grievances, rumors, and interpretations developed on the frontier. These ideas of the grievances, whether truth as much as presupposition or misunderstanding, were strong enough to motivate the frontier farmers to seek a new way of life.

Indeed, one leading trekker stated that they were "incapable of severing the sacred tie which binds a Christian to his native soil, without the most sufficient reasons."[3] Those who would soon migrate north assumed that the government was prejudiced against them and was spreading propaganda impugning their motives. Many recent happenings brought only "vexations and severe losses."[4]

The most complete listing of the grievances was written by Piet Retief and published in the *Grahamstown Journal* on February 2, 1837.[5] In ten points, calm and well stated, he presented the reasons behind the movement. Retief began, "We despair of saving the colony from those evils which threaten it by the turbulent and dishonest conduct of vagrants . . . nor do we see any prospect of peace or happiness for our children." Reformation was impossible; restitution was the only answer. Second, "We complain of the severe losses which we have been forced to sustain by the emancipation of our slaves, and the vexatious laws which have been enacted respecting them." The British Empire abolished the slave trade in 1814 and in 1833 abolished the institution of slavery altogether. Payment to the farmers was arranged, but it was not considered adequate. Third, farmers believed the government had favored the Africans too often, especially when a treaty of 1835 was signed forcing withdrawal of British authority from east of the Great Fish River. The eastern frontier was always unstable. The Dutch East India Company was not interested or able to appropriate either the funds or the personnel to organize the frontier; the British attempted but were unsuccessful. The British government concluded, rightly, that some of the Bantu attacks on the white settlers were in revenge for white forays to capture Bantu cattle. They forbade the Boers to retaliate in case of losses. Governor d'Urban, who annexed Queen Adelaide Province, was a hero for the Boers, while Lord Glenelg, the colonial secretary in London who forced the reversal, was the villain.

Fourth, Retief had the London missionary, John Philip, in mind when he reported: "We complain of the unjustified odium which has been cast upon us by interested and dishonest persons, under the cloak of religion, whose testimony is believed in England, to the exclusion of all evidence in our favor." Missionaries in South Africa, and the London Missionary Society leaders especially, became scapegoats for the settlers' dissatisfactions. The Boers complained that the missionaries assumed Africans were innately the equal of any white man, even though now culturally inferior. The trekkers reiterated their opposing religious concept. "The blacks," J. N. Boshof stated, "are encouraged to consider themselves upon an equal footing with the whites in their religious exercises in church or community, . . . thereby showing a disrespect for the religious institutions of the people."[6] Piet Retief's niece, Anna Steenkamp, later wrote that it was not the freeing of the slaves and Khoikhoi that drove the trekkers to made their exodus. Rather they feared the implication arising therefrom, for the Africans were "being placed on an equal footing with Christians, contrary to the laws of God and the natural distinction of race and religion, so that it was intolerable for any decent Christian to bow down beneath such a yoke;

wherefore we rather withdrew in order to preserve our doctrines in purity."[7]

Various questions of a social and political nature are included in Retief's *Manifesto*. He said they were seeking a place where they would "take care that no one shall be held in a state of slavery" but at the same time where they could "preserve proper relations between master and servant." They would not molest any people but would defend themselves; they would frame a code of laws; and they would inform all native tribes of their peaceful intentions.

A political rejection of British authority was clearly necessary: "We quit this colony under the full assurance that the English government has nothing more to require of us, and will allow us to govern ourselves without its interference in the future." The trekkers underestimated British imperialist designs, however, when they expected they could escape British political domination by crossing the Orange River. "We are now quitting the fruitful land of our birth . . . and are entering a wilderness and dangerous territory; but we go with a firm reliance on an all-seeing, just, and merciful Being, whom it will be our endeavor to fear and humbly to obey."

Thus the ideological basis for the trek was stated. It would lead to restitution of a good society, a new Israel, and a Christian society in a new land, excluding both British ideas and African participation. "The trekkers saw themselves as the Israel which God brought out of Egypt. They must trek through the wilderness in order to plant Christian civilization in the interior."[8]

The synod of the Dutch Reformed church of the Cape Colony officially opposed the trek and did not send ministers. The clergy of the colony urged the people not to go on trek for no ministers would go with them, and they would never head the Word of God; their children would remain unbaptized. The trekkers replied that they were taking their Bibles and song books with them. To the charge that the Cape clergy would refuse to baptize the children, the trekkers responded that they would be baptized by other ministers or would remain unbaptized.[9] In place of regularly ordained men, not plentiful in any case, the trekkers had the religious leadership of a few lay preachers or missionaries of various groups already at work among the African tribes in the north. Often the political leader led in prayer or exhorted his followers in a true patriarchal manner.

As the Boers began their Great Trek out of territory controlled by the British, they had only a minimum of information concerning the territory to which they were going. Explorers and missionaries had traveled along the coast to Natal and knew that the Bantu, especially the Xhosa and the Pondo, were thickly settled for much of that distance. Scouts and traders had also explored territory north of the Orange River where some early Boer settlers were already established. While there were Bantu remaining in the region, there was still much more open land in this region directly north of the eastern Cape Colony. Even the explorers, however, did not know details about the recent disturbances among the Bantu tribes in the territory of the Orange, the region across the Vaal River, and the coastal area of Natal. Into these regions the Boers proposed to go.

At the beginning of the nineteenth century, there was a long-established tribal division resulting in two Bantu nations.[10] Along the coast from north to south were the Zulu, the Pondo, and the Xhosa and several other smaller groups known collectively as the Nguni people. They had related languages and some similar customs. The second Bantu nation was established in the high plains west of the Drakensburg mountains. These were known as the Southern Sotho and included the Tswana along the western edge of the high plains and the Sotho along the mountains on the eastern edge of the same high veld. Associated with these were smaller groups, but in the interior, much of Orangia, there was sparse settlement.

In 1800 these groups were strongly organized around a chieftain, had no military forces, and gave ultimate loyalty to the chief of the tribe. There were, and continued to be, splits or divisions among the groups because of disagreements and rivalry among various leaders within the chiefs' families. This pattern had probably been similar for several centuries. In the 1820s the situation changed, however, because of internal problems among the Bantu groups themselves. The Zulus rapidly expanded under the leadership of Shaka (d. 1828) and drove neighboring Nguni peoples south into Pondoland. Others were driven west into Orangia and the Transvaal, causing special confusion because they were a Nguni tribe replacing or infiltrating groups of Sothos. There were also several groups which migrated north into regions of contemporary Mozambique, Zimbabwe, and Malawi and will not concern us in this study.

While the Zulu drove other groups before them, there were also rival leaders among their own people, resulting ultimately in the organization of different tribal relationships. A list of some of the groups more prominent in this study follows, with the significant chieftains of the early and mid-nineteenth century listed in parentheses:[11]

Southern Sotho
(on the high veld)
1. Tswana
   subgroup of Tswana
   a. Rolong (Moroka)
2. Basuto
   (Moshweshwe, d. 1840)
3. Pedi
   (Sekhukhune, d 1882)

Nguni
(along the coast)
1. Zulu (Shaka, d. 1828;
   Dingane, d. 1840; Mpanda,
   d. 1872)
   a. Ndebele
      (Mzilikazi, d. 1868)
   b. Swazi
2. Mpondo (Faku, d. 1867)
3. Xhosa
   (Gaika—Mgqika, d. 1829)

The result of this aggressiveness among the Zulus was a massive migration of peoples, tribal regrouping and division, and wholesale massacres.
This widespread turbulence is known as the *Difaqane*, or the *Mfecane*.[12]
The terms are from the Sotho and Zulu languages respectively, and with the
several words from the same root, the meaning is disturbance, forced
migration, and confusion in general. This widespread crisis resulted not
only in a regrouping of peoples in new areas under different leaders but in
strengthened internal organizations and in generally large and more cohesive tribal units. Smaller groups or wandering refugees were absorbed into
ever-larger spheres of authority. These people who had withstood their own
troubles would not be passive in the face of another migration, the Boers
from the Cape Colony.

In 1835 the earliest groups of trekkers to leave the Cape Colony were
the parties led by Louis Trigardt and Johannes H. J. van Rensburg.[13] They
migrated in parallel movements into the northern Transvaal where their
movements were observed by African tribes, but at first they were not
molested. In time, however, disastrous disagreements among the leaders
forced them to part company. Van Rensburg and his group of forty-nine
persons headed east toward the coast, and within a few weeks the whole
party was massacred in northeastern Transvaal. No records of their travels
or deaths have been found.[14] (See map III.)

The Trigardt party of approximately sixty-three remained almost a
year in central Transvaal where they erected temporary homes, planted
crops, and established a school. By August 1837 they decided to migrate
east over the steep Drakensberg toward what became Mozambique. Some
of the descent required that wagons be taken apart, carried down, and
reassembled at lower elevations. Their hardships brought several of the
travelers' worst qualities to the fore; arguments among leaders were common. At one point Trigardt revealed his biblical outlook as he attempted to
instill harmony into his party; "I sometimes spoke of the murmuring of the
Children of Israel and said that we would do better if we thanked God for
his protecting hand."[15] This party was ill prepared for life in the tropical
area. Cattle and horses died from disease and men, women, and children
died from yellow fever and malaria.

When they arrived at the Portuguese settlement at Delagoa Bay in
April 1838, twenty-six survived out of the original sixty-three persons.
Trigardt expressed his faith: "I spoke with my wife about the blessings God
had brought to us [April 21, 1838]. I thanked the Almighty for his grace
shown to us, and I hope that our sick may become well again [April 24,
1838]."[16] On May 1, 1838, Mrs. Trigardt joined those who succumbed to
illness. The survivors were taken by ship to Natal where other Boers had
now settled. Trigardt, however, chose to stay behind and later the same
year was buried on Portuguese soil, ending the earliest chapter of the Great
Trek of Boers who fled from British authority.

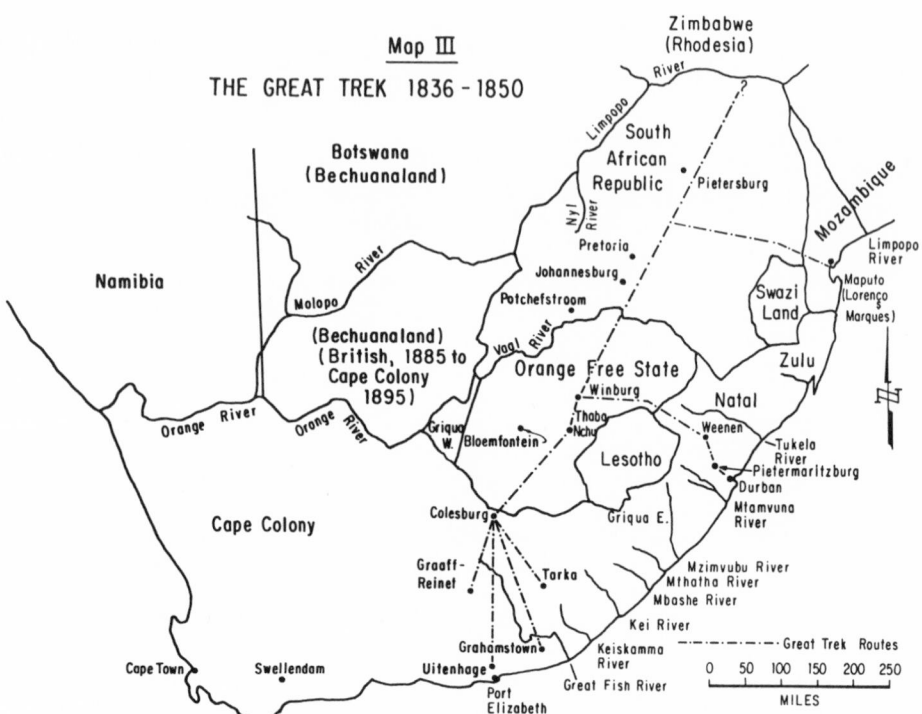

Map III

THE GREAT TREK 1836–1850

Zimbabwe
(Rhodesia)

Botswana
(Bechuanaland)

South
African
Republic

· Pietersburg

Namibia

Limpopo River

Nyl River

· Pretoria

· Johannesburg

Molopo River

· Potchefstroom

(Bechuanaland)
(British, 1885 to
Cape Colony
1895)

Vaal River

Orange Free State

Swazi
Land

Maputo
(Lorenço
Marques)

Limpopo
River

Mozambique

Zulu

Orange River

Orange River

Griqua
W.

· Bloemfontein

· Winburg

Thaba
Nchu

Natal

Weenen

Tukela
River

· Pietermaritzburg

· Durban

Cape Colony

Lesotho

Colesburg ·

Griqua E.

Mtamvuna
River

Graaff-
Reinet

· Tarka

Mzimvubu River
Mthatha River
Mbashe River

Kei River

Cape Town

Swellendam

Uitenhage ·

· Grahamstown

Keiskamma
River

Great Fish River

Port
Elizabeth

------ Great Trek Routes

0 50 100 150 200 250

MILES

Other groups from the eastern Cape Colony began their trek within a few months after these earliest groups. Andries Hendrik Potgieter left from Tarka late in 1835 with a group of approximately two hundred people.[17] He was joined at Colesburg by the party led by Charl Celliers, who became the spiritual guide of the whole movement. They migrated slowly with their families and their herds across the Orange River to Thaba Nchu. Here they remained for a time where they formed a friendship with the friendly Moroka and his African tribe, the Rolong. They were aided by the Rev. James Archbell, a British Wesleyan missionary already working among these Africans. As the Boers later migrated between Thaba Nchu and the Vet River, they were informed that not all Africans were friendly. The much more warlife people were near—the Ndebele, led by Mzilikasi. Since the Rolong people were a subdivision of the Tswana tribe, they were enemies of the Ndebele.

The trekkers were to the west of the main settlement of the Sotho tribe in the mountains, so they met the opponents they had heard about in open country. The Ndebele group had split from the Zulus in the 1820s because of rivalry among the leaders. For self-protection as well as self-aggrandizement, they had migrated over the mountains into central Transvaal, while some settlements extended as far south as central Orangia. It was this well-organized foe which confronted the Boers in October 1836.

Meeting this less hospitable African tribe forced the Boers to develop their own resources. Charl Celliers functioned as a type of lay minister as he called the people together.

> [I] addressed a few words to them, to the effect that we had a holy God, invested with Almighty power in heaven and on earth; and that we must unite in humbling ourselves before Him, and in praying to Him in his heaven, and that all must pray in heart with me. We all knelt down, our wives and children too, and I prayed to God that, in His boundless mercy, He would have regard to us in our great need, and if it were consistent with His counsels, would not forsake us, but would strengthen us to resist our enemy.[18]

The trekkers interpreted this battle at Veg Kop (literally "Battle Mountain") as the hand of God on their side for 430 Africans lay dead compared with two dead among their own number. The pious Celliers concluded: "By God's mercy we are delivered [by guns]."[19] The Boers conveniently forgot that the Ndebele were successful in capturing most of the sheep and cattle and that they had help from the Rolong tribe, enemies of the Ndebele.

Soon after this Veg Kop battle, another party of trekkers arrived from Graaff-Reinet under the leadership of Gerrit Maritz. With him was his brother-in-law, the local preacher, Erasmus Smit, and approximately one

hundred wagons of trekkers and supplies.[20] This expanded group of trekkers, remembering their desire to be free from English governmental
controls, began to take the law into their own hands. In December, 1836,
they chose "judges by the general voice of the people," who were concerned
with the best interests of the people and with peace.[21] Potgieter and
Maritz were among the seven chosen. They composed a primitive constitution exemplifying their wish to organize a new society in the wilderness.

Their respite was short. In January 1937 they attacked the Ndebele
again. The results were victory for the Boers, resulting in death to 400
Ndebele, and the loss of many thousands of cattle. Again, the Rolong
assisted, but the pious Celliers attributed their success to God: "Necessity
obliged us to advance against our powerful foe with only 107 men; and our
God delivered him unto our hands, so that we gave him a severe defeat, and
took 6,000 head of cattle from him, without the loss of a man of our number."[22] In commemoration of the win over the Ndebele, Potgieter established the town of Winburg on the Vet River.

Soon another leading trekker prepared to leave him home in Grahamstown.   Piet Retief crossed the Orange River with approximately one
hundred wagons and arrived with the previous trekkers in April 1837.
Retief's reputation was well-known, and since Potgieter and Maritz could
not agree on the leadership of the trekkers, Retief was unanimously chosen
and asked to assume leadership. As he accepted the offer, he said that he
believed it was the hand of God and that he would do his best and pray for
strength in the interest of all.[23]

At a gathering on June 6, 1837, at Winburg on the Vet River, the Constitution of Winburg was composed. Their ideal, embodied in nine articles,
formed the basis of later constitutions of the Voortrekker republics of the
Orange Free State and the Transvaal. In the first resolution, to be understood against the background of earlier history in the Cape Colony, they
stated that the members of the trekker community, all members of the
Reformed church, should have no further communication with any English
missionary society.   When asked what would be the name of the land to
which they were going, they suggested New Eden, but the the Free
Province of New Holland in South East Africa was adopted.[24] Immediately
they installed Retief as the governor. Erasmus Smit spoke of the importance of this leader and implied a theological basis for their organization as
he used II Chron 19:6-7: "[The Lord] said to the judges, 'Consider what you
do, for you judge not for man but for the Lord; he is with you in giving
judgment.'" Piet Retief then knelt down, placed his left hand on the open
Bible, raised his right hand, and said:

> I, Pieter Retief by the voice of the people (*Volkstem*) lawfully
> chosen to be their Governor and Commander in Chief of the
> United Laager, hereby solemnly swear before Almighty God
> that I, as governor chosen by the people . . . shall protect and

defend the Christian Creed . . . with adherence to the same, to
the catechism and the liturgies of the Netherlands Reformed
Church; and that in my government I shall not permit any official to act as such in the administration of Church and Civil
Government, except such as are members of the aforesaid Reformed Church and are provided with due testimonials. So help
me, God.[25]

Still another group arrived from Uitenhage. Their leaders were Jacobus
and Pieter Uys, father and son, and twelve-year old grandson Dirkie. On
the way English settlers met them at Grahamstown and presented them a
Bible. The inscription indicated further theological understanding of the
trekkers.

This Holy Book has been presented to Jacobus Uys and his
departing compatriots by the inhabitants of Grahamstown and
its vicinity, as a remembrance and a token of esteem and
hearty sympathy with their departure. The desire which they
have manifested to obtain a preacher, and their strict observance of Holy precepts, are clear proofs that, on their journey
to seek another land, they will submit to the guidance of the
command laid down in this Holy Book, and that they will stead-
fastly adhere to its Holy Laws, as the immutable precepts of
the creator of all—the God of all nations and peoples.[26]

This last group joined the organized trekkers in Orangia late in 1837.

Although Retief was chosen governor, Potgieter, Maritz, and now
Jacob Uys had ambitions. Hardly had the ink dried on the Winburg Constitution when tensions mounted and Uys renounced the leadership of Retief.
The divided group then went in separate ways. On September 9, 1937,
Retief and Maritz with several wagons in their party began their journey
toward the east to open a new, although tragic, chapter of Voortrekker
history. The remainder, led by Potgieter and Uys, proceeded farther north
where in November 1837 they attacked the Ndebele again. So successful
were they that after a nine-day battle, the Ndebele retreated north across
the Limpopo River into present-day Matabeleland in Zimbabwe. The Boer
leaders assumed the land was theirs by conquest, but neighboring African
leaders would have other assumptions. Some groups, for instance, displaced
by the Ndebele only within the past generation, would migrate back into
their former homeland areas. From this point the Boers settled in two
areas: the high veld, including Orangia and Transvaal, and the coastal
plains of Natal. Let us follow the Retief group to the coastal region first.

Piet Retief was confident that he could prove that the trekkers wanted
to live at peace with all tribes. He began his eastern trek hoping above all
to obtain land by treaty with the Zulu chieftain in Natal. Earlier than this,
however, the British in 1835 had arranged a treaty with the Zulus at Port

Natal Bay and established a British resident. They named the village after the recent Cape governor, d'Urban.[27] Thus when Retief and his party reached the bay on October 19, 1837, they were welcomed by British residents. Two days later Retief requested an interview with the Zulu leader and stated his peaceful intentions.

The Zulu chief was Dingane, half-brother of Shaka who had led in the Zulu expansion a decade earlier. Within a few days Dingane met the visitors. The Rev. Francis Owen, an English missionary working at Dingane's village of Mgungundhlovo, was one of the interpreters who prepared the way for Retief's visit. Following the meeting with Dingane on November 7, 1837, Retief was convinced that the chief promised them land. No documentary evidence, however, supports this contention.

After leaving Dingane and returning to his followers, Retief sent a letter of theological advice to Dingane:

> What has now happened to Mozelikatzi makes me believe that the Almighty and all-knowing God [will not permit] him much longer to live. From God's great Book [we learn] that kings, who do such things as Mozelikatzi [has done], are severely punished, and not suffered long to live and to reign. And if you wish to hear more fully how God treats such wicked kings, you can enquire of all missionaries in your country. . . . As a friend I must impress on your mind this solemn truth, after all, whether white or black, who will not hear and believe God's word, shall be unhappy.[28]

Although the reference was to another chief, surely Dingane could not fail to realize in the veiled threat that this could eventually apply to him as well.

On January 25, 1838, seventy trekkers, including several young men and boys, began a return expedition to Dingane to complete the treaty. The families following along behind, the men remained in one of the valleys quite some distance from Mgungundhlovo. In the last letter he wrote to his wife, Retief reiterated his confidence that God was on his side in the undertaking:

> Thus far once more, God be thanked, all is well. Until now, I have found everything as I wished: except that I have received five men from Rudolph, my field commandant, instead of fifty, so that with children, I have only *60 men.* Do not worry about this; but rely on Almighty God that on this occasion also he goes with me. . . . Keep God before your eyes [Deut 1:30] and you will have no evil to fear.[29] (dated January 26, 1838)

Retief thought all was well when he arrived at Dingane's settlement on February 4, 1838. The missionary, Owen,[30] was concerned about the expedition for he knew that over two years previously the same Dingane ceded the same land to the queen of England.[31] The Boers' confidence semingly was not lessened by the suspicions of the British missionary. They signed a treaty on February 4. The next day Dingane entertained the trekker party, and on February 6, they planned to return to their families. Suddenly, on a signal from Dingane, all seventy men were seized by Zulu warriors and beaten to death. Afrikaners consider all seventy martyrs for the Christian cause against heathenism. A plaque listing all heroes' names was recently erected in their memory.

As soon as the Zulu warriors completed their historic attack at Mgungundhlovo, they began searching for other Boers in the area and massacred many.[33] The families of the Retief party within twenty or thirty miles of Dingane's headquarters were attacked before dawn on February 17. The gallant fighting on the part of the surprised and ill-prepared Boers allowed some to escape, but in the massacre most were killed.[34]

Boer leaders encamped in different valleys were notified by an escapee and retaliation was planned. Two major leaders in the rally for a counter-attack were Gerrit Maritz and Charl Celliers. As Celliers made preparation he said:

> Our God did not wholly forsake us. We acknowledge that our God, from His heaven, looked down on us in His mercy, and He strengthened with His might those of us who remained alive, to take up our weapons again, and I can affirm that I strove, and that I, like Jephthah, had my life in my hand. [Jephthah, from Judges 10:6, 12:7, concerning the defeat of the Ammonites. The reference to the covenant was Judges 11:31.] . . . I said to my brothers, "Have God before your eyes; let not a hair on your head show fear, and follow me." . . . Had we come five minutes later, the whole laager would have been a bath of blood; but our great God prevented it, and said to our enemy, "thus far, and no farther." [Job 38:11] Our enemies were terrified, and their hands were weakened. Five men liberated the camp, with God's assistance.

The final count of dead in the massacre was 41 men, 56 women, 185 children, and 250 Colored servants.[36] Including the seventy in Retief's party, the number massacred by the Zulus within the ten-day period was over six hundred. The survivors named the settlement on the Blauwkrans River River Weenen ("weeping") and vowed vengeance on the Zulus.[37]

Leaders still in Orangia and Transvaal were informed of the recent happenings, and Potgieter and Piet Uys led fighters to Natal to assist their compatriots. They disagreed on the method of attack, however, and proceeded separately.[38]   Then disaster struck.   Piet Uys was caught by an assegai (a thrown spear) and died very soon; his twelve-year old son Dirkie was also killed. Within a few days Potgieter gave up the offensive in Natal and retreated with his followers over the mountains, where he resumed the leadership of what later became the Transvaal and established the town of Potchefstroom.

The Africans continued their attack on the Boers. On one occasion, in August 1838, when they feared defeat, Erasmus Smit offered prayer of encouragement for the Boer contingent:

> God give us His almighty aid against this numerous foe. May he grant us the victory, if we have to fight; so that we may praise Him. As we have heard so many untrue reports, may the Lord grant that this may prove equally untrue; and, if it be true—He is mighty to strengthen our hearts, and should we die, to have mercy upon our souls.[39]

Although outnumbered, the Boers on the third day were sure that God had given them victory as their attackers fled under continual fire. About this Veg Lager conflict, Mrs. Steenkamp reflected, "Thanks and praise are due to the Lord, who so wonderfully has rescued us out of the hands of our numberless and blood-thirsty foes, and granted us the victory. . . .   The Lord strengthened us and weakened our enemy!"[40]

Further misfortunes came to the children in the wilderness. Gerrit Maritz died of illness on September 23, 1838; the people "were a sheep without a shepherd."[41]   In memory of their two greatest leaders, Gerrit Maritz and Pieter Retief, the Boers named their settlement Pieter Maritz Burg, now a major city in Natal. An assurance of God's favor, however, sustained this small band of pilgrims where those of lesser faith would perhaps have turned back to their former security.

The shepherdless people were not long without a leader. On November 22, 1838, Andries Pretorius, destined to be their most influential spokesman, arrived from Graaff-Reinet.   Pretorius was immediately elected commanding general, which led one author to say he was sent directly from God: "We should be grateful to God that He had provided us with such a chief, who was wise in all his doings."[42] Pretorius inspired renewed zeal and courage for battle as he reminded them that they must "begin this most important task which they had undertaken (and which must be blessed by the Most High, should it be successful) with supplications and prayers to the throne of God"; but "any design undertaken without God is frustrated."[43]

Plans were made for the final and decisive battle against the Zulus. As they marched along toward the battle, the Boers equated themselves with the children of Israel; Pretorius was their new Joshua. With a force of only four hundred men against many times that many Zulus, they wisely considered their disadvantage.

> We saw this, and that if the good God was not with us, there
> was little hope of victory. I saw, to the extent of the light
> granted to me, that we must become suppliants to the Lord to
> entreat that He would be with us at our standards, as he was
> with Moses and Joshua. I made the people sensible that if the
> Lord were not with us we must be overwhelmed. Mr. Andries
> Pretorius was our chosen general in that expedition. He and I
> spoke to each other on the subject of the promises made holy
> by the Bible, and how we, too, were bound to make a promise
> to the Lord, that if He gave us the victory over our enemy we
> should consecrate that day, and keep it holy as the Sabbath in
> each year.[44]

When all gathered on December 7, 1838, Celliers continued the idea of a renewed covenant:

> As nearly as I can remember, my words were these: "My
> brethren and fellow countrymen, at this moment we stand
> before the holy God of heaven and earth, to make a promise, if
> He be with us and protect us, and deliver the enemy into our
> hands so that we may triumph over him, that we shall observe
> the day and the date as an anniversary in each year, and a day
> of thanksgiving like the Sabbath, in his honor; and that we will
> build a temple to His honor where we may worship him; and
> that we shall enjoin our children that they must take part with
> us in this, for a remembrance even for our posterity."[45]

They made a covenant to build a church to honor God in their new wilderness home.[46] Even the preparation for their next battle was chosen by God, for "the Lord in His holy providence had appointed a place for us, in which He had determined that the fight should occur, . . . so that camp, by God's mercy, was protected on two sides."[47] As the superior weapons of the Boers helped to rout the Zulu forces, the pious Boers reflected, "Our God blessed our violent effort, so that we got through without loss on our side, and heavy loss on theirs."[48]

Their complete confidence in God was continually reinforced. "The Word of our Lord was fulfilled: 'By one way shall your enemies come, but by the blessing of the Lord they shall fly before your face'" (Deut 28:7).[49] Pretorius shared this confidence in God: "It pleased the Almighty to give us this victory without the loss of a single life on our part, only three of us being wounded."[50]

This battle, fought on December 16, 1838, gradually came to be considered the most decisive battle for the trekkers. The date of the defeat of

Dingane, Dingane's Day, became a major trekker holiday, later embellished with elaborate theological imagery. The Boers again saved their settlement for their own culture at Blood River. The power of Dingane was broken. Thus in a short time Pretorius had taken his place as undisputed leader as the Boer patriarch. They believed the covenant made with God had brought the victory.

The Boers had thus far developed a theological assurance that God would continually protect and guide them. Many sympathetic Boers remaining in the Cape Colony wrote encouragement. Pretorius, for example, received the following suggestions from a Mr. Hattingh in the eastern Cape:

> Brother, however peaceful the blacks seem to you, trust them not! . . . There are many villains still among you. . . . Pray to God for help and counsel that He may always help you. He shall hear you if you pray in truth. Let this be your trust, as David has withstood, see how the Lord has discovered his traitors, but you must trust that He speaks truth according to his Word, and that you can build the city on Him. . . . When you have overcome your opponent hold a general day of prayer to the Lord, and thank God for his goodness and for the victory. And as you go to the conflict, pray to the Lord for support, counsel and courage. . . . [In all] remember that the Lord is with you and shall stand beside you in all of which he approves. . . . We wish you all God's benediction and a long life, health and peace in your land [and we wish] that the Lord may be pleased to lead you in his way so long as you may live in this tabernacle.[51]

Two weeks later Mr. Hattingh wrote: "Brothers, my only trust is this 'The Lord Reigns' [Psalm 93:1, 96:10, 97:1, 99:1, etc.] . . . . Thank Him in your heart and He shall keep you further. . . . First of all you shall have victory and Dingaan shall be exterminated."[52]

News of the murders by Dingane brought increased sympathy for the Boers from many sources. From Cape Town, Adam Carstens wrote: "For the cruel murder of Retief and his party the monster must answer before God's judgment seat."[53] D. J. Brand at the Cape wrote to "Dear Friend":

> Hold fast to Almighty God, and your trust will be richly rewarded with signs of the Almighty. Move forward, my friend, to fight under the power of God, and he shall struggle among you and before you, and he shall destroy your enemies with the sword. . . . Think of the Children of Israel, how God abandoned them, when they abandoned Him and served strange Gods [I Sam 15:23, Psalm 78:56-59]. This can also be your lot, . . . and if He leaves you, who shall help you?[54]

From Cape Town Pretorius was assured: "Be certain, my true friend, that your lot is felt strongly here."[55] God required men to accept the situation which He sends without complaining or remorse.

> Aaron had remained silent when God killed his two sons, Nadab and Abihu, by lightning [Numbers 3:4]. Also Elijah remained silent, knowing that all which God does is good. Now you, and your friends have to struggle against many difficulties which you will experience, but the God of Jacob which rescued Israel from her slavery, the God who fed Israel in the time of hunger, the same God yet reigns and shall reign forever.[56]

Three weeks later Carstens wrote to Pretorius: "Do away with the monster God's law says: 'Put the heathen out of your way'"[Numbers 33:52, 55; Deut. 20:16-18]. [57]

The Boers, anxious to do God's will lest He abandon them to a questionable fate, were deeply concerned to have regular worship. Consequently, after they tried in vain to secure a minister from the Cape Colony, in January 1840 they chose the Rev. Daniel Lindley to serve them in Pietermaritzburg.[58] Lindley, a Presbyterian sent to South Africa by the American Board of Foreign Missions, had served several years among African tribes in both Orangia and Natal. For seven and one-half years he had served the Boers in Natal, and he traveled extensively. On various trips he preached and baptized in what became the Orange Free State and the Transvaal. He is credited with establishing the earliest churches not only in Natal but also in the other two Boer areas.[59] Lindley's influence among the Boers was far-reaching, but he continued to wish for the opportunity to return to his missionary work among the Zulus. In 1847 after many members of his Boer congregation had departed for Orangia and the Transvaal, he had his opportunity to work again among the Zulus. He remained there many years until his departure from Africa for the United States in 1873.

While God was leading the latter-day Israelites to victory over Dingane's forces, another challenge appeared in this area. In December 1838, the British reinforced their base in Durban "for the better protection of the native tribes."[61] The British flag was hoisted on December 16, the day of the Boers' victory over Dingane in another section of Natal.

Two attitudes of the British now challenged the Boers' concept of their own self-sufficiency. First, they did not agree that the trekkers were no longer British subjects, and second, the British feared the results—slavery or mistreatment—if the Boers were allowed to treat the Africans in their own way. The British commander set the tone for future conflict with the Boers when he wrote to them in January 1839.

> Her Majesty's Government will learn with regret the slaughter of the Zulus and the unwarranted invasion of their country, and

he warns them that any hostile aggression of the kind in the future will assuredly be followed by the strongest marked displeasure of the British government.[62]

He requested Pretorius to march out of the Zulu territory and return to his previous location because he considered the attack on Dingane murder.

At first the trekkers disregarded the implications of the British communications and proceeded to reinforce their group consciousness by establishing the second *Grondwet* at Pietermaritzburg in March 1839.[63] They organized the Dutch Reformed church as the only church of the community and drew up strict standards for relations between master and servant. Africans had no place in the organization. They summarized their experiences on the high plains and the massacre of many in Natal as a type of ritual. They hoped the British authorities would look with more favor on their motives, but "if even here we are to be persecuted and disturbed by undeserved hatred and persecution, we shall be under the necessity . . . of seeking elsewhere for that rest and peace which is refused us in such an ungenerous and iniquitous manner."[64] They referred to their theological covenant in several ways. Part of their land was won by treaty; part was "ratified in his [Retief's] blood."[65] Should the British settlers come with a military force, the Boers resolved to "retreat into the mountains and kloofs . . . and there defend ourselves in small parties, as did the oppressed Spaniards, and according to the principles of Don Carlos, neither give nor take quarters, until we shall have recovered what is virtually ours."[66]

The British were interested not so much in annexing territory as in maintaining order among the suspicious African groups. In March 1839 Sir George Napier, governor of the Cape Colony, thinking the region had been stabilized, issued an order for the British forces to withdraw from Natal. One month later the evacuation was completed, much to the joy and relief of the Natal Boers.[67] As the latter called their new nation Natalia, the Boers assumed that they were at last free, and their ideas would indeed find "new birth." The British did not assume so much.[68]

Soon, however, the Boers became involved in intergroup rivalries among the Zulus. Dingane's half-brother, Mpanda, who was the leader of a lesser force of Zulus in the same area, feared that Dingane was making plots on his life. Mpanda fled to the protection of the Boers and was given land on which to live peacefully. The Boers in turn sought to cooperate with the Zulu followers of Mpanda in an offensive against the superior force of Dingane.[69]

In January 1840 the commando against Dingane began its march. Often when the Boers stopped they spent time "reading the Bible and singing hymns," confident that they were doing God's will on the expedition.[70] Their concept of Christian humanity involved "delivering them [Mpanda's followers] from the tyrant Dingane and taking them under their own protection."[71]   Along the way they reinforced their faith when they held a worship service of hymns and psalms, after which Pretorius read to them "to the honor of God, a sermon applicable to our situation, and taken from the Old Testament."[72]

The approach of the superior force caused Dingane to flee into exile where he was killed shortly after.[73] Mpanda mounted the abdicated throne as king of the Zulus. Pretorius, however, would never allow his followers to credit the victory to their own strength: "Our conquest over the powerful Zulu nation was obtained through Providence alone, . . . We, fully justified in our claim against Dingane, were instruments in the hands of God to put an end to the indescribable cruelties and murders committed by Dingane."[74] In February 1840 Pretorius proclaimed jurisdiction over the territory from the Black Umfolosi to the Tugela on the south and as far inland as the Drakensberg range.[75] Following his declaration a twenty-one gun salute was fired, and the people joined in the victory celebration: "Thanks to the Great God, by whose grace victory has been granted us."[76]

During this period further biblical basis was given to show why this was considered a latter-day Exodus. Pretorius' mother wrote to him that they should keep the eyes on the heavenly father "as the Children of Israel held their eyes on the bronze serpent" (Numbers 21:9). Thus they could withstand the latter-day "stinging serpents," which were the assegais of the enemy.[77] This they had done, and their faith was substantiated by their victory. The Boers had reason to believe that this was their Promised Land.

Hardly had the British occupation ended in Natal when it was reestablished.[78] Information concerning problems with cattle as well as the Boer commando raids against African groups convinced the skeptical British that order would be maintained only if they continued to provide occupying forces in Natal. The independence of the Boers was flatly denied for the country was "devasted by the reckless proceedings of the   Queen's subjects."[79] The British prepared to enforce their policy against the Boers.

The belligerence of the Boers was bolstered, however, by a hope of intervention on their behalf by the Netherlands government. A Dutch adventurer, J. A. Smellekamp, traveled to Natal and suggested, without any authority, that the Dutch government was sympathetic to the Boers' freedom fight. British officials knew of this complicating factor and later had Smellekamp arrested in the Cape Colony for illegal travel. One British official summarized the Boers' attitude that "nothing can as yet take out of their heads that Smellekamp had some direct communication to them from the King of Holland."[80] A year later when the king of the Netherlands was told of the situation, he denied that his government had any connection with Smellekamp's expedition. Nothing, however, could cause the Boers to doubt that in addition to protection from God Almighty they also had the blessing of the Dutch government.

In the meantime the British were preparing to retake Natal and "to bring these misguided people to entertain proper views of their situation."[81] The British began their march north toward Natal while the Boers amassed their strength at Congella, across the bay from Port Natal. Boers surrounded the British forces, killed some, and caused some to be drowned. A traveler reported that the Boers were optimistic: "For a commencement, the Boers might consider themselves fortunate beyond all reasonable expectation. Nor did they fail to thank God, and *to consider themselves His people;* for in their favor the same miracle had been wrought as for the Hebrews: Had not the waters closed upon their enemies?"[82] The same unsympathetic writer continued: "There is nothing in the world so stupid as a people who give themselves up to the dominion of certain ideas." He did not dare remind the Boers that "the tide rises twice each day."

For a short time the Boers seemed to have the advantage but could not persevere because of lack of ammunition. The two immovable forces were posed for stronger opposition, while the status quo was maintained for over a month. Finally, on June 24 and 25, 1842, two British troop ships arrived with troops commanded by Lt. Col. Josias Cloete, and in two days the battle of Congella was over. The Boers retreated to Pietermaritzburg, and the British again hoisted their flag at Natal.

The Boers who considered December 16, 1838, the day of God's victory, conveniently did not consider their defeat at Congella a judgment of God. It was, rather, a further test of their faith, sent by God to give them spiritual stamina. The battle of Congella and subsequent happenings began the second trek, or more properly, a continuation of the first. Many Boers prepared as soon as possible to trek over the mountains into what became the Orange Free State and the Transvaal. British authorities decided, wisely, not to attack Pietermaritzburg but to attempt negotiation. On July 16, 1842, a majority of the Volksraad members submitted to British authority; those who did not submit believed their freedom was betrayed by their own people. The agreement included amnesty for Boers with the exception of Pretorius and a few others and allowed the existing Volksraad of the Boers to continue "until Her Majesty's wishes be made known."[83]

By August 1845 the new commander at Natal forced the Volksraad to accept three regulations: in the eye of the law there would be no discrimination or disqualification whatever, based on color, origin, language, or religion; they were not to attack natives beyond the colony; and, there would be no slavery.[84] There was no real question with respect to the second and third, but the first demanded complete equality between black and white, which most Boers could not accept. Many Boers believed their freedom was betrayed by their own people, for Commander Henry Cloete, younger brother of Josias Cloete, acting as a British authority, was of Afrikaner stock. Mrs. Steenkamp summarized the Boers' frustration concisely: "The second Cloete arrived here, and we were fated to be deprived of the land which we had earned and bought."[85]   Commander Cloete reported that the Boers threatened to "walk by the Drakensberg barefooted, to die in freedom, as death was dearer to them than the loss of liberty."[86] Natal was now recognized as a British colony. The Boers' trek back over the mountains was continuing. In Natal Africans were given a limited franchise to vote in the elections on August 24, 1865, a right they never attained in either the Orange Free State or the South African Republic (Transvaal).[87]

In the meantime the feelings of the Boers intensified. Their faith was tried and twisted but not destroyed. In November 1847, one of the Boers reiterated the faith that had brought them to this point:

> This is my faith, brothers and sisters, there is one Creator of all, to whom I am bound. You know as well as I that we are weak creatures and can do nothing on our own, and so my heart's desire, my brother, is that I as well as you may keep the Lord before our eyes day and night, and ask him to help us in faith that he will not leave us standing alone, for he is yet the revered God of Israel. See how wonderfully he has saved us. . . . To eternity he sits upon his throne in order to watch the earth. Know that the eye of justice looks down, and anticipates the final result which will come to being; and yet, my brother, remember with your most earnest prayer before the throne of Emmanuel, what we poor Afrikaners have yet to experience in our oppressed state of affairs.[88]

Late in 1847 the trek out of Natal gained momentum. Pretorius himself left early in 1848, following the unsuccessful attempt by the Cape governor, Sir Harry Smith, to formulate an agreement with the Natal Boers. This ended the first major attempt to establish a Boer republic free from British "oppression" where the Boers could maintain the "true relation between master and servants," where there would be no equality of the races. Only thus could they be true to their interpretation of the covenant they made with God.

The first chapter of the great South African exodus was over. Seemingly the Boers had met defeat on every side. Rather than submit, however, they continually reinterpreted their frustrating situations and transformed these into theological terminology. Biblicism of the Reformed tradition was developed in a unique way in South Africa due to a lack of trained theologians or ministers and a unique sociological milieu. This resulted in a folk theology sustained by popular piety. The Boers assumed that God's plan for Afrikanerdom was a typological reenactment of various Old Testament episodes on the South African frontier. Consequently they interpreted the situations which seemed to reflect biblical events as direct signs from God. On this basis, the Great Trek became the new Exodus; conquest of the land was blessed by God, with the help of Joshua, Gideon, and others; and Providence was on the side of the Boers' freedom fight against both African and British. In battles against the Zulus the Boers kept the stories of Gideon and Jephthah before their eyes as examples of God's favor. Their success against the Zulu chieftain, Dingane, in 1838 was interpreted as confirmation of the covenant constructed on the basis of the Abrahamic covenant. Furthermore, their theological imagery was developing both an anti-British and an anti-African dimension. This use of unorthodox and unsystematic theological ideas was a significant aspect of their developing group consciousness and gave them increased confidence in persevering in their search for their new Eden. Indeed they were not alone; the God of Abraham, Isaac, and Jacob went with them.

Had the Boers' God failed them in Natal? No; they believed He prepared a way to lead them on another trek, to seek their Promised Land in another area. Although they were defeated in battles their faith remained strong. They were confident their God could not fail.

NOTES

1. Reply to landdrost of Stellenbosch to the Fiscal, April 2, 1812. Quoted in MacCrone, *Race Attitudes,* p. 130n.

2. The term myth in the sense of God's direct actions in human affairs was used in reference to South Africa by Leonard Thompson, "Afrikaner Nationalist Historiography and the Policy of Apartheid," *Journal of African History,* III (1962), 125-41.

3. Piet Retief's *Manifesto,* in Eybers, *Select Constitutional Documents,* pp. 143-45.

4. *Ibid.*

5. *Ibid.* For other summaries of reasons for the Trek, see John Bird, *The Annals of Natal* (2 vols., Pietermaritzburg: P. Davis & Son, 1888); Anna Steenkamp, "Record of Migration," in Bird, *Annals of Natal,* I, 459-468; J. N. Boshof, to editor of *Grahamstown Journal,* February 17, 1839, in Bird, *Annals of Natal,* I, 504; "Journal of Sarel Celliers," in Bird, *Annals of Natal,* I, 251; "Narrative of W. J. Pretorius," in Bird, *Annals of Natal,* I, 230.   See also Louis Trigardt, *Dagboek van Louis Trigardt (1836-8),* (Bloemfontein: Het Volksblad Drukkery, 1917).

6. J. N. Boshof to the editor *Grahamstown Journal,* February 17, 1839, in Bird, *Annals of Natal,* I, 504.

7. Anna Steenkamp, "Record of Migration," in Bird, *Annals of Natal,* I, 459-468.

8. Spoelstra, *Doppers,* p. 87.

9. Gustav Preller, *Piet Retief* (Cape Town: 1906), p. 66, quoted in *Voortrekkermense,* I, 135.

10. This complex period and its many tribal movements is analyzed in great detail in J. D. Omer-Cooper, *The Zulu Aftermath: A Nineteenth-Century Revolution in Bantu Africa* (London: Longman Group Ltd., 1966, 1980).

11. The interrelation among the Nguni groups is summarized by Monica Wilson in Wilson and Thompson, *Oxford History of South Africa,* I, 75-130. She has provided genealogical charts of various groups on pp. 88, 91, 92, and 94.   Dates of death for certain chiefs are in accord with her charts. The Sotho are summarized on pp. 131-167.

12. This extensive movement is summarized in Omer-Cooper, *Zulu-Aftermath,* with his special note concerning this term on p. 5. He uses *Mfecane.* A similar, but briefer discussion of the same phenomenon is by Leonard Thompson in Wilson and Thompson, *Oxford History of South Africa,* I, 391-405. Thompson uses the term *Difaqane.*

13. Trigardt, *Dagboek*, p. 347.

14. Their travels are summarized in a letter writter by Trigardt to Portuguese settlers at Delagoa Bay, May 1, 1837, in Trigardt, *Dagboek*, pp. 90-91.

15. Trigardt, *Dagboek*, October 24, 1837.

16. *Ibid.*, April 21, 24, 1838.

17. Details in Gustav Preller, *Voortrekkermense*, I, 118-119, quoted in Manfred Nathan, *The Voortrekkers of South Africa* (London: Gordon and Gotch, 1937), p. 138.

18. Charl Celliers, October 16, 1836, *Journal*, in Bird, *Annals of Natal*, I, 239.

19. *Ibid.*

20. Erasmus Smit wrote a detailed diary of his experiences on the frontier, which is one of the valuable primary sources of the period. The first entry in the diary is dated November 14, 1836. In Preller, ed., *Voortrekkermense*, II. This is reprinted as *Uit Het Dagboek Van Erasmus Smit, Predikant bij de Voortrekkers* (Pretoria: State Library, 1967).

21. *Voortrekkermense*, I, 297; quoted in Nathan, *Voortrekkers*, pp. 153-54.

22. Celliers, *Journal*, in Bird, *Annals of Natal*, I, 240.

23. Preller, *Piet Retief*, pp. 73-74.

24. Noted in Smit's diary under the date Thursday, June 6, 1837.

25. Retief was sworn in on June 1, 1837. The Rev. Erasmus Smith administered the oath. Preller, *Piet Retief*, pp. 62-63, in Nathan, *Voortrekkers*, p. 166. This appears in Erasmus Smit's diary dated Sunday, June 11, 1837.

26. Nathan, *Voortrekkers*, p. 168. This Bible is preserved in the Voortrekker Museum near Pretoria.

27. Eybers, *Select Constitutional Documents*, p. 149.

28. Retief to Dingane, November 18, 1837, in H. S. Pretorius, D. W. Kruger, and C. Beyers, eds., *Voortrekker-Argiefstukke, 1829-1849* (Pretoria: Staatsdrukker, 1937), p. 22.

29. Retief's letter is dated January 26, 1838. Translation in Nathan, *Voortrekkers*, p. 196.

30. See George C. Cory, ed., *The Diary of the Rev. Francis Owen, M.A., Missionary with Dingaan in 1837-1838* (Cape Town: Van Riebeeck Society Publications, VII, 1926).

31. Eybers, *Select Constitutional Documents*, p. 149.

32. A photograph of the plaque and monument is in Nathan, *Voortrekkers*, p. 208.

33. Erasmus Smith, *Diary*, February 17-18, 1838. Summarized also by Anna Steenkamp, in Bird, *Annals of Natal*, I, 459-468.

34. Anna Steenkamp, in Bird, *Annals of Natal*, I, 459-468.

35. Celliers, *Journal*, in Bird, *Annals of Natal*, I, 241-242.

36. Nathan, *Voortrekkers*, p. 227; Preller, *Piet Retief*, p. 254.

37. Preller, *Piet Retief*, pp. 216-236.

38. Celliers, *Journal*, in Bird, *Annals of Natal*, I, 243.

39. Monday, August 13, 1838, in Erasmus Smit's *Diary*.

40. August 13, 1838; Anna Steenkamp's reflections, in Bird, *Annals of Natal*, I, 463.

41. *Ibid.* Erasmus Smith reports on the religious faith of Maritz on his last day, in his *Diary* for September 23, 1838.

42. Report of Mr. J. G. Bantjes, in Bird, *Annals of Natal*, I, 442. Erasmus Smit confirms the arrival date as November 22, 1838, in his *Diary* for that date.

43. Report of J. G. Bantjes, in Bird, *Annals of Natal*, I, 442.

44. Celliers, *Journal*, in Bird, *Annals of Natal*, I, 244.

45. *Ibid.* This has been compared with the version in G. B. A. Gerdener, *Sarel Celliers, Die Vader Van Dingaansdag* (Pretoria: Van Schaik, 1925).

46. Pretorius "wanted to make a vow to God Almighty if they were all willing, that should the Lord be pleased to grant us the victory, we would raise a house to the memory of His great name . . . and that we would note the day of the victory in a book, to make it known even to our latest posterity, in order that it might be celebrated to the honor of God." Graham MacKeurtan, *The Cradle Days of Natal* (London: Longmans, Green and Co., 1930), pp. 246-247.

47. Celliers, *Journal*, in Bird, *Annals of Natal*, I, 245.

48. *Ibid.*, p. 246.

49. *Ibid.*

50. Andries Pretorius, December 22, 1838, in Bird, *Annals of Natal*.

51. Hattingh to Pretorius, March 30, 1839, in Beyers, *Voortrekker-Argiefstukke,* pp. 60-61.

52. Hattingh from Agter Sneeuwberg to Pretorius, in Beyers, *Voortrekker-Argiefstukke,* p. 64.

53. Carstens at Cape Town to Pretorius, May 29, 1839, in Beyers, *Voortrekker-Argiefstukke,* p. 71.

54. Brand to friend, June 13, 1839, in Beyers, *Voortrekker-Argiefstukke,* pp. 82-83.

55. September 11, 1839, in Beyers, *Voortrekker-Argiefstukke,* p. 91.

56. A. Carstens from Cape Town to Pretorius, September 11, 1839, in Beyers, *Voortrekker-Argiefstukke,* pp. 92-93.

57. Carstens to Pretorius, October 4, 1839, in Beyers, *Voortrekker-Argiefstukke,* pp. 95-96.

58. S. P. Engelbrecht, *Die Nederduitsch Hervormde Gemeente Rustenberg, 1850-1950* (Kerkraad of the South African Republic, n.d.), p. 180.

59. *Ibid.,* p. 2.

60. Edwin W. Smith, *The Life and Times of Daniel Lindley* (New York: Library Publishers, 1952), pp. 421-423.

61. Eybers, *Select Constitutional Documents,* pp. 151-152. The proclamation was issued November 14, 1838, but was effected from December 4, the date of the British landing in Natal.

62. S. Charters to the Boers, in Bird, *Annals of Natal,* p. 495.

63. Bird, *Annals of Natal,* I, 236. The first Trekker constitution was written at Winburg in 1837.

64. Eybers, *Select Constitutional Documents,* p. 158.

65. To Pretorius from his aunt in Cape Town, June 20, 1839, in Eybers, *Select Constitutional Documents,* p. 88.

66. *Grahamstown Journal,* October 31, 1839, in Bird, *Annals of Natal,* I, 546.

67. November 11, 1839, in Bird, *Annals of Natal,* p. 547; cf. their statement of January 8, 1840, in Bird, *Annals of Natal.*

68. Vasco da Gama visited the east coast on Christmas Day, 1497. He named the land "Terra Natalis" by which name it has since been known. Smith, *Life of Lindley,* p. 120.

69. Mpanda's statement to the Volksraad of October 15, 1839, is in Bird, *Annals of Natal,* I, 536-540.

70. January 19-20, 1840, in Bird, *Annals of Natal*, p. 563; cf. Delagorgue, *Travels*, in Bird, *Annals of Natal*, I, 553-75, 712-726.

71. This was A. Pretorius's Journal report of the expedition, printed in *Zuid Afrikaan*, February 10, 1846, in Bird, *Annals of Natal*, p. 578.

72. January 26, 1840, in Bird, *Annals of Natal*, I, 580.

73. Omer-Cooper, *Zulu-Aftermath*, pp. 41-42.

74. February 10, 1840, in Bird, *Annals of Natal*, p. 592.

75. *Ibid.*, p. 595.

76. Delagorgue, *Travels*, in Bird, *Annals of Natal*, p. 576.

77. A. W. J. Pretorius, from his mother, February 9, 1840, in Beyers, *Voortrekker-Argiefstukke*, p. 102.

78. June 18, 1840, Lord Russell to Sir George Napier, in Bird, *Annals of Natal*, p. 605.

79. *Ibid.*, p. 605.

80. Cloete to Napier, June 20, 1843, in Bird, *Annals of Natal*, II.

81. Napier to the Council at Cape Town, January 19, 1842, in Bird, *Annals of Natal*.

82. Delagorgue, *Travels*, in Bird, *Annals of Natal*, I, 721. Italics added.

83. G. S. Preller, *Day Dawn in South Africa* (Pretoria: Wallach, 1938), p. 257.

84. *Ibid.*, pp. 257-258.

85. Bird, *Annals of Natal*, I, 468.

86. Cloete to Montague, August 8, 1843, in Bird, *Annals of Natal*, II, 259.

87. Eybers, *Select Constitutional Documents*, p. 194.

88. M. W. Vorster, November 4, 1847, in Beyers, *Voortrekker-Argiefstukke*, p. 281.

IV.
The Great Trek: II: The Orange River Territory and North of the Vaal, 1837–1860

While the Boers in Natal were conquering the land and being absorbed into the British empire, a second group was forming a culture west of the Drakensberg Mountains north of the Orange River in what was to become the Orange Free State and the Transvaal. When Piet Retief and Gerrit Maritz, and their followers began to migrate eastward in 1837, Hendrik Potgieter and Pieter Uys were the two main leaders among those remaining behind. Following the massacre of Retief and before the coming of Pretorius, both Potgieter and Uys went to Natal to help subjugate the Africans. Uys was killed, and Potgieter retreated back over the mountains in April 1838. It was Potgieter and his followers and later Pretorius who were involved in forming the two Boer republics, especially the Transvaal (the South African Republic).

Potgieter returned from Natal to the group of Boers remaining in Orangia, but in 1839 he moved north to the Mooi River, where he established the village of Potchefstroom, now Transvaal, named after himself.[1] This settlement was the center for the earliest governmental organization in the region north of the Vaal River. Confident that God was yet on the side of the loyal Boers, Potgieter believed that they must do something for the honor of God. After calling attention to the close relation between religious faith and social well-being, he told of his hopes for building a church:

> We the undersigned, of this new section of the world, with a Christian concern, seek each and everyone who is likewise concerned in his own heart, and who wishes to have a part in our aim here to build a building in which we as a whole people can serve our God and creator, so that we may, with an upright heart, by grace, inherit eternal blessedness.[2]

Potgieter was constantly informed of British activities against the Boers in Natal but refused to go to help Pretorius again. Rather, he called a meeting of many leaders at Doornkop to discuss the further British encroachments and to reinforce the Boer promises of unity under oath. He then replied to Pretorius,

> I said that they should be ready to stand even to the death, where I stand and now read your report, in order to confess before God as under an oath. I succeeded in getting a promise that the last man present with me would fight to the death for this land, and would rather die than fall under the English Government.[3]

Based on this widespread attitude, which was to grow stronger in succeeding years, the Boer settlement at Potchefstroom quickly developed a self-consciousness based on theological concerns that equated God's will with opposition to Britain.[4]

On April 9, 1844, Potgieter and his followers at Potchefstroom organized their separate government and drew up a set of rules. This "constitution" consisting of "thirty-three articles" was the basis of the first government in what became the Transvaal. Three sections of the thirty-three are especially important for our study as we remember the stated motives for the trek:

> (6) No half-castes, down to the tenth degree, shall be entitled to sit in our meetings as members or judge; (29) No natives shall be permitted to take up their residence near any town-lands to the detriment of the inhabitants of the town, except with the consent of the full Raad; (33) In the matter of master and servants, every master shall have the right to maintain discipline properly among his servants. There shall be no ill-treatment.[5]

Potgieter, however, was not long satisfied to remain at Potchefstroom. His dissatisfaction was based on his own personal ambition, on tensions arising within the group, and on fears of further British authority.[6] His party moved north beyond the twenty-fifth parallel to the area where they established the settlement of Andries-Ohrigstad,[7] where another new Volksraad was established on August 1, 1845.[8] Malaria caused the deaths of many trekkers, however, and the new town was almost completely abandoned.[9] The surviving population moved to territory several miles to the south, which they named Lydenburg—the Republic of Lydenburg—where the Volksraad sat regularly until 1849.[10]

In Ohrigstad-Lydenburg there was no organized church, but the Boers stipulated that the only religious organization they would recognize was the Dutch Reformed church.[11] Their faith continued even in the absence of an institution. On August 2 the Raad received a message from F. G. A. Wolmarans, later elder of the church, admonishing them to remember their witness before God:

> It appears to me that in order to please God, and that He may rescue us and constitute as a people to his honor, we must be established in His Church that it may blossom in our midst. . . . Remember how in Exodus we are admonished not to join in with the masses, in order to follow Him and to be a witness through which the right direction may be established. . . . Recognize my diligence for our own good in freedom! . . . My own longing is only for peace and love for our freedom. . . . It is the truth that before the Lord nothing is concealed.[12]

While Potgieter and his followers were organizing at Potchefstroom and farther north, another group of Boers was developing a political organization to the south in the Orange River territory (or Orangia) based on the Constitution of Winburg of 1836. A group of Boers had settled at Thaba Nchu and Winburg, and their numbers were gradually augmented by returnees from Natal.[13] Early Orangia history, however, was complicated by the presence of pro-British Boers who migrated there before the Great Trek and who did not share the grievances motivating the trekkers. The loyalist Boers had as their spokesman Michael Oberholster; the Republican trekker Boers were led by Jan Mocke. Oberholster was among the 283 Boers who petitioned the British leader in Natal requesting that they be placed under British authority for the purpose of stabilizing their culture and protecting them from the surrounding tribes "so that we may in future enjoy a peaceable and Christian life, and be enabled to erect a building on the ground, which we may call a Church or House of God, for the instruction of the adult, and rearing of the young."[14]

Mocke, strongly anti-British, was among those who represented Orangia in the Volksraad in Pietermaritzburg and who went to Natal to help defend it against the British in 1842. In July 1843 when the Volksraad at Pietermaritzburg submitted to British authority, Mocke and his followers immediately withdrew from the "disloyal" body, returning to the Orange River territory and joining Boers in and near Winburg who had not gone down to Natal.[15]

By 1844 there were thus three distinct centers of Voortrekker Boer political activity, the earliest settlements of what later became three nations and, still later, three sections of one union. Even at this early period there was interrelationship among the various groups of Boers, and all three groups were motivated by similar social, political, and theological concerns. Natal, however, became increasingly British, and the Boer spirit there came to have limited influence. The Boer ideology was nurtured in the two northern areas, which became the Orange Free State and the Transvaal.

The Boers in Orangia suspected the British would continue their expansion. Their fears were substantiated when in March 1846 Captain (later Major) Henry Douglas Warden was appointed British resident north of the Orange River.[16] He established the center of British authority at a place he named Bloemfontein, which has been the major city of the area since.[17] Furthermore, in December 1847 Governor Henry Smith, realizing the serious problems in the east, began an inspection tour. After visiting on the eastern frontier of Cape Colony and in the Orange River Territory, he proceeded to Natal. On February 1, 1848, he met Pretorius and a large number of Boers and promised them some alleviation of their problems in Natal. Pretorius' plea for independence of Natal was undoubtedly discussed and was flatly refused. Pretorius had attempted to stabilize the Boers after they submitted to British authority, but since the Boers continued to leave Natal, his influence declined. Two days later, writing from Pietermaritzburg, Sir Henry Smith proclaimed all land between the Orange and the Vaal Rivers sovereign territory of Her Majesty, forming the Orange River Sovereignty. This was done "with the sole view of establishing an amicable relation with the chiefs, of upholding them in their hereditary rights, and protecting them from any future aggression . . . and [for] their advancement in the blessings of Christianity."[18]

Pretorius immediately proceeded from Natal to the various groups of Boers in the Orange River Sovereignty and north of the Vaal seeking to organize forceful opposition, but without immediate results. Many Boers refused to serve under Pretorius because of their divided loyalties, thus weakening their whole objective. Pretorius finally settled at his new center of activity at Magaliesberg (now Rustenberg, Transvaal). Gradually Boers loyal to him and his objectives gathered from various other settlements, including Lydenburg-Ohrigstad, the stronghold of Potgieter. Agreement among all Boers was not forthcoming, however, as Pretorius indicated in a reply to a military officer:

> I know not whether it would be advisable for us here to lose all. The British near here are filled with treason, and plot with the blacks. I have received letters from different regions in the span of three or four days. . . . It seems to me that the Hollander [Smellekamp] wants to bring us all together under the command of Potgieter, but this he won't accomplish with me. I, and my followers, will serve under an impartial Volksraad, but *never under Potgieter*.[19]

The people of Ohrigstad, Olifants River, Derdepoort, and Krugerspost countered in a similar vein: "We will never recognize Pretorius as Commanding General over us."[20]

Because of this rivalry, Pretorius found his task difficult. On one occasion, speaking at the Mooi River (Potchefstroom), he summarized at length the grievances and the theological ideas of all:

The British Government promised protection for our land on May 12, 1843, yet we are so disgraced and overrun by the colored, that we were forced to flee than land under British authority. We left with great shame. Now notice also that the land between the Great Orange River and the Drakensberg to the Vaal River, where we seemed to have a legal claim to some land, now even that is taken from us, and all privileges are granted to the natives. We cannot live in the midst of them, nor under the British authority which immersed us in such heavy circumstances because of the proclamation. There are other complaints too numerous to mention.

Now we ask: Where is our legal territory which cost us goods and blood of men, women and children? . . . Yet there is the chance which should always be before our eyes, that the great Creator has caused a great movement over the world; and shall we remain still and allow other powers to take possession?

I came before you that you may escape from the disasters which have weighed heavy on you and yours. Therefore brothers, you should not trek to be free, nor flee; but *take God in your heart and the sword in your hands* and protect your rights and your freedom which is given to all creatures on earth. Have a deep trust among yourselves, and a sincere love, and fear no more the name of those who have chased you from your motherland to the impossible wilderness of Africa; but fear alone the God who shall certainly punish whomever turns father against son and son against father and brother against brother.

O, I should like to proclaim a commmandment to you, that you continually, alone or in groups, hold a day of prayer, so that we the lost sons again may return to the Creator, and that we may certainly be blessed. We ask Him to sustain us in our need, yes, He who *has protected us here in the wilderness.* Now as we wait for the joyous morning to break before us poor Afrikaner Boers, I call to all women, send your men; and the mothers, send your children so you may enjoy those great treasures which we have sought for so long. Let us neither hide, nor indulge in weeping; but let us use the Old Dutch motto that: "Eendrag maag mag en treedrag verbreek krag," [Unity makes might; and discord breaks our power]. So, those who stay home have a strong sword. Women pray for your men; mothers for your children; and you brothers and fathers for all of us together; and deal openly with the needy and the distressed. So shall we receive the hoped for harvest of freedom and religion and the blooming of the church among us; but

before we reach this which justice shows us, the Great Creator
may send to us trials and punishments.[21]

The punishments or trials were not long in coming. In July 1848 Willem
Jacobs, landdrost of Winburg and an old friend of Pretorius, invited the
latter to come to Winburg to help defend it against the British. Pretorius
led his followers there to begin a "war of freedom."[22] Arriving at Winburg
on July 12, he decreed that there would be none who could be neutral.
Those who were not for the Boers' cause were against them, and they must
retreat south across the Orange River within one week.[23] Warden, the
British resident in Bloemfontein, issued a reward of 1,000 pounds sterling
for the capture of Pretorius and urged Smith to proceed with troops. They
would organize both white and black who were available in the Orange
River sovereignty.[24] By August 17 the northward march of the British
began from Colesburg (Cape Colony) to a place fifty miles south of Bloemfontein called Boomplaats. Pretorius, leading his troops in heroic fashion,
stated that "they were as Israel standing before Pharaoh."[25] There on
August 29, Pretorius led his last battle against the British oppression.[26]
Within a few hours when all knew that the might of the hastily organized
British forces would overpower the Boers, Pretorius and all of his men fled
north.

The Boers' defeat at Boomplaats caused them to reconsider their many
personal differences. As long as the parties of Pretorius and of Potgieter
divided the loyalty of the Boers, there was no hope of forming a workable
opposition to British encroachments. Finally at Hekpoort on February 9,
1849, all promised to cooperate more fully for the common good.[27]
Potgieter's representative wrote that they had finally decided that the
supreme authority should be the Volksraad, and every individual—including
Potgieter and Pretorius—would be bound by its decisions.[28] Furthermore,
the Boers should "never recognize the British authority, in whole or in
part."[29]

The development toward united efforts was further strengthened at
another gathering at the Olifants River in March 1849 when all decided
again that the highest authority should be the Volksraad.[30] This was made
official at the General Volksraad of the whole area north of the Vaal held
at Derdepoort in May 1849,[31] when they chose the name the United Confederation of the whole community on this side of the Vaal River.[32]
Speaking for the occasion, Pretorius summarized the folk theology of all
groups there:

> You should always keep before your eyes that I am but an
> unlearned Boer, but trusting in your cooperation and help, and
> the great blessings of the Almighty, which we have already
> tasted and enjoyed, I shall use all my power and might to
> attempt to reach the true joy and freedom which we have so
> long sought. . . . What shall carrying the sword profit us if we

are not of one mind full of love and trust for each other, we
shall never reach the earthly nor the heavenly Canaan or
Jerusalem, but shall wander more than forty years, so that we
are completely destroyed and extinguished. . . . Nothing else
can make us joyful than love, peace, and attachment for each
other, for we know that God thereby promised his sign, and yes
even himself. . . . Remember also that we are all brothers who
left the homes of our fathers and mothers, in order to seek
that which is given to each creature.   Why should we any
longer work into the hands of our opponents; and before hundreds of our friends seem to be a mountain, yes, a sea of
discontent, so that they are apprehensive to come to us?[33]

By 1849 the main movement of the Great Trek was over. The land of
Natal had been annexed by Britain, a temporary sovereignty was proclaimed in the Orange River Territory, and the diverse groups north of the
Vaal were beginning to construct a settled government. Although Potgieter
and Pretorius were still strong-willed persons and would have points of
tension in the months ahead, Potgieter began to recognize their common
interests and common destiny as he wrote to Pretorius later that year.

You stated it well . . . that all issues have vanished between us
and that we alone maintain our differences. In the present
time can there be a portion of the world where the happiness
of a people is more sought than by us. Like the headstrong
Israelites of old we reject what brings happiness and hold to
what leads to our destruction.[34]

The Boers were deeply concerned about their lack of ecclesiastical
organizations.   They had no church in the northern area and only one in
Bloemfontein.   Speaking to the Volksraad that organized the union of the
many northern factions, F. G. Wolmarans again reminded the leaders of the
close relationship between a successful and well-ordered society and a
devout religion among the people. How else could these values be guaranteed except by organizing a church and securing a regularly ordained minister?

How insecure is the government, and what is the justification
of the leader of the people when there is no concern for religion? See how Jehiskia reconstituted the religion according to
the signs of God [II Chron. 28:12, where Jehiskia is a corruption
of "Hezekiah."]; but when religion declines, men expect nothing
but strife, and formidable punishment shall follow therefrom.
. . . One can find many images in the words of God, how land
and people are depraved by the decline of religion .[35]

With this deep religious concern, the Boers were anxious to have a regularly
ordained minister.

On the trek, religious services had been performed by laymen, lay ministers, or missionaries to Africans in the area.[36] The Boers, nevertheless, wished for more leadership, for their children remained unbaptized, and catechism was not conducted regularly. As early as 1839-1840, the organized churches and presbyteries nearest the trekkers realized that they had a responsibility to their compatriots, and certain ministers visited the wandering Boers periodically.[37] In 1842 the first Kerkraad was organized at Potchefstroom, but without a building for many years and without a permanent minister for a decade.[38] Daniel Lindley, an American Presbyterian missionary who came to be minister at the Dutch Reformed church in Pietermaritzburg (1840-1847), visited Potchefstroom several times to baptize children.[39] The Kerkraad at Potchefstroom would have accepted Lindley as its minister, but he believed his calling was to the Zulus, to whom he ultimately returned. He had baptized many children and adults in Winburg also, but the Kerkraad was probably not formed there until 1844.[40]

Not all Boers were sympathetic when the Cape churches attempted to send ministers to them. By this time the majority of pastors in the Dutch Reformed church of the Cape Colony were from Scotland, and although they spoke the language of the Boer people, they were suspected of having pro-British loyalties and hence were out of sympathy with the group feelings and objectives of the trekkers. W. A. Krige went to the territory in 1846, where he met resistance:

> I could not see the Boers at Caledon River, Bosjes Spruit and Klikspruit. Those on the Modder River and farther on, would have nothing to do with me. They said, rather, that they would have no teacher from the West. [If one should come to him he must come from the East by which they meant from the Netherlands by way of the East African Portuguese port, Delagoa Bay.][41]

The Cape Synod undertook several deputations to the northern communities, allowing a few ministers to visit many Boers to perform necessary religious functions and to report back to their synod. The first was undertaken in 1848 by Andrew Murray, Sr., and Pieter Kuipers Albertyn.[42] They visited many settlements in the Orange River Territory and crossed the Vaal River, baptizing and distributing free Bibles.[43] They were accused of being on a political mission, however, which they had difficulty in disproving.[44] In reporting this visitation, an interesting and disastrous typographical error occurred. Sir Harry Smith wrote to "My Friend Kruger," but in publication of his letter a "not" was omitted. The printed letter included the sentence: "The gentlemen [Murray and Albertyn] were sent by the Synod among you, for Christian and [—] political purposes."[45] A loyal member of the Dutch Reformed church in Stellenbosch immediately reacted:

Allow me, through the means of your paper, to ask if this is really the case, that the synod sent the spiritual Commission among the Boers for political reasons. I hope that some member of the synodical Commission will feel it his duty to answer this openly, that their silence will not be taken for agreement.[46]

The necessary reply was given a week later by the Rev. Abraham Faure, clerk of the synod. The meaning, he assured them, was completely reversed by the omission from the published letter.[47]

The second deputation was undertaken in 1848-1849 by the Rev. Philip Eduard Faure and the Rev. William Robertson.[48] The latter, minister at Swellendam and originally from Scotland, was known to be strongly pro-British: "We embrace every opportunity of speaking very candidly with those who are said to be disaffected, in private; . . . and we generally take care to obey the Apostolic Command [I Peter 2:17] by praying for the Queen, and all in authority."[49] Robertson hoped to introduce more Scottish or American ministers into the northern districts. Sir Harry Smith confirmed the basic suspicion of the Boers when he reminded the two men on the deputation: "With the words of Christ and His Apostles in your hands, so full of wisdom and grace, ministers like yourselves kind and energetic were alone required to show them [those who were not willing to submit to British authority] the error of their ways and to prepare them for life eternal."[50]

Faure assured Pretorius that the Cape church and the government were interested in their welfare, and in good Calvinistic style he argued that the Boers should respect the government, for wasn't that constituted by God? Neither blood, war, nor money could help or hinder the plan of God. Because the emigrants had so many friends in the Cape Colony who wished to allow the Boers rest and peace, could not the two groups live together in Christian love and friendship? Pretorius answered in his characteristic way, suggesting their typological relationship to Gideon who won the battle with the smaller army.[51] The Transvaal Boers were not convinced of the sincerity of the Cape Synod, for hardly had the deputations completed their work when the northern Boers asked again for religious leaders and schoolmasters. They repeated that they were north of the Vaal River, "thus outside the bounds of British authority."[52]

In 1847, not unrelated to pleas from South African Boers, a book entitled *De Kaapsche Landverhuizers of Neerlands Afstammelingen in Zuid-Africa* [*The Cape Emigrants or Dutch Descendants in South Africa*] appeared in Leiden. Written by Ulrich Gerhard Lauts, professor of naval history, it was destined to have a far-reaching influence in South Africa. Lauts gave a biased description of the Boers without religious leadership and in need of schools, chased from their homes in Natal by British oppression which they called Egyptian servitude.[53] This book inspired two expe-

ditions from the Netherlands to help the Transvaal Boers. The first group
sailed on the ship *Amino*, arriving at Delagoa Bay, where the Boers who
met them were bitterly disappointed that there was no minister aboard. A
year later another expedition was organized to sail on the *Vasco da
Gamma*. Three schoolmasters were on board, two influenced by Lauts' book
and the third by the Rev. Pieter Nicholas Ham, who himself had been
unable to contact the Boers on an earlier expedition to Delagoa Bay.[54]

Another person influenced by the book was the Rev. Dirk van der Hoff,
the first permanent religious leader in the north and a forceful figure in
Transvaal church history. A native of the Netherlands, he disembarked at
Cape Town in November 1852 and arrived at Potchefstroom on May 27,
1853.[55] Less than three months later at Rustenberg—the new name for
Magaliesberg—on August 8, 1853, without any authority from any Cape
Presbytery, van der Hoff was installed as minister when the Volksraad
declared that they were a church independent of any Cape affiliation
because "the conditions, or promises, of supplying us with ministers have
not been fulfilled; and we cannot submit to the ecclesiastical laws of the
Synods of the Dutch Reformed Church of South Africa."[56] Beyond this,
however, there were more than ecclesiastical reasons behind the schismatic
decision. Old hatreds and erroneous fears concerning the Cape church were
furthered for political reasons. The motivations of the leaders of the
schismatic church were summarized by van der Hoff as he sought to persuade the Lydenburgers to join in the schism. He argued:

> The Cape Synod stood under the supervision of the British
> Government, that ministers of the Cape Church were obliged
> to take an oath of allegiance to the Queen, that Cape ecclesi-
> astical law placed whites and blacks upon a footing of equality,
> and that no modifications in the Church's laws and regulations
> would be granted to the congregations of the Transvaal.[57]

The Cape ecclesiastical leaders sought to convince the schismatics that
although their nations were now separate, the body of Christ, the Christian
church, was one body, and they were all members of the same body. They
had no success. The schismatic church took the name of the Nederduits
Hervormde Kerk (N.H.K.), in contrast to the Nederduits Gereformeerde
Kerk (N.G.K.) of the Cape Colony.[58] While most of the people were united
in their schismatic church, the South African Republic was not yet one.
There were four centers: Potchefstroom, Zoutpansberg, Utrecht, and Lydenburg. Not until 1860 were they finally united, and even then Lydenburg
continued its ecclesiastical relationship with the Transgariep Synod, the
synod in the eastern Cape province related to the Bloemfontein organization. Thus the regular N.G.K. continued to be represented in the northern
republic.[59]

Church developments south of the Vaal River proceeded on a different
pattern. The Orange River Sovereignty received its first permanent

minister when the Rev. Andrew Murray, Jr., was appointed to Bloemfontein in February 1849.[60] His influence was far-reaching both because he was a highly trained theologian and because he was sympathetic with the moderate Boers on this frontier. Murray, almost twenty-one years of age, was born in 1828 in the Cape Colony where his father was minister. He was educated in Scotland and the Netherlands and was one of the major leaders of the South African church for the remainder of the century. He was inducted as minister of the Bloemfontein church by his father on May 6, 1849.[61] The next year the Transgariep (Trans-Orange) Synod of the Cape Dutch Reformed church was formed,[62] bringing the Bloemfontein church into close association with the Cape churches.[63]

Murray was deeply concerned about the spiritual well-being of the Boer people and became mildly sympathetic with the grievances of the trekboers, but at the same time he maintained his close contacts with the Reformed church of the Cape Colony. He recognized the difficulties in this area where Boer and Briton lived side by side, and he conducted services in both English and Dutch. After having been in Bloemfontein only one month he reported: "I feel much more difficulty as to the English than the Dutch congregation as to the preaching, and still more as to the pastoral work. . . . The [English] officers are all unmarried, rather wild (often very drunk) and two of them are living openly with colored women."[64] He recognized also the growing tension between the British authority in the sovereignty and the Basuto,[65] which resulted in several Basuto wars and ultimately the establishment in 1868 of Basutoland as a British protectorate.[66]

Hardly had Murray begun his work in Bloemfontein as the only minister in the present Orange Free State when he undertook a tour of inspection into the area north of the Vaal River. During six weeks between December 1849 and January 1850, he traveled to six Boer centers attempting to placate the fears the Boers had of British appointees (Murray and all other ministers of the Dutch Reformed churches at this time were appointed by the Cape governor). He baptized many children and youth and confirmed them as members of the church.[67] His letters give a first-hand account of the religious developments where there had never been a settled minister, and they are written by an astute observer of human behavior. Especially noteworthy is his interpretation of the most radical group of Boers, the Jerusalem Pilgrims, whose political objections to British influence assumed a religious and even an apocalyptic tone.

Very little is know of the development of this unusual sect. They seem to have been centered in the western Transvaal in the area around Mariko where they regarded Commandant-General J. A. Enslin as a prophet. The Pilgrims traced their lineage back to the families involved in the Slagters' Nek Rebellion in 1815, giving insight into the reasons for their intense anti-British attitude. Indeed, the basis for this sect's existence appears to have been more political than religious.

An eye-witness wrote of his experience a few years later. He went to the Transvaal for the first time in 1855 and while in Rustenberg was interviewed by a group of travelers. They asked, "How far is Jerusalem from Rustenberg?" Trying not to express his surprise at their question, he replied flippantly:

> The northern-most Kaffir tribe which some of the Voortrekkers have visited are called "Manakos." There they saw Arabians and Arabian horses and hastily concluded that these truly were the sons of Ishmael. Thus they could not be far from the sons of Abraham and Jerusalem must be relatively close by.
>
> Later it became clear to me what they really hoped for by using the word "Jerusalem." They used expressions in the Bible such as: the promised land, the cluster of grapes of Joshua and Caleb [Numbers 13:21-24], milk and honey, the balm of Gilead and many other things. They referred to this as a real land of plenty without Englishmen, without taxes, and with very little work [zeer wenig werk]. The thoughts of the trek like that of Dorado [El Dorado, the lengendary city of gold of the six-teenth-century Spanish explorers] had already been considered for a long time and already had many followers. Some actually wanted to know how far it was and if there were deep rivers between Rustenberg and Jerusalem.[68]

The visitor then pointed at the map of Africa on the wall, showing the Red Sea and Jerusalem on the extreme upper edge. Then he compared the distance between Cape Town and Rustenberg with the rest of the journey. They knew that the trip from Cape Town to Rustenberg would take from six to eight weeks by ox wagon and realized that the trip on to the Red Sea would be eight times that distance. Furthermore, there were too many difficulties on the way—rivers, climate, distance, tribes, disease. They had no Moses as a leader. Finally, Palestine was largely desert, rivers were mostly dried up, and foreign and unfriendly people were in control. The Jerusalem Pilgrims argued that the Bible told of palaces in Jerusalem; they would find means for crossing swollen rivers and the Red Sea; "Aunt Grita" had prepared a remedy for the tsetse fly (yellow fever); and they knew the Arabs could not shoot as well as they. Furthermore, Enslin was their Moses.[69]

Nothing more came of the discussion, and in a short time, before they began their trek, their "Moses", Enslin, died. Following his death the party passed into oblivion, but undoubtedly their ideas had significant influence in the ultraconservative politics of the Transvaal for several decades. The only remains of the group are two geographical features. The first is the town they named Enselsberg (in Zeerust). The second is the Transvaal River flowing northward, which they named Nylstroom (the Nile). They undoubtedly believed that in their trek to Jerusalem, they must follow this river to its mouth. They did not know enough geography, however, to realize that the Nylstroom and farther on, the Limpopo, would not drain these waters north into the Mediterranean but eastward into the Indian Ocean.[70]

When Murray came into contact with this unusual group on his first trip into the Transvaal, he reported:

> The most of those who are waiting for the trek to Jerusalem are in that neighborhood [near Magaliesberg or Rustenburg] and I was very sorry that my further arrangements prevented my going among them, though this perhaps was also the Lord's doing, as they might possible have turned me back. . . . On the way we called on one of those who refuse to come to church. After a couple of hours' conversation I left him, deeply grieved at the ignorance of these poor people [the Jerusalem Pilgrims]. England is one of the horns of the beast, and of course those who receive her pay are made partakers of her sins. I hardly knew whether to weep or smile at some of his explanations of the prophecies and of Revelation, all tending to confirm their hopes of being soon called to trek to Jerusalem. By the way, he for the moment quite puzzled me by showing me the *kan-teekening* [marginal notes of the Dutch version of the Bible] on Revelation XVII.12, where all the countries of Europe are mentioned as being typified by the horns of the beast except Holland,—and under it he included, of course, the true Afri-kaners.[71]

A year later Murray met some of the same group who urged him to cease giving service to the anti-Christ and to come to be their minister.[72] On this second visit north of the Vaal River, he was further urged to assume leadership of the Boers in that remote area of the world. Potgieter urged him to help secure a settled minister,[73] while Pretorius emphasized the decay of religion in a land without church and minister.[74] Murray seriously considered assuming this new challenge but finally declined in March 1859.[75] He wrote prophetic words, however, as he analyzed the situation in the north: "I have been brought in the leading of Providence to take an especial interest in this people, which may not be excited in the heart of anyone else. God has now set before the Church an open door across the Vaal River, and if we enter not in, it may soon be shut."[76] The door was not entered at the time, and it was partially shut because of a confluence of religious and political circumstances: the formation of the N.H.K. in the Transvaal in 1853 and the Sand River Convention.

To protect the Orange River Sovereignty from agitation from the north and to avoid further Boer conspiracy with the Basuto, the British leaders were forced to consider the Boers' repeated pleas for independence. The first step was taken late in 1851 when Pretorius was invited to come from Magaliesberg in Transvaal to assume the leadership of the Boers again at

Winburg.[77]   Murray convinced the British authorities that they must consider seriously the possibility of furthering the independence of the Boers
north of the Vaal River.   Representatives of both the British and the Boers
met at the Sand River, near Bloemfontein.   All present agreed to the Sand
River Convention on January 17, 1852, which established the land across
the Vaal River (the Transvaal) independent of British control.[78]   One of the
onlookers who had played a significant part in the preparations was the
Rev. Andrew Murray.[79]   The main Boer protagonist for such action was
Pretorius, who signed as commandant general.

One year later the Volksraad voted to call the new nation the South
African Republic,[80] adding two months later "to the North of the Vaal
River."[81]   The convention provided that there be no interference by either
the British or the South African nation in the affairs of the other, and no
slavery was to be permitted.   In June 1855 the qualification appeared with
respect to the voting franchise: "All colored people are excluded from this
provision, and . . . they may never be given or granted rights of burgher-
ship."[82]

The Sand River Convention was a major victory for the Boers, but
Potgieter feared that there was a secret provision that the Boers would be
subject to British authority.[83]   While Pretorius signed for all Boers, some
were not yet ready to agree to his authority.   To make it official, Pretorius
called a council of the people at Rustenberg on March 16, 1852.   Potgieter
had to be convinced that his influence was needed.   When these two strong-
willed leaders met, it was not known if they would agree or if they would
renew their personal feud.   The tense situation was summarized by Jacobus
Stuart:

> The sun was not yet completely visible when the elders
> gathered near the tents of Potgieter and Pretorius.   Both
> leaders respected the request of the elders and the meeting
> was held in the tent of the former.   The people were outside in
> complete silence, as instructed, waiting to know what the
> outcome would be: enmity or brotherhood; fratricide or
> brotherly love.   Finally the tent was opened.   The two leaders
> stood before the people hand in hand; the Bible lay open before
> them.   The people raised a common rejoicing to heaven for
> love was in their midst.[84]

In the end the two fiery champions of Boer freedom were reconciled
because of their higher religious loyalty.   While they could not agree in
political action, with the Bible before them they submitted to its
authority.[85]

The stormy days of both Potgieter and Pretorius were near an end.
Potgieter died in March 1853 and was succeeded by his son, Piet

Potgieter.[86] In July Pretorius was stricken and lay near death. Expecting his last breath to come soon, he wrote his last letter to his followers:

> Now in my weakness I must admonish you—protect your church. As the Christian religion declines among you, your state declines, and the blessings promised to your land and people decline, so that you will benefit in no way. Watch and pray that no seed of discord roots among you; pull it up immediately. Be true to each other in all that you attempt; and do it with the Lord, ask him for assistance, ask him for power and strength and the Lord will pour out his power in your weakness. . . . Set the way of justice before you, and do nothing outside its bounds; if you remain steadfast in good, then the Lord will bless your work; but if you fall into discord, then the devil will be under your feet. Because of this I say, watch and pray.
>
> I must thank you sincerely for your loyalty and trust that you have shown to me; yes, loyal brothers, foremen of the Almighty God, God will repay you by sending understanding in all things, that you may give adequate leadership. Believe in the God of Heaven, who has spared me this long and allowed me to do His will; thank Him not only for your independence, but also that He sent us a minister of the church among us. May the Lord bless him also that he may have rich fruits from his work, that you may remain steadfast in your religious faith, and that the Lord may do even more for you. Thus let the church not be vacant; let the minister not speak to empty chairs and benches; but to attentive hearers. Protect your religion if you love freedom.
>
> My brothers, in conclusion I warn you that in case the Lord takes me from your midst, let no dissension come among you. Seek not high opinions, but fear the Lord. May the God of eternity bless you from heaven; may the earth bring forth fruits and may these not be hid from you even to eternity.
>
> To you my brother who will take my place, serve the people of God in humility and in courage with all justice and modesty. Know that the Lord watches you from heaven; ask him for his Grace and assistance and he will uphold you. Do nothing for your own honor, but let all that you do be for the honor of God, and for the welfare of land and folk.
>
> This is the wish and prayer of your servant and brother.[87]

To his children he wrote, "See to it that your calling and your election remains fast."[88] On July 23, 1853, Pretorius, fearless leader of God's own chosen Boers, died and was succeeded by his son, Marthinus Wessel Pretorius.[89]

While these developments were unfolding in the South African Republic, changes were coming to the Orange River Sovereignty as well. Some of the people wanted to remain British subjects; others sought independence. The Rev. Andrew Murray sensed the changed policy when he reported in December 1852 that Governor George Cathcart "intends abandoning the [Orange River] Sovereignty."[90] Relations between the British and the Basuto people were at a stalemate, and little advantage could be gained by continuing the controversy, so the British decided to retreat.[91] The Rev. Andrew Murray and Dr. Colin Fraser were elected to go to London to oppose the abandonment.[92] Their mission was in vain, for before they arrived in London, the British withdrawal from the sovereignty was an accomplished fact. Representatives of the people met at Bloemfontein on February 15, 1854, to organize their own government, electing Josias Philip Hoffman as their leader. On February 23 they framed the document, the Bloemfontein Convention, finally giving freedom to the Boers north of the Orange River. The nine articles of the convention provided that there would be no slavery in the new territory and that British subjects would be protected and would be allowed to leave if they desired.[93]

The constitution of the new nation, the Orange Free State, was adopted on April 10, 1854.[94] It provided that all white persons born in the state or who had resided there for three years should be citizens and have voting rights; the Volksraad would be the supreme power over all, including the president; the Volksraad would further religion and education, with only the N.G.K. officially organized.[95] Five days later they passed an ordinance making the Dutch language the preferred language of the state; all documents submitted in English were to be accompanyied by a Dutch translation.[96]

While the Orange Free State was developing as a unified people, there were still noticeable divisions in the north, six years after the Sand River Convention. There was not yet a constitution, and there were still four semi-independent groups. While most of the people wished to have one nation, Lydenburg favored a federal constitution with separate states. As a desperate move toward unity, M. W. Pretorius proposed that the Orange Free State and the South African Republic become one nation. When this idea was flatly rejected, the attention of the northern republicans turned to the formation of their own *Grondwet* (constitution), finally adopted February 2, 1858. Lydenburg, however, remained separate. Among the 232 articles of the constitution, five are important for our purposes:

> Article 1: The people desire to permit no equality between colored people and the white inhabitants, either in Church or State.
> Article 20: The people desire to retain the fundamental teaching so their Dutch Reformed Religion as laid down in the years 1618 and 1619 by the Synod of Dordrecht, and the Dutch Reformed Church shall be the State Church.

Article 21: They prefer to allow no Roman Catholic Churches amongst them, nor any other Protestant Churches than those in which the same tenets of the Christian belief are taught, as contained in the Heidelberg Catechism.

Article 22: They shall appoint no other representatives to the Volksraad than those who are members of the Dutch Reformed congregations.

Article 24: The people desire the development, prosperity and welfare of Church and State, and with this view to provide for the wants of the Dutch Reformed Ministers and teachers.[97]

The consolidation of the Transvaal was completed when the Republic of Lydenburg finally united with the South African Republic on April 10, 1860, with the interesting item in the agreement: "The Dutch Reformed Congregation at Lijdenburg shall never be forced to assimilate its form of church government to that of any other congregation."[98] The church at Lydenburg remained in communion with the Cape Church (N.G.K.), although all other Reformed churches of the Transvaal comprised the N.H.K. The area of the republic was finally constituted substantially as it would remain throughout the century.

In the two republics the Boer group consciousness was developed as a double reaction similar to that in Natal. Anti-British and anti-African feelings were intertwined. There was emphasis on freedom, the Dutch language, purity of culture, rejection of the African as an equal in any way, and a confidence that God is ultimately the leader of both the Orange Free State and the South African Republic.

NOTES

1. *Pot* from Potgieter; *Chef,* Dutch and Afrikaans for "chief"; and *Stroom,* Dutch and Afrikaans for "stream." Cf. Nathan, *Voortrekkers,* p. 321.

2. Spoken at Potchefstroom, November 1, 1841, in Beyers, *Voortrekker-Argiefstukke,* p. 146.

3. Potgieter to Pretorius, April 4, 1842, in Beyers, *Voortrekker-Argiefstukke,* p. 158.

4. Later developments show that although they did not state it specifically, they may well have had the book of Exodus in their minds as they organized the settlement: "Now therefore, if you will obey my voice and keep my covenant, you shall be my own possession among all peoples; for all the earth is mine, and you shall be to me a kingdom of priests and a holy nation. These are the words which you shall speak to the children of Israel." Exodus 19:5-6.

5. Eybers, *Select Constitutional Documents,* pp. 349-356; the original is in *Suid-Afrikaanse Argiefstukke* (Transvaal, vol. I), pp. 5-9.

6. Nathan, *Voortrekkers,* p. 325, suggests that Potgieter was reminded that the British had already claimed authority to the twenty-fifth parallel and that it would be only a matter of time until they would act on this promise.

7. Andries was the first Christian name of Potgieter, and Ohrig was the leader of the Dutch Company that had sent Smellekamp several times to South Africa. The name was later shortened to Ohrigstad and substantiates the high regard the Boers still had for the Dutch expedition.

8. *Suid-Afrikaanse Argiefstukke* (Transvaal, vol. 1), p. 13, records the beginning of business on this day.

9. Andrew Murray, Jr., reported in a letter that "the town and neighborhood have been abandoned, though exceedingly fertile, on account of the disease which has carried off so many victims during the past two years, and all the people have trekked out to the Hoogeveld (plateau)." January 17, 1850, in J. du Plessis, *The Life of Andrew Murray of South Africa* (London: Marshall Bros., 1919), p. 106.

10. *Ly* (Afrikaans) or *Lijden* (Dutch) for "to suffer," reminiscent of their many recent heartaches.

11. *Suid-Afrikaanse Argiefstukke* (Transvaal), I, 12.

12. *Ibid.,* I, 159, written to the Raad of Ohrigstad, August 2, 1845.

13. The missionary was only partly correct when he reported: "The Boers residing in the vicinity of this station, who were the most active of

the Natal war, have all returned, and so far as I can learn, have exchanged their warlike spirit for one more peaceable, at least for a season." J. Allison missionary at Thaba Nchu, to the Rev. William Shaw at Grahamstown, August 3, 1842, in Bird, *Annals of Natal*, II, 60.

14. September 28, 1843, in Eybers, *Select Constitutional Documents*, p. 261.

15. H. Cloete to J. Montagu, Pietermaritzburg, August 8, 1843, in Bird, *Annals of Natal*, II, 256-258.

16. Theal, *History of South Africa*, IV, 403; and Nathan, *Voortrekkers*, p. 365.

17. "Bloom-fountain," or "Fountain of flowers."

18. Eybers, *Select Constitutional Documents*, pp. 271-273.   Cf. the Dutch original in *Voortrekker-Argiefstukke*, pp. 303-306, under the date February 3, 1848.

19. From Magaliesberg, February 12, 1847, in Beyers, *Voortrekker-Argiefstukke*, p. 257. Italics added.

20. *Suid-Afrikaanse Argiefstukke* (Transvaal), I, 304, under the date March 11, 1850.

21. The General Complaint, from the Mooi River, April 8, 1848, in Beyers, *Voortrekker-Argiefstukke*, pp. 313-315. Italics added.

22. Preller, *Pretorius*, p. 354.

23. Theal, *History of South Africa*, IV, 431.

24. August 10, 1848, in Beyers, *Voortrekker-Argiefstukke*, p. 334.

25. F. A. Van Jaarsveld, *The Afrikaner's Interpretation of South African History* (Cape Town: Simondium Publishers, 1964), p. 9.

26. Pretorius and his forces numbered fewer than a thousand; British troops were more than double that number. The battle was actually little more than a skirmish.

27. *Suid-Afrikaanse Argiefstukke* (Transvaal), I, xxvi.

28. *Ibid.*, February 13, 1849, pp. 269-270.

29. *Ibid.*

30. *Suid-Afrikaanse Argiefstukke* (Transvaal), I, 272-273.

31. *Ibid.*, I, 299.

32. Nathan, *Voortrekkers*, p. 335.

33. May 22, 1849, in Beyers, *Voortrekker-Argiefstukke*, p. 385.

34. From Potgieter at Zoutpansberg, to Pretorius, December 20, 1849, in Engelbrecht, *Geskiedenis van die N. H. K.*, p. 64.

35. *Suid Afrikaanse Argiefstukke* (Transvaal), I, 277.

36. For example, Erasmus Smit, Charl Celliers, Daniel Lindley, and James Archbell. In addition, a member of the Berlin Missionary Society, the Rev. Ludwig Döhne, succeeded Daniel Lindley as minister at Pieter-maritzburg (1847-1850). Cf. Andries Dreyer, *Die Kaapse Kerk en die Groot Trek* (Cape Town: Van de Sandt de Villiers, 1929), p. 87, for the details about these men. Dreyer also has collected several biographical references on Erasmus Smit, Daniel Lindley, and Jacob Ludwig Döhne, pp. 193-215.

37. See for example, the discussion in the Graaff-Reinet presbytery, 1839-1840, in Dreyer, *Kaapse Kerk*, pp. 27-33. One of the protagonists for such actions was the Rev. Dr. Andrew Murray, Sr., who himself visited the Boers the next year and whose son lived in the Orange River Territory for more than a decade.

38. S. P. Engelbrecht, *Die Nederduitsch Hervormde Gemeente Potchef-stroom, 1842-1942* (Pretoria: J. H. de Bussy, n.d., p. 10).

39. The visits were March 26, 1842, May 3, June 3, and July 18, 1844; Engelbrecht, *Geskiedenis*, p. 35.

40. Engelbrecht, *Die Nederduitsch Hervormde Gemeente Potchef-stroom*, p. 11.

41. Dreyer, *Kaapse Kerk*, pp. 84-85. This is the report of W. A. Krige, October 7, 1846.

42. Andrew Murray, Sr., minister at Graaff-Reinet, 1822-1865; see Dreyer, *Kaapse Kerk*, p. 88. P. K. Albertyn, minister at Paarl, 1841-1844, at Prince Albert, 1845-1850, and taught at Caledon, 1850-1878; Dreyer, *Kaapse Kerk*, p. 19.

43. Dreyer, *Kaapse Kerk*, p. 89.

44. For example, it was reported later that P. K. Albertyn attempted to clarify their objectives for coming. He insisted that their coming was based only on religious and spiritual motives. A woman at Mooi River (Potchefstroom) replied: "Yes, you preachers say you come with the Bible, but after the Bible comes the English government." Reported in *Die Kerk-bode*, March 18, 1920; quoted in Dreyer, *Kaapse Kerk*, pp. 107-108.

45. The letter was published in the *Commercial Advertiser*, September 2, 1848; quoted in Dreyer, *Kaapse Kerk*, p. 110.

46. September 9, 1848, in Dreyer, *Kaapse Kerk*, p. 116.

47. Reported in the *Commercial Advertiser*, September 16, 1848, quoted in Dreyer, *Kaapse Kerk*, p. 116. Nevertheless, by this slip of the pen the

deputations were open to the same type of criticism that had been leveled against the work of Dr. John Philip—that his activities were for political as well as for religious purposes.

48. P. E. Faure, minister at Wynberg, a few miles from Cape Town, 1834-1882, in Dreyer, *Kaapse Kerk*, p. 123. William Robertson, minister at Swellendam, 1833-1872, in Dreyer, *Kaapse Kerk*, pp. 130-131.

49. Dreyer, *Kaapse Kerk*, p. 121, as Robertson reported to the Cape government.

50. Dreyer, *Kaapse Kerk*, p. 149.

51. Letter to P. E. Faure from Pretorius at Magaliesberg, March 1849; in Beyers, *Voortrekker-Argiefstukke*, pp. 363-364. "O how thankful we are to belong to such a loving God, who directs and controls all, and who furnishes our necessities far above our expectations. How frequently I have tasted His leading as a sustaining hand, yes, I have openly experienced this, but always there is too little true thankfulness. Your coming to us was a refreshing rain on a dry land. Oh, may the good God provide us more visits by true pastors and teachers who come not merely for bread, but work toward the extension of Christ's Kingdom here in this almost waste vineyard. ... We know that the Government of England is stronger than we are, but we know the power of the Lord is stronger than us all, and we also know that England has its stumbling blocks as we do. Yet whenever our power is almost equal, we cannot give the Lord enough praise, but we reflect on Gideon, how he conquered the many enemies of the Israelites with the 300 men [Judges 7:7-8]; and we would rather wander with the Israelites for forth years than be subject to a government which had dealt with us such as this English Government."

52. February 10, 1849, led probably by Wolmarans; Engelbrecht, *Geskiedenis*, pp. 55-56.

53. This work is analyzed briefly by F. A. van Jaarsveld in his *Die Beeld van die Groot Trek in die Suid-Afrikaanse Geskiedskrywing, 1843-1899* (Pretoria: University of South Africa, 1963), pp. 12-14.

54. Engelbrecht, *Geskiedenis*, p. 60.

55. Spoelstra, *Het Kerkelijk en Godsdienstig leven*, pp. 147-152.

56. du Plessis, *Andrew Murray*, p. 141. Cf. *Die Kerkbode*, 1854, pp. 30-32, quoted in Spoelstra, *Het Kerkelijk en Godsdienstig leven*, p. 149.

57. du Plessis, *Andrew Murray*, p. 145.

58. The history of these two denominational names is confusing. When the first settlers came from the Netherlands in 1652, they brought the name of their church with them. The name in both South Africa and the Netherlands was De Nederduits Gereformeerde Kerk in Suid Afrika. This name, the N. G. K., has continued to this day as the major Reformed body established mainly in the Cape Colony but with some congregations in each of the three areas. Cf. C. Spoelstra, *Het Kerkelijk en godsdienstig leven*

der Boeren na den Grooten Trek, p. 438. The name of the church in the Netherlands, however, was changed in 1815 to De Nederduitsch Hervormde Kerk (N. H. K.). *Ibid.,* p. 430. When the Transvaal patriots sought to develop their own church in opposition to British, especially Scottish, influence in 1853, they took what they considered a more authentically Dutch name, the Nederduits Hervormde Kerk. (*Ibid.,* p. 439). Thus the N. G. K. and the N. H. K. were names of the same church in the Netherlands, at different times, but of different denominations in South Africa.

59. du Plessis, *Andrew Murray,* p. 145.

60. H. Smith to Dr. Robertson, Cape Town, February 9, 1849, quoted by Dreyer, *Kaapse Kerk,* p. 150.

61. du Plessis, *Andrew Murray,* p. 86.

62. Dreyer, *Kaapse Kerk,* p. 171.

63. The Transgariep Synod included the following churches: Bloemfontein, Pietermaritzburg, Winburg, Smithfield, Fauresmith, Harrysmith, and Ladysmith. du Plessis, *Andrew Murray,* p. 98. Other early ministers in the Orange River Sovereignty were Dirk van Velden, who went to Winburg in 1850, and P. Roux, appointed to Smithfield in 1852; Engelbrecht, *Geskiedenis,* p. 49.

64. du Plessis, *Andrew Murray,* p. 91, reported June 14, 1849.

65. *Ibid.,* p. 95, letter to his father, June 27, 1849.

66. Leo Marquard, *The People and Policies of South Africa* (London: Oxford University Press, 3d ed., 1962), p. 258. Cf. Cornelis W. de Kiewiet, "The Period of Transition in South African Policy, 1854-1870," in *Cambridge History of the British Empire,* VIII, *South Africa,* pp. 421-423.

67. du Plessis, *Andrew Murray,* pp. 102-105, letter to his father, December 22, 1849.

68. A "Hollander" (pseud.), *Toen en Thans: Mededeelingen en Beschouwingen omtrent de twee Republieken in Zuid Afrika* (Cape Town: Dusseau, 1898), pp. 5-7.

69. *Ibid.,* pp. 7-8.

70. Spoelstra, *Doppers,* pp. 115-118. Cf. Engelbrecht, *Geskiedenis,* pp. 57-58.

71. du Plessis, *Andrew Murray,* p. 104. Letter to his father from Magaliesberg, December 22, 1849.

72. "On Tuesday the 18th [November 1850] we left Magaliesberg. ... On Wednesday ... we were suddenly and unexpectedly stopped. ... Next day I took my seat upon the wagon box, while some forty Boers stood round to put me to trial. À Brakel [an orthodox Dutch theologian, d. 1711] was brought forward, and all sorts of nonsensical demonstrations about the duty

of coming out of Antichrist were urged, in order to prove that I could not be a true minister till I came out from under the English Government to this side of the Vaal River. . . . On Monday there was again a public dispute with the party of those who wish to go to Jerusalem. I was opposed to this, but some of the congregation demanded it, as a good many were sometimes shaken by the arguments adduced. The three heroes, Paul Roos, Stoffel de Wet and Jakob Erasmus came forward, and immediately began to prove that England is a horn of the beast (Rev. 17:3) and that I could not be a true servant of Christ. . . . All but their own party were satisfied with the folly of their assertions about the marks of the Beast, etc. I need not repeat all the nonsense, I may almost say blasphemy, which they uttered. I was very sorry to see them going in fancied security and holiness on the way of destruction; for they literally seek their salvation in their opposition to the Antichrist." du Plessis, *Andrew Murray*, pp. 122-123, letter written from Schoonspruit, November 27, 1850.

73. du Plessis, *Andrew Murray*, to his father, December 22, 1849.

74. *Ibid.*, p. 105, January 17, 1850.

75. *Ibid.*, p. 126.

76. *Ibid.*, p. 125.

77. *Ibid.*, p. 129.

78. Eybers, *Select Constitutional Documents*, pp. 358-359.

79. du Plessis, *Andrew Murray*, p. 131.

80. Eybers, *Select Constitutional Documents*, p. 360, September 19, 1853.

81. *Ibid.*, p. 361, November 21, 1853.

82. *Ibid.*, p. 362, Volksraad June 18, 1855.

83. Engelbrecht, *Geskiedenis*, p. 66.

84. *De Hollandsche Afrikanen en hunne Republiek in Zuid-Afrika* (Amsterdam: 1854), quoted in Coenraad Spoelstra, *Het Kerkelijk en Godsdienstig leven der Boeren na den Grooten Trek* (Kampen: J. H. Kok, 1915), pp. 63-64.

85. Their agreement was solidified in the Volksraad meeting the next day, March 17-19, 1852. *Suid-Afrikaanse Argiefstukke* (Transvaal), II, 54-66.

86. Nathan, *Voortrekkers*, p. 347. A Free State observer added his evaluation to those from the Transvaal. "There seems to be little room for doubting that his great aim was the raising of the Afrikander people into a self-reliant and progressive 'Nation.' He was certainly *one* of the most distinguished; *if not the most distinguished* of the Afrikander Patriots; thus passed away at a comparatively early age the man most deserving to be

regarded as the Washington of the Afrikander people." W. W. Collins, *Free Statia: Reminiscences of a Lifetime in the Orange Free State* (Bloem-fontein: 1907), p. 29.

87. Preller, *Pretorius,* p. 490; July 13, 1853; p. 482, July 20, 1853.

88. *Ibid.*

89. *Ibid.*, pp. 19, 481. In 1853 the Volksraad decreed that a new village be formed, named to honor their great leader. In 1855 the city of Pretoria was established.

90. du Plessis, *Andrew Murray,* p. 148, December 30, 1852.

91. Eybers, *Select Constitutional Documents,* pp. 281-282.

92. du Plessis, *Andrew Murray,* p. 148, September 8, 1853.

93. Eybers, *Select Constitutional Documents,* pp. 282-284.

94. *Ibid.*, pp. 285-296.

95. *Ibid.*, pp. 285-296.

96. *Ibid.*, pp. 296-297.

97. *Ibid.*, pp. 363-409.

98. *Ibid.*, pp. 420-430. Document of the Union with Lydenburg, April 3-10, 1860.

V.
The Development of Afrikaner Theological Self-Consciousness, 1860–1881

The period between the formation of the two northern republics (1852, 1854) and the First War (1880-1881) was a time for developing a new set of Boer leaders, as well as for developing, testing, and solidifying a cultural ideology. By 1860 most of the leaders who had participated in the Great Trek were gone. The republics had made their uneasy peace with Britain and proceeded to establish their states. These same republics were developing the very Afrikaners who would be the leaders toward the end of the century. In addition, many of the political, social, and religious skirmishes of this period served to test the willingness and the determination of the Boers to undergird their preconceived cultural values, with war if necessary. They ceased hoping only for God's intervention in the future; rather they decided to act on God's behalf now. They not only believed that God was on their side, but in addition, that He called them to take the sword in their hands to uphold His place in South Africa. Theological questions thus ceased being only implicit in the cultural development of the two northern republics and became explicit in the theological self-consciousness more understood and more openly stated.

We have seen how the isolation on the eastern frontier led to conservatism in theology as well as in other questions of everyday life and have indicated how this conservatism played its role in the beginnings of the Great Trek. From the beginning of the Transvaal nation, theological assumptions underlay the developing group consciousness and later nationalism. These caused dissension in the two northern republics within months of their formation. In 1853, the N. H. K. was formed in Rustenberg, Transvaal, with strong aversions to the N. G. K. of the Cape Colony because of the latter's Anglicism and its large number of ministers of Scottish and of liberal background. They also suspected the Cape churches were dominated by political concerns. Controversy now arose leading to the formation of still another Dutch Reformed denomination in strife-torn Transvaal. The only explicit criticism presented as a basis for the new denomination concerned the singing of evangelical hymns, but a differing theological interpretation of culture was included as well.[1]   Strict biblical literalism and rigidity of personality were prominent marks of the Dopper outlook. Some of Potgieter's belligerence during the Great Trek period, for example, is attributed to his being an ultra-conservative Dopper.

Theological difficulties appeared at various places. In August 1853, for example, the first general synod of the N. H. K. was held at Rustenberg, when Paul Kruger (later the Transvaal president) was a leader in the fight against evangelical singing in the churches.[2]   The synod finally decided against him, but the congregation remained divided on this one point. Agitation for reformation (rejection of these hymns) continued to spread. Some suggested that they seek the leadership of a minister who was opposed to this singing.[3] Similar dissatisfactions were expressed among the Boers in Bloemfontein where the N. G. K. minister was Andrew Murray, Jr. Murray was a Boer at heart but not a Dopper. He realized the difficulty in ministering to these ultra-conservatives, as he wrote to his brother, John: "We have never been able, even when willing, to reach the real, stiff Dopper mind. Our language was strange to it."[4]   The Dopper leader in Bloemfontein was Jacobus J. Venter, whose family was among the dissatisfied Doppers on the eastern frontier.[5] This family made its way to the Free State and founded the town of Ventersburg. Now Venter and his followers insisted that the gospel they heard from Murray in the N. G. K. was not in agreement with the command of Christ.[6]

One further step was taken in the Free State in February 1858 when Paul Kruger and Philip Snyman made plans for wider influence. Both from Rustenberg, they went to Bloemfontein to meet with Venter. Although they had not specifically considered a separate denomination, they decided to make a direct appeal to a minister in the Netherlands who would come and help them oppose the singing.[7] The leaders contacted officials in the Christelijke Afgeschiedene Gereformeerde Kerk (separatist) in the Netherlands.[8] At this separatist synod meeting in the Netherlands in November 1857, the Rev. Dirk Postma was chosen for the South African assignment.[9] He had a theological education and had been a separatist minister in the Netherlands for several years.[10]   Leaving his home in April 1858, he arrived at Cape Town on July 10.[11]

An era of decisive influence both theological and political began when Postma arrived in the Transvaal in November 1858. He was welcomed by the Rev. Dirk van der Hoff and was afforded many opportunities to preach in the churches. Some questioned his authority in the N. H. K. because his ordination was from the separatist church in the Netherlands, but the relationship he enjoyed with van der Hoff was friendly and sincere. Immediately, however, Postma recognized evangelical singing as a problem, and he told Murray that he could accept hymns only hesitatingly and provisionally.[12]   The tension was brought to the fore officially when the eighth general synod of the N. H. K. of the Transvaal, meeting at Pretoria in January 1859, passed a resolution allowing these hymns. In addition they allowed those who so desired to refrain from singing so they would not violate their consciences.[13]   This was not a strong enough statement for Postma and his followers, however, who insisted the songs be banned. Consequently they separated from the N. H. K. in the Transvaal and formed the Gereformeerde Kerk van Suid Afrika with 310 members.   Although Postma did not cause the schism in the church of the Transvaal, he became the center for organizing those who were already dissident.[14]   Similar schisms occurred in other towns where moderate Boers and conservative or Dopper Boers could not agree.

From our distance in time and our different theological concepts, it may seem that this schism in the Transvaal was over insignificant matters. The theological principle the Doppers kept uppermost in their minds, however, is of major importance for understanding their political actions. They interpreted their covenant with God as their promise to do His will as far as possible in their national as well as in their personal life. They may have meditated on Proverbs 14:34: "Righteousness exalteth a nation, but sin is a reproach to any people." To fail God, knowingly, was to leave oneself and one's nation liable for punishments of various types; any activities that opposed the will of God—equated with the conservative cultural traditions —were to be shunned. The more seriously one took one's promise to God, as that person understood it, the more determined was one's opposition to changes both in religious forms and political policy. In this way the Doppers' theological attitude gave strength to their growing self-consciousness, as they thought of themselves closer to God than other groups.[15]

The separation of the Dopper groups from the N. H. K., based as it was on both theological and cultural considerations, led to further political conflicts. The *Grondwet* of the Transvaal states that none shall hold office but members of the N. H. K.[16]   Early in his career Paul Kruger realized the technical difficulties when he later reflected:

> Now during the recent disputes many members of the Hervormde Church had reproached me with having no right whatever to meddle in public affairs. According to the constitution of the Republic, the Hervormde Church was the state church. Its members alone were entitled to exercise any influence in public affairs. Whoever was not a member of the Hervormde Church was not a fully-qualified burgher. Now I belonged to the Christelijke-Gereformeerde Church. . . .   It is generally known in South Africa as the Dopper, or Canting Church. . . . As for the peculiar tenets of the Dopper Church, they consist

in a strict adhesion to the decrees of the Synod of Dordrecht, of 1618 and 1619, and share the point of view of the Old Reformed Church. The service differs from that of the other Evangelical bodies in this particular, that no hymns except psalms are sung by the worshipers.[17]

Whereas in the early months of the schism, the Reverend van der Hoff and the Reverend Postma were on friendly terms, their followers suspected each other. A few years later, under the leadership of acting President W. C. J. van Rensburg (1862-1863) of the Transvaal, an agreement was reached allowing all persons who subscribed to the Heidelberg Catechism and the Decrees of Dort to hold public office. This would, of course, benefit the Dopper Paul Kruger. Members of the separatist church (Doppers), however, were not recognized as full-fledged burghers until 1882.[18] At the same time the separatists referred to the Hervormde Kerk as a "deluded" or "false" church.[19] The Boers were still plagued by theological differences so that they could not be united. Very soon the idea of a separatist church was carried to the Free State, where Venter was the major leader. Murray reports the situation as he knew it in Bloemfontein: "Postma has been at Venter's since Thursday evening, receiving signatures to the declaration of adhesion to the new church. All my Doppers have joined. Tomorrow elders are to be appointed, and the sacrament is to be dispensed at Johann van der Walt's."[20] In addition, in 1862, R. D. van Wyk of the Free State Volksraad sought to allow further control of the state by the conservative branch of the church. He proposed "that all officials within this state, including all lawyers, shall live by the official faith. As an example he shall live a godly life and shall have knowledge of God's Word. . . . Should one fail in this he shall be deposed from his office."[21] This motion was tabled, and two years later the Volkraad stated that no one would be forced by the government to adhere to a special faith. The more conservative branch of the Dutch Reformed faith, nevertheless, became increasingly influential in the Orange Free State. For example, in May 1889, the Volksraad tried to prohibit trains from running on Sundays in the Free State because this would desecrate the sabbath.[22] What part the most conservative groups, the Doppers, played here is not known. One observer, however, indicated that their activities in the Free State were similar to what we have already noted in the Cape Colony and in the Transvaal.[23]

Let us now follow this theological thread as it weaves itself through several of the significant political developments and other cultural challenges of the next two decades. We are concerned not only with the facts as they can be ascertained from the standard histories of the period but with the Boers' interpretation of their various situations as well.[24] We see that their developing exclusiveness, both theological and political, was not developed in any systematic theology or through the institutional church. Because they did not separate their theological concepts from their concept of their nation under God, their theological assumptions found their basis in their total culture—referred to in our time as a civil religion.

The Boers' relationship with neighboring African tribes proved as troublesome as were their internal political factions. The independence of the Free State, guaranteed at the Bloemfontain Convention in 1854, was one step, albeit not permanent, in the direction of amicable agreements between Boers and British. Hereafter the challenge of British power was felt not directly on the Orange Free State but indirectly through its neighbors and at the point of certain boundary questions left unsettled by the convention. Two major areas of conflict helped to develop the theological ideology of the Free State: the conflict on the Basutoland border to the east and the disagreements over the Diamond Lands (Griqualand West) to the southwest. In both areas, the Boers' image of their calling was intermingled with both anti-British and anti-African feelings, and in both instances the Orange Free State Boers interpreted British actions as favoring the Africans against the "rightful owners" of the land.

The Free State Boers had almost continual conflict with their Basuto neighbors. During the period of the Orange River Sovereignty, Major Warden attempted settlement by proclaiming the "Warden Line" in 1849. This proved unpopular to both the Africans and the farmers in the sovereignty. The Basuto chief, Moshweshwe, decided to bide his time, and the Boers could do nothing about Warden's decision. In 1854, as the Bloemfontein Convention was signed, the people on both sides of the Warden line began their activity. In October 1855, President Jacobus Boshof of the Free State and Moshweshwe the leader of the Basutos met to discuss their grievances. One of their agreements, which later proved prejudicial, concerned an early form of pass requirements for the Africans. Clause 1 of the Free State agreement read: "That whenever any Basuto subject wishes to enter the Free State he shall be provided with a pass signed by his Chief, or by a missionary according to the Free State Law of 31 August 1855."[25] This indicates that the Free State government believed itself somewhat separated from the Basuto people. A few years later, however, when the British annexed Basutoland, the Free Staters feared the British were taking over their territory.

Agreements were short-lived. Moshweshwe successfully organized many tribes into a determined Basuto people, and soon they sought revenge for past grievances.[26] The Basutos suddenly attacked Boer settlements in the vicinity of the border, and the Boers, now independent from Britain, knew they must retaliate. On March 19, 1858, they declared war. The Basutos had the advantages of number and many times sent troops around the battle lines to attack settlements behind the fighting Boers at Smithfield and at Winburg. The Boers were engaged in a type of warfare for which they were not prepared, so they were driven to seek peace. As mediator they called on Sir George Grey (high commissioner and governor of the Cape Colony, 1854-1861). The result was the treaty of Aliwal North, arranged by Grey and signed by both peoples on October 15, 1858.[27] This did little but reaffirm the unsatisfactory Warden Line and served only to postpone the conflict.

Tensions increased, and by June 1865 the Boers were again at war with the Basuto.   Their political necessity had theological overtones.   J. H. Brand, president of the Free State, called his people to fight because of blood and friendship and because of the righteousness of their cause in the sight of God: "Now the hour has come, in which it becomes necessary, yes even unavoidable, if we wish to be true to God, that we take our weapons to defend our rights against the Basutos."[28]   On June 9, 1865, President Brand was even more forceful in his theological justification for the war."

> Rise, then, burghers of the Orange Free State,—gird your armour on for the defense of your rights, for the protection of your property, homesteads, and families,—for the suppression of the arrogance and violence of the Basutos, trusting in God; be courageous, be strong, and put your trust in the Righteous Judge, who hears the prayer of faith.[29]

After some initial victories Brand appealed directly to Moshweshwe stating the theological justification of the cause of the Boers:

> After failing to obtain an amicable settlement of the many causes of complaint; after waiting in vain for the fulfillment of your promises, no other recourse was left to our government than to vindicate our rights by the sword; trusting in God, we took up arms in defense of our rights.   The Lord blessed our arms and prospered our undertakings.[30]

He later gave suggestions as to what should be done "if God gives us the victory."[31]

The Boers were certain that God had approved their action for they had many victories, and ultimately in April 1866 the Basutos were forced to accept a peace settlement favorable to the Boers.   This Treaty of Thaba Bosiu (April 3, 1866) first treated of new boundaries, moved into Basuto territory beyond the Warden Line, and required compensation by Moshweshwe of 3,000 cattle.[32]   At the signing of the treaty, the Boers broke into singing Psalm 100.[33]   Final settlement, however, was not yet a reality. On July 16, 1867, after provocation, the Basutos attacked their Free State neighbors.[34]   The Free Staters rallied to what they saw as a holy cause and were in process of handing the Basutos their greatest defeat when Moshweshwe made another request to the British authorities that he be accepted as a British subject.

The British immediately decided to intervene against the claim of the Free State.   They requested that the Boers accept overtures of peace, to which Brand replied:

> With the experience we have of the reliance that can be placed on the promises of the Basuto chief Moshesh, I think it would

be unsafe to suspend hostilities against the Basutos at the moment that the object of the war is nearly accomplished, and when our arms are, under God's blessing, everywhere successful, trusting merely to the good faith and the inclination and power of Moshesh to make his people comply with the treaty of Thaba Bosigo.[35]

President Brand argued that British intervention in this situation was a violation of two portions of the Bloemfontein Convention of 1854.[36] First, article II states: "The British Government has no alliance whatever with any native chiefs or tribes to the northward of the Orange River, with the exception of the Gricqua Chief, Captain Adam Kok."[37] Second, the British forbade the sale of ammunition to the Orange Free State, whereas it was guaranteed by the Bloemfontein Convention that they could purchase ammunition from any British colony.[38] Meanwhile, as the war continued, the Boers were victorious in many skirmishes.[39] The British, fearing the Boers would subjugate the Basuto and thus gain more land, issued a proclamation on March 12, 1868, declaring Basutoland a British territory.[40]

This was a disturbing event for the Free Staters, who, when they were almost victorious over their old Basuto enemies, were again defeated by the British. Indeed this proclamation was a disappointment to many Europeans in other parts of South Africa, for, based on a widespread anti-Basuto attitude, "there was almost universal sympathy with the Free State."[41] Soon memory of this reversal took its place among the list of grievances from previous decades and was published in emotional tones in the Bloemfontein newspaper, *De Tijd*:

Will you give up your freedom, so dearly bought by your forefathers? . . . Think about the freeing of the slaves in 1834. . . . Think about Slagters Nek. Think about the sheep stealing, the murder and the raids which the Kaffers of the interior inflicted upon those of us living on the borders. Think of how many times your servants have followed you before the law. . . . Have not many of you in 1835 given land back to the Kaffers? . . . Much shame is brought, and is not the blame of the acquisition laid on you? Think burghers of the grounds for the removal of your forefathers out of the colonies, and how they established themselves in Natal after unbelievable losses of goods and health, how wickedly their freedom was snatched from them by the self-seeking British, how they would not bow under the hated British flag so despised by their fathers, fleeing here and there to the present time. Think how the British repeatedly have meddled through interferences and wars, and again disturb the freedom of those who are descendents of those who cleaned up the land and fought against Dingaan, Moselikatze and others.[42]

Since the Free State Boers thought the Cape Town government was prejudiced against them, they sent a delegation to present their case in London, but they were told that the annexation of Basutoland was "an accomplished fact."[43]

Finally in February 1869 the Second Convention of Aliwal North proposed a new boundary approximately halfway between the old Warden Line of 1849 and that of the Treaty of Thaba Bosiu of 1866. In May 1870 the Volksraad of the Free State accepted the treaty, but reluctantly because they wanted more compensation for their losses. This concluded the conflicts between the Afrikaner Boers and the Basuto, but Britain later had its own problems with this nation. By May 1870 Moshweshwe, the strong Basuto leader, had been dead two months.[44] In later years the growing resentment against Britain reminded the Boers again of the injustice of the British intervention in these Basuto wars.

Shortly after the Basuto question was settled unfavorably for the Free State, conflict arose in the second region, over the land on the southwest border of the Free State where the first diamonds were found in 1867 near what became Hopetown.[45] News of the discovery spread, and by 1870 three other sources of diamonds in the immediate area were known: Klipdrift, Pniel, and Hebron.[46] This section of the Free State was not thinkly settled at the time, and governmental control was tenuous. In addition, boundary agreements here had never been concluded. By mid-1870 there were as many as nine hundred white diggers in the area, which led to much confusion.[47] Disputes between white miners were common. Finally, to bring order out of chaos, Stafford Parker, one of the miners, organized a Mutual Protection Committee to arbitrate disputes, and he became "captain" or "magistrate."

To bring further complications in the troubled area the Griqua chief, Nicholas Waterboer, who had a claim on some of the land in the area, made his own appeal. Waterboers's claim went back to a grant the Cape Colony had given to his father, Chief Andries Waterboer, in 1834. The land, which became known as Griqualand West, was north of the Cape Colony, where the British officials did not contemplate expanding. Not only were there Griquas (of mixed race), but sections of other tribes lived there along with some white trekkers who came from the Cape Colony. Part of the land had been presumed to have been part of the Orange River Sovereignty and transferred to the Orange Free State in 1854. Other sections were claimed by other groups. The exact borders were unclear, however, and no one seemed to be very much concerned before diamonds became the issue.

Waterboer appealed to the British authorities that his people might receive protection as British subjects. The authorities believed his claims, which actually involved much more land than he ever had controlled. In August 1870, Lt. Gov. (and acting High Commissioner) C. C. Hay received

the plea from Waterboer and began arguing for establishing British authority in the area.[48] He sent a representative to collect taxes and admonished
the inhabitants not to recognize the authority of the Free State.   The
British argued that "Waterboer's offer is accepted to prevent the irregular-
ities which would arise from a prolonged absence of a regular government
at the Diamond Fields."[49]

At approximately the same time, President Brand began to exert his
influence, and he sent his representative, Olof Truter, to uphold Free State
authority. This move was further strengthened when Brand also sent artil-
lery and attempted to collect taxes from all inhabitants as subjects of the
Free State.[50] Brand argued his cause with the high commissioner, without
results, and immediately called a special meeting of the Volksraad.

British authorities rejected all pleas of President Brand and the Volksraad, and the Cape governor sent an argument of their case to London:

> It is desirable and needful, as well as for the interests of this
> colony as well as a view to the maintenance of peace and order
> on our borders, that the territory commonly designated "the
> Diamond Fields" partly belongs to the Gricquas and West
> Gricqualand under the government of Captain N. Waterboer,
> and partly to other native chiefs . . . should . . . be annexed to
> this colony.[51]

On October 27, 1871, the diamond fields were proclaimed part of the
British empire.[52] A few days later, armed mounted police were sent from
Cape Town to maintain order.[53]

President Brand retaliated in a few days by issuing a proclamation
opposing the British move. The formal protest was issued from Bloemfontein on December 4, 1871, concluding with a theological analysis of the
cause of the Orange Free State Boers: "Believing that the Most High
controls the destinies of nations, and protects the weak, the people of the
Orange Free State humbly but confidently commits its rights and future
well-being to that supreme ruler, feeling assured that such reliance can
never be disappointed."[54] Not only were the Boers of the Free State and of
the Cape Parliament antagonized by the annexation, but British subjects
wrote scathingly about the turn of events.[55] The British admitted the
error of their actions when they wrote a few months later that they should
no longer "uphold the fiction of acting in Waterboer's name."[56] To complete his opposition, Brand traveled to London in 1876 to present his case
directly to the Colonial Office.[57]

As if to soothe irritated wounds, the British authorities allowed a
compensation of 90,000 pounds sterling to help alleviate tensions.[58] This,
however, was not adequate to allay growing Boer hatred of British policies,
and it was one more aspect in the beginning of Afrikaner nationalism in the

Free State. The diamond fields became yet another grievance that brought Boers from all parts of South Africa together in spirit.

Theological questions became entwined with the political in the Transvaal. These were brought to the fore during the career of Thomas Francois Burgers, an N. G. K. minister at Hanover (Graaff-Reinet area) who later became president of the Transvaal (1872-1877). We have noted the reaction against the growing Scottish influence in the Reformed churches of the Cape, which was one aspect of the three-way schism in the churches in the Transvaal and the Free State in 1853 and 1859. All the reaction, however, was not confined to these two republics. Many people in the Cape Colony were concerned about the new and liberal ideas from nineteenth-century France, Holland, and Britain being brought by the ministers.[59] There was no theological school in South Africa at this time, so the church in the Cape Colony was challenged to deal with the threat of theological schism.[60]

The synod of 1862, meeting in Cape Town with Andrew Murray, Jr., of Wellington as moderator, began the first phase of the controversy. Liberals introduced a resolution to exclude ministers from the synod serving outside the borders of the Cape Colony.[61] Subsequently the N. G. K. of the Free State and the Transvaal organized their own synods, as did Natal-Utrecht-Lydenburg.[62] Deeper theological questions were at stake because liberal ministers questioned the literal interpretation of the Bible, the interpretation of miracles and the resurrection in a scientific age, and the idea of redemption and the doctrine of predestination.[63] For our purpose the most important minister in the liberal group was Thomas Francois Burgers, trained at Utrecht (Netherlands),[64] who questioned the existence of a personal devil, wondered whether Christ had a sinless nature, and challenged the traditional doctrine of the physical resurrection.[65] In 1863 Burgers was found guilty on some of the charges and was asked to recant or leave his pulpit. He chose to do neither and continued as minister in Hanover in the Graaff-Reinet Presbytery until elected president of the Transvaal in July 1872, when he resigned from the active ministry.[66]

Compared with the four preceding presidents, Burgers was the best qualified and had the most knowledge of the world outside the Transvaal, but his success was limited. He began several progressive measures meant to bring the Transvaal into the modern world. He suggested that the Transvaal have a railroad to a non-British port (Portuguese Delagoa Bay, Mozambique); he talked of confederation of all South Africa into one nation; and he introduced secular education reforms.[67] He was never accepted by the Doppers, however, and met stiff resistance because of the less-educated Boers' conservatism and their fear of his liberal record. An anti-Burgers reaction, based on religious fears, gained momentum as the years passed.[68] The Dopper party suggested Kruger as the candidate to oppose Burgers, but when Burgers seemed to make concessions, Kruger asked that his name be withdrawn.[69]   Solid support never shifted to Burgers, however, and an impossible situation was developing.   The election due in 1877 was postponed until the rivalry between factions could be redirected.

Much of the intense reaction against Burgers was based on theological and biblical interpretations by the unsophisticated, literalist-minded Dopper Boers.   For example, in March 1876, President Burgers had planned to go on an expedition of which Kruger was commanding general.   The president was flatly told by Kruger: "I cannot lead the Command if you come. For with your merry evenings in Laager and your Sunday dances, the enemy will shoot me behind the wall; for God's blessing will not rest on our expedition."[70]   Another analysis of Burgers' lack of piety and hence his lack of God's support for his causes was printed at the height of the election controversy in *Die Patriot*, the pro-Boer newspaper in the Cape Colony.   The author reacted against Burgers' policy of the gradual equalization of all races and showed the contrast between the situation when Africans had a "proper respect" for Boers and the present situation when the Boers were being threatened by belligerent Africans.   He asked, "What is the answer?" and answered:

> God's word gives us the solution.   Look at Israel, while the people have a godly king, everything is prosperous, but under a godless prince the land retrogrades, and the whole of the people must suffer.   Read Leviticus Chapter xxvi with attention, etc. In the day of the Voortrekkers (Pioneers) a handful of men chased a thousand Kafirs and made them run; so also in the Free State war (Deut. xxxii, 30; Jos. xxiii:10; Lev. xxvi:8). But mark, now, when Burgers became President, he knows no Sabbath, he rides through the land in and out of town on Sunday, he knows not the church and God's service (Lev. xxvi:2, 3), to the scandal of pious people.   And he formerly was a priest too.   And what is the consequence: No harvest (Lev. xxvi:16); an army of 6,000 runs because one man falls (Lev. xxvi:17, etc.).[71]

The contemporary solution to a similar problem is to be found in Paul Kruger "because the Lord clearly points him out to be the man."[72]   No qualifications as to political ability or religious faith are given. The writer assumes only two qualifications are necessary: "He is a warrior.   He is a Boer."[73]

Since this attitude was widespread, Burgers' efficiency was gradually eroded.   One of the major reasons he failed was because he did not capture the religious loyalty of a large portion of the conservative churchmen of the Transvaal.   Needed taxes were not paid, and the postponed election was never held for the British annexed the Transvaal in April 1877, and Burgers resigned and returned to the Cape Colony.   Although they did not realize it at the time, the Transva. Boers could not have hoped to form a stable nation by continuing to reject as un-Christian all attempts at stability and progress. Their concept of their covenant with God was still too narrow and too much divided by strong personalities. They had not yet fully realized the implications of being in the latter half of the nineteenth century, and they rejected what they saw of these implications. The conservative Dopper attitude gradually gained the ascendance during the next few years, allowing Paul Kruger and his followers to remain the leaders of the Transvaal for the remainder of the century. This defeat of their best hope for developing a modern nation had a deep impact on the total culture of the Transvaal.

Because of its limited vision, theology in the Transvaal contributed to weakness rather than to strength, and Britain used these weaknesses as excuses for intervention. In addition to party factions which sapped what energy there was in the struggling government, Britain noticed the various tensions with Africans, fearing they could erupt into conflicts and cause suffering for British as well as Boers. Britain also feared an unsuccessful financial policy. The ultimate intervention of the British became the Boers' most serious grievance and was the situation that proved strong enough to unite the Boers of all South Africa in a common cause.

Behind the problems Burgers faced personally, political realities in both South Africa and Britain complicated the affairs. The air was filled with many misunderstandings in the months leading up to the annexation. Since the British allowed self-government in the Transvaal at the Sand River Convention in 1852, the imperial policy had shifted.[74] In 1852 Britain sought to decrease the tax burden that South Africa required of it. By 1877, however, there were both fears of the unstable government in the Transvaal and a hope for control over more territory there, especially since gold and diamonds were being mined in the northern territories.

There was one further reason, or at least an excuse, which the British used to justify intervention. In mid-1876 in the northeastern section of the Transvaal, the Bapedi tribe led by Chief Sekukuni was restless and threatened to disrupt the republic's administration. President Burgers declared war on these people. Despite difficulties, he was able to mount sufficient forces that the Bantu capitulated and asked for peace. British authorities in the vicinity used this as a further proof that the Transvaal could not maintain peaceful relations with the tribes within their borders. For all these reasons, following the insistence of Lord Henry H. Carnarvon, secretary of state for the colonies in London, the British decided they must annex the colony.

To carry this plan into a reality, Carnarvon sent Sir Theophilus Shepstone, for the last thirty years the successful administrator of native affairs in Natal, to Pretoria. The British leader discovered that there was a sizable group of the burghers, many of them of British background, who welcomed a confederation or an outright annexation, while the majority, the Boers, were opposed. President Burgers and the Volksraad were warned either to modernize the nation or be annexed by Britain.

Burgers was too liberal for Kruger and his Dopper followers, but he was not a partisan of the British authorities, as his critics often suggested. He now showed his true spirit as a South African patriot. On February 16, 1877, he flatly told the Volksraad that annexation was imminent unless the reforms could be passed immediately:

> I cannot believe that the heavens convict us except that our own deeds convict us. I cannot believe that God implants in us a hope, a concept of freedom as an independent people, only to crown us with bitter disappointment. . . . Here I differ from the honorable Paul Kruger, a member of the Volksraad. We need law and order and cannot go to war against the British to gain our freedom. We must have as our weapon "Order, obedience to the law, unity and progress." . . . It is not tasty to drink the bitter chalice of self-denial which we speak of. Yet we must do it. There is no other way.[75]

Two weeks later, on March 3, it was evident that the Volksraad distrusted the motive of the president, believing he counseled them to give in to the British pressures too quickly. Burgers responded:

> Not only are strong burgers necessary for a strong state. But I say to you "when you mistrust your president, then your land is lost. Then like Sampson, you break the pillars which hold the ceiling over your head. Then you will be compelled to do one of two things: either submit to British administrators, or hold the republic with civil law and require regard and obedience thereto." I would rather have fallen in battle than to have come to the day when I must speak to you thus.[76]

With this threat in the open, on March 4, 1877, the Volksraad was finally persuaded to pass the reform bills creating central government control, reorganizing the justice and police departments, and strengthening the government generally. They also postponed the elections until affairs should be sufficiently stabilized for a free election.[77] Shepstone had underestimated the determination of the Boers for the latter disarmed the imperialists by approving some of what was suggested. Consequently, he quickly shifted his method of approach and suggested that the state was not powerful enough to carry out its plans.

On April 12, 1877, Shepstone established British authority in the Transvaal when he read a prepared proclamation of annexation. He referred to the Sand River Convention of 1852 at which time the British government had hoped the South African Republic "would become a flourishing and self-sustaining State, a source of strength and security to neighboring European communities, and a point from which Christianity and civilization might rapidly spread towards Central Africa."[78]   The intervening twenty-five years had proved disappointing.

He called attention to three major problems. First, he spoke with respect to the "increasing weakness of the state," which could only deteriorate further:

> Commerce is well-nigh destroyed. . . .   The country is in a state of bankruptcy. . . . The white inhabitants, discontented with their condition, are divided into factions. . . . The government has fallen into helpless paralysis from causes which it has been and is unable to control or counteract. And the prospect of the election of a new President, so far from allaying the general anxiety, or from inspiring hope in the future, is looked forward to by all parties as most likely to result in civil war, with its attendant anarchy and bloodshed.[79]

Second, the British considered unrest among the Africans a threat to European civilization in South Africa. The decay of the government led to "real strength and confidence among the native tribes . . . which have produced their natural and inevitable consequences." Third, Shepstone was convinced that many European settlers welcomed British protection and intervention.[80]   Many concessions were suggested but never carried out. The Boers were promised that their legal courts and their own government leaders would remain in power and that the Dutch language would be official along with English.[81]   Equal justice was guaranteed to the persons and property of both white and colored, but "the native tribes living within the jurisdiction and under the protection of the government must be taught due obedience to the paramount authority, and be made to contribute their fair share toward the support of the state that protects them."[82] The same day this proclamation was read, Burgers wrote as a South African patriot, believing that God was on the side of the Boers:

> Violence and injustice have triumphed through cunning, but not for all time; from the grave of the Republic will arise a youth, who will revenge this injustice. We yield and bear our fate, but the day of vengeance will dawn. God is righteous, and the judgment of history sure. . . . Never will the desire to overthrow the tyranny one day, ever perish. . . . May my children grow up in this spirit and disposition; may they one day honour the memory of their father by their triumph over the enemy. May God help us.[83]

The high ideals and liberal policies of President Burgers—the development of education, the railroad project, and the strong central government

—were carried out, surprisingly, by Burgers' major opponent. What was too liberal before 1877 and what was first mentioned by a "heretic" ex-minister became the orthodox basis of a strong Transvaal under the long and fruitful leadership of four-times President Paul Kruger. Burgers died in 1881 and did not live to know of the ultimate success of many of his maligned and temporarily defeated ideas.

Kruger carried out the details of organizing a relatively stable government in the Transvaal, however, not on the basis of a liberal democracy as Burgers had envisaged, where the final authority is only the best progress for the greatest number of people. Kruger developed, rather, a "Calvinist democracy," in which the final judge was not the people but the voice of God reflected through the voices of a select group of people—the Boers.[84] The result might have been similar had Burgers' program been continued, but the interpretation the Boers gave to their cause and the constant reliance on God's will as they interpreted it gave their whole enterprise a totally different basis.   Only faithful Boers were entrusted with the national destiny. It is this theological basis that forms the foundation for the discussion of the next three years, and it is this theological basis on which the war of 1880-1881 was fought.

THE INTERREGNUM, 1877-1880

During the three years between the annexation and the outbreak of the First War of Independence, the attitude of the Transvaal leaders changed markedly. From an almost passive acceptance of the annexation to an armed resistance against the mighty British Empire, there was a major development of public opinion augmented significantly by an intensified theological imagery. This change of attitude was enhanced by several mass meetings of Boers where their national aspiration was thoroughly interwoven with their theological literalism.   During this three-year period, Afrikaner nationalism came into its own,[85] Cape citizens of Dutch background began to sympathize with their northern brothers, and the cause of Afrikaner nationalism took on the character of a holy cause.[86]

When he learned of the annexation, President Burgers immediately issued his protest against the British decision, but he had no influence. He reminded the British authorities of the guarantee of independence promulgated at the Sand River Convention of 1852 and argued that the South African Republic had never given Britain any cause for hostile acts; rather, they had been willing to cooperate in all things. Furthermore, he was optimistic when he suggested that the British government did not wish to coerce any people against their will. The government of the South African Republic, on the other hand, did not wish to cause dissension between the sections of the white people of South Africa and was willing to use all peaceful means toward reversing the British decision. Therefore, in addition to making formal protest against the action, the South African government would send a delegation to Europe to protest in London or to other nations which recognized the independence of the South African Republic.[87] Following his proclamation and because the British controlled the government, Burgers resigned on May 5, 1877, and left for the Cape Colony, where he lived until his death on December 9, 1881.[88]

In the meantime a new era for the Transvaal began. Paul Kruger and E. P. Jorissen, with Eduard Bok as secretary, left for England on May 1, 1877, to make formal protest. Arriving in England at the beginning of July, they gave their report to Lord Carnarvon, the minister for colonial affairs, but their effort resulted in no action. Carnarvon was not convinced that the annexation was really opposed to the wishes of the majority of the people.[89] He had heard about the warm welcome Shepstone received as he traveled around the newly annexed territory and had also seen letters and petitions from Transvaal Boers supporting the annexation.[90] Kruger asked that the British authorities allow a vote of the people to determine where their sympathies lay.[91] Carnarvon countered by stating that the annexation was an accomplished fact and that the British Parliament had already approved 100,000 pounds sterling to help the Transvaal overcome its financial difficulties. This promised payment was meant to satisfy the delegates, but it did not. They left England in November, arriving home late in December 1877.[92]

Continued frustration caused the Boers to begin organized opposition. They believed that Shepstone might allow the Boers their Volksraad as they continued self-government under British authority, but he declined to allow such gatherings. The Boers thus took the matter into their own hands and called a meeting at Pretoria to hear the report of the first deputation to England. On January 7, 1878, Kruger told the assembled gathering of approximately one thousand that he was convinced that Carnarvon was misinformed concerning the wishes of the Boers, and if he could be convinced, he would reverse the annexation. At a second meeting two weeks later at Nauwpoort, near Potchefstroom, a committee was constituted, with M. W. Pretorius as chairman. Their purpose was to arrange details of a large mass meeting at Doornfontein, on April 4, to obtain the opinion of a large number of Boers. Kruger stated, "I think I can say in good faith that Lord Carnarvon *will* consider the matter."[93]   During the intervening months, the plan was circulated widely among the inhabitants of Transvaal.

The Boers made their plans carefully and thoroughly. Paul Kruger wrote about the details of the Boers' planning and sent these to Shepstone. He stated that they would attempt to determine the Boers' wishes about the annexation; if the majority was in favor, he, Kruger, would abide by their wishes and become a loyal British subject.[94] By now Shepstone was convinced that the leader of the agitation was Paul Kruger and that he should be imprisoned, but at the moment Shepstone did not dare to make such a move. Rather, he issued a stringent proclamation against agitators.

> I do also hereby make known that all meetings convened for seditious or any other unlawful purpose whatever, at which are proposed, discussed, or passed any resolution or resolutions aiming to weaken, resist, or oppose the power and authority of the Government, or to incite the taking up of arms by the people of this country against the said government, or in any way whatsoever tending to disturb the peace of this country, are contrary to law.[95]

He stipulated punishments for persons who should attend such meetings, especially for the leaders. These intemperate words of Shepstone convinced many Boers of the unfaithfulness of the British administration, and Kruger won the initiative he sought.

The changed attitude caused by Shepstone's proclamation was reflected at the next Boer meeting when results of their petition were reported. At Doornfontein, near Pretoria, on April 4, 1878, Kruger received the vote he expected. There were 6,591 signatures opposed to the annexation and 587 in favor—that is, over eleven to one in favor of independence.[96] The people at the gathering decided there should be another deputation to London, composed of Kruger and Bok again, but with Piet Joubert replacing Jorissen. Kruger related the cause to the sovereignty of God; the decision was His. Kruger, however, was convinced that he and his close followers reflected God's wish accurately: "Where is the hope if it is not in God, who holds the hearts of Queens and Monarchs in his hands?"[97] Later in April the second deputation left for London armed with the petitions with the thousands of signatures. Arriving in Britain, they were confronted by a new minister for colonial affairs, Sir Michael Hicks-Beach. They were told again that the annexation would not be reversed; the Transvaal would remain under the queen's authority.[98] The petitions with seven thousand signatures bore no results. When the members of the deputation returned to the Transvaal in December 1878, they were convinced that further argument would produce nothing. Action was necessary.

The report from the second deputation was given on January 10, 1879, when between two thousand and three thousand burghers gathered at Wonderfontein.[99] They were dissatisfied with the reaction of Sir Hicks-Beach. One asked, "What shall we say about our subjugation to England?" and then answered, "We would rather die."[100] While some talked of armed rebellion immediately, Kruger, joined by Joubert and Pretorius, warned that they must make careful preparation for this opposition.[101] At present they were militarily too weak to oppose Britain.

They began their preparation for the revolt, still two years away, not with weapons but with prayer and with a covenant between themselves and God:

> In the presence of Almighty God, the searcher of all hearts, and prayerfully waiting on His gracious help and pity, we burghers of the South African Republic, have solemnly agreed, as we do hereby agree, to make a holy covenant for us and for our children, which we confirm with a solemn oath.
>
> Fully forty years ago our fathers fled from the Cape Colony in order to become a free and independent people. these forty years were forty years of pain and suffering.
>
> We established Natal, the Orange Free State and the South African Republic, and three times the English Government has trampled our liberty and dragged to the ground our flag, which our fathers had baptized with their blood and tears.
>
> As a thief in the night [I Thess. 5:2] our Republic has been stolen from us. We may not nor can we endure this. It is God's will, and is required of us by the unity of our fathers and thy love to our children, that we should hand over intact to our children the legacy of the fathers.
>
> For that purpose it is that we here come together and give each other the right hand as men and brethren, solemnly promising to remain faithful to our country and our people, and with our eye fixed on God, to cooperate until death for the restoration of the freedom of our Republic.
>
> So help us God.[102]

Thus the Boers adapted their religious tradition and used it as a tool for their social and national ends. They were completely sincere about their actions, but the results of such a policy were soon to produce disaster.

The Boers prepared for a meeting with the newly arrived high commissioner for Natal and Transvaal, Sir Bartle Frere. This was to have been held on March 19, 1879, at Kleinfontein, but Frere did not arrive. Although he was detained at Natal with details of an invasion of the Zulus, where the British were soundly defeated, the Boers interpreted this as only procrastination and as a broken promise. When between four thousand and five thousand Boers gathered at the appointed place, Joubert set the tone for the meeting with a theological interpretation:

> We recognize that we have seen that England is powerful; so powerful that one would think that we would no more resist England than that we should touch heaven with our hand. England can shatter us; but I would rather be shattered into dust than to surrender my freedom. I am comforted by a Higher Hand, and by God's help. I have most clearly told Your Excellency, that the people want their independence back, and will be satisfied with nothing less.[103]

A few weeks later with the conclusion of the disastrous Zulu battle at Kambula in Natal, Frere was able to proceed to the Transvaal where he faced the alternatives of either peaceful settlement or civil war. He was met in the Transvaal by hundreds of Boers, all armed, who had remained in the area after the meeting concluded two weeks before. He began the meeting at Erasmus' farm, Hennopsrivier, near Pretoria, on April 12. Immediately after the spirit of the preceding gathering was reported, he accused the Boers of using force and bribery against those loyal to Britain and added: "You know that you are guilty of rebellion and can be severely punished."[104] Kruger answered quickly: "I have heard what your excellency has said, and I am more dissatisfied than you know. . . . They were gathered of their own free will. . . . Those who wished to do so, came; others stayed away."[105] The commissioner told them that the question of annexation stood and could not be reopened. Other than this, he would attempt to please the Transvaalers. Frere sensed, however, that the agitation was becoming more serious. "The Boers, submissive and acquiescent two years ago, are now clamoring for the repeal of the annexation."[106] Some measure of pacification was necessary. Consequently, he arranged for certain recommendations he would propose to the queen, including an executive council on which some Boers would have seats and a temporary legislature, looking forward to a reestablished Volksraad.[107]

Afrikaners, still discouraged, made an appeal directly to the queen, hoping in vain to influence her policies. The communication dated April 17, 1879, was drawn up by a committee headed by Pretorius and included these words:

> We continue to cherish the confident hope that by our expectant attitude we have rather gained than lost in Your Majesty's eyes. . . . [We report so that you will know] the sacred will of the people. . . . What else can we do? Must we draw the sword? . . . Your majesty cannot desire to rule over unwilling subjects. Unwilling subjects, but faithful neighbors, we will be.[108]

Planning for further agitation continued. A special meeting was called for December 1879 to reject the authority of Britain and to reconstitute the government of an elected Volksraad. This meeting was not a secret, for British authorities knew of its proposed date as well as its proposed objectives. Sir Garnet Wolseley, the British representative, stated the case of the government as he gave warning:

> In my opinion there can be nothing more hurtful to the interests and welfare of the people than any attempt to unsettle their minds and disturb their allegiance by concerted occasion of public excitement, and I have reason to fear that certain designing and evil-intentioned persons are in this matter pro-

moting an agitation by which many through timidity or ignorance may be betrayed into irrevocable trouble.[109]

He warned them of the dangers involved and urged people not to attend.
Those who chose to attend would be violating the law and would be liable to
punishment. Frere, still underestimating the strength of the growing agitation, wrote to Hicks-Beach in London that the Boer agitators are "neither
numerous nor formidable, the leaders and instigators being many of them
foreigners . . . who induced others to join them by intimidation."[110]

The threats were of no avail, however, for when the Boers' meeting
opened at Wonderfontein on December 10, 1879, a reported six thousand
were in attendance.[111] In stately procession with both political and religious implications, several leaders carried the flags of the old South African Republic. Nicholas Smit began with an emotional appeal concerning the
sacredness of their mission that day: "Men, the flag which waves here is
the flag of our fathers, dear to them, and double dear to us. Let us respect
this flag, let us remember the sacral duties for which we are assembled
here; if necessary, let us sacrifice our blood in order to plant it again in
free soil."[112]

Joubert brought all hearers up to date on events of the past few
months:

> [You have heard enough to know]that deputations, resolutions,
> meetings, etc., are of no further avail. You know now the will
> of the English Government. The Committee now desires to
> know from the people what their will is. Joshua says, "Choose
> ye this day your Lord whom you will serve." [Josh. 24:15].
> Now then brethren choose; submit or show us the way we are
> to follow.[113]

The people answered: "We want our country back." Hans Steyn added his
theological observations: "The time of passive resistance is past, let us
proclaim our own government and by God's help the country will soon be
ours again."[114] Joubert then added: "Do you wish to submit? I don't
advise you to do so. It is true, England is powerful, and when we think of
that we shudder; but do not forget the cause we uphold. It is sacred, and
God will give us strength."[115] Later that evening while Kruger was walking through the camp, he reflected on the day's activities: "I returned to
my tent and thanked God that my people were so firmly determined to
recover their independence."[116]

During the meeting held from December 10 to 15, the Boers drew up a
set of ten resolutions embodying their official rejection of British authority. Some of these are especially significant for our study. They vowed not
to recognize British authority, and whoever called them "agitators" was "a
liar." They made provisions to reestablish their government, including the

Volksraad. Finally, they wrote: "The people declare that, by God's help, they desire to have a strong government for the South African Republic, respect for the law, and development and advancement of the country, and they promise man for man to cooperate for that purpose, to defend their government till death, so help us Almighty God."[117]

Sir Wolseley heard about the meeting before he read the resolutions sent to him a few days later. His immediate reply in a speech at Pretoria included his evaluation. The Boers showed their ignorance when

> a section of [the] population . . . take upon themselves to establish themselves in camp on the High Veld, coquet with rebellion, and utter high talk about their destinies and their future. . . . I think the Transvaal has never had such formidable enemies either outside or within its limits than the 1500 or 2000 Boers assembled near this town. . . . [It is surprising to see] a few thousand Boers meeting together, and presuming to speak for all those of the Transvaal [assuming] that they, and they alone, are authorized to speak in the name of its people. Another curious phase of their ignorance is the manner in which they have been persuaded by the few designing men who lead them, that there is a chance of this country being given back to the former miserable state of affairs.[118]

Shortly after this speech, a copy of the document containing the ten resolutions reached Wolseley with the request that he should notify British authorities that the Transvaal was no longer British territory. He retaliated by arresting two leaders of the meeting, Secretary Eduard Bok at Pretoria, January 3, and Chairman Pretorius at Potchefstroom on January 5, 1880.[119] Several hundred Boers began immediately to organize to free their ex-president, Pretorius, but were discouraged from this hasty act by Kruger, Joubert, and others.[120] The wise counsel of these leaders caused the heightened tension to remain under control until further plans could be considered.

During the course of the trial when several Boers were questioned about the attendance at the meetings, Wolseley was informed that had it not been for the efforts of Pretorius, Kruger, and others, there would have been violence.[121] The trial of the two was never completed, and to pacify the Boers, Wolseley offered Pretorius a place in the British administration as a representative of the Transvaal people. Pretorius declined, stating that if he would do so, he would lose the influence he had with his people. The Boers departed from Wonderfontein at the end of December 1879 with the plan that they would come together again in April 1880 to elect the Volksraad and reconstitute the government. This meeting was not held, however, for tensions subsided due to political events in England. The Liberals, led by Gladstone, increasingly criticized the Conservative government of Disraeli, especially its policy in the Transvaal. The Liberals argued that the Transvaal annexation should not merely remain a *fait accompli,* but if it were shown to be of more advantage to England, a retrocession should not be opposed at least for face-saving reasons.

When the Gladstone government was victorious in 1880 the Boer leaders were again optimistic. Kruger and Joubert wrote, with hope, to Gladstone, who replied that although the annexation could not be revoked, the Transvaal people could win their own rule and freedom as part of the South African confederation.[122] Discouraged and disgusted, the Boer leaders began another phase of their political history. Before turning to the last meeting of the Boers that led directly to the beginning of the First War of Independence, we must note briefly the growing sympathy for the Boers' cause arising among Boers outside the Transvaal.

The British authorities thought the various deputations to London, arguments with British leaders, and several Boer mass meetings would have no results. Throughout South Africa, however, there were many persons of Dutch-Boer background whose sympathies were being aroused.[123] Whereas a generation earlier the catalog of grievances which resulted in the Great Trek was repeated only in the north, by 1877 these were published at Cape Town as well. An attempt was made to unite the Boers of the south and the north into one group consciousness. One of the organs for this sympathetic movement was *Die Patriot,* a pro-Boer newssheet published by the Rev. Daniel François du Toit in Paarl. In 1877 he summarized the Boers' grievances for the Cape Town Boers as they were previously summarized for the trekkers:

> Our grievances we have almost forgotten . . . the question concerning the Hottentots, the freeing of the slaves in an unbecoming manner, the disastrous Kaffer wars, the shame of paper money, the injustice in Natal, etc. How can we bring this back to memory? But now England continues to bring us pain—think of partiality for the Basutos; the taking of the Diamond Fields; the annexation of the Transvaal. How can we forget these things now? No, we think about them. We shall remember these; our children shall drink this with their mother's milk.[124]

Two years later the Afrikaner Bond (a religio-political association) was formed by the Rev. S. J. du Toit of Paarl, a brother of the publisher of *Die Patriot.* These two—the newssheet and the Bond—became active Afrikaner political and religious forces crossing all national boundaries in South Africa.

The Volksraad of the Free State quickly provided support for the oppressed Boers of the Transvaal.[125] Pretorius served as chairman of a delegation from the Transvaal to seek support from pro-Boer elements in Natal on the assumption that this was God's cause:

[there] is constantly increasing bitterness between the burghers of England and Afrikaner descent. The old wound was almost healed; it was again opened by Sir Theophilus Shepstone. God knows how long this evil seed, sown by him, will continue to grow. Help us then, by your cooperation, to extirpate, root and branch, this weed of division.[126]

Recognizing this growing pro-Boer unity, on November 8, 1879, Frere called a meeting at Cape Town with the pro-Boer members of the Cape Parliament. Frere summarized the situation well when he said, "The meeting illustrated the strong and intimate connection in feeling which exists between the Transvaal Dutch farmers and their relatives, who form so large a portion of the conservative country party in this colony."[127]

Several workable suggestions were presented, all indicating the growing sympathy of the southern Boers for their northern compatriots. For example, P. J. Stigant stated that there was daily contact between the Transvaal and other sections of the area, especially the eastern part of the Cape Colony. Some of the Cape inhabitants had actually opposed the annexation: "You cannot set aside the sentiments of these people, and the fact that there are very strong blood relationships between them and the inhabitants of the Cape Colony, who sympathize to a very great extent with their brethren in the Transvaal."[128] John X. Merriman added his observation that agitation had taken deeper root: "There is hardly a farmhouse in the country in which this matter of the Transvaal annexation is not talked about, and there is a strong and bitter feeling growing up against the British government."[129] H. P. du Preeze reflected that in his travels to the outlying towns, he found much feeling in support of what Stigant and Merriman had reported.[130] J. H. Hofmeyr reiterated what Paul Kruger had said before—that a Volksraad should be called to let the people decide their own future. If the majority freely voted to remain British, the agitation undoubtedly would disappear.[131]

This counsel from highly respected parliamentary members should have shown Frere that the reaction was deeper than he imagined. He was not deeply moved, however, by the discussion; he believed that the decision of the past was fair and honorable. In addition, how could a free vote be taken at the present time? Which party or which group would one trust? He concluded what might have been a fruitful discussion with a closed mind: it is "hopeless to expect a free vote on any question."[132] Gradually the reaction spread to other towns in both Natal and the Cape Colony. On December 9, 1880, a deputation arrived in Cape Town from Paarl, requesting something be done to ease the situation.[133] The Paarl newspaper, *Die Patriot,* had supported the Boers' cause for some time. Stellenbosch also added its criticism of governmental policy.[134]

In Europe there was also sympathy. In the Netherlands a petition had been signed by over six thousand persons, pleading with England for a change of policy for the Dutch were alarmed at the treatment of "our own flesh and blood."[135] When this petition was signed, however, the Boers' compatriots in Europe did not know that war was already in progress between the two white European factions in the Transvaal.

Later in 1880 the tension in all of South Africa increased. Immediately before the war began the lieutenant-governor of Natal, Sir Henry Bulwer, reported that "there are ugly rumors in Natal of active sympathy with the Boers throughout the Orange Free State and Cape of Good Hope Colony."[136] Always sympathetic to the Boers, J. H. Hofmeyr, a moderate Boer leader in Cape Town, tried one last-minute idea. He suggested that someone respected by both sides, such as Justice J. H. de Villiers, be sent north to negotiate. His suggestion also came too late.[137]

England was not satisfied merely to maintain authority in the Transvaal; it continued to press for further jurisdiction, especially with respect to taxes. The Boers had never had a strong central government and had no efficient method of collecting taxes.[138] They resented taxes even when demanded by their own government, but to pay taxes to the British authorities would be, in their eyes, a recognition of British right to rule in the Transvaal.[139] Sir Owen Lanyon, the new administrator of the Transvaal, despite his knowledge of the tension, chose a specific instance to force the issue. A Boer, Piet Bezuidenhout from Potchefstroom, accused of refusing to pay taxes, became the focal point. British authorities decided that either he should pay taxes and the costs of his trial or be imprisoned. He chose the latter course and went to prison for one week.[140] To achieve partial payment for their expenses, the government seized the only real property Bezuidenhout had—his wagon—and announced that on November 11, 1880, it would be sold at auction. Early that morning approximately one hundred Boers sympathetic to Bezuidenhout appeared at the office of Landdrost Goetz and forcibly took the wagon from him and dragged it away. The British official sent for reinforcements although he believed no "serious trouble will arise out of the affair."[141]

This minor incident was an outward indication of an intense hatred that was growing against British authority. In addition, the Boers gained historical understanding and made the most of it. As it happened, this Mr. Bezuidenhout was the son of Frederick Bezuidenhout, one of the heroes of the Slagters' Nek revolt (1815). Earlier in the century, British authorities had sought to punish the Boers who had mistreated their Khoikoi servants, and in the conflict Bezuidenhout and six others were killed. This later incident with the wagon and the younger Bezuidenhout was quickly interpreted as a repetition of Slagters' Nek, another "great example of bitter enmity against British power."[142] Slagters' Nek was also mentioned in the Petition of Rights as one of the situations remembered by all loyal Afrikaners.[143]

While tempers were almost uncontrollable, the Boers assumed that they could no longer profit from discussions with British officials; they must reconstitute their government by force, always confident that God was on their side.[144] During the last six months of 1880 the Boers collected weapons in secret and received help from certain sympathetic landdrosts in the Transvaal, as well as in the Free State.[145] To take the law into their own hands, another meeting was called for January 8, 1881, but actually took place a month previous—December 8 through 15, 1880—at Paardekraal. Between four thousand and five thousand Boers attended. After the meeting was opened with prayer, they chose Paul Kruger as spokesman. He had been one of the most devoted workers on their behalf during the interregnum and had been continually upheld, so the gathering was told, by thought of "his poor oppressed people, confident in the righteousness of his own cause, and an inner faith in the all-wise and all-knowing Creator of all, and the Source of all Justice."[146] Kruger responded:

> I stand here before your face, chosen by the people; in the voice of the people [*Volkstem*] I have heard the voice of God, the King of all people, and I am obedient. . . . The people have never forsaken the rule of law. After the annexation they protested, have resisted and suffered, and would have attempted every other peaceful means had not English authority in Pretoria made this impossible. The rights of the people are on our side; and although we are very weak, God is a just God. My friends! May the Lord bless your activities and protect our Fatherland.[147]

Another Boer comment heightened the theological imagery of the occasion:

> We have heard the words of our Honorable Vice President with warm feelings of thankfulness, because he has the courage, in this difficult situation, to take the law into his hands in the name of the People. . . . The people will never forget the work of the Committee whose activities and vigil was on behalf of the people during the four years of our subjection. We are here with you, and with our people, ready to the last man, to offer our lives for the independence of our beloved fatherland.
>
> With God's help we are all ready to take any suggestions you have to recommend for the good of the land.[148]

To begin reconstituting their government, the Boers chose Paul Kruger, Piet Joubert, and Marthinus Wessel Pretorius as a triumvirate to lead them. On December 13, 1880, they presented a proclamation of independence: "Notice is hereby given to every person that the government has been restored as of December 13, 1880, and that Mr. S. J. P. Kruger is acting as Vice President, who together with Messrs. M. W. Pretorius and P. J. Joubert, will form the Triumvirate to execute the control of the country. The Volksraad has resumed its session."[149]   The proclamation included thirty-eight points. Three are important to this study:

> Point 28: "We presented a proclamation two days ago asking that a choice be made. Are we to be considered rebels; or can we maintain our eternal rights as a free people?"
> Point 29: "We affirm, before God the knower of all hearts and before the world that anyone who calls us agitators is a liar! The people of the South African Republic have never been subjects of Her Majesty, and we will not be."
> Point 38: "The Republic is ready to agree with the Colonies and States of South Africa on a confederation. . . . [They concluded:] From today let it be known that we are in a state of siege, and under the rule of martial law."[150]

WAR AND PEACE, 1880-1881

For the proclamation to be official it needed to be printed and distributed widely, but the only two printers, at Pretoria and Potchefstroom, were administered by British officials. P. J. Cronje was sent with a force of eight hundred armed men to force the printer in Potchefstroom to publish it. The printer was sympathetic, but British officials prevented the printing. Several Boers then rode into Potchefstroom on December 15 and took control of the printing press.[151]   The next day British officials sought the leader of the Boers, without success. In the process of investigation, shots rang out; the war had begun. These first shots were fired on Dingane's Day, December 16, 1880, and the Boers soon gained control of the city of Potchefstroom.[152]

A second group of Boers rode into Heidelberg where they set up their government, hoisted the flag of the South African Republic, and cut the telegraph cable linking Pretoria with Natal, the source of British reinforcements. The Boer leaders sent a copy of their proclamation of independence to Sir Owen Lanyon, the British representative in Pretoria. Kruger asked for a peaceful takeover.

A third group of Boers went toward Pretoria to intercept any possible British reinforcements coming from Natal. A few days later, the first open conflict occurred between the Boer and British troops coming from Natal. At Bronkhurst Spruit on December 20, the Boers, with the larger number of troops, surprised the British marching between Middleburg and Pretoria. In ten minutes the Boers defeated the British, who did not realize the Boers had already begun the war.[153]

When he heard of this victory, Kruger again saw the hand of the Lord:

Inexpressible is the gratitude of the Burghers for this victory,
grateful their feelings toward the valiant General Franz
Joubert and his men, who have maintained the honor of the
Republic on the battlefield. We are bowed down in the dust
before God Almighty who has been so near to them and who, as
against the hundred soldiers killed, had caused only two of our
men to perish. . . . We are thus at war. A war of self-defense,
thrust upon us, but never declared to us. We know not against
whom, but every one does his duty, and the God of our fathers,
who has been with us till now, will remain with us.[154]

Others were quick to see the theological implications in this victory. A
clergyman responded: "Behold the armies of salvation of the Lord; we were
as Israel of old—before us lay the Red Sea, behind us was the Egyptian host
and on either side of use were lofty mountains. We could but look up and
cry to God and He heard our voice."[155]

The reaction against British authority intensified immediately. From
all parts of South Africa, people of Dutch background were driven to sympathy with the oppressed Boers. John X. Merriman, later to become Cape
prime minister, captured the nationalist spirit:

It is no use disguising the fact that there is a great deal of
sympathy and fellow feeling between the inhabitants of the
Cape Colony and the inhabitants of the Transvaal, and in the
present state of affairs anything that takes place in the Transvaal cannot fail to have a most prejudicial effect on Cape
Colony or on a large portion of the population. Each shot fired
up there will find its echo down here in the Cape Colony, and
every drop of blood that is shed there will sow the seeds for
the continuance of that bitter feeling which existed before, but
which happily was dying away between Dutch and English.[156]

A Mr. Strahan, also of the Cape Colony, reinforced the idea: "There can be
no doubt that a very strong sympathy exists among those of Dutch descent
in this colony with the Boers in the Transvaal. . . . There is scarcely a
family of Dutch descent in one colony which has not relations or connections in the other."[157]

In the eyes of many Boers of the Cape Colony, Britain had overstepped
the bounds of justice. Almost immediately Stellenbosch sent a deputation
to Cape Town to ask for immediate settlement. M. L. A. Hofmeyr and
J. W. L. Hofmeyr, among others, argued that the longer the conflict continued, the more difficult would be any confederation policy. "Blood is
thicker than water," they said, and it was quickly becoming a conflict not

of north against south but Boer against British. Furthermore, the Boers far outnumbered the British in all sections of South Africa.[158]

The scene of the battle now shifted from the center of the Transvaal to the border the republic shared with Natal. Since the Free State was officially neutral, there was no way for British reinforcements to reach the Transvaal except to come through Natal. The initiative was then taken by Sir George Colley, the British commander in Natal, who wrote to the "misled" and "deluded" Boers asking them to cease their unjust rebellion. The Boer triumvirate replied:

> Perhaps, after all, we are misled and deluded. By what and by whom? By our faith in a living God, who will be the defender of the weak against the strong, of the oppressed against the oppressor, who will raise a feeling of shame amongst the English people for the evil deeds which are perpetrated in their name in South Africa. In the name of our Lord, we will fight until death.[159]

General Joubert gathered his troops on the eastern border of the Transvaal, and Sir George Colley gathered the British forces at Newcastle near the same point. On January 23, the British officers offered a final ultimatum for the Boers to disperse. The Boers responded: "We have only to submit to our fate; but the Lord will provide."[160] The stage was set for the three major conflicts of the war. The first was at Laing's Nek. On January 28, 1881, the British marched to the top of the hill beside Laing's Nek in an attempt to outflank the Boers, but without success. Many of the British leaders were killed, and within a few hours the British retreated down the way they had come. In reporting the day's activities, General Joubert told P. A. Cronje, assistant commanding general: "I have the honor to inform you that the enemy made an attack upon us. With the help of God, they have been repulsed with heavy losses. . . . Thus they have been prevented to do more at this moment. Looking up to God that He may further bless us."[161]

In two further battles, the Boers attributed the miscalculations and faulty tactics of the British to God's protection. On February 8, 1881, the two forces came together in Ingogo Heights, and after an all-day battle the British retreated. Finally, three weeks later the British walked to the top of Majuba Hill under cover of darkness, hoping to gain the advantage. When Sunday, February 27, dawned, however, the battle began, and brought heavy casualties to the British. Among the dead was their commanding leader, Sir George Colley. The Boers were again convinced that God fought on their side for freedom against oppression. Joubert at the battle line reported to Kruger in Heidelberg:

> Beyond all our expectations the Lord assisted us, and we all ascribe it to the most wonderful deliverance and help of an all-

governing and mighty God. . . . Our God who gave us the true victory and protected us, exceeded gloriously all acts of courage and tact. . . . I conclude with wishing your honor joy at the successful issue of today's battle, and that this day may be considered for the future a day of Thanksgiving and Prayer.[162]

Kruger answered in the same vein:

We know that the South African Republic looks up to you with gratitude. We glory not in human power, it is God the Lord who has helped us—the God of our fathers, to whom for the last five years, we have addressed our prayers and supplications. He has done great things to us, and hearkened to our prayers.

And you, noble and valiant brothers, have been in His hands the means of saving us. . . . The God who guides the hearts of kings like running brooks will deliver us. Trust in Him.[163]

On learning of the death of Sir George Colley, Sir Evelyn Wood took command of the British forces. Even before the disaster of Majuba Hill, peace negotiations were discussed in many areas. Hardly had the war begun when President Brand of the Free State corresponded both with the triumvirate and with Sir Evelyn Wood about peace efforts. Brand had spent many years stabilizing the government of the Free State and knew that a long battle between the two powers around the Free State would result in trouble for his own people.[164] It was his suggestion that J. H. de Villiers, chief justice of the Cape Colony, himself a Boer by background, but educated in English schools, be mediator. This paralleled the same suggestion made shortly before at the Cape by J. H. Hofmeyr.[165] The British government offered to discuss peace if the Boers would first lay down their arms, but Kruger rejected this stipulation.[166]

Kruger offered the British a way out as he interpreted the cause as God's cause and stated that the British could take the initiative:

I have found that we are compelled against our will to proceed in a bloody combat, and that our positions, as taken, are of that nature that we cannot cease to persevere in the way of self-defense, as once adopted by us, so far as our God will give us strength to do so. . . . I should not be answerable before my God if I did not attempt once more to make known to you our meaning, knowing that it is in your power to enable us to withdraw from the positions taken by us. . . . Should, however, the annexation be persevered in, and the spilling of blood proceeded with by you, we subject to the will of God, will bow to our fate, and, to the last man, combat against the injustice and violence done to us.[167]

Sympathy came from other areas of South Africa. Although the Free State was officially neutral, British officials suspected that many Free State citizens were fighting with their Boer compatriots. Nevertheless, in the midst of peace negotiations, some of the Boers were not certain they would be successful. Consequently from Potchefstroom they made a specific plea for help from the Orange Free State, confident that they knew the will of God:

> Therefore, brethren and fellow countrymen, we appeal to you! Come and help! Thus far the Lord has assisted us and blessed our arms, and providence will further help us. . . . Consider our cause. God rules and is with us. It is His will to unite us as a people; to a unified South Africa, free from British authority. The future lightens for us. His will be done.[168]

Ministers of the Cape Synod of the N. G. K. also expressed sympathy with the Boers:

> By reason of a common national descent, a common religion and the continual influx of people into the Transvaal from the Dutch portion of the inhabitants of this colony, there are strong ties uniting the Dutch churches in the Transvaal, with our own. Since the annexation a deep sympathy with the Transvaal has been awakened among our people. . . . We are convinced that nothing short of the restoration of their independence will satisfy and appease the Transvaal people.[169]

Sir Evelyn Wood sincerely wanted peace but only after the surrender of more Boer strongholds. Kruger and his followers also wanted peace but could not accept the proffered terms. Finally, through the untiring mediation of President Brand, a truce of eight days was arranged.[170] Negotiations began when the Boers were represented by all three of the triumvirate. Between March 21 and 23, 1881, the British agreed to accept the triumvirate as the legal heads of the Transvaal, and the Boers agreed to negotiate with the British.[171] The armistice was signed, and the Transvaal again was allowed its self-government.[172]

While negotiations were proceeding, the theological interpretation was also continuing. *Die Patriot,* published at Paarl, gave its own interpretation of the end of the war: "God's hand has been visible in the history of our people so as it never has been since the days of Israel. [It was] fear from God which made the English soldiers powerless."[173] Paul Kruger added his comments also: "With a feeling of thankfulness to the God of the Fathers, who is near us in struggle and danger, it is an unexpressible privilege to be able to hand over to you the peace agreement concluded between us and Sir Evelyn Wood."[174] A newspaper, the *Volksstem,* reflected the same theological attitude of the man soon to be elected president of the Transvaal: "He [Kruger] expressed his confidence that at that moment no one stood with a feeling of self-exaltation. Rather, each felt condescendingly meek with thankfulness to God for the signs he had sent them. Now our flag can truly be unfurled."[175] Later in the century a Transvaal official summed up the First War of Independence: "At Bronkhurst Spruit, at Laing's Nek, at Ingogo, and at Majuba, God gave us victory, although in each case the British troopers outnumbered us, and were more powerfully armed than ourselves."[176]

The war-weary Boers agreed to the armistice on March 23, without being certain of the exact meaning of some of the terms. These were further interpreted—by the Pretoria Convention, which they were asked to sign on August 8, 1881. The thirty-three items included one that seemed to be more restricting than the Boers had expected. They had consented to British suzerainty, but whereas in March they had signed a statement that their foreign relations must be conducted with the *permission* of the British resident, now in August they read that the British government would have "*control* of the external relations . . . and the conduct of diplomatic intercourse."[177] Other measures of the Convention included the following:

Point 4:   "The rule of the Triumvirate who were thereby authorized to call the *Volksraad*."

Point 14: "Natives will be allowed to move as freely within the country as may be consistent with the requirements of public order . . . subject always to the Pass laws of the said state."

Point 16: "No slavery or apprenticeship" will be allowed.

Finally, the decision was announced to the people by proclamation: "On this 8th day of August 1881 the country has once more come back under our government. . . . With the deepest gratitude to our God we announce this to all the inhabitants."[178]

Kruger espoused their theological self-consciousness as he spoke at the opening session of the Volksraad the next month:

It is with a feeling of inexpressible gratitude toward God, the creator of all things, that at an extraordinary period we can again bid you welcome here in this building, and see you assembled to discuss the affairs of our beloved Fatherland. . . . We are . . . sure that that God who has so visibly led us hitherto, will not withhold from you His support and help, but will complete the work of his hands. . . . When at Paardekraal the Government undertook its important task, the people bound themselves by a solemn oath. The oath is faithfully fulfilled, and the unity of purpose of the people will be the strength of the land.[179]

This change of attitude among the Boers from passive resistance in 1877 to the active insurrection in 1880 and 1881 sparked new hopes of nationalism in other parts of South Africa. One group of the nationalistic Afrikaner Bond from Kroonstad spoke for many:

A trance-like resignation to British injustice and oppression constrained the Afrikaner's love of liberty entirely. Indeed, at a moment's notice Great Britain can and will destroy us and deprive us of our freedom. . . . By the stubborn defense of your rights you have roused the entire South Africa from the slave-like stupor to which every oppressed nation descends. Now every true Afrikaner doubly appreciates his dignity as burgher, his rights and regained liberties. He shall know how to defend and respect these for the future. There is no doubt that many of us living will behold in full growth the tree of patriotism and of complete liberty of South Africa, the seed of which you have planted in fertile soil.[180]

Undergirded by a theological interpretation, Afrikaner nationalism came into full bloom. The eventful year and the eventful two decades were concluded by a great festival at Paardekraal in December 1881, a "festival of the people, for the worship of God, where all who have suffered, striven and prayed with us may thank the gracious Father who has saved us."[181] It was here at Paardekraal just one year before that they decided to oppose Britain with force, and now at the same spot they held a religious remembrance. Theology, nationalism, and emotion—"freedom," "God's will," "Afrikaner Cause," "preservation of our culture"—were intermingled among the estimated twelve thousand to fifteen thousand persons attending, who had come from Natal and the Orange Free State, as well as from Transvaal.[182] While some suggested it was merely good shooting that gave the Boers their victory, the orthodox General Joubert gave his own interpretation: "No, it was not the good shooting of the Boers that has procured for us the victory, but the Lord's help. The Lord has done it."[183]

The eloquence of Paul Kruger carried the throng to new heights and convinced some who had not yet sympathized with the Afrikaners. He spoke for most of the faithful people as he related their cause to the will of God:

We have come here to celebrate a feast and you know it. Our and your object is nothing else but to let us understand the will of the Lord and to point out his guidance, so that parents can relate to their children and grandchildren to their most distant generations what God has done for us. You know that our country had been snatched away from us more than four years ago, perhaps for transgressions, but you know it also that God chastises whom he loves. . . . Now give due regard how the Lord has guided us so that we can stand today on this spot to thank Him for the deliverance vouchsafed to us. It is true that there were leaders, but God has made use of them solely as the means of His hands to carry out His work. . . . Now we have assembled to thank the Lord for His blessings vouchsafed to us. . . . The Lord has led us hitherto. Let us then in our after life remain true to him and serve him faithfully.[184]

The Boers again had reason to be confident that God delivers His faithful from oppressors, as was the case with Moses' escape from Egypt. Their election by God had been proved in several situations as the attempted oppression by the superior British forces was turned back as if by a miracle. God sustains, they reasoned, that society that maintains the pure Reformed faith. So clearly was the biblical typology in their minds that as they constructed a platform the speakers used, they also constructed a monument of small stones nearby (Joshua 8:30-31; Deut. 27:5). Now they were latter-day children of Israel; pharaoh was now British; and the whole biblical story had been reenacted. One speaker, H. Lemmer, called their attention to the Old Testament story:

> Even as Aaron had raised the hands of Moses on Pisgah [Exodus 17:12] so had the people raised the speaker's hands in the battle. What did Moses do after the battle? He erected a stone and called it "The Lord is our banner" [Exodus 17:15]. Let us do the same here. Let us abide with that God and endeavor in the name of the Lord to unite for time and eternity.[185]

These two decades formed a significant period of the theological history of the Boers. They were strengthened by new leaders, a clarified ideology, and deepened confidence that their cause was just because it was God's cause. They had been true to their covenant. They had faced a challenge strong enough to unite them above party faction. They now had a common destiny, and it included not a single nation but all God's elect people—the Afrikaner Boers—in all sections of South Africa. With the Boers' determination, undergirded not only by nationalism but with deep religious conviction as well, they had gained a group consciousness and envisaged their true destiny as upholders of God's culture. They were opposed, however, by a British determination equally strong. The stage was thus set for the catastrophe that ended the century.

NOTES

1. The argument, as in previous generations, concerned the propriety and even the orthodoxy of singing "man-made" hymns (those not part of the Calvinistic metrical versions of the Psalms).

2. Engelbrecht, *Geskiedenis,* p. 147.

3. *Ibid.,* p. 147.

4. du Plessis, *Andrew Murray,* p. 178, letter to his brother, John, May 1, 1859.

5. Engelbrecht, *Geskiedenis,* p. 147.

6. *Ibid.*

7. *Ibid.,* pp. 147-148.

8. The Gereformeerde Kerk van Suid Afrika (the Doppers) was related to the Christelijke Afgeschiedene Gereformeerde Kerk of the Netherlands. Spoelstra, *Doppers,* p. 192. This separatist church was organized in 1834, mainly by Hendrik de Cock. Cf. J. Reitsma and J. Lindeboom, *Geschiedenis van de Hervorming en de Hervormde Kerk gedurende de 18^e en 19^e eeuw* (Amsterdam: Meulenhoff & Co., 1912), pp. 299-304. One of the major differences in the Netherlands, as in South Africa, concerned the use of evangelical hymns that were not part of the metrical Psalter. The hymns were rejected by the more conservative separatist groups both in the Netherlands and in South Africa.

9. G. C. P. van der Vyver, *Professor Dirk Postma: 1818-1890* (Potchefstroom: Pro Rege Pers, 1958), p. 168. On his attitude toward evangelical singing, see p. 188.

10. *Ibid.,* pp. 50-90; cf. Engelbrecht, *Geskiedenis,* p. 149.

11. van der Vyver, *Postma,* pp. 89, 174, 178; cf. Engelbrecht, *Geskiedenis,* p. 151.

12. du Plessis, *Andrew Murray,* p. 176, letter to John Murray, November 30, 1858.

13. Engelbrecht, *Geskiedenis,* p. 157.

14. *Ibid.,* pp. 157-158; cf. G. D. Scholtz, *Die Geskiedenis van die Nederduitse Hervormde of Gereformeerde Kerk van Suid-Afrika* (2 vols., Cape Town: N. G. Kerk-Boekhandel, 1956), I, 155.

15. Krüger, *Ontstaan,* p. 77; cf. *Die Kerkbode,* March 24, 1860.

16. Eybers, *Select Constitutional Documents,* p. 366.

17. Paul Kruger, *The Memoirs of Paul Kruger* (New York: Century Co., 1902), pp. 74-75.

18. Engelbrecht, *Geskiedenis*, p. 168.

19. *Ibid.*, p. 169; cf. Scholtz, *Geskiedenis*, I, 154.

20. du Plessis, *Andrew Murray*, p. 178, to John Murray, May 1, 1859. Cf. W. A. Venter, "Die Geskiedenis van die Nederduitse Gereformeerde Gemeente Bloemfontein gedurende die Pioniersjare, 1848-1900," *Argief-Jaarboek vir Suid-Afrikaanse Geskiedenis*, XXV (1962), 163-306.

21. Johannes David Kriel, "Die verhouding tussen kerk en staat in die Republiek van die Oranje-Vrystaat, 1854-1902," *Argief-Jaarboek vir Suid-Afrikaanse Geskiedenis*, XVI (1953), p. 183.

22. *Ibid.*

23. "The 'Doppers', so called, are a very peculiar 'sect', extremely conservative, and clannish toward their own fellow worshippers, or creedsmen, but exclusive, and suspicious to a degree, as regards the adherents, or religious doctrines of other churches; they have seceded from what is known in South Africa, as the 'Dutch Reformed Church', from whose religious tenets they differ somewhat widely,—claiming, as they are understood to do, to be the *genuine* Reformers of the Dutch Church; the Old Testament—good old book—seemingly finding more favour with them, than the New,—though the writer does not, by any means, intend to imply that they discard the latter; David's Psalms—and not hymns—forming the chief metrical portion of their religious services; these they sing in a kind of 'monotone', and are, as a rule, against the use of musical instruments in their churches.
"Jehovah's wonderful manifestation to his ancient peoples, and his interpositions on their behalf, in Old Testament times, and his specially raising up men, and endowing them with supernatural wisdom, as his instruments for doing his work amongst their brethren, has evidently laid great hold on their imagination, so much so, indeed, that they seem to be possessed with the idea that they too are a specially Divinely favoured people, in the same sense that Israel was, and have been signally endowed by the Almighty, with sufficient intuitive knowledge and understanding to undertake, and acquit themselves satisfactorily, of any mental, or other duties, without the necessary secular training for the efficient performance of same, which, other ordinary mortals regard as essential; this idea appears to be inherent, and has come down from Father to Son,—from generation to generation,—and is not calculated to raise them much above their present level, their manner of dress too is unique—they wear large hats, short jackets, rather wide trousers pinched up at the back, with an opening at the side, in which they carry a kind of bowie knife, for use in several ways, chiefly to cut their food,—though the writer wishes to add here, that he has from time to time known many intelligent and thoughtful men among the Doppers, who, if their minds had been developed by a liberal, secular, and religious educational training, would have surely left their mark, and have been a blessing to their friends and neighbours." Collins, *Free Statia*, pp. 158-159.

24. Examples are: F. Lion Cachet, *De Worstelstrijd der Transvaalers aan het Volk van Nederland Verhaald* (Amsterdam: 1881); C. W. de Kiewiet, *British Colonial Policy in the South African Republic, 1848-1872* (London: 1929); W. J. Leyds, *The First Annexation of the Transvaal* (London: R. Fisher Unwin, 1906); Theal, *History of South Africa*, IX, *The South African Republic, 1870-1872*, VIII, From 1858-1870 (London: George Allen and Unwin, 1919); Cornelis Janse Uys, *In the Era of Shepstone, Being a Study of British Expansion in South Africa, 1842-1877* (Lovedale: 1933).

25. Collins, *Free Statia*, p. 77.

26. Leyds, *First Annexation*, p. 102; cf. Jean van der Poel, "Basutoland as a Factor in South African Politics, 1858-1870," *Argief-Jaarboek vir Suid Afrikaanse Geskiedenis*, IV (1941), pp. 171-228.

27. George M. Theal, *Basutoland Records* (3 vols., Cape Town: W. A. Richards & Son, 1883), II, 476-479; cf. Godfrey Lagdon, *The Basutos* (2 vols., New York: D. Appleton Co., 1909), I, 267-273.

28. G. D. Scholtz, *President Johannes Henricus Brand* (Johannesburg: Voortrekkerpers, 1957), p. 50.

29. Collins, *Free Statia*, p. 213.

30. August 25, 1865, c. 4140 of 1869, pp. 11-12. Extensive records of South African society appear in the "Blue Books" or the *Accounts and Papers* of the British House of Commons. These are indicated by the letter "C" followed by the paper number, the year of presentation, and the page.

31. Theal, *Basutoland Records*, III, 360-362.

32. C. 4140 of 1869, pp. 98-100.

33. Scholtz, *President J. H. Brand*, p. 60.

34. Leyds, *First Annexation*, p. 108.

35. C. 4140 of 1869, p. 27.

36. *Ibid.*

37. C. 4140 of 1869, p. 27; cf. Eybers, *Select Constitutional Documents*, p. 283.

38. Article VIII, the Bloemfontein Convention, in Eybers, *Select Constitutional Documents*, pp. 283-285. Wodehouse issued the ban on ammunition March 10, 1868; cf. C. 4140 of 1869, p. 39; Brand complained of the action December 4 of the same year; cf. C. 4140 of 1869, p. 77.

39. Not many records of the Boers' theological analysis during the war have been preserved. One source, however, contemporary with the events, gives an interesting sidelight on Brand's personality. This is perhaps typical of other Boers' thoughts and actions of the time. A contemporary witness

reported: "I remember his [Brand's] relating some of his Basuto war experiences, and how, worn out and tired at a critical time of the struggle, he spent a sleepless and bitterly cold night in a disconsolate frame of mind, when on opening his tent flap the following morning before the sun was up, he noticed a small printed paper lying near by on the frost-covered ground. He picked it up, and found it to be a leaflet from a Dutch hymn book, containing the following lines taken from Psalm 121: 'Geen kwaad zal u genaken, de Here zal u bewaken' [No evil shall approach you, the Lord shall guard you, Psalm 121:7]. The good President, seeing in this the hand of Providence, took courage and mentioned the incident to the men with him on commando, which likewise stimulated them to renew their efforts." Sir John Kotze, *Biographical Memoirs and Reminiscences* (Cape Town, n.d.), p. 793, quoted in Scholtz, *President J. H. Brand,* p. 53.

40. C. 4140 of 1869, pp. 44, 78. Cf. *Basutoland Records,* III, 892.

41. Theal, *History of South Africa,* VI, 268f; cf. Leyds, *First Annexation,* p. 111.

42. *De Tijd,* August 22, November 4, 1868; quoted in J. A. van Jaarsveld, "Die Afrikaner se Geskiedsbeeld," *Mededelings van die Universiteit van Suid Afrika,* Pretoria: Part VI (1958), p. 71.

43. C. 4140 of 1869, April 9, 1868, p. 68; December 16, 1868, p. 78.

44. C. 99 of 1870, p. 3. He died March 11, 1870.

45. C. 459 of 1871, p. 22.

46. *Ibid.,* pp. 29-30.

47. *Ibid.,* p. 37.

48. *Ibid.,* p. 37.

49. C. 732 of 1873, July 21, 1871, p. 19.

50. C. 459 of 1871, p. 161.

51. To the Earl of Kimberly, July 26, 1871, C. 508 of 1872, p. 6.

52. C. 508 of 1872, pp. 33-34.

53. *Ibid.,* p. 49.

54. C. 732 of 1873, p. 20.

55. See, for example, Augustus F. Lindley, *Adamantia: The Truth about the South African Diamond Fields* (London: Collingridge, 1973), where he analyzes the "false evidence" used by Britain to confiscate land not actually its own. Lindley, a British subject, concluded that Britain was completely wrong and the Boers were correct in their claim. James A. Froude, who traveled in South Africa in 1874, called this incident "perhaps the most discreditable in the annals of English Colonial History." He

argued that the British should have been frank to say they took the diamond fields because of economic motives; rather, they "poisoned the wound" by attempting to make a case as "protectors of the rights of native tribes." James Anthony Froude, *Oceana: or England and Her Colonies* (London: Longmans, Green & Co., 1886), pp. 46-47.

56. C. 508 of 1872, p. 4, August 15, 1871.

57. Scholtz, *President J. H. Brand*, pp. 182-187.

58. C. 4190 of 1884, p. 3.

59. T. N. Hanekom, *Die Liberale Rigting in Suid Afrika: 'n Kerkhistoriese Studie* (Stellenbosch: Die   Christen-Studentenvereniging-Maatskappy van Suid-Afrika, 1951), p. 59.

60. The theological school in Stellenbosch was established in 1859 specifically to counteract liberalism from European countries. Sheila Patterson, *The Last Trek: A Study of the Boer People and the Afrikaner Nation* (London: Routledge & Kegan Paul, 1957), p. 187.

61. du Plessis, *Andrew Murray*, p. 213.

62. Walker, *History of Southern Africa*, p. 300.

63. Hanekom, *Liberale Rigting*, p. 442.

64. Malherbe, *Education in South Africa*, pp. 235-236.

65. du Plessis, *Andrew Murray*, p. 223.

66. *Ibid.*, p. 224. Cf. C. 732 of 1873, p. 84; cf. S. P. Engelbrecht, *Thomas Francois Burgers: 'n Lewenskets* (Pretoria: J. H. de Bussy, 1933).

67. Malherbe, *Education in South Africa*, pp. 236-248.

68. Looking back on the situation, Burgers analyzed the problem. "The clerical faction . . . was active in seducing the people. Slips were printed and distributed, everyone was roused in the name of God and religion to abandon the Liberal President. Faint-hearted friends were induced to sit quiet while a constant cross-fire of lies was kept up and the pulpit degraded into a political catapult." Engelbrecht, *T. F. Burgers*, p. 191.

69. Kruger wrote to Joubert, November 7, 1876, in Engelbrecht, *T. F. Burgers*, p. 192: "You are aware that I had opposed the President's election, and you also know the reasons for it. I feared his liberalism which might cause the fall of Christianity. In particular did I fear that the Education Act was a state measure which could deprive the Church of the children, who in turn would receive a secular education. During the last session, however, a motion by the President was adopted, whereby the children were returned to the Church. The cloud has thus vanished."

70. Marjorie Juta, *The Pace of the Ox: The Life of Paul Kruger* (London: Constable and Co., 1937), p. 140.

71. H. Rider Haggard, *History of the Transvaal* (New York: New Amsterdam Book Co., 1900), pp. 77-78.

72. *Ibid.*

73. *Ibid.*

74. C. 1776 of 1877, pp. 1-2.

75. Burgers' speech to Volksraad before annexation, published separately as a pamphlet by the *Volksstem*, Pretoria. Now in the State Archives, Pretoria.

76. *Ibid.*

77. Cf. Engelbrecht, *President T. F. Burgers.*

78. Eybers, *Select Constitutional Documents*, pp. 448-453.

79. *Ibid.*

80. *Ibid.* "I have been satisfied by numerous addresses, memorials, and letters which I have received . . . a large proportion of the inhabitants of the Transvaal . . . earnestly desire the establishment within and over it of Her Majesty's authority and rule."

81. *Ibid.*

82. *Ibid.*

83. Engelbrecht, *President T. F. Burgers*, p. 287.

84. This distinction is drawn by Spoelstra in *Doppers*, p. 16.

85. F. A. van Jaarsveld, in *The Awakening of Afrikaner Nationalism, 1868-1881* (Cape Town: Human and Rousseau, 1961), has studied thoroughly the development of this nationalism, which began, as he shows, at the time of the British reversal of the Sand River Convention and the annexation of the once-free Boer state, the South African Republic (Transvaal), between 1868 and 1877.

86. This was Joubert's statement in C. 2505 of 1880, pp. 113-114.

87. April 11, 1877, in Eybers, *Select Constitutional Documents*, pp. 447-448.

88. Engelbrecht, *President T. F. Burgers*, p. 332.

89. A petition from the Transvaal had arrived in England with these words: "Said deputation represents only a small minority of the influential inhabitants of the country." Dated Transvaal, June 9, 1877, in C. 1883 of 1877, p. 23.

90. For example, a petition signed by 527 individuals, including leaders of the Volksraad, went to great lengths to convince Carnarvon of what he secretely hoped. Cf. C. 1883 of 1877, pp. 11-12, written June 5, 1877. Sir Bartle Frere, the newly arrived British official in Natal, reported: "It would be very difficult at the present moment to find in the Transvaal anyone to avow a wish averse to the acceptance of the annexation as the best solution of their difficulties, and as a fact that everyone recognized and desired to remain as irrevocable." C. 1883 of 1877, pp. 15-16, June 12, 1877. Shepstone, as administrator of the Transvaal, reported that he was impressed at "the general feelings of acquiescence, relief, and satisfaction with which the announcement was received throughout the whole territory." He wrote to express "admission of the fact that there has been no expression of opinion in the Transvaal itself, from any class whatever, indicating the slightest desire to undo what has been done." C. 1883 of 1887, p. 15, dated June 12, 1877.

91. J. F. van Oordt, *Paul Kruger en de Opkomst der Zuid-Afrikaansche Republiek* (Amsterdam: Jacques Dusseau, 1898), p. 188.

92. Kruger, *Memoirs,* p. 127.

93. C. 2100 of 1878, p. 29.

94. Letter January 31, 1878, in van Oordt, *Paul Kruger,* pp. 193-194.

95. March 11, 1878, in C. 2100 of 1878, pp. 83-84.

96. C. 2128 of 1878, p. 9.

97. van Oordt, *Paul Kruger,* p. 202.

98. C. 2220 of 1879, p. 365. Further correspondence concerning the London visit is to be found in C. 2220 of 1879, pp. 361-365; in Dutch in van Oordt, *Paul Kruger,* pp. 218-239; and in C. 2128 of 1878, pp. 1-19.

99. van Oordt, *Paul Kruger,* p. 243.

100. *Ibid.,* p. 244.

101. John Martineau, *Life and Letters of Frere* (2 vols., London: J. Murray, 1895), II, 307.

102. Published in the *Zuid Afrikaan,* February 15, 1879; translated in C. 2316 of 1879, pp. 1-2.

103. March 18, 1879; van Oordt, *Paul Kruger,* pp. 250-251.

104. C. 2367 of 1879, pp. 79, 86; van Oordt, *Paul Kruger,* p. 255; Martineau, *Frere Letters,* II, 291.

105. van Oordt, *Paul Kruger,* p. 257.

106. Frere's letter to Hicks-Beach, May 2, 1879, in Martineau, *Frere Letters,* II, 306.

107. Martineau, *Frere Letters*, p. 309.

108. Koolfontein, April 16, 1879, in C. 2367 of 1879, p. 99.

109. van Oordt, *Paul Kruger*, p. 281, November 16, 1879.

110. Martineau, *Frere Letters*, II, 361, December 2, 1879.

111. A witness at Pretorius' trial, in C. 2584 of 1880, p. 45.

112. C. 2505 of 1880, pp. 113-114, December 10-11, 1879.

113. *Ibid.*

114. *Ibid.*

115. *Ibid.*

116. Kruger, *Memoirs*, p. 141.

117. C. 2505 of 1880, p. 118, December 12, 1880.

118. C. 2505 of 1880, pp. 111-112; Wolseley was speaking December 17, 1879.

119. C. 2584 of 1880, p. 44. Proceedings of the trial of Pretorius are in C. 2584 of 1880, pp. 43-48.

120. C. 2584 of 1880, p. 43, January 16, 1880.

121. So stated a trial witness, in *ibid.*, p. 46.

122. C. 2676 of 1880, p. 46B.

123. F. A. van Jaarsveld has argued conclusively that it was in this period that Afrikaner nationalism reaching outside the borders of one Boer nation was first developed. Cf. van Jaarsveld, *Awakening of Afrikaner Nationalism*.

124. *Die Patriot*, June 15, 1877; quoted in F. A. van Jaarsveld, *Die Afrikaner en sy Geskiedenis* (Cape Town: Nasionale Boekhandel, 1959), p. 94.

125. C. 2454 of 1879, pp. 105-106, May 9, 1879.

126. *Ibid.*, pp. 54-55, April 18, 1879.

127. C. 2482 of 1880, p. 444.

128. *Ibid.*, pp. 446-447.

129. *Ibid.*, p. 448.

130. *Ibid.*, p. 449.

131. *Ibid.*, pp. 450-451.

132. *Ibid.*, p. 453.

133. C. 2783 of 1881, pp. 61-65.

134. *Ibid.*, pp. 68-71.

135. *Ibid.*, p. 73, December 24, 1880.

136. *Ibid.*, p. 75, December, 1880.

137. *Ibid.*, p. 72, December 23, 1880. The war had begun a week before this date.

138. Thomas Fortescue Carter, *A Narrative of the Boer War, Its Causes and Results* (London: John MacQueen, 1896), p. 98.

139. In a speech President Burgers had said, "Public meetings had been held in presence of members of the Volksraad, where it had been unanimously resolved not to pay taxes." This was February 20, 1877, before the annexation. Also cf. C. 3782 of 1881, p. 46.

140. Carter, *Narrative of the Boer War*, p. 105.

141. *Ibid.*, p. 107.

142. The *Volkstem*, December 14, 1880, quoted in van Jaarsveld, *Die Afrikaner en sy Geskiedenis*, p. 134.

143. The Petition of Rights was issued February 7, 1881, and is in C. 2866 of 1881, pp. 169-176.

144. "We now had to admit that it was of no use appealing to England, because there was no one to hear us. Trusting in the Almighty God of righteousness and justice, we armed ourselves for an apparently hopeless struggle in the firm conviction that whether we conquered or whether we died, the sun of freedom in South Africa would arise out of the morning mists." *Century of Wrong*, 1900, p. 32.

145. van Oordt, *Paul Kruger*, p. 299.

146. *Ibid.*, p. 304.

147. *Ibid.*, p. 304.

148. *Ibid.*, p. 306.

149. *Ibid.*, pp. 307-312.

150. *Ibid.*, pp. 311-312.

151. C. 2794 of 1881, p. 9.

152. Carter, *Narrative of the Boer War*, p. 116; Lanyon's analysis of the beginning of the war is in C. 2838 of 1881, pp. 4-5.

153. Lanyon's analysis of the beginning of the war, C. 2838 of 1881, pp. 4-5.

154. Kruger and the triumvirate wrote from Heidelberg, December 23, 1880, in C. 2794 of 1881, p. 11.

155. *De Express*, February 9, 1882, quoted in van Jaarsveld, *Afrikaner's Interpretation*, p. 56.

156. C. 2783 of 1881, pp. 70-71.

157. *Ibid.*, p. 67.

158. *Ibid.*, pp. 68-69, December 24, 1880.

159. Carter, *Narrative of the Boer War*, pp. 150-151.

160. *Ibid.*, p. 155.

161. *Ibid.*, p. 173.

162. *Ibid.*, p. 300.

163. *Ibid.*, p. 301.

164. John Morley, *The Life of William Ewart Gladstone* (3 vols., London: Macmillan Co., 1903), III, 32.

165. C. 2783 of 1881, p. 57; cf. Eric A. Walker, *Lord de Villiers and His Times: South Africa, 1843-1914* (London: Constable and Company, 1925), pp. 151-152.

166. C. 2783 of 1881, pp. 6, 8, 10, 77.

167. C. 2866 of 1881, pp. 186-187, February 12, 1881.

168. Potchefstroom, February 19, 1881, signed by 645 individuals, in Carter, *Narrative of the Boer War*, p. 242.

169. C. 2866 of 1881, pp. 168, 187-188, February 23, 1881.

170. Carter, *Narrative of the Boer War*, p. 330.

171. C. 2837 of 1881, p. 29; C. 2892 of 1881, pp. 1-6.

172. C. 2837 of 1881, pp. 16, 23; C. 2950 of 1881, pp. 84-85; C. 3219 of 1882, p. 71.

173. *The Patriot*, quoted in Theophilus Lyndall Schreiner, *The Afrikander Bond and Other Causes of the War* (London: Spottiswoode and Co., 1901), p. 20.

174. *Staats-Courant van den Vrijheidsoorlog*, 1881, Pretoria, pp. 53-54.

175. *Die Volksstem*, August 10, 1881.

176. Reitz, *Century of Wrong*, p. 32.

177. Article II of the Convention of Pretoria, August 8, 1811, in Eybers, *Select Constitutional Documents*, pp. 455-457; C. 2998 of 1881, pp. 108; *Century of Wrong*, Appendix E, pp. 130-139.

178. Eybers, *Select Constitutional Documents*, p. 463.

179 C. 3381 of 1882, p. 30, September 21, 1881; cf. van Oordt, *Paul Kruger*, pp. 364-365.

180. Engelbrecht, *T. F. Burgers*, p. 161.   The burghers of Kroonstad wrote to the Transvaal leaders, December 21, 1881, subsequently published in the *Volksstem*.

181. Leyds, *First Annexation of the Transvaal*, pp. 332-333.

182. C. 3098 of 1882, p. 150.

183. *Ibid.*, p. 152.

184. *Ibid.*, pp. 150-159; December 13-14, 1881.

185. *Ibid.*, pp. 150-159, December 13, 1881.

VI.
Continued Frustration, 1881–1895

In 1881 the South African Republic (Transvaal) again was at peace with Britain, but it was a peace based on mutual misunderstanding. The British underestimated the Boers' determination for an absolute independence unrelated in any way to British authority and on this basis wrote the Convention of Pretoria. This document came under immediate suspicion as Boers began agitation to modify several sections. Furthermore, confident in the correctness of their cause and encouraged once again by what they interpreted as direct signs from God, the Boers disregarded sections of the convention and attempted to expand their restored Zion. The British retaliated in each case. Neither power could have foreseen, however, the increased complexity that would be posed because of an unknown factor in South African relations—gold. Consequently, the peace of 1881 was no settlement but merely a suspension of conflict beginning an interval during which time added complications developed.

Even before the peace was negotiated, there was unrest and reaction. On February 7, 1881, the Boers indicated the direction their thoughts were taking when the triumvirate wrote to President Brand of the Free State what became an important statement of the Boer objectives. In their Petition of Right when they called for rejection of the British yoke, they declared:

> We lay our case before the whole world, be it that we conquer
> or that we die, liberty shall rise in South Africa like the sun
> from the morning clouds, as freedom rose in the United States
> of America. Then shall it be Africa for the Afrikander, from
> the Zambezi to Simon's Bay.[1]

Further evidence of heightened theological-nationalist feelings was noted by observers. A citizen of the Free State, for example, stated, "I consider and believe that this land is the land ordained by God since time began in which we should wage our final fight for freedom."[2]   The Rev. Andrew Murray, now minister at Wellington in the Cape Colony, observed

> how strongly the feeling of nationality is asserting itself and mingling with the religious sentiment of the people. . . . The development of a strong national life among our half-slumbering Dutch population will offer a stronger race in which the Christian life can be inspired.[3]

Two means for developing such strengthened group consciousness among the Afrikaners were emphasized at this time. The first of these was education in the language of the Afrikaner. They developed a yearning for Afrikaner historiography, retelling the stories of the heroes of the past and inspiring the present generation: "It is high time that our children in school are taught in their own tongue the glorious history of the land of their birth. . . . Long enough we have received stones for bread, serpents for fish, and scorpions for eggs."[4] The second emphasis toward renewed group consciousness came when the triumvirate reestablished what it considered an adequate educational system in the Transvaal. One of the conservative reactions against President Burgers was at the point of educational policy. Kruger now stated the conservative idea:

> School education must be under the guidance of the Church. The Government does not want to establish *State* Schools; they must be Church schools. . . . I not only see no harm in giving of doctrinal instruction during school hours, but I am strongly in favor of it, because it will contribute toward conciliation between the different denominations.[5]

To implement the new church-directed school system, the triumvirate in 1881 invited the Rev. S. J. du Toit, leader of the Afrikaner Bond in Paarl, Cape Colony to be the superintendent of education, a post he held from 1882 to 1891.[6] His educational philosophy included a glorification of the Boer heroes and a reiteration of their exploits as signs of God's work among the faithful Afrikaners. Hence the theologically oriented politics of Kruger and others was reinforced by the theologically oriented education of the Bond leader. The government acted on its presupposition that the elect people of God must be faithful to God's will, as they understood it, in all areas of life.

Later that year the Transvaal Volksraad began to discuss the ratification of the Convention of Pretoria. This was signed August 3, 1881, by all three of the triumvirate, but in the September *Volksraad*, questions were raised on two points. First, the Boer leaders had understood from the terms of peace offered in March that the British suzerain would be given supervision (*toezicht*) of foreign affairs, but now in the Convention of Pretoria the suzerain was to have "control" of external relations of the Transvaal.[7] In this light many Boers wondered exactly what they had won in the war. This led to the second misunderstanding. The suzerain, they were told, had authority to approve or reject laws passed by the Volksraad. They questioned this because the suzerain was a foreigner and could not act wisely with respect to local laws. This was the case especially with laws pertaining to the relationship to the Africans, for England had already proved to be unsympathetic with the Boers' presuppositions of superiority in these matters.[8]

The Volksraad embodied these objections in a telegram sent to the colonial secretary in London, asking for modifications.[9] The British government replied that no change could be made before the convention was ratified. Kruger, again a mediator, urged the Volksraad to ratify now then to press for needed changes. He said in effect: "You have two choices: approve the Convention or we go back to Laing's Nek" to war.[10] Many were tempted to choose the latter alternative.[11] Kruger did not disagree with the major objectives of the Volksraad members, but he took a longer view of the problem. Throughout the remainder of the century, the Boers sought ways to eliminate the last vestige of subjection to British government, but they found frustration on all sides and became more and more defensive. They slowly came to realize that Britian did not intend to release its hold on the Transvaal but rather sought ways to strengthen its authority.

The general trends of the next few years were suggested by Kruger during the election campaign of 1883. The authority for governing the country had been vested in the triumvirate following the armistice, but many believed that a well-organized state should have a duly elected president. An election was planned to be held between January 15 and February 15, 1883. The two candidates were Paul Kruger and the second person of the triumvirate, Piet Joubert. J. H. Hofmeyr, the highly respected parlimentarian of the Cape Colony and a leading figure among Cape Afrikaners, was suggested as a third candidate, but nothing developed from this suggestion. He was an Afrikaner, but a moderate, and the Transvaal wanted nothing but an orthodox Dopper leader who would be extremely pro-Transvaal and anti-British.[12]

Kruger and Joubert each made speeches explaining his concept of the state's needs and the objectives he would seek if elected. Kruger's summary of the problems proved to be the main challenges he had faced for almost twenty years. All was done, however, with the assumption that God was leading the nation and would help the people choose the right leader. He reminded the people again of their past heroes and their evidence of God's leadership when he suggested: "We as a republic, have been reared on the roots of our own folk history, with due recognition of God's leadership in the past. These memories going back to our beginnings inspire in us a united striving for national growth."[13]

Kruger predicted three problems they would face: transportation and the problem of railroads, immigration, and the relations between political powers in South Africa. He made some comments about each:

> It is necessary that our transportation be improved, not only by improvements of roads and opening new ones, but above all we need a direct railroad connection to the sea, especially a railroad from Pretoria to Delagoa Bay. I hold this to be a live question for the Republic, and I have promise of a speedy completion with cooperation of the Portuguese government. I shall work for this with all the power which our young republic has at its disposal.[14]

He envisaged gradual immigration from Holland, but could not have known that the major immigration of the next decade would be neither gradual nor Dutch. Rather, it was a veritable flood of Englishmen:

> I am for immigration. Our sparsely populated land has a need for this, but under certain conditions. To begin with this stream of imigrants must not be too strong, so that there would be a danger that our nationality would thereby be over-run. The influx of new blood must be strengthened to such an extent that they can rather become identified with our nationality.[15]

The relations with England as well as with other South African nations were hinted at:

> I shall do all within my power to remain in peaceful coopera-tion with the Suzerain power of Great Britain and her repre-sentative here, as long as such can be done without offending the dearly-bought rights of the Republic. I shall constantly lend my support to any attempt to establish a new relationship between the states and colonies of South Africa, yet without giving up the rights and freedom of the Republic.[16]

He repeated the theological terminology to instill loyalty and group feeling among the hearers:

> Our Republic is born, reborn and bound together under all types of dangers and difficulties; our people are what they are be-cause of clear leading by a Higher Hand. Our most noteworthy evidence is our recent struggle for right and freedom. There-fore it is the holy duty of our people to continue to honor God's name and to follow His Word.[17]

In a Calvinistic manner, the state and church were to be coequal agencies, alike under God's leadership. Neither was to be subject to the other:

The political leader, who also wants authority in the Church of Christ, is animated with the spirit of anti-Christ, for Christ is the head of His Church and He has entrusted the leadership of the church to his disciples under the guidance of the Holy Spirit, not under the worldly authority.[18]

He concluded his preelection speech by placing the outcome in the hands of God and His chosen people: "Hoping that our trustworthy God, who has thus far so graciously helped us through all things, shall also lead our people to His Will in the choice of their state President and leader, I lay the choice in your hands."[19] Kruger was elected a three-to-one favorite.[20]

During the first Volksraad after the election, dissatisfaction with the Pretoria Convention was again voiced. After receiving a telegram from the new colonial secretary, the earl of Derby, suggesting that some adjustments were possible in the convention, the Boers sent a delegation to London to discuss differences. The three representatives were President Kruger, S. J. du Toit, the Bond leader now superintendent of education in Transvaal, and Nicholas Jacobus Smith, Volksraad member and hero of the recent Transvaal war.[21] They left Transvaal August 1883, arriving in London three months later.

The discussions in London centered on foreign relations and suzerainty. In the Convention of London, signed February 27, 1884, the Transvaal delegates were assured of certain concessions, at least on paper.[22] *Consul* was substituted for *suzerain* in the agreement. The debt the Transvaal owed to Britain was reduced. The title *South African Republic* was restored in place of *Transvaal*, the designation the British had given to the land across the Vaal. The Boers were also allowed to conduct their own relations with the Africans, within certain limits, and to continue the pass laws. Two other portions of the London Convention, identical with sections of the earlier Pretoria Convention, were the sources of much misunderstanding in the next few years. The fourth section includes the words: "The South African Republic will conclude no treaty or engagement with any state or nation other than the Orange Free State, nor with any native tribe to the eastward or westward of the Republic, until the same has been approved by Her Majesty the Queen."[23] A portion of the fourteenth article reads:

All persons, other than natives, conforming themselves to the laws of the South African Republic . . . will not be subject, in respect of their persons or property, or in respect of their commerce or industry, to any taxes, whether general or local, other than those which are or may be imposed upon citizens of the said Republic.[24]

While one objective of the delegation's visit to Europe had been concluded in London, another lay before them. The Transvaal needed other friends in Europe, especially help to build the railway to the east. Consequently, after the signing of the convention in London, the delegation made its way to Edinburgh, Amsterdam, Paris, Madrid, Lisbon, Antwerp, and finally to Berlin.

In the Netherlands they were feted as compatriots, as *onze Broeders te Zuid Afrika* ("our brothers of South Africa"). They had maintained the Dutch *Taal* ("tongue") whereas Dutch settlers of Australia, America, and the East Indies had ceased to use the language.[25] Reflecting the recent war, the Dutch leaders played on the emotions of the visitors: "Freedom and independence were not merely exalted slogans with you, but were deeply felt hopes that you might live according to your own insight and responsible to your own laws according to God's decree."[26]

The delegation responded in like spirit. Smit stated that the Transvaal had won the war by remembering many times the eighty-year struggle the Dutch had waged for their freedom (1568-1648).[27] Reflecting feelings more deeply entrenched in South Africa than the newly won concessions of the London Convention, du Toit answered on behalf of the deputation. He suggested that in Paul Kruger the whole history of the republic was embodied in one person and continued with the warning: "Sometime the South African flag shall wave from Table Bay to the Zambezi, whether this must be accomplished by ink or by blood. If by blood it must be, we shall not lack the men to spill it."[28]

In Lisbon the discussion revolved around the question of the railway to the sea at Delagoa Bay (Lourenco Marques, now Maputo), in Portuguese territory. The Portuguese agreed to cooperate.[29] Then the delegates went back to the Netherlands to seek finances for what ultimately became the Netherlands South African Railway Company. The plan moved slowly for several years. The delegation then met Bismarck in Germany and began to develop the friendship that gave the republic courage in their anti-British actions in the next few decades.[30]

They returned to Cape Town in July 1884 reporting two weeks later to the Volksraad in Pretoria that a new day was dawning for their republic. Indeed, Kruger thought that "the Suzerainty has fallen," and he was supported by newspapers from Germany and the Netherlands but not in the English press.[31] With Kruger's interpretation, the Volksraad ratified the Convention of London on August 8, 1884. They assumed they had complete independence as a true republic. The British did not carry the assumption so far, however, as they merely negotiated certain points hoping to restore good feelings on the South African frontier before continuing their drive for a South African confederation.

Kruger then related his experiences in Europe and discussed the railway question. Interestingly some objected to the plan. They reasoned that this much-needed modernization would be evil because it would drive some ox wagon drivers out of work. Kruger again used his ability to persuade when he first admitted that he could do nothing without the approval of the people for the president is only "the mouth-piece of the people," but "the State must and shall with the Lord's help, push forward without undermining the authority of the people."[32] He persuaded them to vote favorably by arguing from the need for economic advantages in their developing state.

The president believed that ultimately he was responsible to God for the conduct of the state. All of his actions had some bearing on the future of the Transvaal depending on whether God's will was discovered and fulfilled. In the Volksraad a year later, he summarized his concept of the close relation between the church and the state:

> All citizens are members of the church in this land, and all are united in the faith. The Christian builds on the foundation of the church; the state is built on the Church. We are upheld by the Church and no one can deny this. . . . It is only just and right that we should protect the church; . . . for if one hinders the church, he also harms the state.[33]

If they failed God, the nation would be weakened. His very forceful—and at times repressive—leadership of the next two decades must be seen against his view of himself and of his responsibility for his nation under God. Already there were complications arising that gave evidence of Kruger's principal objectives but at the same time caused increased conflict with British plans in South Africa. Kruger's concept of God's election was closely associated with maintaining the integrity of the Transvaal government against several attempts by Britain to frustrate the Transvaal.

The western, eastern and northern boundaries of the Transvaal were areas of contention for many years. In all three directions, the attempted expansion of the Transvaal was frustrated, and within little over a decade Britain had control of all the disputed areas. In 1868 President Pretorius had proclaimed Transvaal territory west as far as a line from Lake Ngami south to the Langeberg Mountains. This would have placed almost all of Bechuanaland (now Botswana) under Transvaal authority.[34] In 1871, after further disturbances, Pretorius consented to arbitration by the lieutenant governor of Natal, Robert W. Keate. This resulted in the Keate Award, which the Volksraad rejected and which in turn caused the downfall of Pretorius' presidency.[35] Both the Conventions of 1881 and 1884 suggested boundaries increasingly favorable to the Transvaal, but they could not be enforced.

Many Boers had migrated to the area outside the Transvaal to the west, and in 1882 and 1883 established two republics for which they asked Transvaal protection. These were "the land of Goshen" on the north and "Stellaland" on the south.[36] British interests were threatened so the Cape Town government sent the Rev. John Mackenzie, a former missionary in Bechuanaland, as mediator.[37] Following his failure a younger, but more forceful British official became the mediator—Cecil Rhodes. Rhodes argued that the British should annex all of Bechuanaland, including Land of Goshen and Stellaland, for otherwise the "Suez Canal to South Central Africa" would fall to a foreign government.[38] Some assumed that the Boers wanted to continue their republic west to the Atlantic Ocean to join the German settlement at Angra Pequena (Lüderitzbucht), in South West Africa (now Namibia).[39]

The Boers and British authorities were near the point of armed conflict when in September 1885 Britain followed Rhodes' suggestion and proclaimed all Bechuanaland, including the two infant republics, British territory.[40] The pro-English population was pleased; the majority, from the Transvaal, were disillusioned. The Dutch language was outlawed, and those who wished to remain were required to become subjects of Britain. Many Boers abandoned the area.[41]

The solution of the western boundary question in favor of British interests was a frustrating experience for Kruger. He had hoped to establish peaceful relations with the Africans and the immigrants in the west and thus to strengthen his struggling nation in the eyes of the world. The defeat of his vision in the west caused him to look instead to the east, where he considered the coastal area between Natal and the Portuguese port of Delagoa Bay. The area was peopled with the Zulu tribes, remnants from the opponents of the first trekkers into Natal when their king was Dingane. Boers who possessed land in the Zulu territory organized a government led by Lucas Johannes Meyer, and on August 16, 1894, declared the "New Republic" duly constituted.[42]

British officials assumed that this was part of a major plan for Transvaal to reach the sea.[43] Germany had annexed the west coast of southern Africa in May 1884, and there were rumors that it was interested in Zululand.[44] Cooperation with the Germans would have strengthened the Boers' position against England. Britain immediately reacted and in December 1884 hoisted its flag at St. Lucia Bay north of Natal, a likely goal of Boer expansion, and in May 1887 annexed the whole of Zululand, excluding the section known as the New Republic, which remained part of Transvaal territory.[45] The South African Republic was frustrated in another attempt to expand and failed to secure a seaport.

The last attempt to expand to the east concerned the area of Swaziland. For many years Boers had infiltrated into the area of the Swazis to find additional pasture. In 1886 British settlers discovered gold in the area.[46] By 1890 it was estimated that among Europeans in the area, three-fourths were Boers.[47] Would the mining rights of the British or the grazing rights of the Boers predominate? Transvaal decided that it should annex the area and petitioned British authorities accordingly.[48] The latter objected, however, and several conferences were held, in 1890, 1893, and 1894. Britain then annexed the strip of territory to the east of Swaziland, controlled by two independent tribal leaders.[49] It also extended a protectorate over the last bit of coastline between Zululand and Portuguese territory, assuming control of Tongaland on May 30, 1895.[50] Including the settlement of Rhodesia (Zimbabwe) along the north, the South African Republic was completely surrounded by the British Empire and was cut off from the sea forever. Their only contact with the outside world would be by way of railroads, two of which led to ports where Britain controlled the tariffs.

Two internal developments did much to complicate the theological image in South Africa during the 1880s. First, the awakening of Afrikaners to their own political responsibility, especially in the Cape Colony, up to now heavily dominated by leaders of English background. This was not without its theological overtones and pious justifications. Second, the Transvaal, and in turn, the whole of South Africa, experienced an economic revolution centering around gold. Both internal factors challenged Kruger's almost undisputed one-man rule—critics called it "Krugerism"—in the Transvaal. Kruger's reaction was to reiterate his theological concerns for God-given culture as he understood it. These concerns in the South African Republic and developments among other sections of the Afrikaners are the basis for the increased Afrikaner nationalism late in the nineteenth century.

Sympathies for the Transvaal Boers before and during the war of 1880 led Afrikaners in all parts of South Africa to a feeling of oneness. This was enhanced by their religious attitudes of uniqueness in the sight of God. There were at least four aspects of this new nationalism.

The first aspect concerned the Afrikaner Bond, organized in 1879 in the Cape Colony by the Rev. S. J. du Toit and his brother D. F. du Toit. Most Afrikaners resented the predominance of the English language but were not united enough to oppose it. In the 1870s the du Toits formed the *Afrikaner Taal Bewegung* (Afrikaner Language Movement) and *de Genootskap van regter Afrikaners* (the Society of true Afrikaners) "to stand for our language, our nation and our people."[51] S. J. du Toit suggested that God placed Afrikaners in Africa and gave them the Afrikaans language.[52] This nationalist spirit was circulated among the people by *Die Afrikaanse Patriot,* a newspaper published at Cape Town from 1876 by Daniel F. du Toit.

These movements helped to solidify the ultranationalist spirit previously so segmented that it had had no effective voice. It was anti-British and looked to the day when British influence, represented by their flag, should disappear completely from South Africa. The language desired by this nationalist group was Cape Dutch (Afrikaans), whereas a sizable group

of Afrikaners wished to retain high Dutch and also to retain close connections with the Netherlands. This narrow nationalism is not fully developed
in the rules of organization first published by S. J. du Toit on July 4,
1879,[53] but the true spirit was expressed by his brother in the *Patriot*
shortly after the war was concluded:

> The Transvaal war is now happily over. While we now sing
> praises to God for His deliverance and the victory of our
> brethren, and the restoration of pure and righteous government
> . . . can we better employ our thoughts than by considering
> what we have already gained by the war and what we may yet
> further gain by it?
>
> England's power has been repeatedly beaten and humbled.
> The little respect which an Afrikaner still had for British
> troops and cannon is utterly done away . England has learned
> so much respect for us Afrikaners that she will take care not
> to make war on us again. Think of it: no English soldier had
> the honor to set his foot on Transvaal ground. . . .
>
> The Transvaalers have now got what they wanted, and what
> they for four years vainly solicited from England, namely, the
> revocation of the annexation. . . .
>
> The Free State shall now also remain a free State, and
> England must now keep her claws off from the Transvaal long
> enough for us Afrikanders to recover strength a little and pull
> things to rights.
>
> The Afrikaners have now a little time and opportunity to
> develop themselves as a people. . . .
>
> This is now our time to establish the Bond, while a national
> consciousness has been awakened through the Transvaal war.
> The Bond must be our preparation for the future confederation
> of all the states and colonies of South Africa. The English
> Government keeps talking of a confederation under the British
> flag. That will never happen. We can assure them of that. We
> have often said it; there is just one hindrance to confederation,
> and that is the English flag. Let them take that away, and
> within a year the confederation under the free Afrikaner flag
> would be established.
>
> As long as the English flag remains here, the Afrikander
> Bond must be our confederation.[54]

These nationalist Afrikaner organizations are significant because they
provided a means whereby Afrikaners could express themselves and in turn
could read of the feelings of their compatriots in various parts of the
land. As such these were significant developments toward a full-blown
nationalism and held out a warning to the almost unchallenged British
domination of the Cape Colony.

The Bond, organized in the Free State by Judge Francis William Reitz, later president of the Free State, and the German Carl Borckenhagen, was not completely welcome there.[55] President Brand had worked among the English and did not share the Bond's insistence that the British contribution to South Africa was only negative.[56] The administration of the Transvaal, however, was so completely in sympathy with the Anglophobia of the Bond that there was little need for organizing the Bond as a separate movement. The Transvaal government indicated its sympathy with the movement when the triumvirate invited S. J. du Toit to become part of the Transvaal government immediately after the war. Henceforth the Bond had sympathizers in all parts of South Africa but was most thoroughly organized and most active in the Cape Colony.

The second aspect of theological nationalism was the appearance in 1877 of S. J. du Toit's *Geskiedenis van ons Land,* the first history of the Afrikaners in their own language.[57] The book was widely circulated immediately after the war. To be sure, it evinced a pro-Boer bias and a type of pious nationalism; nevertheless, it provides insight into the attitudes of many Boers of the period. Patriotic Boers could read and reminisce about God's concern at the time their slaves were freed (1835):

> Be quiet! "God meant it to be good" [Gen. 50:20]. Unexpected and out of time—in the heart of the summer—our Dear Lord, who manages everything so wisely, allows 8 consecutive days of rain, such as has happened never before nor since that time in the Colony. Then the freed slaves could not wander around so much in troops; they had to go to work again in order to buy food; most of them went back to their old bosses to offer themselves for hire; that was better for boss and boy, and however much was wrong in the way in which the English government freed the slaves today we thank the Lord that He arranged it all so wisely.[58]

They were also presented with an emotional story of the insurrection at Slagters' Nek (1815):

> Weep, Afrikaners! Here lies your flesh and blood; martyred in the cruellest manner. Wrong was it to rebel against their government; but truly they did not do it without reason! Wrong it was to take up arms; but only because they were too weak! Guilty they were, says the earthly Judge! But what shall the Heavenly Judge say some time?
> But come! It is getting darker! Come, if we sit here too long, then we too shall be regarded as conspirators! Come— another day will dawn—then we shall perhaps see the grave in another light! Come, we go home with a quiet sigh![59]

The Great Trek played its part in the drama of the heroes:

The trekking-out of the Boers is certainly one of the most significant happenings in the history of the colony under the English. What Afrikaner is there whose heart-beat does not rise when he reflects on the events of the Great Trek? There is none who carries the name Afrikander who can remain cool as he reads of the oppression, unlawfulness and the wretchedness which the poor Boers endured. This is not to be minimized, for no less than 6,000 quiet and peaceful persons felt it necessary to leave all their possessions and go into the wilderness land to find a new home.[60]

Later there was grievance concerning the Boer loss of Basutoland. The writer expressed the bitterness of the Boers after the British had ended the war between the Basutos and the Boers and had declared the Basutos were their subjects:

Look! What then comes to pass? Yes, ask it! Hear and understand! The English government first breaks Article VIII of the Convention [Convention of Bloemfontein, 1854] and prohibited the purchase of arms and ammunition by the Free State. Then, even easier, they broke Article II of the Convention, and on 12 March, 1868, took the Basutos under their wing—English wings——and made them British subjects! What shall we have as our proclamation? Bismarck said it: "Might is right."[61]

We also read of the "robbery" of the diamond fields, the British occupation of Natal and Boomplaats, and several other grievances. "What hate and grudge remain between Afrikaners and Englishmen . . . shall not be forgotten quickly."[62]

The third illustration of theological nationalism appeared shortly after the book by du Toit. This was a historical tract published in Bloemfontein, Orange Free State, in 1883.[63] Although this tract has not been translated, the English title would be "The History of the Afrikaner People from 1688 to 1882." Although the date 1688 refers to the coming of French refugees to South Africa, the first section of this so-called history actually concerns the Slagters' Nek battle of 1815. This document is interesting because it shows in clear outline and in crude analogy the way biblical stories were used to help interpret various happenings in the South African past.

The author, C. P. Bezuidenhout, has the same family name as the hero of Slagers' Nek. Whether some relationship between the two exists has not been established. The man whose wagon was auctioned off in 1880 was another Bezuidenhout, the son of the hero of Slagters' Nek. C. P. Bezuidenhout began by delineating his purpose in a short foreword and then introduced the biblical reference of which he made extensive use.

It is the wish and the prayer of the author that his nation and descendants may learn the history of their people; and may gain wisdom therefrom. May they be convinced that, just as Israel of old in Egypt was planted as a vine in Canaan and protected, so also our nation, this people who came from Holland, France and Germany and were by God's Providence planted in Africa, may be preserved.[64]

The motif of the vine that God planted referred to Psalm 80:9-15, which the author quoted in full.

Thou didst bring a vine out of Egypt; thou didst drive out the nations [The Dutch here is *heidenen*—"heathen."] and plant it. Thou didst clear the ground for it; it took deep root and filled the land. The mountains were covered with its shade, the mighty cedars with its branches; it sent out its branches to the sea, and its shoots to the River. Why then hast thou broken down its walls, so that all who pass along the way pluck its fruit? The boar from the forest ravages it, and all that move in the field feed on it. Turn again, O God of hosts! Look down from heaven, and see; have regard for this vine; the stock which thy right hand planted (and upon the son whom thou hast reared for thyself). (Psalm 80:9-15).

He related other comparable Scriptures:

Open up your Bibles and read the Lord's Words: "Let me sing for my beloved a love song concerning his vineyard; my beloved had a vineyard on a very fertile hill. . . . The vineyard of the Lord of hosts is the house of Israel, and the men of Judah are his pleasant planting." (Isa. 5:1-7).[65]

Finally, he noted the comparison used in the Gospel of John where Jesus is made to say, "I am the vine and you are the branches" (John 15:5). He showed to his own satisfaction that God's people are to be compared with a vine with many branches; the branches are the faithful people who are attached to the vine, which is Jesus Christ himself. He still must show how this refers directly to South African society. That is the purpose of this treatise.

That the author equated South African experiences with those of the Old Testament is quite clear as he continued his story.

Whenever we know the history of our folk as the Psalmist knew the history of his people, should we not make the same comparison when we compare the happenings within our experience with the holy Word of God? We say: "Lord, you have brought this vine stalk over the sea from France, Germany and Holland." The Psalmist says: "You have driven the heathen [heidenen] out, and planted it." We know what the Lord has done for Israel in Canaan; He has done the same for His vine stalk of our people in Africa. Previously Africa was inhabited only with wild barbarians. A child can understand that, and no man of understanding will dispute that. The Psalmist said that God has prepared the plants and the roots have grown so as to cover the earth. Whenever we think of all the storms which have blown over this vine stalk of our people, then we are convinced of the truth that God has helped this vine stalk prosper so that the land is covered. The Psalmist said further that the mountains are covered with shadows of the vine, and the branches are as cedar trees.

Interwoven in the spirit of the history of our folk from Cape Town to Natal, and on mountain and cliff, you will find our people in the midst of roaring lions and wild barbarians, standing as cedar trees of God. Their songs of praise are reflected in forest and valley. Whenever we meet it is clear that they have been planted by God. . . .

The vine stalk was not allowed to grow too long before it was transplanted to Canaan. . . . Likewise, the vine stalk planted by God in South African soil on mountain and in valley was not allowed to grow long before passers-by began to pick the fruit. Swine out of the forest, wild beasts of the field came to root up the plants and pull the branches. . . . What the passers-by were for Old Israel, that is what the British authority is for our people in the past and even today.

The Psalmist calls the Canaanites, Jebusites and Amorites "Swine of the forest, beasts of the field" because they live in the wilderness. What they were for the vine stalk of Caanan, that is what the British government is for the people whom God brought over seas to a distant land.

Follow me in the spirit and back into history, and you shall be convinced, beloved branches of the vine stalk of our people, of the truth of what is related above. You will be convinced of the similarities of our people with those related in the Biblical Word. Whenever we think back on these things we can rejoice as did the Lord as recorded in Isaiah 27:2 and 3: "A pleasant vineyard, sing of it! I, the Lord am its keeper; every moment I water it. Lest anyone harm it, I guard it night and day."[66]

After each brief section of his history the author included a verse account of the history. These were to be sung as the Psalms, but the content was strictly South African. A few verses will show the method of his emotional appeal:

There came a vine stalk young and tender,
Brought by the Heavenly Lord;
It was brought from a distant land,
And then planted in Africa.

How briskly its branches shot out,
It was not stunted in its growth;
Its shadows came on cliff and valley,
As cedar trees over all.

The vine stalk grew in wood and valley
From Cape Town to Natal.
Then came the swine from the woods
And damaged the branches.

Red swine came out of the sea,
The black came with them;
In order to root up the vine shoots;
They thirsted for its sap and blood.

To these tender shoots planted by God
Came the beasts and swine of wood and beach;
Onto this prepared good ground,
And rooted around the stalk.

But this stalk was planted by God
In this land he prepared,
They are protected by God himself
With stem and roots in the earth. . . .

Now the noble vine stalk does not fear
As the swine bites with his teeth;
Even as some of his sap or blood flows,
The swine can never root it out.[67]

With this framework the author proceeded to analyze several crises and related each to the vine and branch motif. The first crisis he related was of Slagters' Nek.[68] The author related the tale with a minimum of theological interpretation.

When I was young I was told about these happenings (hellish deeds) often, and by many different people. . . . Whenever I relate to you how our people were provoked and oppressed, your blood shall cook in your veins. . . . A barbarous deed was here committed by an enlightened government. . . . We compare the five martyrs with Psalm 137:7-9. "Remember, O Lord, against the Edomites the day of Jerusalem, how they said: Raze it, Raze it! Down to its foundations. O daughter of Babylon, you devastator! Happy shall be he who requites you with what you have done to us! Happy shall be he who takes your little ones and dashes them against the rock."[69]

Again, the verse forms a summary and a connecting link.

> We are now far from Slagters' Nek,
> And from the horrible deeds;
> Let us leave the disgusting place,
> Let us go farther.
>
> Come, follow the vine stalk place after place,
> From here all the way to Natal;
> And see how God covers the branches
> And plants on mountain and valley.[70]

The Great Trek became a reality when farmers decided to leave their land "because of the injustices they had to suffer under the British government."[71] Along the way the trekkers met many Africans who "stormed upon them with wild noise and battle. It was a struggle of life and death, which the Boers won in the name of the Lord. How stealthily the swine came out of the under-brush to attack the noble vine stalks, to dig them out root and branch."[72] Then God intervened. "They [the Boers] destroyed the swine who were able to cut off only 53 branches of God's vine stalk."[73]

After the trekkers got to Natal and Retief's party had been murdered, the author reflected: "Yes, Natal is a land bought with the sweat and blood of our forefathers":

Natal is a justified and legal domain for our fathers, whom I call nothing less than "Martyrs"[74] . . . Dingaan was not to remain supreme in Natal. You can imagine, dear readers, how the noble man [Pretorius], the hero of old, has fought with his eyes to the God of vengeance. . . . They [Boers] have driven the swine out of the woods in the name of the Lord—those swine who destroyed so many branches of the noble vine stalk.[75]

Then the British took control of Natal and they

agitated among the tribesmen again to destroy our beloved forefathers by plunder and murder. The trekkers then left Natal, but it remains today the rightful territory of Boers who now live in Transvaal, Orange Free State and other places. Each Afrikaner who feels love for fatherland and nationality must feel his blood boil in his veins. All happenings have their time under heaven, and God brings things to happen in their predetermined time.[76]

Now he turned to the settlement within the Orange Free State. On February 3, 1848, when the Boers were organizing their settlement, the British declared that they controlled the country. "What do you think now, beloved readers, about the happenings in our land?"[77] A few months later the Boers decided to oppose Britain by force at Boomplaats, in the Orange Free State.[78] The British had nineteen hundred men while the Boers mustered only four hundred. "Well balanced, wasn't it, dear friends, 1900 to 400? Our forefathers built their hope on the justice of God which had not yet failed them."[79] The Boers lost five men, the British many more.

> Shall we not clearly see the finger of God in this? . . . Dear
> Readers, shall we tell about what happened to the noble vine
> stalk which God also planted in the Orange Free State? Shall
> we forget Joshua's admonition: "As for me and my house, we
> will serve the Lord"? (Joshua 24:15).[80]

After the British had retaken Natal and the Orange Free State, many Boer refugees from both areas settled in the Transvaal at Potchefstroom, (under Potgieter), and at Magaliesberg (Rustenberg, near Pretoria) under Pretorius.

> As it gets to the Wonderland, Transvaal
> The vine stalk shoots up a dozen-fold.
> It grows up in each place
> As cedar trees everywhere.
>
> O God, the Lord of all,
> Seek the fruitful vine stalk again,
> Which you have now planted
> Here in Transvaal the Wonderland.[81]

He sensed that all was not well in the Transvaal.

> There was a snake in the grass, with the nature of a swine,
> waiting in the prepared field of God's vine stalk—of our people.
> On the 12th day of April, 1877, England's minister, Shepstone,
> came, under false pretenses, and annexed the South African
> Republic to England. . . . Our leaders had besought England in
> all possible ways to explain what wretchedness might follow
> this evil deed, but she [England] was like Pharaoh, and would
> rather go into the sea than be stopped in her proceedings. The
> gold, the precious stones, and the profit from the fruitful land
> of Transvaal beckoned on Mr. Englishman, and then clawed out
> his eyes.[82]

During the few years after the English annexed the Transvaal in 1877, the reaction among the Boers grew gradually more aggressive:

It was in Transvaal as with Israel's queen against the Canaanites and Amorites, that the swine of the woods came upon
them. See II Chronicles 20:12: "We are powerless against this
great multitude that is coming against us. We do not know
what to do, but our eyes are upon Thee".[83]

God heard about the wretchedness. We had no ammunition,
but God was our shield and weapon. . . .

If Mr. Englishman was foolish enough to attack with power
of weapons, he might have been compared with ancient Israel:
"As a rock which one cleaves and shatters on the land, so shall
their bones be strewn at the mouth of Sheol". (Psalm 141:7)
Then He [Mr. Englishman] reconsidered.[84]

Finally, the Boers planned their mass meetings and reiterated their
faith in God's providence.   They made their convenant to fight the
British:[85]

The commemoration and covenant ceremony was meant to
remind the people not only what was done on that day, but also
what was believed. The ceremony was a witness to the covenant made by all in the name of the Lord, that according to the
faithful oath they should struggle and suffer for fatherland and
freedom. The day should be, thereafter, a feast of thanksgiving to God's goodness for our people.[86]

The First war of Independence began December 16, 1880. After the
first battle at Bronkhurst Spruit, when the Boers were victorious, our
author reported: "We have a song of praise and jubilee to sing, while we
leave Bronkhurst Spruit—a song to the honor of God of Jacob."

Praise, honor and thanks be brought
By us and by our descendants
To Israel's God which we have trusted;
From now to eternity.

We go now away from Bronkhurst Spruit,
And thanks to God is our resolve.
His help will be remembered by our progeny
Spoken or recalled to memory.[87]

The Boers won all four battles. We note only one of these typical
reactions of Bezuidenhout, related to the Laing's Nek battle.

Stand still, reader of our historical chronicle, and praise God,
for he has done great things for us. Our elders will tell to their
children and grandchildren and to many more generations, the
great deeds of God. One would have expected that the 80
noble vine stalks would be roooted out [eighty Boers against

seven hundred British]. No beast of the field ate them up, for they were vines planted by God and protected by him.[88]

In another battle it was 160 Boers against 600 British. God sided with the Boers, we are told:

Their faith and trust in the Lord was their strength and they did not fear the enemy. They had acted as heroes in the conflict. Now we must remind our readers that this was obviously a battle of the Lord; the later generations should praise and thank God their father. They should build their hope on Him, in case the time may come that they must trust Him as heroes of a later time, to withstand the British nation as their forefathers did.[89]

The war of freedom had a good side, as we look to the future of South Africa; and it signifies a thread of God's action in the history of the Boer people. God's work has been written into the history of the war of freedom. His works have been entered on memorial monuments in great and clear letters, written by Afrikaners of Cape Colony, Orange Free State, the Transvaal and Natal: "Africa for the Afrikaners." May the day come speedily when the Afrikaners' freedom flag waves over the whole of Africa from Cape Town all the way to Natal; when the foreign yoke of oppression shall have been permanently removed.[90]

The end of the First War of Independence came in March 1881. A song was necessary.

> The freedom war is now passed,
> Our four-colored flag stands planted;
> We threw off the tyranny
> And freed the Transvaal land.
>
> The blood which guiltless flowed here
> God demands from England.
> The Almighty holds [England] in tow
> Toward the pirate ship's shore.
>
> Now let Transvaal praise the Father God,
> His arm has upheld us.
> He remained our deliverer, steered our fate,
> And heard our supplication.
>
> The freedom has cost us much,
> The price was goods and blood;
> But the Lord's power has delivered us,
> His arm has upheld us.

> God's power, God's help has freed us
> From England's hard tyranny which
> Pressed us down as lead;
> So our love is great.[91]

A fitting conclusion puts the whole into its theological and nationalist framework.

> May the Lord bless the reading of this historical record, in order that our descendants may place their trust in the God of their fathers. They shall not be ashamed, but may experience what we have experienced: that faith in God is the victory of the world.[92]

The fourth aspect of theological nationalism was the culmination of the above three. As a national recognition of this religious attitude, a special festival was instituted, a renewal of the covenant. In 1881 the first annual religious festival was held at Paardekraal, on Dingane's Day, December 16. Here the Boers celebrated two major religious and nationlist happenings: the covenants of 1838 and 1879. This has become an increasingly significant festival each year since 1881 and has grown with the spirit of theological nationalism. In 1890 Kruger gave the theological oration, including several biblical allusions:

> All ye multitude listen with full attention that you may take hold of what I say. God is in our midst. I shall first address the true burghers who are here to praise God for His Almighty deeds, favoring our entire people in the past days and now also. Unbelievers say God does not do signs and wonders as in days of the old Covenant, but I can show you from our own history that the dear Lord does everything to give a good time to those that are the people of the Lord.
> [Then they sang Psalm 89, including these two verses: "Thou hast said, I have made a covenant with my chosen one, I have sworn to David my servant; I will establish your descendants for ever, and build thy throne for all generations' (Psalm 89:3-4).]

On unveiling a monument for the occasion, he concluded:

> Let this be kept as a religious festival from generation to generation. For this purpose alone let this hallowed spot be used, and in the Holy Words let each one say, "Make me to live up to thy mercies, and so shall I keep the laws of Thy mouth."[93]

During and following the war, patriotism, nationalism, hero worship, and theological assurance that the Boers were God's elect went hand in hand. The emphasis on the negative aspects of the relations with Britain in the past was so intensified that they assumed the British were sent by God to test their faith and to help make them strong in their resolve to oppose anti-Christ. This extremist tendency, beginning long before in the Dopper groups, was now organized into a political party and continues to have influence in South African religious nationalism.

Opposed to the extremists among the Afrikaners were many people who were loyal Afrikaners but did not harbor hatred of British influence. The moderates believed that their true destiny would be built with British cooperation rather than through rejection of British cultural influence. Individiuals who became moderate leaders were persons who had been trained in British-administered schools in the Cape Colony or in Europe and who knew first-hand the contribution that Britain had made to their total national life.   Leaders among the moderate Afrikaners were President Burgers of the Transvaal and President Brand of the Orange Free State. Two extremely significant moderates of the last part of the nineteenth century were Johan Hendrik de Villiers, later chief justice of the Cape Colony and after 1910 of the Union of South Africa (he died in 1914);[94] and Jan Hendrik Hofmeyr,Jr., strong parliamentary influence and long-time leader of Afrikaner moderates not only in the Cape Colony but in other sections of the land as well (he died in 1909).[95]

In comparison with the nationalistic but narrow Bond, we must note briefly another Afrikaner organization that was to have significant influence among moderates. Through South African history an estrangement existed between the more prosperous coast—Cape Town and environs—and the less-developed interior. This was true before the Great Trek; it was in fact one of the factors that led to the Trek.   The situation remained throughout the nineteenth century. In 1873 several farmers in the eastern section of the Cape Colony banded together in *Boeren Verenigingen* (Farmers' Associations).[96] Their main concern was economic.

Shortly thereafter a crisis arose in the west when government raised taxes on wine producers, who were mainly in the western section of the Cape Colony. The wine producers were mainly Afrikaners who up to that time had taken little interest in Cape politics and who had not produced candidates for public office.   With this crisis before them the farmers organized in 1878 into *Boeren Beschermings Verenigingen* (Farmers' Protective Associations) with expressly political objectives. They sought to make their influence felt in government affairs where they had previously taken little interest. One of their champions was J. H. Hofmeyr, the publisher of the Cape newspaper, *Zuid Afrikaan*.[97] He wrote and spoke widely, always insisting that if the Afrikaners wanted to have influence, they must organize and vote for candidates who would listen to their interests and needs. The farmers of the east and the west were now organized into two similar but separate organizations. Gradually the eastern and western organizaions grew together. The objectives of the organization, with branches in many towns across the Colony, were contained in their "Rules and Regulations."[98]

Soon Hofmeyr realized that the two nationalist organizations—the Bond and the Farmers' Associations—were competing with each other. An Afrikaner population pulling in two directions was no better than an Afrikaner population unorganized. Hofmeyr urged the use of Dutch; the Bond, Afrikaans. Hofmeyr believed the emphasis on Afrikaans with no literature or history could hardly hold a chance in competing with English. In this respect he said the Bond was "fighting a losing battle."[99] He urged cooperation with the British; the Bond rejected British influence. Hofmeyr summarized the problem:

> Is there indeed only a choice between two alternatives? Must the Dutch Afrikander either fight an endless battle ever growing more and more bitter, against all that is English—or must he content himself with a resolution to commit moral and national suicide, to try to forget his language, and to strive to quench every aspiration, every sentiment, yes, his whole conscience as an Afrikaner? Is there in South Africa no place for the one as well as the other? Can we not be true Englishmen and true Afrikanders and at the same time loyal British subjects?[100]

Thus Hofmeyr urged cooperation for the good of all Afrikaners under the British flag; the Bond insisted on a united South Africa under a South African flag. The only realistic solution was to unite the competing organizations for the good of all. After the Rev. S. J. du Toit, the moving force of the Bond, became part of the Transvaal government, Hofmeyr gradually assumed leadership of all Afrikaners of the Cape Colony. In May 1883 delegates of both organizaions came to Richmond where after much discussion, the two groups voted to merge as the Afrikaner Bond.[101]

Hofmeyr succeeded in his first objective, to help Dutch Afrikaners to take their rightful place along with citizens of British background. He also succeeded in his attempt to merge two contending Afrikaner organizations into one. In still another area Hofmeyr's influence was decisive. He desired to have his national group fully recognized as a responsible section of the population. Up to now all business of government and of law was conducted in English. In 1881-1882 he won his case, and by 1884 Dutch and English were used equally, and bills were presented to Parliament in both languages.[102] With broad support behind him, Hofmeyr was elected to the Cape Parliament in 1879, where he was the leader of the ever-increasing Afrikaner section until his retirement in 1895. His stature was such that he was invited to be a candidate for the presidency of the Transvaal in 1883, for the presidency of the Orange Free State at the death of President Brand in 1888, and premier of the Cape Colony in 1884.[103] He declined all these opportunities, preferring to work behind the scenes.

Much of the remainder of South African history is concerned with Afrikaner attempts to fulfill their God-given destiny of a South Africa united "from Cape Town to the Zambezi." Afrikaner influence was growing in the Cape Colony, and it had always been strong in the two republics. The real question was, however, which vision of Afrikaner destiny: the extremes of Kruger and du Toit or the moderation of Burgers, Brand, Hofmeyr and de Villiers?

The developing political activity of the Afrikaners was only one of the decisive changes that occurred in South Africa during the 1880s. The more drastic change was in fact an economic revolution, a revolution concerning gold. The presence of this precious metal had been known for some years but had not been exploited to any extent. In 1882 deposits were discovered in the Transvaal town of Barberton, in the eastern section of the country.[104] Many diggers came from outside the country, but the development was limited. Then gold was discovered in 1886 on the Witwatersrand by two Struben brothers.[105] Almost immediately the news spread, and a sizable number of diggers headed for the sparsely populated area. A new city began to take shape, named Johannesburg after Johannes Rissik, surveyor general of the Transvaal.[106] Most of the diggers were *Uitlanders* (outsiders, foreigners), and a large percentage were British. Indeed, by 1896, ten years later, out of a population of 50,907 in Johannesburg, only 6,205 were from the Transvaal.[107] The stage was set for the problem of the decade: How would the Transvaal deal with its new-found wealth, and even more important, how would it deal with these large numbers of new inhabitants?

When the extent of the gold deposits was only partially known, Paul Kruger saw again the hand of God coming to bring a sign to His elect. God hid the gold and let the Boers discover it at the right time.

> See, it was concealed by God until our freedom was regained. Then at the appointed time the simple Boers found the gold. The earth was opened and unlocked her treasure. From far and near many came into the land. A great debt rested on the land, and with anxiety the question was asked: "How shall the debt be paid?" But in His own time the Lord gave the treasures of the earth and we received more than seven-fold what we had lost. God's power, wisdom and goodness was also very clear and certain here. Folks of the land . . . let us here gathered confess our debts and recognize God's hand leading us.[108]

In preparation for the election of 1888 Kruger further indicated the direction he would lead his people in the new challenges brought to them by the gold discoveries. Theological allusions are plentiful:

> My ideals are to be seen sufficiently only from my whole political career. Above all I wish to give the impression that

my main objective always shall be to maintain and strengthen
the independence of this Republic. God has shown that He is
well-pleased in our independence so that both unbelievers and
heathens must recognize that it was His Hand which made us
free.

I feel that I would be under a curse if the independence and
freedom should ever be diminished by me. As a valuable gem
these basic rights of all the people must be preserved. If we do
not protect these basic rights; if we commit acts as Esau who
wasted his rights, so shall God take His blessings from us.[109]

After Kruger was reelected by a large margin (Kruger 4,483; Joubert,
834) he continued in a similar vein:

I am weighted down with reflections, and my heart is filled
with thankfulness to God as I see you people of this land before
me. It is with a trembling and anxious heart that I again
undertake to lead this state, for I feel that *I must give an
account to God for the way in which the folk of this land make
use of the advantages and the drawbacks which the Lord has
granted to us.* Again the people have chosen me to lead them
as I have in the last five years; and again I have placed my
trust in the Almighty, pledging to serve the Republic to the
best of my ability. . . . I offer you my thanks for the support
you have given me in the past years. I mean support in the
deeper sense, for what did Moses say—The man whom God
himself chose to be leader of his people?—He asked immediately that his people strengthen him by their belief, so that he
as well as they would be sustained. I say this: You have supported me; you, the representatives of the people, have always
supported in a most forceful way. On the other side, you have
also supported the government, by interpreting it to the
people. Through the grace of God, your determination in the
past has been a blessing for the land, and you can be the same
in the present. May you always be the representatives of the
people in the Volksraad and the interpreters of its views. . . .
God has thus blessed you, and the treasures of the womb of the
earth are revealed to you, and our beloved land is rich. Therefore I say to you; *may the curse of heaven destroy me if the
independence of the state is ever brought into danger by me.*
Following the discovery of riches here, new people have come
into the land, and we take pleasure that they have done so. [To
the newcomers] I welcome you, yet I set you under the concern
of the old burghers. Work in unity together, and the blessing of
heaven shall rest upon you, and you shall be the means for
furthering the welfare and prosperity of the land[110]

Kruger stated clearly the policy he believed God called him to pursue. He must maintain independence at all costs; he would be led by God as a new Moses; and he would attempt to have the newcomers in the area add their part to his concept of the order of the land.

President Burgers, hoping to advance his country economically, had sought support to build a railroad to Delagoa Bay, but he had not been successful with his followers, who suspected his progressive vision.[111] Now with the growing population and the need for more food and equipment in the Transvaal, interest again turned to the railroad. Kruger was insistent, however, that before any connection was made between his state and the Cape Colony, he must complete a railroad to the Portuguese port. He had discussed this in Europe in 1884, but no progress had been made. (See map IV.)

British interests were progressing on their railway from Cape Town to the Kimberley diamond mines, and they hoped to persuade the Free State to allow a rail through their territory, ultimately to reach Johannesburg and the goldfields. Fearing the results, Kruger hurriedly called a meeting in his home in Pretoria. He included President Brand and delegates of the Free State. In the face of growing British pressures, Kruger thought the two republics should be more closely associated. In addition, he hoped to persuade Brand not to allow the railway until the Delagoa Bay line was completed. He expressed his opinion to the Free State delegates:

> The strength of our position lies in our making the British Government understand that the Republics hold together. Then we can be sure that we will be taken into account. . . . Let us speak frankly. We are not going to be dependent on England. Take no railway union—remain without a railway. That is better than to take of their money. The future will provide greater blessings if you work with us. Let them keep their money. Let them not bind you. The Lord reigns—none other— the deliverance is near at hand.[112]

A. D. W. Wolmarans of the Transvaal added to the interpretation of the underlying fears: "Let us first get to the sea and achieve our independence. Wait a few years. Why are we today worried at Delagoa? English influences! They wish to keep us in bonds and dependence; that is what we struggle against."[113] The conference concluded on the promise that for the time being, the Orange Free State would not allow a railway from either the Cape or Natal without the consent of the Transvaal.

A few months later, between October 6 and 22, 1887, another meeting was held between the leaders of the two republics in Bloemfontein.[114] Still hoping to stem the tide that seemed to be going in Britain's favor some considered a federal union between the Free State and the Transvaal, modeled after that of the United States. The moderate Afrikaners of the

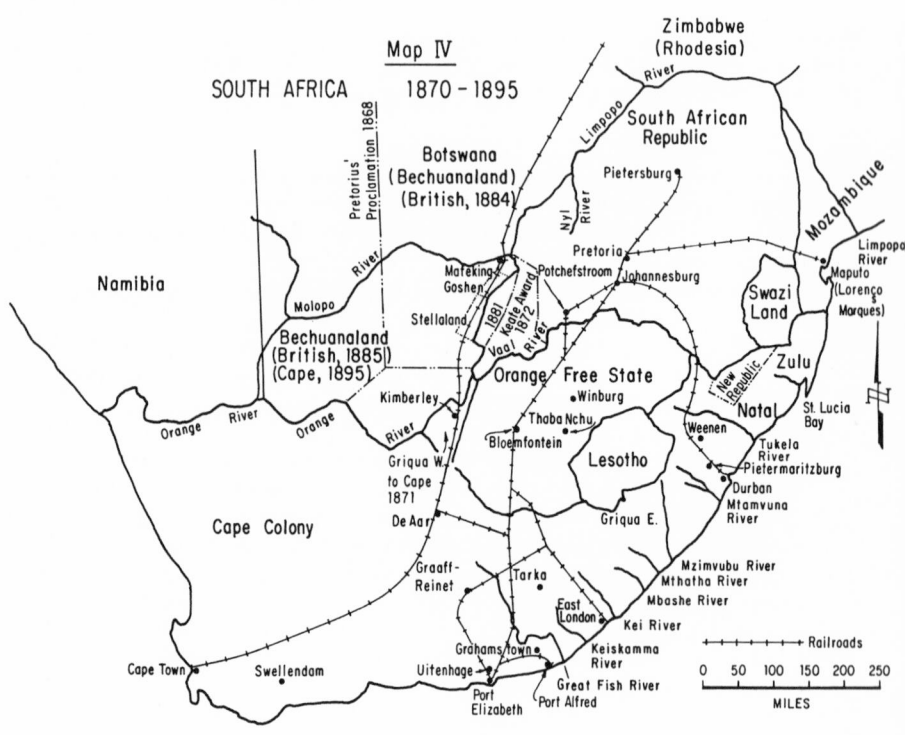

Map IV
SOUTH AFRICA   1870-1895

Zimbabwe
(Rhodesia)

Namibia

Botswana
(Bechuanaland)
(British, 1884)

Pretorius' Proclamation 1868

_____ River

Limpopo River

South African
Republic

Pietersburg

Nyl River

Pretoria
Mafeking•
Goshen•   Potchefstroom
Stellaland   Johannesburg

Molopo

Bechuanaland
(British, 1885)
(Cape, 1895)

1881
Keate Award 1872
Vaal River

Swazi
Land

Mozambique

Limpopo
River
Maputo
(Lorenço
Marques)

Kimberley

Orange Free State

•Winburg

New Republic

Zulu

Orange   River   Orange   River

River

•Thaba Nchu
•Bloemfontein

Griqua W.
to Cape
1871

De Aar•

Lesotho

Griqua E.

Weenen•

Natal

St. Lucia
Bay

Tukela
River
•Pietermaritzburg
•Durban
Mtamvuna
River

Cape Colony

Graaff-
Reinet•

•Tarka

Mzimvubu River
Mthatha River

East
London•

Mbashe River

Kei River

Cape Town•

Swellendam•

Grahams town•

Uitenhage•

Port
Elizabeth

Keiskamma
River
Great Fish River
Port Alfred

•——•——• Railroads

0   50   100 150 200 250

MILES

Cape Colony feared that Brand would be persuaded to repudiate his Cape sympathies, thus jeopardizing Afrikaner unity. Consequently a long statement was drawn up by Bond leaders, notably Hofmeyr, and sent to the president of the Free State. The Bond committee argued against Transvaal's policy of aloofness and obstruction of the railway plans. They pleaded that the Afrikaners of the north not finally separate themselves from the south: "We lay bare the position before Your Honor, because, when once a division arises between kinsfolk, one cannot foresee where it will end, and the *Afrikander cause* is far from being strong enough to be able to face division between Transvaal and Colonial sons of the soil."[115] In the end it was Kruger who refused to join such a confederation, fearing, perhaps, that this would mean an eclipse of his major vision and God-given goal for his country.[116]

There was a precarious three-way balance of power among growing British influence, the moderate Afrikaners who were in the majority and who were supported by President Brand, and the extremist Boers of the Transvaal. Suddenly the balance shifted when on July 16, 1888, President Brand of the Free State died and was succeeded by Justice Francis William Reitz, much more Republican and sympathetic to the Transvaal cause than his predecessor.

Knowing the change of attitude in the Free State, in March 1889 Kruger invited President Reitz to Potchefstroom to discuss their common problems. They made three agreements that later affected both countries. They agreed to eliminate customs dues on goods passing between the two states; they agreed on a defensive alliance whereby if either was attacked, the other would offer support; and, they agreed that no rail connection except to Delagoa Bay should be plannned without approval of the other republic.[117] The British had railways to Kimberley and to Colesburg, and following an agreement negotiated with President Brand just before his death, they planned to continue one or both lines to Bloemfontein. For a time, based on the agreement of common cause and common defense, Kruger's policy of isolation from British influence in his Zion seemed to be moderately successful.

Economic progress drove relentlessly forward, however. The Transvaal could not long remain aloof, especially when the major industrial development was within its own borders. In December 1889 Bloemfontein was joined to the Cape economically and physically by the railway from Colesburg, and negotiations were under way to continue north to the Transvaal border. The industries of the Transvaal demanded action, and the proposed route to Delagoa Bay seemed plagued with difficulties. The Transvaal was finally forced to allow a railway. The line from Delagoa reached the Transvaal border in 1889, completed to Pretoria in 1894.[118] In the meantime another connection had already been completed; the Cape line through Bloemfontein reached the goldfields in 1892. The line from the British harbor at Durban was progressing rapidly, reaching the Transvaal border by

1891 and Johannesburg in 1895.[119] Thus in 1895 the Transvaal was joined to the outside world in three directions.[120] The economic revolution was pressing harder on Kruger's fortress and on his concept of his own destiny as a leader of God's people.

The two republics were already surrounded by British territories on both the east and west sides. There were opportunities for Boer expansion remaining only north of the Limpopo River, a fact not overlooked for long by British interests. One of the major figures in this expansion to the north was Cecil Rhodes who came to Natal in 1869 at the age of sixteen.[121] He first visited the diamond fields two years later, and except for his college education in England and various trips, he remained a substantial figure in South Africa for the remainder of the century until his death in March 1902 at age forty-nine. Rhodes had vision and administrative and financial ability, which resulted in his amalgamating various diamond companies into his own company, the De Beers Consolidated. When gold came to be South Africa's main export, again Rhodes gained a large control of the industry in his company, Consolidated Goldfields of South Africa. His company, how-ever, was not able to gain the monopoly of the Johannesburg mines. In addition to the two giant projects of gold and diamonds, he had a vision for developing the land to the north of the Transvaal for the British Empire.

To this end he secured the charter of the British South Africa Com-pany, which allowed his company to push from Bechuanaland toward and beyond the Zambezi.[122] The charter allowed them to promote trade and commerce, to bring "civilization" to the African tribes, and to exploit other mineral deposits they might find. Although this area later known as Rho-desia was not a British protectorate, the company control there made Transvaal expansion to the north impossible. Rhodes stated his objective in 1885: "Do not be led away by the assertion that I am pro-Dutch in my sympathies. I had to consider the best mode of permanently checking the expansion of the Boer Republics into the interior. The only solution I can see is to enclose them by the Cape Colony."[123]

President Kruger suspected this was the British policy before he knew of this particular statement. He realized that for the present his govern-ment could not oppose Britain but must maintain its strength from within. There were, however, Transvaalers who did not have this realistic under-standing of political affairs and decided to move north. In 1891 the Trans-vaal newspapers reported a trek to the north. This plan was later widely circulated across South Africa:

> The men, who wish to go to the new land, not in their own
> strength, but in the power of the Lord who has made Heaven
> and earth, and still administers it, propose to go as a lawful
> and law-abiding people under law and order. . . . Their govern-
> ment and judicial body shall be regulated and chosen . . . as

soon as the "trek" has got outside the borders of the South African Republic, or inside the *promised land.*

Who are to be their Joshuas or Calebs, we do not yet know, but as temporary leaders are nominated: [here follow fourteen names, representing the Transvaal, the Free State, and the Cape Colony].

The God of Heaven, who administers all things, can alone put a stop to this trek, but men cannot. . . .

We hope for better things, that no Afrikander will allow himself to be misled by the Charter of Rhodes to come and quarrel with us, and just as unrighteously as the Transvaal was once annexed, now come and trouble us in our own lawful land.[124]

The document was signed by L. D. Aldendorff, otherwise unidentified. Leaders were secured from all parts of South Africa, including S. J. du Toit, then in Paarl (Cape Colony), and Joubert from the Transvaal.[125] Two thousand people were to gather at the Limpopo River on June 1, 1891, and to proceed as a group.[126]

Such a planned "invasion" held grave consequences for the relations between the two national groups in South Africa. The British leaders north of the Limpopo had been warned and were taking precautions. Afrikaner leaders in the Cape Colony, headed by Hofmeyr, also gave warning. Finally, although the trekkers had said, "The God of heaven . . . can alone put a stop to this trek, but men cannot," President Kruger stepped forward and presented a proclamation, passed by the Volksraad, forbidding the trek.[127]   Nevertheless, over a hundred Boers did meet at the appointed place, where British officials invited them to cross the river to the north if they wished, as soon as they signed a deed of submission to British authority. With this turn of events, the trekkers abandoned their holy cause and returned home. Kruger now felt himself "shut up in a kraal."[128]

Frustrated in its attempts to expand into the surrounding territory, the Transvaal was becoming aware of another major problem, immigrants or Uitlanders. The new arrivals in the Transvaal were confronted with frustration of their own, and increasing pressure was put on the Transvaal government to come to terms with this flood of immigrants, by now nearly equal to the number of the original inhabitants of the area. From Kruger's viewpoint, Johannesburg, with a larger population than any other city in South Africa, was fast becoming a foreign city in his domain. The situation was further complicated as he realized that the prosperity of the Transvaal was dependent on the industries of this foreign enclave. Furthermore, this large group of Uitlanders was almost completely without a voice or vote in government because this area was controlled by a minority government. Kruger and his followers sensed that this was their most pressing internal problem. They might have met the situation with a constructive approach to integrate the newcomers into their already established republic; they reacted in just the opposite manner, however, becoming more entrenched and more belligerently defensive. How long this anomalous and tense situation could remain was not certain, nor was it certain how the change would be brought about.

The offensive was taken by the Transvaal National Union, formed August 20, 1892, and supported by a large number of Uitlanders. The objectives of the union were "the maintenance of the independence of the Republic; the obtaining, by all constitutional means, equal rights for all citizens of this Republic; and the redressing of all grievances."[129] One of the leaders of the union, and its chairman from 1894 to 1896, was Charles Leonard, formerly an attorney in Cape Town. Leonard collected and published many documents of this period, and his work remains a valuable primary source for understanding the stormy period of Afrikaner-Uitlander relations.[130] The union proceeded to hold public meetings, to write petitions to the government, and to publish pamphlets concerning their plight and their plea for the right to full citizenship in the Transvaal.[131] On one occasion President Kruger discussed the objectives of the union with one of its members. To their plea, he replied, "Go back and tell your people I will never give them anything. I shall never change my policy; and now let the storm burst."[132] What was the background for the turmoil among the Uitlanders and of the strong recalcitrance on the part of the Transvaal government?

When Transvaal won the war in 1881, the leaders were overjoyed and set about to establish a new Zion with the help of God. The in-rush of prospectors that began shortly thereafter, however, threatened to undo what the Boers had accomplished. The Transvaal had been invaded not by an army of soldiers but by an army of diggers and company officials. Population statistics are not available for the period, for President Kruger had a biblical reason for refusing to "number the people" (Exodus 30:12).[133] However, as we have noted, a census of the city of Johannesburg in 1896 listed only 6,025 Boers out of a total population of 50,907.[134] On the strength of later census figures, it is assumed that by 1892 there were probably at least as many male Uitlanders as male Boers in Transvaal as a whole.[135] Many in the flood of newcomers came only for profit and at first were not concerned about the government under which they happened to live. Soon even these became critical of a government that put too many controls on their business and where they had no voice in that government to influence their own affairs. The agitation among the Uitlanders grew from month to month.

Immediately after 1881 the financial status of the republic was precarious; more income was needed, from the outside if possible. One means by which Kruger and his government attempted to acquire needed finances and also to continue their control of their land was by granting concessions— monopolies—often to European interests. In the first election campaign, Kruger asked the Volksraad for authority to grant monopolies, and after

some debate this right was granted. He sold a concession for the manufacture of liquor, much of which was consumed by the Africans (the Transvaalers preferred imported German liquor).[136] He granted a concession to
Transvaalers for developing the mines in such areas as Rustenberg and
Lijdenburg to exclude as many foreign diggers as possible.[137] The first
railway project was a monopoly granted to a Netherlands-based company.
The discussions about railways and customs agreements between the Transvaal and the Cape Colony were part of the Transvaal's attempt to hold a
monopoly on such transportation and hence to set their own prices.

The concession that caused most agitation concerned explosives, especially dynamite. In 1887 this was first granted to a German, Mr. Lippert,
provided he would build a plant and manufacture "dynamite and other
explosives" in the Transvaal.[138] Their first need was for ammunition, but
dynamite for mining was soon in great demand. During the agitation concerning grievances, they discovered that no factory had been built. Rather,
dynamite was being imported duty free by the owner of the concession, who
then set his own price, evidently with tacit approval of the government.
When criticism became strong enough, the government revoked the concession to Mr. Lippert and awarded it to a partner of the original company. It
became a government concession, and criticisms from the mining industry
continued.[139]

Other sources of grievances continued to reflect the government's
concern to maintain its preferred status. The Transvaal government imposed taxes unequally, leading the Uitlanders to believe their leaders were
taking advantage of them. The authorities controlled imports so that the
cost of foodstuffs was kept high. A new customs act of 1892, which would
have worked undue hardship on the Uitlanders, finally brought the Transvaal National Union into being.[140] Another grievance concerned language.
Most Uitlanders were English, but only the Dutch language was allowed in
the Transvaal, including the schools.[141] Only Boers could serve as jurors,
and only Boers were appointed policemen. Finally, a new press law allowed
President Kruger virtual censorship of all printing of a political nature.[142]

The president also kept a tight rein on any political organization
thought to compete with the absolute rule of the state. In December 1888,
for example, the city of Johannesburg applied for status as a municipality
with its own city government. Kruger refused, stating that this could lead
to a state within a state.[143] His fears concerning Johannesburg's growing
influence were not allayed when on a visit to the city in 1890, the Transvaal flag was ripped down by agitators before his eyes! He replied that he
would not return to the troublesome city again.[144] The absolute control
that Kruger kept was strongly felt by the Uitlanders who reflected the
underlying theological motif: "The Government [Transvaal] is absolutely
rotten, and we must have reform. The alternative is *revolution* or *English
interference*. Kruger seems beyond himself, and imagines he is guided by
Divine will."[145]

An analysis of the grievances of the Uitlanders could easily give the impression that this was only a tension between Boer and Briton, but the problem of the African was always only slightly under the surface during this period. A pro-British writer analyzed the anti-African attitude of the Afrikaner: "In regard to external policy, the Boer is definite—clear the blacks away, or let them crouch before the white man. . . . Drive out of your head any notion of native rights."[146] The theological justification of a chosen people and a special destiny was also obvious to an outsider: ""The belief in a providence caring for the white man at the expense of the black, is as strong as it ever was in the mind of the ancient Israelite. They are like the ancient Hebrews too, in their continual pious acknowledgement of God's existence and providence."[147]

The fear that outsiders would upset the *status quo* through political maneuvering was epitomized in the lengthy and involved debates concerning the franchise for Uitlanders. A contemporary writer during the period of the agitation suggested that the basis of the problem was economic. There was "a reluctance of the majority of the burghers to throw open their lucrative preserve by their extension of the franchise."[148] Undoubtedly this was part of the problem, but more important, the Transvaal government intepreted it as God's will that the Boer leadership should remain in power and not be diluted by outsiders. Up to 1882 settlers were allowed the franchise on obtaining property or after having lived in the Transvaal for one year. When some outsiders living in the Transvaal, however, were among the agitators for annexation in 1877, the government decided to raise the standards. In 1882 the time limit was raised to five years.[149] By 1890 Kruger realized that under the five-year law, thousands of Uitlanders who came in 1886 or 1887 would be eligible to vote in the presidential and Volksraad elections of 1893. The freedom of the Transvaal might be lost at the ballot box as surely as on the battlefield.

The president again became defensive as he proposed an ingenious modification in the government machinery, introducing the idea of a Second Volksraad. The time limit was to be reduced so that now only two years' residence was required to be eligible to vote for members of the Second Volksraad. After being eligible to vote two years, one could be elected to the Second Volksraad. Only after ten more years, a total of fourteen years after coming to the Transvaal, would one be eligible to vote for the First Volksraad members. The First Volksraad voters controlled the main business of the state, including the taxes and questions of monopolies, and they could vote for president.[150] Truly the new law was designed to continue control in the hands of the old burghers and give the agitating Uitlanders only enough vote to calm their feelings, not enough to have any real effect in the state.

The argument over the concept of the Second Volksraad continued for three days, with sharply divided opinion. Joubert was one of the leaders opposed to the new legislation and became continually more progressive and favorable to the Uitlanders in later years.[151] The day was won by the president, however, as he justified himself:

> You all know that God has found pleasure in the independence of the land, and to such an extent that blind heathen and unbelievers must recognize that things took place here which were almost impossible. . . . You know that the number of newcomers and their children grows daily. . . . Following the old law these strangers can become registered voters after five years; after five more years there will be perhaps five times as many of them as of us; and then I have my suspicions about the security of our independence. . . . We must use the means which God gave us to determine what the choice will be. . . . The Lord has taken pleasure in our independence, but in five years it can happen that others will sit in your place.[152]

Kruger was called an autocrat in proposing such a radical change to prohibit the franchise from so many. His sympathetic biographer, however, argues that Kruger was merely better equipped to know the needs of the state than most of his opponents.[153] The final step in the franchise reform came in 1894 when the government declared, contrary to the 1890 law, that children of Uitlanders, even though born in the Transvaal, were under the same limitations as their fathers.[154]

Kruger was continually encouraged in his undertakings and encouraged his followers in turn by remembering the mighty acts of God in South Africa over the past three-quarters of a century. He repeated much of past exhortations at the Paardekraal festival on December 16, 1891:

> God is in our midst whether we recognize him or not. . . . It is for God that we have prepared the feast in His honor. . . . In the Old Testament God said to Abraham: "The covenant which I made with you and your descendants, excluding none, shall remain before you and your seed from now to eternity" [Gen. 17:7].[155]

He continued with a long recitation of past history in which God's hand had been assumed many times before. He began his story of the Great Trek, "When I was ten years old . . ."[156]

Kruger's extremism brought reaction from both the Uitlanders in his midst and from his own Boer compatriots. Not only did the Uitlanders react because of the decisions he made but because of the way in which he used biblical examples to justify what he had already decided. For example, in 1890 the president was asked why he did not outlaw horse racing and gambling. He replied that "gambling and lotteries were in conflict with the Word of God, but it was also the duty of man to have exercise and to exercise his horses. For that reason an exception had been made in the Bill as to horse races."[157]   In 1891 Kruger was asked if he would consent to having his name given as patron of a ball. His secretary replied: "His Honor considers a ball as Baal's service, for which reason the Lord ordered Moses to kill all offenders; and as it is therefore contrary to His Honor's principles, His Honor cannot consent to the misuse of his name."[158]

In 1892 locusts were a plague and should have been exterminated. There was objection, however: "Mr. Roos said Locusts were a plague, as in the days of King Pharaoh, sent by God, and the country would assuredly be loaded with shame and obloquy if it tried to raise its hand against the mighty hand of the Almighty."[159]   Charles Leonard summed up the Uitlanders' attitude when he stated:

> The Boer knows very little from books, and what he has gained
> by experience of business relates only to stockbreeding and
> agriculture. Yet he legislates by Divine Right on all the intri-
> cate questions raised by a complex modern civilization, which
> has come upon him almost as suddenly as if it had dropped
> from the moon.[160]

The tensions generated among the Boers were partly theological in nature and seriously affected the outcome of the election of 1893. All three Dutch Reformed churches were organized in the Transvaal: the N. G. K., the original denomination, strongest in the Cape Colony; the N. H. K., which severed relations with the Cape church in 1853 as a mark of Transvaal independence; and the ultra-conservative Gereformeerde Kerk, the Dopper, with its most illustrious member, President Kruger. The first two denominations attempted a union in the Transvaal after the war of 1881.[161]   A segment of the N. G. K., however, objected to the merger and formed a splinter group. Property rights were involved, and confusion reigned. The president, who believed the tensions over church problems were foreboding of more serious things to come, sought to negotiate a settlement. He did not have authority to participate in ecclesiastical affairs except as a layman; furthermore, this question did not even involve the church of which he was a member. Nevertheless, for the good of the state, in August 1891, he called a meeting of delegates from the two groups to construct a workable arrangement.[162]   Those who had reason to oppose Kruger now had one further criticism: they felt that as a state official, he attempted to influence church policy.[163]   Many also remembered that the Grondwet of the Transvaal specified that the state church to which state officials must belong was the Hervormde Kerk, and their president belonged to a different group.

This election was significant because it reflected a growing reaction against Kruger, even among his own Boer compatriots. The opponent again was Piet Joubert, but now there was a difference. Joubert had become sympathetic to the cause of the Uitlanders and supported more progressive views. He had openly differed with Kruger a few years earlier when he advocated a railway from Durban to the goldfields.[164] Although Joubert was rejected by many religious leaders because of his progressive ideas, he had a strong following among anti-Kruger Boers.   When the vote was counted, there was real question whether Kruger had a majority, but the official figures were Kruger 7,881 and Joubert 7,009.[165] Personal and theological as well as political tensions engendered throughout the area did not fail to have their effects.

The Transvaal National Union continued its agitation against the government. In 1894 it mustered 13,000 signatures on a franchise petition and in 1895 38,500 signatures.[166] Neither had any appreciable effect, however. In 1895 the First Volksraad held what was called the Great Franchise Debate in which the "monster Uitlander petition" was discussed.[167] Lucas Meyer, who had been a supporter of Joubert in the recent election, carried the offensive for the eight (out of twenty-four) who wanted a more progressive law with respect to the franchise.

The sixteen who voted in favor of the *status quo* argued from curious presuppositions. One argued that to extend the franchise was "contrary to Republican principles."[168] He had evidence that the Uitlanders were not law abiding because they were against the law, otherwise why should they attempt to change it rather than follow it? One suspected that they might give the franchise to "persons who shot kaffirs . . . but people who came here only to make money and that only did not deserve the franchise."[169] Jan Meyer assumed that many of the 38,000 signatures were forgeries.[170]

President Kruger failed to realize that there was a difference between just and well-founded grievances among loyal settlers on the one hand and direct imperial infiltration and subversion on the other. He assumed that suppression of Uitlanders was the only way to maintain the supremacy of Afrikanerdom. After the debate when he and another Boer were discussing the question of the franchise, Kruger said: "You see that flag? . . . If I grant the franchise I may as well pull it down."[171] To this Gert de Jager replied with insight: "Now our country is gone. Nothing can settle this but fighting, and there was only one end to the fight. Kruger and his Hollanders have taken our independence more surely than ever Shepstone did."[172]

In December 1895, the Transvaal National Union composed a comprehensive *Manifesto* giving in detail their grievances of the past decade. After summarizing the tensions, Leonard, the chairman, reiterated in ten points what the movement sought. He stated "we want the establishment of the Republic as a true Republic. . . . an equitable franchise law . . . equality of the Dutch and English language."[173] Then he asked, "How shall we get it?" This manifesto was to be circulated to all Uitlanders in preparation for a protest and strategy meeting when they would decide their next move. The meeting, called for January 6, 1896, was never held, for in the meantime the history of the Transvaal took another turn.

NOTES

1. C. 2866 of 1881, p. 176.

2. J. D. Weilbach and C. N. J. du Plessis, *Geschiedenis van de Emigranten Boeren en van den Vrijheidsoorlog*, (1892), quoted in van Jaarsveld, *Afrikaner's Interpretation*, p. 19.

3. March 26, 1881; du Plessis, *Andrew Murray*, p. 420.

4. *Die Express*, July 7, 1882; quoted in van Jaarsveld, *Die Afrikaner*, p. 100.

5. Volksraad discussion, October 5, 1881, quoted in Malherbe, *Education in South Africa*, p. 261.

6. *Ibid.*, p. 259.

7. Articles 2c and 18(4) of the convention, in Eybers, *Select Constitutional Documents*, pp. 455-463.

8. Sections 3, 13, and 26, in Eybers, *Select Constitutional Documents*.

9. C. 3098 of 1882, p. 87.

10. van Oordt, *Paul Kruger*, p. 336.

11. *Ibid.*

12. J. H. Hofmeyr, *The Life of Jan Hendrik Hofmeyr* (Cape Town: Van de Sandt de Villiers, 1913), p. 217.

13. van Oordt, *Paul Kruger*, p. 380.

14. *Ibid.*, p. 379.

15. *Ibid.*, p. 381.

16. *Ibid.*

17. *Ibid.*

18. *Ibid.*

19. *Ibid.*

20. *Ibid.*, p. 387. Kruger 3,431; Joubert 1,171.

21. *Ibid.*, p. 404.

22. C. 3947 of 1884, pp. 47-58; also printed in full in Eybers, *Select Constitutional Documents*, pp. 469-474.

23. Eybers, *Select Constitutional Documents,* p. 471.

24. *Ibid.,* p. 473.

25. van Oordt, *Paul Kruger,* p. 415.

26. *Ibid.,* p. 415.

27. *Ibid.,* p. 413.

28. *Ibid.,* p. 419.

29. *Ibid.,* p. 420.

30. *Ibid.,* p. 421.

31. *Ibid.,* p. 422.

32. *Ibid.,* p. 422.

33. *Ibid.,* pp. 451-452.

34. C. 1361 of 1875, p. 33.

35. C. 3947 of 1884, pp. 11-18, including the map where the 1881 and 1884 boundaries are compared.

36. C. 4194 of 1884, pp. 7-8; C. 3486 of 1883, pp. 71-72.

37. His very interesting and influential story is told in a biography written by his son, William Douglas Mackenzie, *John Mackenzie, South African Missionary and Statesman* (New York: A. C. Armstrong & Son, 1902).

38. C. 4194 of 1884, pp. 85-105.

39. van Oordt, *Paul Kruger,* p. 400.   This German settlement had just been declared, August 15, 1884; cf. Raymond Walter Bixler, *Anglo-German Imperialism in South Africa, 1880-1900* (Baltimore: Warwick and York, 1932), pp. 23-26.

40. C. 4643 of 1886, p. 93.

41. C. 4839 of 1886, p. 29.

42. C. 4214 of 1884, p. 69.

43. C. 4587 of 1885, p. 15.

44. C. 4290 of 1885, p. 5; cf. Bixler, *Anglo-German Imperialism,* p. 6.

45. C. 5143 of 1887, p. 41.

46. van Oordt, *Paul Kruger,* p. 493.

47. C. 6201 of 1890, pp. 8, 11.

48. C. 6200 of 1890, p. 56, January 20, 1888, C. 7611 of 1895, pp. 2-3, 34-37.

49. C. 7780 of 1895, pp. 40, 50, 53.

50. Ibid., pp. 41ff.; C. 7878 of 1895.

51. Hofmeyr, Hofmeyr, p. 144.

52. van Jaarsveld, Afrikaner's Interpretation, p. 19.

53. The Afrikaner Bond published its first set of principles as follows:
"I Principles
"1. The Afrikaner Bond starts from the principle, that we as Afrikaners have our own general as well as special interests, which each true Afrikander is called upon to protect.
"2. In order, however, to exercise influence socially and politically, there is need of an Association or organization, that will unite all forces; and that means the Bond.
"3. To that end it includes every one that has chosen Africa as his fatherland, and aims at Africa's prosperity, irrespective of his national descent, or the ecclesiastical or political party to which he otherwise belongs.
II. Objects
"1. The Bond sets forward as its object the promotion of the prosperity of South Africa in general, and in particular the growth of true national feeling.
"2. For that purpose it takes under its protection the rights and interests of each section of the population, but more particularly of our farming population, which hitherto has been placed too much in the background.
"3. Especially it considers itself called upon to take under its protection the language of the people, where it is neglected, in the church, socially or politically, and especially in the schools.
"4. In politics its chief object is to provide, that the various classes of the population are properly represented in the various legislatures, according to their numerical strength, and by such representatives as are in agreement with the principles of the Bond.
"5. The bond shall watch over the press, to prevent harmful principles being published and to take care that the development of the population is promoted in a right and proper fashion.
"6. Special attention shall be paid by the Bond to the promotion of fitting and appropriate education, especially for our farming population."
These principles were presented July 4, 1879; printed in full in Hofmyer, Hofmeyr, pp. 196-197.

54. Quoted in Leopold Stennett Amery, ed., The Times History of the War in South Africa (6 vols., London: Sampson, Low, Marston and Co., 1900), I, 80-81.

55. Ibid.

56. Hofmeyr, *Hofmeyr*, pp. 200, 209.

57. S. J. du Toit, *Die Geskiedenis van ons Land in die Taal van ons Volk* (Paarl: 1877).   This document was located in the Johannesburg Public Library, and the author secured a photographic copy. The translations of this history are all from this document by the author.

58. du Toit, *Geskiedenis*, p. 58.

59. *Ibid.*, p. 62.

60. *Ibid.*, p. 87.

61. *Ibid.*, p. 120.

62. As quoted in van Jaarsveld, *Afrikaner en sy Geskiedenis*, p. 98.

63. C. P. Bezuidenhout, *De Geschiedenis van het Afrikaansche Geslacht van 1688 tot 1882* (Bloemfontein: 1883). This document is not available in the United States. I obtained a photographic copy from the Johannesburg Public Library. All translations are mine.

64. *Ibid.*, p. I-II.

65. *Ibid.*, p. 1.

66. *Ibid.*, pp. 1-2.

67. *Ibid.*, p. 3.

68. See Chapter II for further mention of Slagters' Nek battle.

69. Bezuidenhout, *Geschiedenis*, p. 3.

70. *Ibid.*, p. 5.

71. *Ibid.*

72. *Ibid.*, p. 6.

73. *Ibid.*

74. *Ibid.*, p. 7.

75. *Ibid.*, p. 8.

76. *Ibid.*, p. 10.

77. *Ibid.*, p. 11.

78. See Chapter IV for further mention of the Boomplaats battle.

79. Bezuidenhout, *Geschiedenis*, p. 11.

80. *Ibid.*, p. 11.

81. *Ibid.*, p. 16.

82. *Ibid.*, p. 18.

83. *Ibid.*, p. 19.

84. *Ibid.*, p. 21.

85. For further information, see Chapter V.

86. Bezuidenhout, *Geschiedenis*, p. 22.

87. *Ibid.*, p. 40.

88. *Ibid.*, p. 32.

89. *Ibid.*, p. 35.

90. *Ibid.*, p. 42.

91. *Ibid.*, p. 43.

92. *Ibid.*, p. 44.

93. *The War against War in South Africa,* a weekly periodical published during the War by Stop the War Committee of London; December 1, 1900.

94. Walker, *Lord de Villiers.*

95. Hofmeyr, *Hofmeyr.*

96. *Ibid.*, p. 144.

97. *Ibid.*, p. 145.

98. The complete set of rules is in *ibid.*, pp. 643-645.
    "I. The Association shall be called the South African Farmers' Protection Asociation.
    "II. The object of the association is to watch over and protect the farming interests of this Colony.
    "III. The Association proposes to attain these objectives:
    "a. by promoting the election of members of both Houses of Parliament who will generally oppose all measures calculated to press unduly on the farming population—who will resist the imposition of all export duties or other one-sided taxes on articles of Colonial produce or industry—who will avail themselves of every favorable opportunity for repealing or rendering less oppressive the excise tax on colonial spirits—who, in all proposed legislation on the relations of Masters and Servants, will keep in view the special wants of the farming population, and who will advocate the judicious application of grants out of the public revenue for the development of the agricultural and pastoral resources of the country;

"b. By endeavouring to secure the registration as Parliamentary voters of all men interested in the farming pursuits of the Colony and to guard against all abuse of the franchise.

"c. By providing proper machinery for informing the farmers of all measures proposed in Parliament, by which their interests may be endangered."

99. Hofmeyr, *Hofmeyr*, p. 80.

100. *Ibid.*, p. 214, April 1879.

101. *Ibid.*, pp. 205-206. For the Constitution adopted in 1883, see pp. 649-652.

102. *Ibid.*, pp. 222-225; Eybers, *Select Constitutional Documents*, p. 166.

103. Hofmeyr, *Hofmeyr*, pp. 247-248.

104. van Oordt, *Paul Kruger*, p. 389.

105. Walker, *History of Southern Africa*, p. 408.

106. Amery, *Times History*, I, 108-109.

107. J. S. Marais, *The Fall of Kruger's Republic* (Oxford: Clarendon Press, 1961), p. 1.

108. van Oordt, *Paul Kruger*, p. 558, December 16, 1891. Translation by the author.

109. *Ibid.*, p. 470.

110. *Ibid.*, p. 485. Italics added.

111. Engelbrecht, *T. F. Burgers*, pp. 113-138.

112. Amery, *Times History*, I, 98.

113. *Ibid.*

114. *Ibid.*, I, 99.

115. Hofmeyr, *Hofmeyr*, p. 330.

116. Amery, *Times History*, I, 99.

117. van Oordt, *Paul Kruger*, p. 498.

118. *Kruger's Memoirs*, p. 225.

119. Cornelis de Kiewiet, *A History of South Africa* (London: Oxford University Press, 1941), p. 125.

120. Jean van der Poel, *Railway and Customs Policies in South Africa, 1885-1910* (London: Longmans Green & Co., 1933), pp. 72-105.

121. Lewis Mitchell, *The Life and Times of the Right Honourable Cecil John Rhodes* (2 vols., London: Mitchell Kennerley, 1910), I, 23.

122. C. 5918 of 1890, pp. 224-232, October 29, 1889.

123. Michell, *Life of Rhodes*, I, 223, June 7, 1885.

124. Hofmeyr, *Hofmeyr*, pp. 411-412. Italics added.

125. van Oordt, *Paul Kruger*, p. 520.

126. Hofmeyr, *Hofmeyr*, p. 414.

127. *Ibid.*, p. 416.

128. Amery, *Times History*, p. 106.

129. Charles Leonard, ed., *Papers on the Political Situation in South Africa, 1885-1895* (London: Arthur L. Humphreys, 1903), p. 44.

130. *Ibid.*

131. *Ibid.*, p. 44.

132. *Ibid.*

133. Marais, *Fall of Kruger's Republic*, p. 1.

134. *Ibid.*, pp. 1-2.

135. *Ibid.*, p. 3.

136. van Oordt, *Paul Kruger*, p. 370.

137. *Ibid.*, p. 370.

138. Leonard, *Political Situation*, p. 138; Amery, *Times History*, I, 122.

139. Leonard, *Political Situation*, pp. 138-144.

140. Amery, *Times History*, I, 136.

141. *Ibid.*, p. 128.

142. Leonard, *Political Situation*, pp. 56-58.

143. van Oordt, *Paul Kruger*, p. 497.

144. Amery, *Times History*, I, 136.

145. A letter written by Lionel Phillips, one of the Uitlander agitators, on July 25, 1894; published in John Scobie and H. R. Abercrombie, *The Rise and Fall of Krugerism* (London: Wm. Heinemann, 1900), p. 273.

146. James McKinnon, *South African Traits: Sketches of his Life at the Cape of Good Hope* (Edinburgh: George Gemmell, 1887), pp. 274-275.

147. *Ibid.*, p. 285.

148. Amery, *Times History*, I, 127.

149. C. 3219 of 1882, p. 25; cf. van Oordt, *Paul Kruger*, p. 388.

150. Leonard, *Political Situation*, pp. 65-72, where he gives a history of the franchise question.

151. van Oordt, *Paul Kruger*, p. 505.

152. *Ibid.*, p. 143.

153. *Ibid.*, p. 492.

154. Leonard, *Politcal Situation*, p. 66.

155. van Oordt, *Paul Kruger*, p. 554.

156. *Ibid.*, p. 554.

157. J. P. Fitzpatrick, *The Transvaal from Within* (New York: Frederick A. Stokes, 1899), pp. 189-190, where the Volksraad debate is printed.

158. Fitzpatrick, *Transvaal from Within*, p. 385; the Volksraad debates, 1891.

159. *Ibid.*, p. 389; Volksraad debates 1892.

160. Leonard, *Political Situation*, p. 52.

161. Spoelstra, *Het Kerkelijk en Godsdienstig Leven der Boeren*, pp. 364-382.

162. van Oordt, *Paul Kruger*, p. 519.

163. Spoelstra, *Het Kerkelijk en Godsdienstig Leven der Boeren*, p. 365.

164. Amery, *Times History*, p. 133.

165. Walker, *History of Southern Africa*, p. 438.

166. Leonard, *Political Situation*, pp. 23-24.

167. Fitzpatrick, *Transvaal from Within*, pp. 396-403, gives selected statements from the debate.

168. Mr. Tossen, in Fitzpatrick, *Transvaal from Within*, p. 397.

169. Mr. Jan de Beer, in Fitzpatrick, *Transvaal from Within*, p. 400.

170. *Ibid.*, p. 400.

171. *Ibid.*

172. Amery, *Times History*, I, 144.

173. Leonard, *Political Situation*, pp. 38-39, sections of the Manifesto. Cf. C. 7933 of 1896, pp. 65-72.

VII.
Collision of Afrikaner and British
Policies: Trial by Fire, 1895–1902

The conflicts revolving around the franchise debate, the demands of the Uitlanders, and the agitation that grew out of various grievances kept the situation tense. The Boers' self-confidence and continuing trust in their God-given destiny, however, kept them optimistic. Had Kruger made a misstep, moderate opinion throughout South Africa would have surged to the side of the British imperialists for redressing grievances and for justice. Suddenly, however, the advantage was shifted to the Boers' side in a way they could not have foreseen. The misstep was taken by Prime Minister Rhodes of the Cape Colony, which in turn intensified the Boers' determination to oppose the British and to exert their own nationalistic ambitions. The moderates, fearing further intervention by the British, shifted their sympathies to the Pretoria government. Kruger again gained the ideological offensive. In a real sense the mobilization of the Boers in the Jameson Raid was the first skirmish along the escalating road to the Anglo-Boer War four years hence.

The Boers had been secretly arming themselves for several months, and by 1895 the Uitlanders knew that the Boers had placed large arms and ammunition orders in Germany. Furthermore, German officers were coming to train the Boers.[1] Germany continued to encourage the Transvaal to maintain its anti-British policy in order to safeguard German investments there.[2] This knowledge caused a stir of unrest among the Uitlanders, who were becoming desperate for reforms. They appealed to the Rhodes government in Cape Town. Some even hoped for intervention by British forces.[3] In response the Rhodes government conceived a plan, secretly backed by Joseph Chamberlain, colonial secretary in London.[4] They conceived of an uprising among the Uitlanders in order to have an excuse to intervene directly in affairs in the Transvaal. To this end British sympathizers began to smuggle arms to the Uitlanders in the Transvaal.

Still determined that he would not be bound to Britain by economic ties, Kruger attempted to modify rail rates to force incoming goods to be transported via Delagoa Bay rather than on Cape Colony railways. As a last move in this direction, the Transvaal government in August 1895 placed a prohibitive tariff on all goods entering the Transvaal by rail from the Cape Colony. Rather than transfer to a different port, the shippers chose to unload trains at the Transvaal border and transport their products by ox wagon through the Transvaal. Not to be outdone, Kruger retaliated and on October 1, 1895, forbade ox wagons to cross at any of the Vaal "drifts" (fords), again stifling trade.[5] This act of obstruction was a violation of article XIII of the Convention of London, which stated that "no other or higher duties shall be imposed . . . on any article coming from any other place."[6] British sympathizers reported to London, and Chamberlain replied with a telegram strong enough to force Kruger to "climb down" from his lofty position.[7]

In the meantime, organization for the planned insurrection continued. This called for an uprising in Johannesburg when a plea would be sent to Cape Town for assistance to "restore order." Sir Hercules Robinson, the British high commissioner of South Africa, would be sent immediately after receiving the "invitaion." In addition, Leander Starr Jameson of Rhodesia would be called from Bechuanaland with his troops, and the international insurrection would overturn the Pretoria government. The plan miscarried. Uitlanders complaining that they had not received as many weapons as they were promised sought to postpone the insurrection. Fearing his carefully laid plans would be scuttled, or would be postponed by command of Rhodes, Jameson decided to serve his country by fomenting the rebellion himself. He cut the telegraph lines from Cape Town to Mafeking, Bechuanaland, so he could not receive the message of postponement Rhodes was in fact sending, and on December 29, 1895, he began his march from Bechuanaland to Johannesburg. On January 2 he and almost five hundred men were captured at Doornkop, near Johannesburg. There was no major uprising, Sir Hercules Robinson disclaimed knowledge of the raid, and Chamberlain in London did the same. Jameson was jailed, Prime Minister Rhodes—who had been elected and supported by moderate Afrikaners—was toppled from office, and Afrikaners across South Africa united behind the victims of this conspiracy.[8] The Pretoria government was further encouraged when it received a telegram from the German emperor offering congratulations for withstanding "foreign aggression."[9]

The conspiracy roused the deepest animosities of both the Afrikaner and the British communities and became a major foundation stone for the forthcoming Anglo-Boer war. The Boers attempted to capitalize on the punishment and relate this symbolically to their own past grievances. Someone located a beam of wood, purported to be the one on which Boers were hanged after the rebellion in 1815. It was suggested that the prisoners be hanged without trial to avenge Slagters' Nek.[10] Kruger wisely declined such advice as he reflected, "You shall not return evil for evil"

(Romans 12:17).[11]   He did, however, relate this incident as the third treacherous attack on Boers. The first was that of Mzilikazi when the trekkers first arrived in the Free State, and the second the attack by Dingane in 1838. This was the worst of all, however, because it was perpetrated not by "black barbarians" but by civilized whites.[12]

If the insurrection had been initiated from within the Transvaal, perhaps the sympathies of the world would have supported their cause. The unfortunate invasion from without, however, exposed the whole plot. The Boers used the incident to prove once more the theological justification for their society. A few months after the raid, Ons Land published its analysis:

> Has not Providence over-ruled and guided the painful course of events in South Africa since the beginning of this year [1896]? Who can doubt it. . . . This Providence sent a stab which was intended to paralyze Afrikanerdom once and for all in the Republics, [but rather this became] an electric thrill direct to the national heart.[13]

"Providence" purposely approved and supposedly supported the sudden surge toward Afrikaner nationalism that followed the abortive Jameson Raid.

As a step toward the Boer War, the Jameson Raid was but one of many, but as an incident around which the Boers' sympathy could cluster, it was decisive. This was the next major challenge following the crisis of 1877-1881 in which the Boers clearly saw God's approval of their cause. The Jameson Raid hardened the Boers' attitudes toward Britain and brought wavering or moderate Boers to the support of freedom and the Transvaal government. The raid should have taught the Pretoria government how vulnerable its status was, when the Transvaal was but an island in the British sea and when half the population could easily be driven to appeal for British intervention.   Rather than recognize their precarious situation, however, the Boers looked in the opposite direction. They said, in effect, "In an impossible situation, look how much God has done for us." This interpretation gave Kruger a mandate from God not to modify past policies but to strengthen them. He felt justified to push relentlessly forward. many sympathetic Boers agreed wholeheartedly with his interpretation, and they loyally closed ranks behind him.

Kruger intensified his hold on government by appointing promising Afrikaners to significant government posts. This was a welcome change for those who had criticized his policy of importing so many government officials, business leaders, and monopoly holders from Europe. Among these he appointed Jan Smuts as state attorney in 1898. Smuts, from the Cape Colony, trained in the law both in the Cape Colony and at Cambridge, migrated to the Transvaal after the raid.[14] Kruger appointed Francis W. Reitz, another native of the Cape Colony and a lawyer, formerly president of the Free State. He became state secretary, replacing W. J. Leyds who had often been criticized for being more a Hollander than a Transvaaler. To strengthen his political organization further, Kruger appointed some opponents of government positions, thereby winning support from ever-expanding groups of people.

Several new laws were introduced that helped to strengthen the walls of Zion. To keep the state pure, the Alien Exclusion Bill was passed into law in September 1896.[15] The bill was designed to exclude anyone deemed a menace to the public peace and order; it was directed especially against Uitlander leaders. British officials immediately insisted the law was unconstitutional according to article XIV of the London Convention, which stated that "all persons . . . other than natives . . . will have full liberty . . . to enter, travel, or reside in any part of the South African Republic."[16] Questions were also raised with respect to the immigration law, passed late in 1896, requiring foreigners to register and carry a passport when in the Transvaal. The government tightened its control on the press by passing a censorship law in 1896 designed to suppress two newspapers hostile to the regime.[17] Large groups had been forbidden to hold outdoor public meetings although they were permissible inside.[18] Evidently the Boers remembered that it was through the medium of such large mass meetings that they began their agitation in 1879, which led to the war little over a year later.

Concessions that were approved and investigations undertaken were for the purpose not of discovering truth but to keep the Pretoria government in control. In 1897, for example, the government appointed an industrial commission to inquire into why the mines were not producing as they should. The government attempted to place the blame on the mine officials. The commission, led by Schalk Burger, a progressive Afrikaner, turned rather to the relation between the mines and the government. After investigating, they recommended a reduction of the exorbitant taxes to which mines were subject and suggested a committee composed of both government and mine leaders to work out an equitable policy.[19] The Kruger government, however, branded Burger a "traitor" and proceeded to appoint a Volksraad committee to revise the recommendations to make them acceptable to the government.

In other ways the Kruger government showed that it wanted to remain in complete control of all aspects of society. One example of this was a reform of the city of Johannesburg, which was allowed municipal status in September 1897. The authority for action, however, centered in a town council, some members of which were appointed by the government. The townspeople realized this was no reform.[20] At about the same time J. G. Kotze, chief justice, became the leader among lawyers questioning the legality of some of the governmental procedures. Kruger responded by dismissing Kotze from office.[21] In the celebrated Edgar Case, unnecessary policy brutality was charged. Edgar, an Uitlander, had knocked a man down in a fight. Police, all Boers according to Transvaal law, followed Edgar home and shot him. When the police were tried by their peers and given a light sentence, the case became a political weapon for the Uitlanders.[22] Other Uitlanders prepared a petition of grievances to be sent to the queen, but this was refused and their leader summarily arrested.[23]   A protest meeting in Johannesburg was broken up in riot, instigated by Boers sent by the government.[24]

One of Kruger's ambitions of the period was to substantiate his idea that the London Convention had been superseded and Transvaal was a sovereign state.   Many times he used this idea to gain sympathy for his cause against the aggressive British.   A long correspondence with London proved once again that the two governments argued from different pre-suppositions.   In the controversy over the alien-exclusion and immigration laws, Kruger maintained that article IV of the London Convention did not apply to them any longer.[25]   He reasoned that since they were a sovereign state, not one requiring approval from the British, points of dispute must be solved by an independent third party, such as Switzerland.[26]   Chamberlain replied that the Convention of London did not allow complete sovereignty but self-government with certain conditions; there could be no arbitration by a foreign power.[27]   Leyds reminded England that the word *sovereign* was dropped from the London Convention; hence the Transvaal owed its inde-pendence to an agreement between two sovereign powers, and its condi-tions were equally binding on both nations.[28]   Chamberlain countered with the statement that the word *sovereign* may have been dropped, but the concept remained.[29]   Reitz, the new Transvaal state secretary, carried the idea one step further: "The now existing right of absolute self-government of this Republic is not derived from either the Convention of 1881 or that of 1884, but . . . from the inherent right of this Republic as a sovereign international state."[30]   The correspondence was concluded by Chamberlain in July when he suggested that Britain had no intention to continue the discussion.   A conditional suzerainty concept remained despite the Trans-vaal arguments.[31]

Kruger was not short-sighted or naive in political affairs.   He did not have the formal training of most of his opponents, but he was a shrewd planner and had much political success in achieving what he believed was necessary.   Rather, his hesitance to accept change was based on his prior loyalty to a covenant with God.   With this higher loyalty, he saw no reason to come to terms with British leaders or with Uitlanders.   He must bear his own responsibility for his nation and the blessings would come from God, not from men.

Support for the Afrikaner cause, now embodied in the Kruger govern-ment, came from the Free State and the Cape Colony. Earlier President Reitz of the Free State had swayed his people toward Transvaal sympathies from their moderate position under President Brand.   Reitz stepped down from the office and was succeeded by Marthinus Theunis Steyn, who was even more wholeheartedly a supporter of Kruger.[32]   When chosen president on December 11, 1895, President Steyn gave the theological basis for his government.

> In case I must rely on my own power, then I surely will flinch from the difficulties incumbent on this office. As I rely on the voices coming to me from all sides, and as I think that the God which has led our honored Presidents with so many signs for our Fatherland, I have confidence. Today the same God is prepared and remains ready to help those who ask, and I can do nothing less than accept the invitation extended to me by this election.[33]

As he was sworn in in 1896 he was told, "In the task which is laid on his shoulders, may he rely not only on his own powers, but on the power from the God who shall help him, and Who shall remain with the *Volk* (people), and above all Who shall remain with the people's elected representatives— the Volksraad."[34] In March 1897 Kruger went to Bloemfontein to discuss another treaty with President Steyn of the Free State, similar to that he had concluded eight years before with President Reitz. Each leader promised mutual protection if the other were attacked, and they laid the basis of an eventual federation or union of the two republics.[35]

In the Cape moderate Afrikaners were leaders of the government where W. P. Schreiner was elected prime minister in 1898. Many were still skeptical of British imperialist plots, and many had strong sympathy for the Transvaal. *Ons Land*, the moderate newspaper in Cape Town, was undoubtedly read by a large number of sympathetic Afrikaners when it editorialized:

> Afrikanerdom has awakened to a sense of earnestness and consciousness which we have not observed since the heroic war for Liberty in 1881. This has given birth to a new inspiration and a movement amongst our people in South Africa. Now or never the foundation of a wide-embracing nationalism must be laid. . . . Let us now lay the foundation-stone of a real United South Africa on the soil of a pure and all-comprehensive national sentiment.[36]

On February 22, 1897, the Cape *Times* proposed a movement that was to be for Afrikaners against British. It suggested that all Afrikaners set aside their differences and unite in a more aggressive policy for "right for Transvaal."[37]

There were still moderates who were loyal Afrikaners and who were strongly critical of Kruger's tactics and believed the worst was yet to come. De Villiers, chief justice of the Cape Colony and a long-time leader of the moderates, attempted to alleviate tensions as he suggested to Steyn: "If I had any influence with the President [Kruger] I would advise him no longer to sit on the boiler to prevent it from bursting. Some safety valves are required for the activities of the new population."[38]   John X. Merriman, also a Cape moderate, told Steyn that the moderation of the Free State was all that stood between the Transvaal and disaster, but even Steyn was hardly a mediator for he was bound by treaty to the cause of the Transvaal.[39]

The British government knew that the situation was near the breaking point.   Consequently when Sir Hercules Robinson resigned in 1897, an aggressive and determined high commissioner and cape governor was appointed.   He was Sir Alfred Milner, a careful but determined imperialist. He had no illusions about his duty but knew there was tension on both sides.   In a speech at Graaff-Reinet a few months after he arrived, Milner made it clear what the problem was and how it might be solved:

> The political controversy of the country at present unfortunately turns largely on another question—I mean the relations of Her Majesty's government to the South African Republic, and whenever there is any prospect of any difference between them, a number of the people in the colony at once vehemently, and without even the semblance of impartiality, espouse the side of the Republic. . . . They seem to care much more for the independence of the Transvaal than for the honor and interests of the country to which they themselves belong.[40]

Afrikaner feeling was intense in South Africa, based on their concept of what they thought God called them to do. British emotions also ran high against the "injustice" in the Transvaal. While the Afrikaners were taking their place in the Cape Colony as a responsible Afrikaner party, the pro-English group was also developing in intensity. They believed that the British government should intervene in the Transvaal or else cease being the paramount power in South Africa.

Afrikaner nationalist ideology was firmly based on the idea that God grants special favor to those who are true to their covenant and who take special precautions to maintain a pure society.   Transvaal leaders attempted to keep their society pure both politically and religiously in order to be assured of God's continual advantage. While various leaders were instilling enthusiasm for this religious nationalism—one Dutch Reformed minister took a different look at his society. The tension among the three Dutch Reformed denominations, not yet settled, was still considered a mark of disloyalty before God. Added to this, the unrest generated with relation to the Uitlanders augmented the confusion. On June 13, 1897, the Rev. Coenraad Spoelstra of the N. H. K. of Pretoria preached a sermon for the occasion. He based it on the destroyed vineyard of Isaiah 5 and predicted similar destruction through God's displeasure unless peace and harmony befitting a true Christian nation were established. He asked three searching questions and in each case compared the biblical story with the Boers' life in the Transvaal.

> I. What did the Heavenly Landlord do for Israel—What for our land and people? . . . The vineyard of the Lord is Israel's house and the men of Judah are a plant of his pleasure; therefore the whole Israelite people, and the kingdom of Judah are His. We understand the vineyard to be Israel, one and undivided.

He then continued to allegorize all aspects of the beautiful vineyard:

> Brothers and sisters, there are many noteworthy examples which exist by which we compare Israel's history and the history of our land and people. . . . Israel's God led our fathers out of servitude with a powerful arm. He helped them in such a wonderful way to triumph over the heathen peoples. We say "That is God's finger." . . . Therefore, the Spirit of the Lord rests in our midst to make us into noble wine, into men and women of faith and filled with the Holy Ghost, who yearn for Him, in order to be a sign for the two hundred million [sic]men who live in South Africa. . . . He has devoted all concern to us and all gracious happenings are on our behalf—that from noble winestocks we might grow into noble fruit—justice and righteousness.
>
> II. Yet, what type of fruit has Israel—And what fruits have we offered?

He summarized all the sins mentioned in Isaiah 5, such as love of money, drunkenness, falsehood, and evil-doing:

> What Isaiah said is in all instances coming to pass in the South African Republic. . . . He was angry against the lovers of money; against the detestable covetousness of those who take possession of the best land for themselves while they take the land away from the poor. . . . Do not the covetous in our midst seem to be the root of all evils? . . . The prophet opposes carousers and drunkards. Are there not also many in the land who are so under the influence of wine and strong drink that they pay no attention to what the Lord says, and they have no eye for the works of His hands? . . .
>
> Shall the prophet not also oppose the blasphemers and liars in our midst? . . . Do our leaders always take refuge in the God of wisdom and power—or are they too satisfied to stand on their own wisdom and understanding? Are Christian statesmanship and worldly politics always held strongly opposed to each other? . . . Where one is guilty, there the whole people is guilty. (Joshua 7).
>
> Search yourselves, beloved brethren and sisters. What

have you offered: noble wine, or vermin? . . . The Great
Winegardener asks: "What was there to be done in my vineyard
that I did not do?" How shall we answer Him? . . .

I am deeply humble about our shameful and guilty appearance of fruitfulness!
III.   Shall Israel's dreadful lot be ours also? The Landlord says
to the unfruitful vineyard . . . I shall make it a wilderness. . . .
Thorns and thistles shall shoot up from it; and I shall command
the clouds that there shall be no more rain on it. . . . The land
shall become a dry wasteland. . . . Brothers and Sisters, let us
examine ourselves in relation to Israel! Whoever does Israel's
sins shall undergo Israel's lot. Israel's God is not to be mocked.
As we take on the appearance of serving Him; as we sustain
only the form of God and religion; if we call "Lord, Lord" in
place of doing the daily work of the Heavenly Father; if there
is no real conversion—no deep-felt repentance; no shunning and
hating sin; if no good comes out of our shortcoming; . . . then
our day of prayer is indeed an abomination.

He then listed the possible evils that will come from the Lord:

As He sees that the riches which He entrusted to us are placed
above Him; . . . then he chastens us to make us search our own
hearts to bring us to our senses. . . . Our land, which was
purchased by the blood and the prayers of our fathers will be
given into the hands of our enemies; our free and self-governing existence will come to nothing, and our nation will be
removed from the list of nations; our own law, our customs,
our government authorities will be gone. We will no longer
have our language, but that of strangers. Our land will be
waste, our homes burned, our churches ineffective. Our land a
waste land and a people forsaken by God. . . .

We should then turn again to the Lord as one man.
Because of his promise, he will in no way cast out those who
come to him.[41]

A few years later, the same minister concluded that this prophecy had been
unusually accurate, and credit was given to God that this was revealed to
the people.[42]

There was at the same time another aspect to the Boers' religious
nationalism. Theophilus Lyndall Schreiner, a German who had settled in
South Africa and was sympathetic with the moderate Afrikaners, was more
critical. He was skeptical of the place of the Dutch Reformed ministers
and the Afrikaner Bond in keeping South Africa divided and agitated.
Looking back to this period just before the Boer War he reflected:

Another cause of the war is to be traced to the successful efforts of the Afrikaner Bond to gain the cooperation of the ministers of the Dutch Reformed Church. . . .

While the loyalty of some of them is beyond question, and deserves grateful recognition and while we acknowledge their generally pious and spiritual character, it is not too much to aver that they have as a rule fostered and strengthened the Dutch Republican sentiment, as opposed to the interests of England in South Africa.[43]

He criticized the religious nationalism that was untrue to the authentic Christian faith:

The idea referred to seems of late years, perhaps unconsciously in some cases, to have been elevated into an article of religion by many of the ministers and members of the Dutch Presbyterian churches, whose teaching has tended to foster the belief that the Dutch people of South Africa *are the people of God par excellence, like Israel of old,* and that the English are by comparison the enemies of God, like the Amelekites, the Phillistines, etc.; that *the Dutch language is the language of God's people,* while English is a poor and worldly tongue; that *the Dutch Presbyterian Church is the Church of God,* all other churches, even the English and Scotch Presbyterians occupying a much lower level. . . . So widely, deeply and firmly have these ideas taken root that even the spiritually-minded among the ministers and their flocks . . . have not escaped the contagion of this unjust and puffed-up *religion of Dutch Republican patriotism.* . . . This religion of Dutch pseudo-patriotism has misled Presidents Kruger and Steyn into dragging themselves and the states over which they ruled to their doom. Their speeches are saturated with it. They assume all the promises of national blessing to Israel in the Bible to be theirs.[44]

The situation had so conditioned the Transvaal leaders that they confused their preconceived goals with God's will without fully realizing what they were doing. Their patriotism was based on theological ideas that deeply motivated them, but this was an unauthentic theology, unworthy to be the foundation of a true religious nationalism.

In February 1898 seventy-three-year-old Paul Kruger was elected to his fourth five-year term as president. At his inauguration on May 12, he summarized his theological ideas in a speech that lasted over three hours and in printed form covers thirty pages. He emphasized the same theme as in the past. To the Volksraad he said:

I stand here before you, in obedience to the voice of the people, in which I believe I recognize God's voice, in order once more, as State President, to take upon myself the government of the country. . . . When I look back and see how the Lord has guided the people and that God has set the people free, then I know, now that I am to govern the people, what would follow if I were to falter, for I have not only to give an account to you honorable gentlemen, but also to God, and my life is short; I shall have to appear before Him, and when I think of that, my heart fails me, and I can only pray.

His promise is that to them who expect aid and strength from the Lord he will teach the plain path, and him that feareth the Lord He will guide. . . . He who acknowledges this in his heart looks to the Lord, our faithful God of the Covenant, for light, wisdom and divine strength. He will give us everything out of His infinite wealth of mercy. Yes, I trust in that faithful God of the Covenant, because He has so clearly led us along various paths. So I accept this post in the fear of God and in all uprightness; yes, it is my innermost desire and the wish of my heart to live for Him and to govern the people according to His will.

Directing his attention to the burghers of the country he continued:

An array of thoughts comes up within me, all of which lead to one point, namely, that we must observe God's ways. To go over all these with you I have not now the time; but I trust that you will recall everything in your own thoughts and consider those ways, those proofs of the faith that God has shown us,— that He has rescued us from oppression and given us other blessings; and the ways in which God has punished us and we have been oppressed by our adversaries.

Let us stand in sincerity this day before God's countenance. We see that God's arm is stretched out; he is chastising us; and we shall find that everywhere we are breaking God's commandments. . . . We often ask "Why does the Lord chastise us so?" Is this not in order that we may return to him?

To the judicial leaders he said:

From you there is no longer any appeal, and therefore you are called "gods;" but God stands in the midst of the council of the gods and pronoounces judgment upon good and evil. If you act to the best of your knowledge and conscience and remain within the law, then one day it shall be said of you also: "Thou good and faithful servant, thou hast been faithful over a few things, I will make thee ruler over many things". [Matthew 5:21, 23].[45]

As long as the president maintained the support of the majority, the nation could withstand all attempts to modify its policies. Discussions were used only to pacify dissent, not to change governmental policy; discussions were expedient but were not used to gain information. The president believed this his government was based on truths more basic than any discussion could elucidate and on national assumptions backed by confidence that they were doing God's will. Increasingly the Transvaal became a formidable fortress, less and less likely to allow new light or any gradual modification.

By now it was evident that the basic grievances of the Uitlanders revolved around the franchise. By the law of 1890, which included the creation of the Second Volksraad, the Uitlanders became no more than "half-burghers" in a land where they hoped to remain. They could see no prospect for any improvement. The British official, Milner, sought a meeting with the Transvaal leaders to discuss specifically the franchise question.[46]   Arrangements were made for the discussion to begin in Bloemfontein on May 31, 1899. Milner believed that the situation was serious, and this must be a successful last-minute attempt to avert severe consequences. He knew he must not press for a franchise modification so drastic that Kruger would refuse immediately, but he still must seek a modification significant enough that the Uitlanders would believe progress was being made. Kruger came with apprehension about the whole question. He did not recognize the right of the Uitlanders' pleas to become full citizens, and since he was attempting to ignore the London Convention, he saw no justification for the British intervention in Transvaal government procedures.

As the conference convened, Milner came to the point directly. He urged a change of policy with respect to the Uitlanders. If the Pretoria government would make a liberal and workable adjustment, Uitlanders would not continually appeal for outside help, and hence the Transvaal would have less, not more, British intervention.[47]   Kruger raised his defenses immediately, however, as he replied: "If those who rushed in speedily get a vote equal to our burghers, and they can vote in the Volksraad, then in a very short time those who are brought in can turn the laws topsy-turvy, and do as they like, and with that my independence would fall, in that they could make laws as they like, and the burghers would be crushed out in that way."[48]   Milner did not suggest a drastic reform; he asked only that Uitlanders have a few seats on the Volksraad. A more significant difference remained between the two men. Kruger had repeatedly stated, "Don't touch our independence." Milner reiterated that he saw no connection between discussing the franchise and the Transvaal independence. Kruger, however, could not separate the two. He believed that soon he would be voted out of office, and if he should consent, "it would be worse than annexation."[49]   "If I were to go further [in lowering the franchise requirements] I should be giving my land away." Burghers who "paid for that country by their blood," would be outvoted.[50]

Milner then suggested that any Volksraad, no matter how constituted, should vote the will of the majority of the people.[51] They would not necessarily undo laws of the present Volksraad. Kruger did not understand this reasoning for he had a much narrower concept of who was a true Transvaal citizen. He remarked, "It is wholly against God's word to let strangers carry on the administration," suggesting that they cannot serve two masters at the same time.[52] Milner countered by reminding Kruger that they were discussing not strangers but fully naturalized citizens who had taken the oath of loyalty to their new homeland. Kruger never saw a distinction between Uitlander citizens and imperialist outsiders, and thus in his eyes all who sought change were instruments of Britain, a foreign conspiracy.

Because of the differing presuppositions with which the two leaders came to the conference it was doomed to fail before it began. On the fifth day, June 3, 1899, the two parted, but not before Kruger summarized his ideas with a homely parable:

> If I gave it [the franchise] away . . . I would be giving away my land. You must admit that it would be as unfair as if I had a rich farm and lots of water, and I said to others "Come and help work my farm for me, and you must give me a little of what you win on that farm," and when they have got rich on my farm they said "Give me the title deeds of that farm." They actually have more rights than I have myself, because the gold fields form the richest part of my land. Instead of being thankful for what they get here, they now begin to want title deeds and because they are more numerous they would like to have my farm.[53]

Kruger's real fears were based on his concept of the Boers' covenants with God—at Blood River in 1838 and at Wonderfontein in 1879—renewed at every religious and national gathering subsequent to 1881. They had promised to do His will and to be faithful with the gifts they had been given. God had proved himself many times and would do so again. It was those who had covenanted with God who owned the land, and even the profit from the gold was theirs—God's gift to faithful Boers. When put in such theological terms, Kruger's fears concerning the franchise for the English settlers become clear. He was not arguing political expediency, nor could he sympathize with the logic of the British official. He was obeying his interpretaion of his responsibility before God, and he would be held accountable if he did anything to jeopardize the freedom of his Zion.

The failure of the Bloemfontein Conference brought tension on all sides, a political calm in the midst of swirling unrest. Both sides began to build their armaments and their defenses "to protect peace." The South African League, formed after the demise of the National Union in the Jameson Raid, organized and promoted pro-British sentiment throughout

the land. No longer were the leaders interested only in redressing grievances under the banner of the republic; they began, rather, to agitate for
subjugation of the Kruger policies and for loyalty to the British Empire.[54]
Enthusiasm mounted daily for Milner's offer of a compromise at the Bloemfontein Conference.[55]

The Transvaal Boer leaders realized the changed situation as well.
Secretary of State Reitz stated the case for the Transvaal in June 1899:

> Owing to the presence of races [nationalities] in South Africa
> ... principally a legacy of the past, South Africa is today in
> this fatal position, that, as soon as a dispute arises between the
> Government, and Her Majesty's Government, war is spoken of
> by one party, and thereby again the slumbering suspicions of
> the other party are awakened. In this manner party feeling and
> race hatred are more and more increased, and the minds of the
> Republic are held in such a state of tension, that the whole of
> South Africa suffers most deeply under it.[56]

Now that any compromise seemed unlikly, the future held only two possibilities for the Transvaal: surrender completely, or go to war against the
agitating Uitlander, and ultimately against the Britsh Empire. Diplomat-
ically they were being backed slowly into a corner. Enthusiasm for the
inevitable was built on a theological foundation. Kruger addressed the
Volksraad on July 14, 1899, stating that he did not want war, but to make
any more concessions would be to surrender. "The Lord had protected their
independence in the past; He would never let them lose it."[57] Three days
later an emotional meeting of four thousand Boers was held at Paardekraal.
General P. J. Cronje admonished them "never to surrender to any power the
privilege they had inherited, and if they were required to shed their blood,
to put their trust in the Almighty."[58]

Not only were the Boers fearful of the consequences of the situation,
but the Uitlanders of the Transvaal became concerned as well. They met in
secret and complained that the Pretoria government was building forts
overlooking Johannesburg.[59] Reitz did not commit his governemnt when he
replied that there was no need for uneasiness. The forts were only for
"protection," and he had no idea of any reason to take extreme steps. The
Pretoria government had no intention of making any attack on the city,
except in self-defense.[60]

Preparations for war continued. British troops were concentrated in
Natal on the Transvaal border "to protect British interests." Great numbers of Uitlanders were leaving the two republics. They suspected that the
Boers were preparing to expel all Uitlanders and destroy the city of Johannesburg.[61] The Free State closed its borders to British subjects; mines
were idle; the Transvaal government confiscated a large shipment of gold

prepared for export.[62]   As the tensions mounted and war seemed inevitable, President Steyn of the Free State answered questions of his
people and gave his own justification for their preparations.

> See, then, the questions which must be answered before God
> and before you people. What concerns me has forced me to
> days of reflection and has cost, also, nights of prayer. I have
> done what I can for the peace with true honor, and shall con-
> tinue to do so. I now say to you, however, openly and with a
> free conscience: I would rather lose the independence of the
> Orange Free State with honor than to maintain it with dishonor
> or deceit. . . . Many think that I have not thought seriously on
> this question. I know what it is for two weak Republics to
> oppose the mightiest nation the world has ever seen. I know
> that if this comes to war, we will fight not only for the right of
> speech, but for the preservation of the Afrikaner people. Our
> cause is just. I have the faith that nothing happens without the
> will of the Almighty. He who has so wonderfully helped our
> forefathers, shall also take pity on us. In either case: His Will
> be done.[63]

Legal authorities in the Transvaal justified government seizure of property
of any British subject.[64]   Some Uitlanders who did not escape were imprisoned. Finally, on September 27, Kruger announced that any who agreed
to fight for the Transvaal would be given the franchise.[65]   By a treaty in
1897, the Free State was bound to support the Transvaal, and secret meetings were held to plan strategy.[66]

There were yet some Afrikaners who considered compromise preferable
to destruction, but their voices were not heard. J. H. de Villiers made a
plea as late as September 28, hoping that disaster could be averted.[67]   An
interesting telegram was sent to President Steyn urging hesitation rather
than war. The telegram from Cape Town simply referred to I Kings 22 and
was signed "Micaiah."[68]   Steyn, however, was bound to the Transvaal by
treaty and could not heed this biblical warning.

The two governments now decided to make one final statement of their
principles; each would prepare an ultimatum. The British authorities began
by outlining all of their grievances against the Transvaal since 1881. From
London, Joseph Chamberlain summarized the British point of view early in
October 1899:

> It must be clearly borne in mind that what we have to deal
> with is not the individual cases of grievances, numerous as they
> may have been. . . . but it is the general situation which has
> been created by the policy uniformly pursued by the South
> African Republic since 1881 and directed against any assertion

of supremacy on the part of Her Majesty's Government and any claim to equality for British subjects.

What is at stake is the position of Great Britain in South Africa, and with it the estimate formed of our power and influence in our colonies and throughout the world.

The Dutch in South Africa desire, if it be possible, to get rid altogether of the connexion with Great Britain, which to them is not a Motherland, and to substitute a United States of South Africa which, they hope, would be mainly under Dutch influence.   This idea has always been present in their minds. . . . But it would probably have died out as a hopeless impossibility but for the evidence of successful resistance to British Supremacy by the South African Republic.[69]

The ultimatum the British presented posed three main topics: maintenance of their position as paramount state of South Africa and the exclusion of all foreign influence; equal rights for all white inhabitants of the Transvaal; and just and considerate treatment of the African population. They stated that the Transvaal "deliberately designed to oust Her Majesty's Government from the supremacy restored to her by that [Pretoria, 1881] Convention." To this end they made seven stipulations, of which we need mention only the first three. The British demanded: "(1) repeal of all legislation since 1881 injuriously affecting the rights and privileges of aliens . . . ; (2) full municipal rights to be granted to the mining districts . . . ; [and] (3) a guarantee of independence of Courts of Justice." British authorities were not specific as to the consequences of failing to fulfill the wishes of the ultimatum:

If these conditions are agreed to, Her Majesty's Government are still prepared to give a complete guarantee against any attack upon the independence of the South African Republic. . . . [But] failing such acceptance, Her Majesty's Government will hold themselves at liberty to take such steps as may seem necessay to secure their objects.[70]

The British ultimatum was never presented, however, for the Boer government presented an ultimatum of its own. Kruger prefaced the document with an admonition to his people. He now believed that war was inevitable because their enemies "did not want the Afrikaners to be a nation; [but] The Lord would be with them, and would be the Final Arbitrator."[71] Then he asked them to read Psalm, 118:7-8:

The Lord is on my side to help me;
I shall look in triumph on those who hate me.
It is better to take refuge in the Lord than
to put confidence in man.

Boers should not fear the shots of the enemy, for "who directs the shots but the Lord?"[72]

On October 9 the Boers presented their ultimatum, including four main ideas: points of difference should be regulated by friendly arbitration; British troops on the borders of the Transvaal should be immediately removed; all troop reinforcements having arrived in the last four months are to be removed; and British troops on the seas are not to be landed in any port of South Africa.[73] The Boers asked for an unequivocal affirmative reply to all four points by five o'clock in the afternoon of October 11, only two days hence. In case no reply was received, the Transvaal would "regard the action of Her Majesty's Government as a formal declaration of war."[74]

No reply came, and on October 12, 1899, the Anglo-Boer War began as the Boers captured a train in British Bechuanaland, south of Mafeking. It has been suggested that the two powers went to war merely over a franchise question or over the interpretation of a word, *suzerainty*.[75] In reality the war came because two conflicting ideologies were juxtaposed in one nation, and no compromise seemed feasible. The British, driven by motives of imperialism, economics, and desire for equality of their subjects could not compromise with what they interpreted to be a class rule and a closed society, inefficient, hopelessly outmoded, and with little knowledge of the ways of modern goverment. Neither could the Pretoria government compromise. They were God's chosen people. They had a mandate from God to continue uncontaminated that which He had given them and which they had sealed with a covenant before God and with the shed blood of their ancestors. Their pious interpretation of their Bible supposedly gave them proof, and their successes in face of heavy odds confirmed their theological assumptions. Not without good reason did the Kruger government argue that to extend the franchise was tantamount to losing one's freedom by invasion. The political, social, and theological maneuvering of a half-century seemed to make war the inevitable outcome. Indeed, Chamberlain, speaking to the House of Commons, concluded: "War was always inevitable."[76] He was probably right, when we remember that what seemed to be the ultimate concerns of both powers were thoroughly opposed.

Immediately after the war began, it took on aspects of a holy crusade. President Steyn issued his statement concerning the Boers' ultimatum:

> We declare solemnly and as if in the presence of the Almighty, that we are compelled to take this course through the injustice done to our kith and kin. . . . In carrying on the conflict which we are now compelled to undertake, let the deeds of none of you be such as to disgrace a Christian and a burgher and the Free State. Let us look forward with confidence to a successful issue of the struggle, trusting to that Higher Power without Whose assistance human weapons avail nothing. To the God of our fathers we humbly commend the justice of our cause. May

He defend the right and may He bless our weapons! Under His banner we proceed to battle for freedom and for fatherland.[77]

In similar vein, F. W. Reitz spoke for many Afrikaners when he placed this war in context of many previous conflicts through which the real strength of the Transvaal was tested and sharpened:

> The British Empire is a mighty empire; but we know that whoever may be mighty, the Lord our God is Almighty. Brother Afrikanders! the great day is at hand. The God of our fathers will be with us in our struggles: the Lord, whose arm has not been shortened so that He cannot help those who call to Him in their time of trouble. Let us lay aside our trust in princes, and raise our eyes in supplication to God, our Banner. By His help we will do great deeds.
> Even as the mighty Spain, with her blood-thirsty Alva and her invincible armies, had to swallow the bitterness of defeat, so too, will God give our enemies into our hands. . . . [He then repeats the major grievances of the past century] Brother Afrikanders! I repeat, the day is at hand on which great deeds are expected of us! War has broken out. What is it to be?—a wasted and enslaved South Africa, or—a free, United South Africa?
> Come, let us stand shoulder to shoulder and do our holy duty! The Lord of Hosts will be our leader.[78]

Just when the war seemed imminent, a fiery partisan book appeared to excite further religious patriotism among the Boers. *A Century of Wrong* cataloged the injustices of the British occupation since 1806 and showed how God was always on the side of the Boers against tyranny.[79] The author used the imagery of a tree (Psalm 1?) planted as a "seed germ of liberty," which has grown into a mighty tree of today and "will yet, in God's good time . . . stretch out its leafy branches over the whole of South Africa."[80] God has led the Boers through many trials to test them, and "that we may be, as it were, sanctified and prepared for the conflict which lies before us, bearing in mind what our people have done and suffered by the help of God. In this way we may be enabled to continue the work of our fathers, and possibly to complete it."[81] A catalog of events of history is offered to inspire the people:

> Once more in the annals of our bloodstained history has the day dawned when we are forced to grasp our weapons in order to resume the struggle for liberty and existence, entrusting our national cause to that Providence which has guided our people throughout South Africa in such a miraculous way. . . . [If God proves to be on our side in this war] by the grace of God the last stone will now be built into the edifice which our fathers began with so much toil and so much sorrow. . . . [Then we

shall know for sure] whether the sacrifices which both our fathers and we ourselves have made in the cause of freedom have been offered in vain, whether the blood of our race, with which every part of South Africa has been, as it were, consecrated, has been shed in vain.[82]

Some say that British power is too much for a sparsely settled land with its inadequately armed and partially trained soldiers.

Do not be disturbed by such men as Milner, Rhodes and Chamberlain, or even by the British Empire itself, but cling fast to the God of our forefathers, and to the righteousness which is sometimes slow in acting, but which never slumbers nor forgets. Our forefathers did not pale before the terrors of the Spanish Inquisition, but entered upon the great struggle for Freedom and Right against even the mighty Philip [of Spain], unmindful of the consequences. . . . If it is ordained that we, insignificant as we are should be the first among all peoples to begin the struggle against the new-world tyranny of Capitalism, then we are ready to do so.[83]

Others summarized the grievances in similar fashion. Ben J. Viljoen, a Boer general, circulated a statement widely throughout South Africa at the beginning of the war. He reminded them of the

murder at Slagters' Nek . . . Natal was taken . . . diamond fields were stolen from the Orange Free State . . . and look how God snatched us, as if by a miracle, from the claws of mighty England in 1881. . . . Providence placed them [Jameson raiders] in our hands. . . . England's persecution ceases not. . . . The two Afrikaner Republics have been driven by Great Britain like the old people of Israel, to the Red Sea, and our liberation and redemption lie in the hand of God. We trust in God. He extricated our fathers from many serious dangers and can and will probably do say [sic] again.[84]

The deep theological commitment of the Boers was substantiated by their major opponent, Milner, realizing they interpreted Majuba (1881) and Doornkop (1896) as divine signs of God's pleasure with their regime. "It is small wonder that the pious parsons of the Dutch Reformed Church really believe that the Lord of Hosts is always on the look-out and will get them out of any tight spot."[85]   Another opponent of the Boers analyzed the theological dimension of their courage:

The Boers have been confirmed in the belief that they have only to ask long and loudly, with a veiled threat of serious consequences, to obtain what they may happen to desire. Shreds of Old Testament history have led them to consider that the God whom they profess to worship will direct their bullets so as to bring about a victory to their arms. President Kruger's recent exhortation to the Commandoes in the field to trust to God rather than to marksmanship, as He would direct their bullets so as to secure the defeat of their enemies, is a tolerably clear proof that *they consider themselves the chosen people among the moderns,* and, like the Hebrews of old, under the protection of the Most High.[86]

With this confidence not in their own power but in the righteousness of God, the Boers entered the battle against overwhelming odds, singing their national song:

> Know Ye this young Republic small?
> Outnumbered though it be,
> It has resisted British thrall,
> And was acknowledged free.
> Transvaalers, nobly have we striven,
> 'Gainst wrongs and insults great.
> By God alone the power is given
> Our land to vindicate.
> Praise be to God, Praise be to God,
> For our Republic State.[87]

After General Cronje led one section of commandos to attack the train in Bechuanaland, another group, led by Generals Wessel and de la Rey, surrounded Kimberley. The largest Boer forces were deployed to Natal under the leadership of such generals as Piet Joubert, Christiaan de Wet, and Louis Botha. Indeed, de Wet stated that the war was a "war of religion" in which God was seeking to strengthen them and to make "a nation worthy of His name."[88] Britain had not yet landed all its forces in South Africa; consequently all seemed to favor the Boers. Suddenly, on February 27, 1900, General Cronje on the western front was forced to surrender. Kruger, trying to instill confidence, hurried to the eastern front, his Bible under his arm, where he told his army: "I am searching the entire Bible and can find no other way possible than that adopted by us, and we must continue to fight in the Name of the Lord."[89] He based his confidence, he said, on Psalm 33:12, 20-22:

> Blessed is the nation whose God is the Lord, the people whom he has chosen as his heritage! . . . Our soul waits for the Lord; he is our help and shield. Yes, our heart is glad in him, because we trust in his holy name. Let thy steadfast love, O Lord, be upon us, even as we hope in thee.

He warned against overconfidence, for he was certain the British also used their Bibles for their guide: "They say 'Come, let us wipe them out as a nation; let the name of Israel be remembered no more' (Psalm 83:4)."[90]

The deep religious attitude which appears time and again throughout the military adventures was analyzed by a French leader with the Boers during the war. Colonel Villebois-Mareuil observed:

> The laagers are chiefly interesting for the spirit that animates them. An atmosphere of deep religious feeling pervades the camp, which commits everything to God—the fate of the Transvaal, the defense of its liberties, and the rights of the people against the aggressors. If you compliment a general he says "God has permitted it." The Boer whose secret aspirations are thus encouraged lifts eyes of faith to heaven. . . . The pastors are among the men, living their life, present at their death, simple, like the others. . . . There is something on our side that is invincible—God is fighting for us.[91]

The theological enthusiasm, however, was not matched by military success. On February 28, 1900, Ladysmith, Natal, was captured by British forces, and the success of the Boers was at a standstill. General Hertzog went into the Cape Colony to lead agitation among the Afrikaners there, with some success. The British planned massive attacks on Natal and the Free State and on March 13, 1900, the British army marched into Bloemfontein. This fall of the capital city of the Orange Free State did not cause discouragement for President Steyn. He said instead: "Our power is not dependent on a *single City*. Have courage and stand firm in the faith. The Lord's plan for us will not be frustrated. Persevere in the struggle. Whenever the night is the darkest, the daylight is soon to come."[92] Two weeks after the fall of Bloemfontein (March 28) Commandant General Piet Joubert died in Natal, succeeded by thirty-six-year-old Louis Botha. Speaking at Joubert's funeral, Kruger said to his compatriots: "The Lord will stand by you against the ruthless hand of the foe."[93] On May 24, British officials annexed the Free State, calling it the Orange River Colony. Just before fleeing from Pretoria, Kruger spoke to the Volksraad, reiterating his faith and attempting to justify their cause before God:

> O God of the Volksraad and of the Republics, shall this be our final act? No it shall not, it cannot be. God will be merciful and strengthen the right. . . . [Britain said] "This miserable nation of Afrikaners must cease to exist"; But God said "It shall not." . . . [He said further that] the same Lord who worked the wonders chronicled in the Bible was still awake. God would surely listen to such prayers as theirs, and soon would say to England "This far and no farther" [Job 38:11].[94]

The Boers seemed unable to stop the British success. Desperately Kruger repeated himself: "The Almighty, in spite of our recent loss [of General Joubert] is still on our side! . . . Brothers, is it not the same God who cleft the Red Sea assunder and punished Pharaoh with his hosts when Moses remained firmly trustful?"[95] On May 31, the British occupied

Johannesburg and on June 5 reached Pretoria.   The war seemed to be almost over, but the widely scattered Boers continued their resistance. Kruger spoke to the commanders on June 20, giving a detailed theological background for their inspiration.   He said that "the time is at hand when God's people shall be *tried in the fire* [Malachi 3:2-3]."   The situation was serious, and Kruger launched into the apocalyptic vision:

> The Beast shall have power to persecute Christ, and those who fall from faith and their Church will know Him not, nor shall they be allowed to enter the Kingdom of Heaven.   Those who are true to the faith and fight in the name of the Lord, wearing their glorious crown of victory, they shall be received in the church of a thousand years and enter into glory everlasting. Brothers, I beseech you abandon not your faith, but hold fast by it, and so go forth and fight in the name of the Lord.   Look well into your hearts.   If cowardice hiding there whispers to you "fly" you are blasphemers, for listening to the Tempter you deny your God, your faith is dead.   Believe as you would be saved that *nothing happens here below without the will of God*. Victory and the sword are in His hands and He gives both to those who fight in His name.   Is not our God the *same God who led Israel* under the power of His miracles out of the land of Pharaoh?   Did not He lead them safely through the Red Sea?   Did he not hide them in the thick cloud which was darkness to the enemy, but light to His children; for the column of cloud was Built upon the Word of the Lord, and if we trust Him as they trusted Him, it shall be our guide also, through the darkness, leading our feet safely to the light. . . . And this same God our Lord and Savior, *who has brought us here from our distant home,* and given us our liberty, and performed miracles on our behalf, dare we doubt that He who commenced this work will finish it? . . . He is the same Lord who helped Gideon and his three hundred warriors, who led and strengthened them in battle and in whose hand lies every victory. . . . He often leads his children through the barren desert, where it seems as if they would never get through.   But if we will only trust Him, I assure you He will be our guide.   He who trusts in God's guidance is under the protection of the King of Kings and safe through the darkest night.[96]

Finally, knowing that Kruger was the major enemy of the British forces, the generals persuaded him to flee from the Transvaal. He became an exile in Europe but not before he designated Schalk Burger to govern in his name.   Kruger was almost seventy-five years old and feared he would be captured by British forces.   In addition, he hoped that in Europe he would be able to muster further reaction in favor of the Transvaal.   Kruger fully intended to return as president as soon as God gave his devastated forces their victory.   Sailing from the Portuguese port of Lourenco Marques, he arrived at Marseilles in November 1900, where the reception was that of a victor rather than an exile. On arriving in France he stated his case:

> The war which is being waged against the two Republics has reached the utmost limits of barbarity. In my life I have had occasion many times to fight with the savage tribes of Africa, but the barbarians with whom we have now to fight are much worse than the others. They have gone so far as to arm the kaffirs against us. They burn our farms, which we have built with so much difficulty. They hurt our women and children whose husbands and fathers have been killed or taken prisoners. They leave them without protection, without word, and often without bread. But whatever may happen we shall never surrender. We will keep until the end our great and immovable confidence in the Almighty—in our God. Our cause is just, and if the justice of men fails us, the Almighty God, who is above all nations and to whom the future belongs, will not abandon us. I can assure you that if the Transvaal and the Orange Free State are to lose their independence, it will be because the two Boer people will have been destroyed, with their women and children.[97]

When the British formally annexed the Transvaal on October 25, 1900, many thought the war was over. Although both the Republican capitals were occupied and all the land was annexed by Britain, the determined Boer spirit was not quenched. Loyal Republican Boers began waging guerrilla warfare, and the Afrikaners of the Cape Colony, led by Generals Hertzog, de Wet, and Smuts, were near insurrection. Martial law was declared in order to control the Cape Colony, and intensive drives were begun to attack the republics, farm by farm.[98] Massive concentration camps were built to house women and children and thus to demoralize the fighters. Since the people in camps were overcrowded, underfed, and had inadequate medical attention, disease took its toll. By the end of 1901 it was reported that almost 14,000 had died in concentration camps, 10,000 of them children.[99] Even when the concentration camps were filled, the guerrilla warfare continued. At the end of the war it was estimated that as many as 40,000 Boer women and children were in the camps. Boers counted approximately 6,000 soldiers dead in battle; the British lost nearly 22,000.[100]

Early in 1902 the alternatives were peace or annihilation of the Boers. From Europe Kruger urged them to continue to fight, but Louis Botha, the general who succeeded Joubert, and Schalk Burger, Kruger's successor, assumed leadership to negotiate for peace. During March, April, and May 1902, they gathered enough support that on May 31, 1902, they could agree on the Treaty of Vereeniging. The bloody war that brought the sympathy of the world to the side of the Boers was over.

President Kruger was in the Netherlands when he heard of the negotiated settlement of the war. Although the settlement was made contrary
to his own judgment, he saw God's hand even now, as he reacted to the
peace:

> So far as I myself am concerned, I will not consent to lose
> courage because the peace is not such as the burghers wished
> it. For quite apart from the fact that the bloodshed and the
> fearful sufferings of the people of the two republics are now
> ended, I am convinced that God does not forsake his people,
> even though it may appear so. Therefore, I resign myself to
> the Will of the Lord. I know that He will not allow the af-
> flicted people to perish. He is the Lord and all hearts are in
> His hand, and He turneth them whithersoever He will.[101]

The same confident attitude is not evident in one of the Afrikaner soldiers
on the battlefield. He expressed the disappointment that hundreds of
thousands of other Afrikaners must have felt. In his diary he wrote:

> Think of it! After fighting for thirty-two months, against such
> odds and after keeping alive the flame of freedom for so long,
> to hand up our arms, forfeit our independence, so dear to us,
> yield up this fair country, lose our separate existence, and
> become merged in that of our conqueror! . . . To me everything
> in which hope was, seems gone and I feel as if our liberty has
> been buried alive and our future still-born. Our opportunities
> seem forever past and gone.[102]

High-ranking officials within South Africa also expressed their
disappointment. F. W. Reitz, president of the Free State from 1888
to 1895, later judge in the Transvaal and finally Transvaal state
secretary, reflected his disappointment when he wrote the following
during the Vereeniging meeting on May 30, 1902:

Farewell to the Vierkleur[103]

No longer may our Standard wave,
And flaunt its colours to the sky,
'Tis buried with our heroes brave
Who on the field of glory lie.

Oh, happier far were they who fell
Ere yet its tints began to fade
Than we, who loved it passing well,
Yet in the dust have seen it laid.

For it there bides no glad tomorrow,
And this farewell must be our last,

Wet with a Nation's tears of sorrow
We consecrate it to the past.

To those who bore our Flag on high
And dared the haughty foe to face,
And who, when death was drawing nigh
Clung to it with a last embrace.

Forever be their story told
As long as there are men at all,
Until the very heavens grow old,
And earth shall totter to her fall.[104]

The British won the war, but could they win the peace? Many observers thought so. The Boer organizations were completely broken; their republics as self-governing nations had disappeared; Paul Kruger, their major leader, was no longer in South Africa; and moderate Afrikaners were negotiating for the defeated Boers. In addition, the peace was written on British terms, and British officials were at the head of the governments of both the occupied Transvaal and the Free State. Soon it became evident, however, that the Boers clung to their dreams. They had been severely chastened, but God still had a destiny for them.

The period leading up to the Anglo-Boer War was marked by increasing frustration of the Boers' objectives to expand and to stabilize their society. The more Kruger's government saw itself as a reinforced Zion, the more they interpreted the British presence as anti-Christ. Consequently, in this period the theological justifications were based more on opposition to Britain than on anti-African concerns. By comparison, the magnitude of the British threat dwarfed the racial problem. Under constant threat the Boers maintained their faith and were belligerently defensive of their *status quo,* but they could not maintain their composure unceasingly. With the confidence that they were fighting God's war for Him the crusading Boers launched their holy cause. Their nationalism and their protection for Christian civilization against the anti-Christ were made even stronger because they interpreted their destiny as God's destiny. Even though they were weak in their own nation, God would make them strong to do His will.

As the British failed to understand the theological basis of Afrikaner national aspiration, they failed also to understand the strength this ideology gave to their militarily weak opponents. The Boers who fought with theological assurance possessed a strength unknown to those who fought only for their nation. Whether the Boers lived or died, they believed they were sustained by God; their loyalty to God called them to take up His Cause against heavy odds. God gave strength to Gideon and Joshua, and he would not fail them and their "promised land" of the "covenant" in South Africa.

NOTES

1. Leonard, *Political Situation*, p. 36.

2. Bixler, *Anglo-German Imperialism*, pp. 77-78.

3. Amery, *Times History*, I, 152.

4. Marais, *Fall of Kruger's Republic*, pp. 64-95.

5. C. 8474 of 1897, pp. 2-3.

6. Eybers, *Select Constitutional Documents*, p.473.

7. Chamberlain's telegram, November 7, 1895, in C. 8474 of 1897, p. 15.

8. Jean van der Poel, *The Jameson Raid* (London: Oxford University Press, 1951).

9. Hofmeyr, *Hofmeyr*, p. 495.

10. Fitzpatrick, *Transvaal from Within*, p. 230.

11. van Oordt, *Paul Kruger*, p. 718.

12. C. 8063 of 1896, p. 60.

13. *Century of Wrong*, pp. 49-50.

14. W. K. Hancock, *Smuts: The Sanguine Years, 1870-1919* (Cambridge: Cambridge University Press, 1962).

15. C. 8423 of 1897, pp. 40-41, 51.

16. Eybers, *Select Constitutional Documents*, p. 473.

17. C. 8423 of 1897, pp. 56-58; the "Critic" was suppressed, C. 9345 of 1897, pp. 3, 57-58; the "Star" was also suppressed, C. 9345 of 1897, pp. 53-55, 63.

18. Amery, *Times History*, I, 223.

19. C. 9345 of 1899, p. 35.

20. *Ibid.*, pp. 65-70.

21. Marais, *Fall of Kruger's Republic*, pp. 203f.

22. C. 9345 of 1899, pp. 108-139, 147-159.

23. *Ibid.*, pp. 113-116, 133.

24. *Ibid.*, pp. 159-175.   There were signatures of 21,684 protesting, January 14, 1897.

25. C. 4823 of 1897, p. 71.

26. C. 8721 of 1897, pp. 6-14, May 7, 1897.

27. *Ibid.*, pp. 18-22, October 16, 1897.

28. C. 9507 of 1899, pp. 7-19, April 16, 1898.

29. *Ibid.*, pp. 28-30, December 15, 1898.

30. *Ibid.*, pp. 31-33, May 9, 1899.

31. *Ibid.*, pp. 33f., July 13, 1899.

32. N. J. van der Merwe, *Marthinus Theunis Steyn 'n Lewensbeskrywing* (2 vols., Cape Town: Nasionale Pers, 1921).

33. J. J. Oberholster and M. C. E. van Schoor, eds., *President Steyn aan die Woord: openbare geskrifte en toesprake van Marthinus Theunis Stuyn* (Bloemfontein: Sacum, 1953), p. 21, December 11, 1895.

34. *Ibid.*, January 1896.

35. Van der Merwe, *Steyn*, I, pp. 109-111.

36. Quoted in Amery, *Times History*, I, 190.

37. C. 9345 of 1899, p. 182.

38. De Villiers to Steyn, May 21, 1899, in Walker, *De Villiers and His Times*, pp. 336f.

39. Amery, *Times History*, I, 211.

40. Milner's speech at Graaff-Reinet, March 3, 1898, in C. Headlam, ed., *The Milner Papers, 1897-1905* (2 vols., London: Cassell, 1931-1933), I, 245.

41. Printed in full in Spoelstra, *Het Kerkelijk en Godsdienstig Leven der Boeren*, pp. 385-393.

42. *Ibid.*, p. 394.

43. Schreiner, *Afrikaner Bond*, p. 10.

44. *Ibid.*, pp. 10-12. Italics added.

45. Kruger's election speech is printed in *Kruger's Memoirs*, pp. 333-367; selections pp. 338-339, 345-347, 354.

46. C. 9345 of 1899, pp. 226-231.

47. C. 9404 of 1899, pp. 15-16.

48. *Ibid.*, p. 16.

49. *Ibid.*, p. 23.

50. *Ibid.*, pp. 40-41.

51. *Ibid.*, p. 25.

52. *Ibid.*, p. 40.

53. *Ibid.*, p. 38.

54. Marais, *Fall of Kruger's Republic*, p. 161.

55. C. 9415 of 1899, p. 15, July 13, 1899.

56. Reitz to Green, British resident in Pretoria, C. 9518 of 1899, p. 3.

57. Amery, *Times History*, p. 288.

58. *Ibid.*, July 17, 1899.

59. C. 9521 of 1899, p. 36, July 18, 1899.

60. *Ibid.*

61. Amery, *Times History*, p. 366.

62. C. 9530 of 1899, p. 45.

63. Oberholster and van Schoor, *President Steyn aan die Woord*, pp. 81-82, September 22, 1899.

64. *Ibid.*, p. 45.

65. Amery, *Times History*, I, 366.

66. *Ibid.*, p. 353.

67. Walker, *Lord de Villiers*, p. 355; Amery, *Times History*, I, 363.

68. The scripture tells of the coming of Jehoshaphat, king of Judah, to Ahab, king of Israel. The latter tried to induce Jehoshaphat to join in war against Syria. "Do you know that Ramoth-Gilead belongs to us, and we keep quiet and do not take it out of the hand of the King of Syria? . . . Will you go with me to battle at Ramoth-Gilead?" Jehoshaphat asked advice from the prophets who said: "Go up; for the Lord will give it into the hand of the king." Not completely satisfied he continued asking others until Micaiah was approached. Finally Micaiah answered: "I saw all Israel scattered upon the mountain, as sheep that have no shepherd and the Lord said 'these have no master; let each return to his home in peace'." Micaiah

was not heeded but was imprisoned as a false prophet. Ahab was killed in battle fulfilling Micaiah's prophecy.

69. G. H. L. Le May, *British Supremacy in South Africa, 1899-1907* (Oxford: Oxford University Press, 1965), pp. 25f.

70. The *Ultimatum*, printed for use of the cabinet on October 9, 1899, appears in full in *Bulletin of the Institute of Historical Research*, XXVII (1954), pp. 182-186.

71. Amery, *Times History*, I, 367.

72. *Ibid.*, p. 368.

73. The complete *Ultimatum* appears in C. 9530 of 1899, pp. 65-67.

74. *Ibid.*

75. Amery, *Times History*, I, 376.

76. *Ibid.*, I, 377f.

77. Oberholster and van Schoor, *President Steyn aan die Woord*, under date October 11, 1899.

78. *War against War in South Africa*, a weekly periodical published by Stop the War Committee of London, October 1899-August 1900; cf. for date November 17, 1899, pp. 68f.

79. There is disagreement about the true author of *A Century of Wrong*. It was issued by F. W. Reitz, state secretary of the Transvaal, but he was only the editor. In "Afrikaner Nationalist Historiography and the Policy of Apartheid," *Journal of African History*, III (1962), pp. 125-141, Leonard Thompson argues that it was the work mainly of Jan Smuts; the discussion concerning this book, p. 129. F. A. van Jaarsveld, on the other hand, attributes it to Jacob de Villiers Roos with the introduction and conclusions only by Smuts; his *The Afrikaner's Interpretation of South African History*, 1964, p. 159, n. 45. Three editions of the work appeared immediately: *Een Eeuw van Onrecht* (Dordrecht: 1899); *A Century of Injustice* (Baltimore: 1899); and *A Century of Wrong* (London: 1900).

80. *A Century of Wrong*, p. 4.

81. *Ibid.*, p. 2.

82. *Ibid.*, p. 1.

83. *Ibid.*, pp. 97-98.

84. *War against War*, October 20, 1899, p. 15.

85. Headlam, *Milner Papers*, II, 268.

86. Scobie and Abercrombie, *Rise and Fall of Krugerism*, p. 13.

87. Transvaal Song, 1899, in *War against War*, December 1, 1899.

88. *Cambridge History of the British Empire* (South Africa), VIII, 610.

89. *War against War*, January 19, 1900, p. 215.

90. This discussion is reported in *ibid.*, p. 215.

91. Letter from Colonel Villebois-Mareuil, in *War against War*, March 2, 1900, p. 308.

92. Oberholster and van Schoor, *President Steyn aan die Woord*, under date March 19, 1900.

93. *War against War*, June 1, 1900, p. 438.

94. *Ibid.*

95. *War against War*, June 1, 1900.

96. *Kruger's Memoirs*, pp. 399-402. Italics added.

97. Coenraad Beyers, "Laaste Lewensjare en Heengaan van President Kruger," *Argief Jaarboek vir Suid Afrikaanse Geskeidenis*, IV (1941), p. 27.

98. For a detailed account of the Boer War, Rayne Kruger, *Good-bye Dolly Gray: The Story of the Boer War* (London: Cassell, 1959).

99. "Concentration Camps," in Pamphlet File entitled "Causes of the War," I, November 1901.

100. These are the statistics of Eric Walker, writing in the *Cambridge History of the British Empire*, VIII (South Africa), pp. 611-612.

101. Juta, *Pace of the Ox*, p. 322.

102. Roland William Schikkerling, *Commando Courageous: A Boer's Diary* (Johannesburg: Hugh Keartland, 1964), under date June 6, 1902.

103. The Vierkleur, literally translated "four-color," was the flag of the proud Transvaalers, still preserved as part of the design of the flag of the Republic of South Africa.

104. From pamphlets of Reitz filed in the Library of the University of South Africa, Pretoria.

VIII.
Forming a Nation, 1902–1910

The period between the Treaty of Vereeniging and the Union of South Africa began a new era. It was both an epilogue to all that had gone before and a prologue to the future. The Afrikaner Zion had been badly battered, but it rose from its own destruction to keep its theological goals before the people. In this eight-year period (May 31, 1902 to May 31, 1910) many of the objectives for which the Boers had fought were realized at least in part, and the details of the Constitution of the Union indicated the direction the new united nation would follow for a half-century. The surprising aspect of the period, however, is that the Boers who hesitatingly accepted unconditional surrender at the hands of the British were the statesmen who constructed the Constitution of the Afrikaner nation. When the British allowed self-government to the four colonies, the three largest—Cape, Orange River Colony (as it was now called), and the Transvaal—were led by Afrikaners. In the National Convention of 1909 the Afrikaner parties in each of these three largest colonies held the majority. Even when we note that all five delegates from Natal were pro-British, the Afrikaners were sure exactly half the votes were theirs.[1] This was the Afrikaners' only home; many who were pro-British had a higher loyalty, the British Empire. The Afrikaners were organized to accomplish certain objectives. Furthermore, a new generation of leaders was emerging now that Paul Kruger, Piet Joubert, and J. H. Brand were handing over leadership reins to younger men. In 1902 the three men who were to control the government until 1948 were all generals of the Boer forces and were relatively young men: Louis Botha was thirty-nine, J. M. B. Hertzog was thirty-six, and Jan Smuts was only thirty-two. The British were not so definite in what they hoped to acccomplish now that peace was a reality.

The Boers who lost the war on the battlefield won the initiative through eight years of negotiation because they had clear-cut goals and unflinching statesmen. We also must credit a portion of their success to the magnanimity of the British who encouraged South African Boers to participate in the developing governments. After the peace treaty was signed, one of the chaplains of the war saw God's directing hand at work even then.

> It is true the English government probably aimed to break the power of Afrikanerdom once and for all in the war of 1899-1902. God disposed things quite differently. He who directs the destiny of nations, used the war as a means to end Afrikanerdom as it had been known. In its place he formed a still greater *volk* for South Africa. The war which was meant to bring the two Boer Republics to extinction, brought, instead, the possibility that Afrikaners from four states could be fused together to make one *Volk*.[2]

When the Boers decided to sign the Treaty of Vereeniging, there was no unanimity among the leaders. The commandos were almost completely routed, imprisoned, or demoralized. Concentration camps were filled with their families and friends, and Britain clearly had overwhelming power. Louis Botha and Schalk Burger saw no alternative but to make peace and then to attempt to negotiate for their objectives, now impossible to obtain on the battlefield. They were opposed, however, by some who wished to fight on. Theirs was a "Holy Cause" and this was a "sacred war."[3] "Faith in God compelled them to fight for their independence."[4] Hertzog and de Wet, both of the Orange Free State, were leaders of the faction that decried peace as compromise. Their nation had entered the war hesitatingly, and now they felt their Transvaal allies were deserting them in the fight. Peace was made, but this deep seated divisiveness remained among the Afrikaners.

The Treaty of Vereeniging was written on British terms but included many concessions to make it more acceptable to the Boers.[5] Among the ten points the Boers were asked to accept without modification, four are especially important to this study. Boers were asked to lay down their arms and to acknowledge themselves subjects of Edward VII (sec.1); the Dutch language was to be allowed in the schools (sec. 5); self-government for the defeated republics would be allowed as soon as possible (sec. 7); and there would be no discussion of the franchise for black Africans until after self-government was instituted (sec. 8).[6]

Within these limitations, Lord Milner, now governor of both the Orange River Colony and the Transvaal, envisaged a strong British South Africa with a broad Anglicizing policy for the defeated republics. In place of narrow provincialism and education in the Dutch language, he considered it imperative to broaden the outlook of the two peoples so that they could join the other nations of the world on an equal basis. Most education should be in English, and governmental affairs should be conducted in English.[7]

Milner did not realize the strength of the Afrikaner spirit, driven by a theological assurance of God's protection. He was almost immediately opposed by this rejuvenated ideology furthered by the Dutch Reformed churches. As the only major Afrikaner organizations to survive the war, the churches and ministers had a strong stabilizing influence on their people. For example, on December 16, 1903 (Dingane's Day), the Rev. J. B. du Toit urged the people to be loyal to their faith and oppose all Anglicizing. Basing his sermon on Deuteronomy 6:6-7, he told of the unique commands God had given to the Afrikaner people: "The lines must be drawn anew, in hearts and lives, which indicate the boundaries between us and all uitlanders. . . . In the isolation of our principle lies the strength of Afrikanerdom."[8] The Anglicizing education policy was challenged as the two former republics organized private schools (the Christelijk Nationaal Onderwijs, C.N.O.) to continue their Christian tradition in the language of the people.[9]

The challenge of their ideology also centered around the question of language. The Boers organized the second language movement. Similar to the Bond program a generation earlier; they simplified Dutch spelling and began to make way for the development of a new written language for their people—Afrikaans. Cape Dutch, the forerunner of Afrikaans, had been spoken for over a century, but high Dutch was maintained as the written language. The need for a simplified spelling and grammatical structure, however, worked against those who hoped to maintain Dutch, for it was almost as foreign to many in South Africa as was English. In 1907 those who argued for Afrikaans and those who pleaded for Dutch agreed to cooperate to oppose undue English influence.[10] The three largest colonies initiated programs of written Afrikaans, and impetus for more literature in the new language continued. Thus the language question united them as a people. Afrikaans, the newest Germanic language, became one of the official languages of South Africa in 1925 when it was accepted by Parliament.[11]

The funeral of former President Kruger was one of the occasions which helped to further Afrikaner theological-political consciousness among the defeated colonies.[12] The aged president had visited in most Western European countries since his exile in 1900. He had never lost his confidence in God and continued to encourage his followers in South Africa. Theologically he was able to interpret the defeat not as God's judgment against the Afrikaners but rather as a further test of their faith. God was still all powerful and all knowing; he said "I am convinced that God shall make His *Volk* free, but when and in what manner I know not. The Lord knows the time."[13] After the peace he was urged to return to his homeland, but he could not accept the requirement of being a subject of Britain: "Born under the English flag, I shall not die under it."[14] No one was certain whether Britain would have allowed his return in any case. He became seriously ill in Switzerland and died on July 14, 1904.[15] Louis Botha obtained permission to have his body returned for a South African funeral and made the necessary arrangements.[16] Some thought he should have a military funeral on his seventy-ninth birthday on October 10, but his people requested instead that it be a religious service. Knowing how Kruger lived, what more appropriate date for the funeral could be chosen than December 16 (Dingane's Day), 1904?[17] People came to Pretoria from all parts of South Africa.

Emotions were at a high pitch, for the funeral reminded everyone again of the vision of Afrikanerdom that had motivated Kruger throughout his life from the founding of the republics to the present day. The Rev. H. S. Bosman, Transvaal moderator of the Dutch Reformed church, spoke of their theological destiny:

> Then referring particularly to the words "By the waters of Babylon there we sat down; yea, we wept when we remembered Zion," [Psalm 137], he said the Afrikander people grieved, but not as those who had no hope. . . .
>
> As the people of Jerusalem had never lost faith in their God, but had prayed continually for deliverance, so must they be constant in their faith, and acknowledge their sins because when sin was acknowledged so did deliverance follow the sins of the people of Jerusalem. Having been forgiven their sins they were brought back to the land from which they were taken. . . .
>
> The speaker then likened the people of this country to those men of God and urged them to keep to that word which remained forever. . . . He urged them, by the God of Paul Kruger, not to let that national feeling die out. . . .
>
> Paul Kruger was dead, but his people were not dead. Neither was his spirit dead, and they could go along the lines that he had laid down under the flag that now waved over them, and still be true to it, but they would always remain Afrikanders, God helping them.[18]

Another observer added to the imagery. Paul Kruger had been not only head of state; he was the patriarchal leader of his people:

> The relation between President Kruger and his people reminds one of the relation between Moses and the Israelites, and not without reason. Even as the Israelites were led from the authority of the Egyptians so also Kruger's people were taken from the governmental authority, and both found their freedom in another land, where they made their own laws and served God in their own way.[19]

Thus in spite of military defeat, the Boer imagery of their state as an elect nation was still alive. The defeat was rationalized so that they still could assume the sovereign God was in control of events. To be true to the spirit of Paul Kruger and to their God, they must capture the initiative, and this could be done only if they reorganized their political institutions.

Following the war, both republics were governed by British appointees, but the people had been promised self-government. Botha took the lead in the Transvaal and called secret meetings even before Kruger's death. In January 1905 he helped to organize *Het Volk* (the People), the Afrikaner political party in Transvaal. Leaders in addition to Botha were Jan Christiaan Smuts, Schalk Burger, Jacob H. de la Rey, and Christiaan Frederik Beyers—all Boer War heroes.[20] Botha's policy emphasized conciliation of differences between the two nationalities in the Transvaal for a better South Africa. Even this was not accepted unanimously, for C. F. Beyers believed that this was tantamount to giving up the faith.

Transvaal led in the reorganization. By a decree from London, self-government was allowed the Transvaal on December 6, 1906.[21] The election held two months later, following extensive town-by-town cultivation by the Boers, resulted in victory for *Het Volk*. There was only token opposition from the less-organized pro-British Progressive party. The acknowledged leader, Louis Botha, ex-commander-general on the battlefield, was asked to form the government of this British colony.

A similar development was transpiring in the Orange River Colony. During 1904-1905 meetings of Boers were held, and in May 1906 the *Orangie Unie* (Orange Union) party was organized, again with the Boer War heroes as leaders: J. B. M. Hertzog, Abraham Fischer, and Christiaan H. de Wet. Behind the scenes was ex-President Marthinus W. Steyn, now in ill health, who admonished them to bear their burdens "until the Almighty achieves His purpose with this people."[22] Self-government was allowed in the Orange River Colony on June 5, 1907, and in the November 1907 election, Afrikaners were again successful, easily defeating the pro-British Constitution party.[23] The prime minister was Abraham Fischer, but both de Wet and Hertzog had significant roles in the cabinet.

The Afrikaner group in the Cape Colony finally came of age. The South African party, the new name for the Afrikaner Bond, was victorious in February 1908, gaining the majority without the necessity of a coalition. The leader of the party, John X. Merriman, became prime minister. Although English in background and the son of an Anglican bishop, Merriman had lived most of his life in the eastern part of the Cape Colony and was thoroughly sympathetic with the moderate Boer cause.

Natal, the smallest of the four, had been a self-governing colony since 1893, was strongly British, and sympathized with neither the republics nor with Cape Colony. There was no strong Afrikaner organization in Natal, and this nation had played little or no part in the British-Boer tensions of the past generations.

Within six years after the end of the war, Afrikaner political organizations gained control not only of the two former republics but of the Cape Colony as well. It was indeed a "strange defeat."[24]

As early as 1906 British officials conceived of a Union of South Africa to further their imperial interests.[25] The Boers, now having political channels through which to operate, also considered union, but their ideological bases for a union were quite different. Boers seized the initiative and began working toward a plan that would embody their major objectives. One of the main inspirations for this movement was Afrikaner leader Jan Christiaan Smuts, probably the best-educated lawyer and the most intellectual leader in South Africa. Most Afrikaners believed that only through union would their objectives with respect to economic development, race problems, and inter-sectional cooperation be furthered. They did not agree, however, with respect to some of the major aspects of a union. The major concern for both the British and the Afrikaners centered on union, but concern for the settlement of the problem with the African peoples as thus pushed into the background. This remained the major unsolved problem in 1910 and was to have its influence on a later generation.

In May 1908 an intercolonial conference was held at Pretoria.[26] Those attending began by discussing customs agreements, but the only real item on the agenda concerned plans for a federation or a union. All delegates decided that union was imperative, and they planned an officially delegated national convention to meet in Durban on October 12, 1908. In the meantime Afrikaner leaders worked behind the scenes so that real progress could be made when the delegates met. Jan Smuts wrote a draft of the new constitution and many of his ideas were adopted with little change.[27] Three sessions of the national convention were held: Durban, October 12-November 5, 1908; Cape Town, November 22-December 18, 1908, and January 11-February 3, 1909; and Bloemfontein, May 3-11, 1909. Between the second and third sessions the preliminary plans were adopted by parliaments of all four areas, and the South Africa Act was ready to be submitted to London.

Major points of difference that appeared at various times during the disccusions give insight into their objectives as a special nation in God's sight. Three colonies desired a union with a strong central government, but Natal knew it would thus lose its coveted sovereignty among the three larger groups.[28] It was defeated, and for a time there was fear that it would withdraw from the discussions.[29]

The problem of language was discussed thoroughly.[30] All agreed that both the Dutch and the English languages should be used and on an equal basis. Orange River Colony delegates, led by Hertzog, suspicious of what they considered an extreme conciliation policy of both Botha and Smuts, insisted strongly on absolute equality of language so that Dutch would not be gradually replaced.[31]

A more knotty problem arose concerning the franchise, especially with respect to non-Europeans.[32] The Cape Colony allowed the franchise to all qualified persons regardless of race, and consequently many Colored and Africans were qualifying to vote in Cape elections. Cape delegates insisted that this was the only realistic goal and that the constitution should leave room for extending the franchise to non-Europeans in all areas. Natal allowed non-European voters but so qualified the requirement that there were few who were actually registered. The two republics had a strict color bar around the privilege of the franchise and were unwilling to discuss any change. The Act of Union was thus a compromise. It was agreed that no person qualified to vote in the Cape Colony should be denied that privilege, but nothing was said about extending this franchise to the north (sec. 35 of South Africa Act). Each side hoped that its idea would triumph. Only persons of European extraction, however, were to be qualified to sit in either the Senate or the House of Assembly (sec. 26 on the Senate; sec. 44 on the Assembly).

The delegates reverted to sectional rivalries when the site of the national capital was discussed.[33] Cape Town was the oldest city and the major seaport; Pretoria was nearest the growing industrial section; Bloemfontein was most centrally located. Natal hoped to suggest Pietermaritzburg in case the three became deadlocked. Instead, a curious compromise was adopted. Pretoria would become the capital and the seat of the executive (sec. 18), Cape Town the seat of the legislature (sec. 23), and Bloemfontein the seat of the supreme court (sec. 109).

Although these compromises were being made relatively smoothly, there were forebodings of difficulties to come. Hertzog did not share the breadth of vision that motivated both Botha and Smuts. He was more insistent on the question of language and was adamant about the relations with the African peoples.[34] Slowly he began to embody the suspicions and the doubts of Kruger and felt that South Africa must become an Afrikaner South Africa. All relations with or cooperation with the British were suspect. Undoubtedly many people sympathized with Hertzog but were swept along by the persuasiveness of Botha and the challenge of the moment. This basic difference between Botha and Hertzog was widely known, and in one speech in which Botha was explaining his education policy, he was interrupted by "What about Hertzog?"[35] Botha expected that even this difference would be overcome in time, and after serious considerations he included Hertzog in the first cabinet. In 1913, however, their differences became so pronounced that Hertzog was excluded from the cabinet. At Bloemfontein in January 1914, Hertzog proceeded to organize his more conservative followers into the Afrikaner Nationalist party, which was to have its greatest influence yet in the future.[36] The question of an anti-British Afrikaner nationalism and a more rigid racial policy were unsolved problems of the future.

In the enthusiasm of the moment, these problems were by-passed, and

Botha and Smuts carried the day. For the time being the Afrikaners were certain that they had secured their major objectives. In spite of their being British subjects, the Afrikaners were self-governing, they held the majority of the votes, and their national ideas revolving around race and language were preserved. They had achieved more than they might have expected.

Three colonies accepted the draft version of the South African Act between June 2 and 4, 1909, and it scored a sizable victory in the Natal referendum on June 10. The next destination was London, where a delegation led by Botha presented it in person. On September 20, 1909, King Edward VII approved the South Africa Act after it had been passed by both houses of Parliament. On May 31, 1910, the Union of South Africa became a reality, just eight years to the day after the end of the bitter war.

When Herbert Gladstone, son of the great prime minister, was appointed the new governor general of South Africa, he asked Botha to form a government. The first cabinet was composed almost exclusively of Botha's Afrikaner supporters, but Botha envisaged, nevertheless, a greater and unified South Africa. In one of his earliest statements, he reminded all of God's place in their society: "The political union of South Africa is no longer an ideal, but has under the guidance of Providence become an accomplished fact through the joint labours and sacrifices of the White races and of all parts of British South Africa."[37] Shortly thereafter referring to the British Boer tension, he urged all to help him "sweep South Africa clean of racialism": "Brothers, let us recognize God's finger in these things during the past 12 years. . . . There will be toleration and broad-mindedness, and there will be no room left for exploitation and small-mindedness in the minds of the people of South Africa."[38]

For the time being Afrikaner hopes seemed near realization through Boer-British cooperation. The Rev. D. Bosman found biblical support for this inclusive concept. Preaching a sermon in September 1910 he compared the Boer people with the Jews in the age of Nehemiah:

> Nehemiah was also troubled "by strangers and uitlanders." He had to defend himself against a raid. Attempts were made to discredit him by offers of cooperation; his own people fell away, married wives from Ammon and Moab, and refused to speak their native language. In spite of all trials, however, Jerusalem was ultimately rebuilt and populated by the tribes of Judah and Benjamin. Similarly let Pretoria be converted into a strong fortress.[39]

As the union became a reality, the history of the Boer people was summed up by Jan Smuts. With deep insight, he suggested that a greater power was hovering over their attempts to make one people out of two:

In the creative Spirit of History the blunders of men are often more valuable than their profoundest wisdom. . . . From the blood and tears of nations which human passions have caused she proceeds calmly and dispassionately to build up new nations and to lead them along new undiscovered paths of progress. When the darkness of the night has passed at last and the light of a new national consciousness forms, the scales fall from men's eyes, they perceive that they have been led, that they have been borne forward in the darkness by deeper power than they ever apprehended to a larger goal than they ever conceived, and they stand silent in the presence of that greatest mystery in the world, the birth of the soul of a new nation.[40]

President Steyn suggested a more traditional and nationalist statement at the 1910 Dingane's Day celebration:

As we look back on the high points of our own history, we see events such as the landing of Jan van Riebeeck, Slagters' Nek, 31 May [1910, Union], and many others. We see how all works together in God's hand to lead our folk along His way, how he uses all that happens to further His will. We see clearly from our own viewpoint; but God reveals to us the other side. True, his thoughts are not our thoughts and his way is not our way.

As we look back on the suffering of our people, and our own personal hardships, we see thorns, thistles and precipices, and it is as though we have gone through the valley of the shadow of death [Psalm 23]. Then we are in a mood of doubt and feel like crying "O God, why all this suffering?" And the echo of our voice answers, "Why?" But now that we see that this was not the chastening hand but the great Almighty Love, then we can not help but cry "Praise the Lord, O My Soul, and all within me Praise his Holy Name." [Psalm 103:1].[41]

NOTES

1. Fifteen out of thirty. This included J. H. de Villiers, the chairman, who was sympathetic to the Boer cause but was registered as an Independent. Leonard M. Thompson, in his *The Unification of South Africa* (London: Oxford University Press, 1960), has included a biographical sketch of each member of the National Convention in an appendix, pp. 501-512.

2. A. J. V. Burger, ed., *Worsteljare: herinneringe van ds. A. P. Burger, veldprediker by die republikeinse magte tydens die Tweede Vryheidsoorlog* (Cape Town: Nasionale Pers, 1936), p. 1.

3. Amery, *Times History*, V, 601.

4. *Ibid.*

5. C. 1096 of 1902, pp. 12ff.

6. *Ibid.*

7. Malherbe, *Education in South Africa*, pp. 315-320.

8. Reported in *Volksstem*, December 19, 1903; quoted in J. Albert Coetzee, *Politieke Groepering in de wording van die Afrikanernasie* (Johannesburg: Voortrekkerpers, 1941), pp. 346-347.

9. Malherbe, *Education in South Africa*, pp. 321-323.

10. Thompson, *Unification of South Africa*, pp. 19-20.

11. Afrikaans had been spoken before 1800, especially in remote parts of the nation unaffected by the continuing cultural contact with Europe that Cape Town enjoyed. Soon after the British came, they made English the official language and thereby caused reaction. During the rise of Afrikaner nationalism during the 1870s, the language question was again brought to the fore. In 1909 the South African Academy, using Afrikaans, was organized. Schools adopted the new language in 1914, the churches in 1916, and parliamentary acceptance came in 1925. T. J. Haarhoff and C. J. van der Heever, *The Achievement of Afrikaans* (South African Central News Agency, n.d.), p. 26.

12. Walker, *History of Southern Africa*, p. 514.

13. Coenraad Beyers, "Laaste Lewensjare en Heengaan van President Kruger," *Argief-Jaarboek vir Suid Afrikaanse Geskiedenis*, IV (1941), p. 45.

14. *Ibid.*, p. 52.

15. *Ibid.*, p. 53.

16. *Ibid.*, p. 61.

17. *Ibid.*, p. 55.

18. *Cape Times,* December 17, 1904, quoted in Thompson, *Unification of South Africa,* pp. 18-19.

19. Coenraad Beyers, "Laaste Lewensjare, Pres. Kruger," p. 60.

20. Amery, *Times History,* V, 163-164; Thompson, *Unification of South Africa,* pp. 21-22.

21. C. 3250 of 1906, pp. 1-13. This decision was promulgated in Britain by the Liberal prime minister, Sir Henry Campbell-Bannerman. Cf. Nicholas Mansergh, *South Africa 1906-1961: The Prince of Magnanimity* (London: George Allen and Unwin, 1962), chap. 1.

22. Van Jaarsveld, *Afrikaner's Interpretation,* p. 21.

23. C. 3526 of 1907, pp. 1-13.

24. "Strange Defeat" is the title of one chapter in Hancock, *Smuts,* pp. 164-204.

25. Thompson, *Unification of South Africa,* pp. 61-135, gives an extensive summary and analysis of this discussion, on which this section is largely based.

26. Thompson, *Unification of South Africa,* pp. 82-94.

27. *Ibid.*, pp. 152-165.

28. Edgar Harris Walton, *The Inner History of the National Convention of South Africa* (Cape Town: T. Maskew Miller, 1912), pp. 42-96.

29. The South Africa Act, section 2, states that it should be a Union. The final version of the South Africa Act of 1909 is to be found in C. 297 of 1909, pp. 179-299.

30. Walton, *Inner History,* pp. 97-116.

31. Section 137. With the integration of Uitlanders into Transvaal politics, the Orange River Colony now had the highest percentage of Afrikaners of any of the four colonies.

32. Walton, *Inner History,* pp. 117-157.

33. *Ibid.*, pp. 264-283.

34. In the Orange River Colony, Hertzog urged the passage of his Hertzog School Act of 1908. He was not only attorney general but minister of education as well. This act was more sympathetic to Afrikaners than to English. Throughout South Africa, it was feared that he would become the successor of Kruger's shortsighted policies. Indeed, the epithet "Hertzogism" was often used as a successor to "Krugerism." Malherbe, *Education in South Africa,* pp. 381-383.

35. D. W. Krüger, ed., *South African Parties and Policies: A Select Source Book* (Cape Town: Human and Rousseau, 1960), p. 3.

36. *Ibid.*, pp. 68-72.

37. *Ibid.*, p. 48; Botha's Manifesto concerning the South African Party, June 2, 1910.

38. Botha's speech, November 21, 1911, in Krüger, *South African Parties*, pp. 50-52.

39. *Times*, September 23, 1910, quoted in Thompson, *Unification of South Africa*, p. 469n.

40. Quoted in *ibid.*, p. 308.

41. Overholster and van Schoor, *President Steyn aan die Woord*, December 20, 1910, when the statement was originally published in the *Volkstem*.

IX.

On the Eve of the Formation of the Union of South Africa: An Analysis of Afrikaner Theology

This study is presented as one example in theological history; it is an analysis of how one theological motif developed and changed through a long span of cultural history. We have followed the doctrine of the elect people through its many manifestations in South African society, from its inception to the formation of the union. The idea of one people in South Africa chosen by God for a certain cause appeared in different forms at different times. For example, the concept was used to bolster loyalty to an unsteady Afrikaner regime illustrated in President Kruger's use of the covenant to instill anti-British loyalty. It was almost always used as an attempt to justify or rationalize various aspects of cultural development already accomplished.

Three general conclusions may be advanced before proceeding to a more detailed analysis. First, the doctrine of an elect people was not explicitly stated for the first century and a half of Reformed settlement in South Africa. The Afrikaners gradually conceived of themselves as a people, but the impetus for this was economic, political, and racial. As the settlers during the eighteenth century proceeded farther inland, they left educational and other social advantages behind in the Cape Town area, but they took their Bibles with them. Their piety developed and deepened as they assumed they had a mission to accomplish for white civilization, but they did not frame this in theological terms until the period of the Great Trek. Following the Trek, this concept of an elect people, more thoroughly anti-British than anti-African, played an increasingly important role in their developing nationalism.

Second, while the Boers were migrating eastward during the eighteenth century, a significant change appeared in their theology. In orthodox Reformed thought, the Old Testament is of Christian significance because Christ is prefigured there. This tends to infuse the Old Testament narratives with a certain Christian tolerance and compassion. In South Africa, however, this assumption that Christ is prefigured in all Old Testament narratives disappeared. The Afrikaner theological nationalism did not have a Christological dimension, but rather, the Old Testament narrative was taken literally. This may account for the fact that the Europeans' oppression of the indigenous peoples of South Africa is much more severe and merciless than in most other examples of European colonialism.

Third, while the Boers migrated in the general direction from Cape Town to Pretoria, the theological ideology of the Afrikaners proceeded in precisely the opposite direction—from Pretoria to Cape Town. The theological dimension of nationalism arose during the Great Trek period, developed in both the Orange Free State and the Transvaal, and became a national ideology in the government of President Kruger. Subsequently, the nationalist theological and racial ideology extended its influence southwest to Cape Town. In the election of 1948 the nationalist ideology that had its origin among the Republican Boers largely in Pretoria was victorious.

One further aspect of this complex symbolism may be noted. Before the Boer War, the area north of the Vaal River was known among Afrikaners as the South African Republic; the name *Transvaal* was a British designation. In 1961, after the Union of South Africa withdrew from the British Commonwealth, it took the name *Republic of South Africa*. The ideology formed by fugitive trekkers and even the name of their nation had now conquered their oppressors. Cecil Rhodes had envisaged a pro-British Union of South Africa stretching from Cape Town to the Zambezi, controlled from Cape Town. Hardly more than a half-century after the death of Cecil Rhodes, there was a nation stretching from Cape Town almost to the Zambezi (except for Rhodesia), but it was anti-British and was controlled from Pretoria. The trekker ideology, originally fleeing from the Cape Colony, returned victorious to its original home.

The mutations of the doctrine of an elect people assumed six forms, often interrelated. The Afrikaners assumed that: (1) their election by God was assured to those who maintained the scriptural pattern in organizing their government and their personal lives; (2) their election was substantiated by the cultural advantages they enjoyed; (3) their election must be defended in the face of British imperialism that sought to compromise the Afrikaner cause; (4) their election must be maintained through their own language, Dutch or Afrikaans; (5) their election assured them of an innate superiority when contrasted to African races; and finally, (6) their different interpretations of the doctrine of election were functionally related to the total social development. We shall analyze each of these assumptions in systematic, rather than in chronological outline, although the actors in the drama up to 1910 were not systematic and usually did not realize the roots of their ideas and traditions.

SCRIPTURAL FRAMEWORK

The Christian Scriptures provide a framework for organizing a society and a government and indicate probable results if this God-given pattern is violated. The basic elements of the Reformed faith—Bible, Psalter and Creeds—were influential in shaping the national self-consciousness in South Africa. From the earliest days, the Bible was basic to the way of life in the new South African settlement. As frontiersmen moved farther to the east, the Bible and the Psalter were often the only books they had. Because of its continual use as a devotional help, the Bible took its place at the center of the society. When the eighteenth-century Boer father gathered his family for evening devotions, he read from the Bible as the word of God given for their particular situation. During the Great Trek, the Boers believed that they were very real companions of Joshua and Gideon. In the newly developing republics, the Bible again had a significant place in the thoughts of the leaders, who used proof texts to justify their rejection of the policies of liberal President Burgers, for example. The personal animosities between Pretorius and Potgieter were mitigated by common reference to the Bible. President Kruger used biblical ideas to justify his opposition to the British. In his theology, the British were interpreted not only in opposition to the Afrikaner regime but were opponents of God as well. Kruger directed part of the Boer War with Bible in hand for guidance. In the developing society, the leaders assumed the Bible contained a model for life, and as Christians this must be their model. When President Kruger rejected horse racing on biblical grounds but finally approved it as an excuse to exercise horses, we see the tension that can develop between the biblical concept and a more pressing concern when they seem to be opposed to each other.

The Psalter, the Calvinist songbook, was perhaps even more widely used than the Bible. From this source, the Boers gathered their theological ideas of reward and punishment and were reminded of the Scriptures as they hummed songs or often quoted Psalms to justify their decisions or their warnings. The Psalms used in worship provided the pattern of life. To transgress or to forget God's plan would invite criticism or even destruction of their society. Through continued devotional use, these theological ideas became deeply ingrained in the lives of all people, valid for the leaders of the nation as well as for the common man. If we were to choose one section of scripture to illustrate the Afrikaner way of life, we might well suggest the first Psalm.

In addition to the Bible and Psalter, the settlers even in remote areas knew of the estalished catechisms of their faith and referred to both the Heidelberg Catechism and the Decrees of the Synod of Dort. Citizenship in the South African Republic was originally limited to those Christians who subscribed to the Heidelberg Catechism. When Piet Retief was chosen leader of the trekkers in June 1837, before God he promised to defend the Christian creeds and the catechism of the Dutch Reformed church. Although most of the people had never read these creeds, they undoubtedly knew of the close correlation between these guides to the faith and the Bible itself. Again, although the content of their faith was not consistent with European Calvinism, their method of approach presupposed a Reformed systm of belief, transmitted not by trained scholars but by tradition.

Biblicism and Folk Theology

Biblicism of the Reformed traition was developed in a unique way in South Africa due to a lack of trained theologians or ministers. It led to a folk-theology sustained by popular piety. Until the Boer War, the institutional church in South Africa played a much less significant role than in almost any other comparable modern nation. Organized churches and trained theologians or ministers were not plentiful enough to be a decisive influence in many areas of the frontier. This is not to suggest, however, that the Reformed tradition had no influence. Rather, the Bible was used regularly in private and family devotions. The settlers believed it was their duty to interpret these religious resources for the good of their people. In the absence of an organized church, the settlers developed for themselves churches in the wilderness, with the father as patriarch interpreting for this family. Many travelers to the frontier, especially in the eighteenth century, corroborated this functional use of the Book of Life.

Typology of Covenant, Exodus, Conquest

God's plan for Afrikanerdom was seen as a typological reenactment on the South African frontier of various Old Testament episodes, notably the making of the Covenant, the Exodus, and the conquests of Joshua and Gideon. The Boers assumed that if they looked to the Bible in humility, they could find answers for their needs; nothing would be hidden from them. Consequently, the situations which seemed to reflect a biblical event were interpreted as direct signs from God. On this basis the Great Trek became the new Exodus; conquest of the land was blessed by God, with mention of Joshua, Gideon, and others; and Providence was on the side of the Boers' freedom fight against both African and British. In battles against the Zulus, the Boers kept the stories of Gideon and Jephthah before their eyes as examples of God's favor. The freedom fighters at Slagters' Nek were bound by a religious covenant in opposition to the British. The Boers' success against Dingane in 1838 was interpreted as a confirmation of the covenant constructed on the basis of the Abrahamic covenant, and the victory in 1881 against Britain was further confirmation of the covenant of 1879 drawn up in anti-British terminology.

These Biblical parallels which seemed to be re-enacted in South Africa formed a proof of the correctness of preconceived strategy in battle or in government. In every success God was given credit for various conquests of Africans. The Boers believed that they could never have achieved victory on their own, although they never mentioned the part their superior weapons played. God brought victory against the British in 1881, again corroborating the Boers' conception of the rightness of their cause. Boer fears for a government led by liberal President Burgers were based on biblical injunctions, mainly Leviticus. The religious orthodoxy and the pious speeches, filled with biblical allusions, of President Kruger gave the nation the strength it needed, for their confidence was now in a higher power. God's favor seemed assured.

Old Testament Theology

Afrikaners used the Old Testament almost exclusively; Christology was almost nonexistent. When we say that Afrikaner nationalism was based on a Calvinistic framework insofar as it used and interpreted the Bible, the Psalter, and the creeds of the Reformed faith, we are faced with one further question. Calvinism was not only bibliocentric but was Christological as well. John Calvin assumed that acquaintance with the prophets and the Psalms would lead everyone to recognize the need for Christ. The Boers did not develop this aspect of the faith. Why? Their strong group consciousness, which developed in their isolation, caused them to be extremely conscious of themselves as a group. Their need to feel part of a larger whole—while still a minority in South Africa—caused them to seek a theological interpretation of their total society. Thus they placed very little emphasis on individual salvation. They considered themselves not new creatures in Christ but a new Israel, a holy commonwealth bound together and to God by their covenant, solemnly renewed each year.

ELECTION BECAME SOCIO-CULTURAL

This brings us to a further presupposition concerning social election. Afrikaners adopted the idea of election from the Reformed tradition, but unconsciously they changed it from a theological doctrine to a sociocultural term. Consequently, they came to believe that there were certain sociocultural proofs for their assurance of God's favor. The social development of those who break new ground on a frontier is always slow. The South African settlers on the newest frontier lacked certain cultural advantages of more settled people, whether in Europe or later in cultural centers such as Cape Town. On the frontier there were few schools, few qualified teachers, no city worthy of the name, few trained theological leaders, few churches. Many of the frontiersmen, including the leaders, could hardly read and write. All thought of themselves as Christians, however, members of the Dutch Reformed church. Although born in South Africa, they traced their unbroken religious traditions back to the origin of the South African people, the fighters for religious freedom in the Netherlands, or the Huguenots in France.

On the frontier these pious Reformed people, using their Bibles, quickly developed their own theological interpretations. Although the main interests of the people revolved around their land and their flocks, they maintained a simple piety. As they perused their Bibles around the campfire and read of the struggles of their theological forefathers wandering in the deserts of Egypt and Palestine or watching their flocks, they identified themselves as a new Israel. They indulged in pious speculation and assumed that God similarly elected them, protected them, and placed them in their situation with a special purpose. Their culture was biblical, and because of their Reformed background—both Dutch Reformed and French Huguenot—they called themselves Calvinists.

In the absence of trained theologians among the Boers on the frontier and in the republics, a lay piety developed among respected and pious leaders. Consequently, South African theology was not explicit, seldom systematic, seldom orthodox, and not based on educated theological leadership. Most religious leaders knew little more about Calvinism than the name. In this case the term *theological history* is justified, however, for in the absence of sophisticated or informed theological opinion, the Boers developed a folk theology of their own. They equated their ultimate concern at a given time with God's concern and assumed that God was on their side if they remained faithful to Him. This folk theology became the rallying point for cultural developments in later years, only slowly modified by, but never completely replaced by, precise theological thought as it came later in the nineteenth century.

In their unsystematic, pious theological constructions, the Boers introduced many modifications into their thought. One of the most far-reaching was their assurance of election. According to Calvin, the elect are known only to God. The Boers modified this, however, as they took the idea from its theological context and gave it a sociological and cultural basis. Thus they came to recognize election by outward appearances. Their Calvinism lost its Christological character and was built much more on the Old Testament than the New. Their thorough reading of the Bible revealed several instances similar to their own: Moses in the wilderness, Joshua and the Judges opposed to "heathens," and Nehemiah's problems with "uitlanders." They read about the covenant between God and Abraham establishing the old Israel as a people, and they assumed that their convenant made in 1838 and renewed in 1879 and every year thereafter was the origin of their modern Zion in South Africa. As they renewed their covenant with God before certain crises in their history and as they knelt in prayer before every battle, they were, they thought, faithful to the example of Abraham. The more they read and reread the narratives about Moses, Joshua, and the Psalms, they were reassured of God's favor. Their faith was biblical and

Calvinistic, but neither term was used in its accepted interpretation. Both were now strictly South African terms, modified by the culture for specific purposes.

Nationalistic History

Before the twentieth century there was no authoritative exposition of the distinctively Afrikaner doctrine of election, which was nevertheless widely assumed and acted on. In the nineteenth century the nearest Afrikaners came to official statements were the nationalistic histories or the charters of organizations such as the Afrikaner Bond. In order to substantiate the suggestion that a culture is based, at least in part, on a theological interpretation, one would expect to read a semiofficial theological analysis. This does not appear in South Africa. A beginning interpretation first appears in the period of the Great Trek with the *Manifesto* of Piet Retief, with even more detail in the sermons and prayers of Charl Celliers, and the layman who acted as minister on the trek, Erasmus Smit. This concept received further elaboration from various people who wrote letters to the editor in the early days of the republics. The first systematic presentation in which theological assumptions were read back into Afrikaner history were nationalistic histories of S. J. du Toit (1877) and C. P. Bezuidenhout (1883). The Afrikaner Bond was formed in this same period as one aspect of "praise to God for His deliverance from British control." In these works the guiding hand of providence was seen in each crisis with respect to both the Africans and the British. These histories were only two among many that formed the basis of later Afrikaner nationalist thought such as the violently anti-British *A Century of Wrong* (1899). Through this type of interpretation, God's favor throughout the generations was proved.

Invisible Church Became Visible Society

Having constructed their concept of election more in sociological and cultural terms than in a theological context, the Boers made many un-Calvinistic and bold assumptions. They carried theological thinking beyond Calvin as they confused the visible church-society with the invisible church and ultimately equated the two. Those who were faithful members of the Afrikaner community were automatically part of God's faithful invisible community of the elect. The elect were those responsible for carrying through the plan of God in their society. In 1838 the elect were those who covenanted together before God in opposition to Dingane and his Zulu followers. In 1858 they were the loyal Afrikaners who marched behind Pretorius at Boomplaats. While President Kruger was in office, the elect were the loyal Afrikaners who opposed the growing population of Uitlanders—supposedly pro-British settlers. In the wars of 1880 and 1899 the elect were those who protected God's people from British aggression.

Education and Election

They assumed, further, that education, culture and skin color were marks of, or proofs of, God's election. If God already made distinctions among people, they must not challenge the *status quo* by attempting to bridge the cultural chasm separating the Europeans and the African groups. In the eighteenth century, the Boers were culturally superior and came to refer to the Hottentots as "heathen," while Europeans were "Christian." In the nineteenth century the various Bantu groups "proved" their inferiority by attacking the well-laid plans of the Europeans. That these attacks were probably provoked by European opportunists was overlooked. The trekkers sought to maintain the proper relation between master and servants, for to allow "heathens" in the church was to show a "disrespect for the religious institutions of the people."

Racial Distinctions are God-Given

For the sake of God's plan they were required to uphold the divinely determined distinctions between the races. If there was this theologically justified distinction between peoples, they felt it was their privilege and responsibility to enhance their favored culture by exploiting Africans for their own purposes. Early in the settlement, a baptized African could not be kept a slave. This theological rite released his physical bonds and made him a free man in Christ. This was soon changed, however, as the slave could be baptized—free, spiritually—while remaining a slave in this life. During the Great Trek, Mrs. Steenkamp probably spoke for many when she suggested that equality between "Christians" and "heathens" was "contrary to the laws of God and the natural distinction of race and religion."[1] Afrikaners felt that there was a great difference between slavery and apprenticeship. Outsiders assumed it was a subtle change in terminology for the same basic attitude. The longer the Boers persisted in favored positions, educationally, culturally, and economically, the more they were certain of the truth of their theological interpretations. They were assured many times that God automatically favored any quest they attempted if they were faithful. Their cause would surely prosper because it was to the glory of God.

Afrikaner Cause Equated with Exodus and Covenant

The biblical imagery of the Exodus and of the Covenant were used by the Voortrekkers to justify a radical move in Afrikaner society—a retreat to a wilderness to maintain purity of doctrine. In later generations biblical imagery was chosen more to bolster the *status quo*. The Boers developed a group consciousness but not a historical consciousness so that they could consider their cause from any objective approach. They did not analyze the internal contradictions of their culture, nor were they able to look at themselves from the standpoint of either the British or the Africans. Their viewpoint was too much limited by other factors to allow this possibility.

neither could they look at themselves in the light of true Calvinism as it filtered in from Europe during the nineteenth century. Their main reaction was to frustrate European influence because it was rationalistic and would undermine their faith and challenge their *status quo.* This fear led to their founding the theological seminary at Stellenbosch in 1859 to provide pure theological training for Afrikaner leaders. They sensed, but did not specifically state, that a fresh look from the outside would shatter the faulty foundations on which their whole society was based. The Boers on the Great Trek, or fighting the Battle of Boomplaats, equated their position with the Israelites fleeing from Egypt under the leadership of Moses. As the Afrikaners' regime settled in the two republics, and especially during the presidency of Kruger, the Afrikaner leaders acted much like Pharaoh themselves. Their response was defensive, resulting in a heightened interest in "God's Will" and in the Afrikaners' "Cause." While the South Africans were anxious to use orthodox Calvinistic terminology, the theological ideas of Calvin were never thoroughly applied by the Boers; rather they were modified in a distinctive Afrikaner manner.

FREEDOM

They believed that freedom is a God-given privilege and true believers are challenged to maintain what God has provided.

Freedom from Dutch or British

Freedom on the frontier included freedom from direction by both government and the confessional establishments of Cape Town, whether Dutch, British, or Afrikaner. Almost from the beginning of the settlement in South Africa, the cry of freedom was heard. In the earliest days, this was synonymous with the burghers' desire for self-determination and a rejection of all restraints. Within the first five years, some burghers became free from the domination of the Dutch East India Company. A few years later they demanded freedom from economic oppression by the governor. When the frontiersmen demanded freedom on the frontier, they meant freedom to handle affairs as they wished and freedom to possess all the land they could amass, tax free. Before the British came, freedom had no political or nationalistic meaning. The basis of even the short-lived republics of Graaff-Reinet and Swellendam was economic.

World politics, which were far removed from the Afrikaners, introduced British armed forces and British cultural influences into South Africa, challenging the Afrikaners' view of their culture to the core. Britain wished to import its ideas to replace the South African orthodoxy.

Britain demanded systematic law courts, asked equal and universal taxation, and established a system of state control of many aspects of life. The Boers, especially on the eastern frontier, were accustomed to acting according to their own convenience, and they enjoyed their self-sufficient independence. Such restraints were interpreted as slavery or oppression.

The Volkstem Operative through Freedom

Only through freedom could the opportunities presented by God be fulfilled by Afrikanerdom. The divine directive through the concept of the *Volkstem* would be thwarted if there were no freedom. Consequently, freedom for them was slavery or oppression at the hands of the Dutch or British. The Patriot movement in Cape Town in the late eighteenth century, although basically economic, had a theological dimension. The people opposed oppression because it thwarted the gift of God—self-determination—implanted in all. The concept of the voice of the people (*Volkstem*) as a divine directive led the patriots to demand freedom and to make their complaints known in the Netherlands. To do less would be to deny the basic right of human nature—the right and the responsibility to work for the well-being of all. In the first thirty years of British domination of the Cape Colony (1806-1836), the Boers became sharply conscious of their many differences from British ideals. They sensed their God-given freedom was being challenged and began gradually to develop their main cultural ideals around this concept of freedom from British ideas. When Piet Retief was chosen president in 1837, he believed the divine directive came through the voice of the people (*Volkstem*) who elected him. This helps to explain the importance the Transvaal later put on the question of election and the fear they harbored of allowing the franchise to the Uitlanders or the Africans. Not being part of God's elect people, these outsiders would subvert the whole nation, and freedom would be lost "as surely as if on the battlefield," so Kruger concluded. To fail to maintain freedom would be to fail God.

Freedom and Exploitation

With respect to the African tribes, freedom was construed as license to build a society at the expense of Africans, whether through slavery or apprenticeship. It has been stated that the early introduction of slavery into South African society contributed immeasurably to the assumed difference between the races. The Europeans were the builders of white society; the various colored races were delegated to menial tasks—"the hewers of wood and drawers of water." The early settlers felt justified in encroaching on more and more land even in the face of Khoikhoi opposition. When the Boers met the San, they felt justified in exterminating those who attacked as a "menace" to the progress of "civilization." The nineteenth-century British philanthropic optimism toward the Bantu was interpreted merely as condescension, for Boers supposed Bantu had only the capability of children and must be protected. Apprenticeship in the Transvaal legally was not slavery, but the distinction was more academic than real.

Election Implies Opposition to Britain

As the Boer War approached, Britain was more the enemy than were the Africans. Divine election, at this point, was defined in anti-British terms—freedom for Afrikaners from British control. When Afrikaner nationalism finally arose between 1868 and 1881, it was for the sake of freedom and was one defensive means to oppose Britain. No longer could the Boers take the initiative and retreat. There was no place to go. They must establish God's rule and God's kingdom where they were by excluding all foreign influences. In the covenant they made in 1879, the concept of God's will and freedom are equated with oppositon to the British. The concepts of freedom, biblical justification, and pride of language coalesced. President Kruger, one of the original trekkers, became the prototype par excellence of the Boer on the defensive, chosen by God through several free elections. The British annexation in 1877, its insistence on the suzerainty after 1881, and its attempts to redress grievances of the Uitlanders in the 1890s all strengthened the Boers' defensive attitude and solidified the intransigence of leaders such as President Kruger and leading conservative Afrikaner nationalists not only of the republics but of the Cape Colony as well. Through these attempted interventions, the British seemed to be denying nationhood to the Boers who had no secure freedom. What their situation demanded continued to be their ultimate hope and goal—national status or freedom. Their continuing argument was "look at what God did for us in the past. Let us have confidence that He will do so again."

The close association between church and state was common in all nations of Europe, as well as in South Africa at the time. Consequently, whatever enhanced the Boers' political group consciousness also enhanced their view of themselves as a people of God. Conversely, their success in battle—especially in 1881 and the Jameson Raid in 1895—taken as God's signs, solidified their confidence that they were a unique people in God's sight. When late in the nineteenth century, the idea of a united South Africa from Cape Town to the Zambezi arose, the concept was theological as much as political. Any partial eclipse of Afrikanerdom by Britain or by a new concept of the relation with Africans was seen as a partial denial of the Afrikaner religious faith. Their nationalism was as much for defense of preconceived theological status as vice-versa.

One of the surprising aspects of the later period is that the Afrikaners so quickly rose from defeat to be masters of South Africa. By 1908 the war had been concluded only six years when three of the four nations were controlled by Afrikaner parties, and since the union in 1910 none but Afrikaners have been prime ministers of South Africa. This phoenix-like rebirth is not explainable on purely economic, or social, or even cultural grounds. Something more pervasive was necessary. The concept of Afrikanerdom had a theological dimension, and this vision of a mission under God assisted the Afrikaners in rising above the defeat of war in a surprisingly short time. Their freedom was a gift of God. This confidence gave them a strong group feeling and instilled in them a spirit of fiercely loyal cooperation.

The concept of freedom that was so prominent in the anti-British discussions in the last century had a deep theological basis. The freedom given by the sovereign God must be maintained against political intrigues by Britain or cultural invasions by Africans. It was for the glory of God that they must maintain their freedom against all challenges. This was the destiny and the cause of Afrikanerdom.

LANGUAGE AND GROUP CONSCIOUSNESS

They assumed that language was closely related to freedom and group consciousness. The insistence on using Dutch in place of English was a continuing factor in the growing national self-consciousness. The emphasis on the Dutch language in the Cape Colony was a reflection of the proud Dutch spirit. This common language tied Cape Town citizens closely to the glory of the Dutch nation and its high concept of its calling. This also resulted in the early subjugation of the language of the French refugees who landed in South Africa in 1688. The Dutch insistence that there be no French-speaking area in South Africa was based in part of their desire for a strongly unified culture. Division in language would be divisive in their infant settlement.

When the British occupied the Cape Colony permanently, they also understood the importance of language, and when they had been in South Africa only twenty years, they attempted to modify the language. They required English in government, hoping Dutch would disappear through disuse. The Dutch settlers were too numerous for this plan to succeed, and their cultural pride was so strong that the subjugation of Dutch was not possible.

Whereas after a few generations most Afrikaners in the Cape Colony spoke better English than Dutch, not everyone accepted the change willingly. The language question underlay part of the reaction and subsequent exodus of the Great Trek. The change in language was interpreted, probably rightly, as one attempt to subjugate the Dutch-speaking people and to eliminate this one strong bond that held them together. It was quite natural that the two republics founded by trekkers for freedom insisted on Dutch as the language of freedom. During the agitation for Afrikaner nationalism, the emphasis on Dutch and later on Afrikaans was a major unifying bond extending from one end of South Africa to the other. The Act of Union was a compromise for both the strongly British and the strongly Afrikaner factions. Each wanted its own language at the expense of the other.

Afrikaans as a New Language

The development of Afrikaans as a spoken language after 1750 and as an official written language in the twentieth century was a major impetus toward Afrikaner national self-consciousness. When the Dutch first settled in South Africa, their own language was not yet systematized. There were many discrepancies in both spelling and use. Widely separated from their European homeland, the Afrikaners solidified their language in a way different from the Netherlanders. Afrikaners adopted some African and some French words. Both their spelling and grammar were simplified. Even after they had developed many distinctive differences from high Dutch, they assumed their language was the same as their forefathers brought with them. Within a century, the Afrikaans language developed its uniquely South African character, and it was spoken by the Afrikaners in place of true Dutch. Since the Afrikaners assumed the British sought to eradicate this language, it is not surprising to see the vital role that language played in the developing nationalism. S. J. du Toit's book (1877) was not only a nationlist history, but as the title indicates, it was a history "in the language of our people." Immediately Afrikaners began developing their own literature written in their language.

It may be suggested without exaggeration that only when Afrikaans was adopted as a separate national language in 1925 did the Afrikaner people come of age as a nation. Previous to this they were only an extension of the Dutch people. Now their "God-given" language was recognized in the world.

New Language is God-Given

The assumption that Afrikaans is God-given provides the language question with a religious sanction. Language is a vital aspect of national consciousness and in this case of theological self-understanding as well. It is not accidental that the Afrikaner Bond leader, S. J. du Toit, suggested that "God gave us the Afrikaans language."[2] So basic is language to culture that when the society thinks of itself as directly led by God, the language of the culture is decreed by God also. Thus a common language, a vital and all-pervasive aspect of any group consciousness, is an emotional rallying point in any time of tension or challenge. The Dutch language, and more especially Afrikaans, played a significant role in the development of the theological nationalism of Afrikanerdom.

RACIAL DIFFERENCES

Racial differences were assumed to be God-given, and the differences between people must be preserved when challenged. There was no emphasis on segregation or overt racial prejudice in the first century of the European settlement in South Africa. The early settlers were able to exploit the Khoikhois for the development of their settlement, and many of these Africans were content to be servants and herdsmen for the Boers. The unusual case of the baptized Khoikhoi, Eva, who married a European without any expressed concern from other settlers, assures us that race was not a distinguishing mark in the early settlement.[3] The theological presupposition that all baptized persons were equal in the sight of God was taken seriously until challenged later in the course of social development.

Challenge of African Tribes

The reaction against African tribes was in direct proportion to the assumed challenge they made on the European way of life. At first the gulf between the Europeans and Africans was so great that comparison or challenge was remote. The growing resentment the Africans felt against the encroachments on their lands and cattle resulted in growing antagonism and conflict. During the eighteenth century while the Afrikaners were migrating from the environs of Cape Town to the eastern frontier, they came to refer to themselves as "Christian" and their opponents as "heathen." Indeed, the Africans who were trained by European missionaries were considered heathen, while those European farmers or cattlemen who had no religious affiliation were considered Christian. These terms originally had religious connotation, but before the end of the eighteenth century, Boers took the offensive and organized in commandos to hunt Africans as though they were animals. The documents of the eighteenth century record many forays against the San in which the numbers of slain or captured are noted with as little compassion as they might record a daily catch of grouse or rabbits. The Boers' sociological terms, now translated back into a theological concept—heathen—justified their actions.

The necessity for protection on the frontier gave rise to the Europeans' use of extermination as a practical requirement. This gradually evolved into an ideological assumption. One could exterminate an African as an effective means of protection. Later when this became immoral or illegal, the same ideological interpretation encouraged the idea of absolute separation to fulfill the same function. In both situations the dominant attitude of protection prevailed, and such qualifying secondary thoughts such as compassion or religious questions were subordinated and of little effect.[4]

After the terms *Christian* and *heathen* were modified into sociological and cultural terms, they easily coalesced with the assumption that the African was inferior. Afrikaners came to regard the Africans as less than human, calling them creatures (*schepsel*), not people. Pseudotheological interpretations reinforced the sociological distinction and helped to imbed it deeply in the group's self-image. The sociological assumption of the inferiority of non-Europeans, reinforced by a theological interpretation, made each challenge seem all the more unjust and instilled growing resentment against the developing African peoples.

The challenge developed in three areas: where the Africans competed for the same land and flocks; where they approached cultural equality; and where the Afrikaners needed inexpensive and docile laborers in the growing industrialization. The ideology of strict separation of racial groups developed slowly and only as challenges developed.

The Afrikaners faced their first formidable challenge of land and flocks at the Great Fish River when the Xhosa tribes were first confronted (1779). The resulting century-long skirmish was significant because the Xhosa and other Bantu challenged the Afrikaner settlers at the heart of their developing frontier life. Both the white and the nonwhite groups were dependent on land and flocks for their livelihood. The Boers who already assumed superiority over the Hottentots and the Bushmen were repeatedly forced to defend this assumption against well-organized tribal groups. Each successful victory against great odds was added proof that the theological idea was valid, and group confidence mounted continually.

The challenge of education and culture caused the Boers to become more defensive. Late in the eighteenth century, the missionaries arrived in South Africa with the implicit assumption that the Africans had potential if they but had a chance for education and for learning the ways of the Europeans. The Boers opposed the missionary movement on religious grounds, which were at the same time sociological and cultural. They believed that anything which would help to equalize their cultural differences would be to their disadvantage. Consequently, the Boers looked with suspicion on any move in religion, government, or law which would make the African any nearer their equal. They were suspicious if laws were applied equally to African and European, for they assumed partiality should be shown to Christians. They questioned taxation for Africans, for this would lead them to think they had the right to citizenship. They denied that a Khoikhoi should be compensated by receiving any of the booty of a raid, for such recognition would give the Khoikhoi some sense of their own worth.

Especially severe was the Boers' criticism of the educational ventures the missionaries organized among the Afrikaners. The criticims concerned immorality and laziness, but actually the Boers were afraid. Their cultural superiority was being challenged by the elevation of an inferior cultural group toward equality in the name of the missionary's religion. Again, the Boers' assumed status, based on social and cultural presuppositions, was confused with religious values, and their *status quo* was championed in the name of God and religion.

Late in the ninetenth century, the elect Boers were further challenged by the new capitalism of an industrial nation. The miners needed inexpensive labor, and Africans from many tribes were willing to work for low wages. Consequently, certain menial tasks were reserved for the blacks, and it was considered beneath the dignity of whites to perform "Kaffir work."

The low wages the Africans were paid, however, allowed them a slightly higher standard than they had known before. They were often able to better themselves gradually through the generations. As the mining industry expanded, the number of needed unskilled laborers also increased. The economic situation produced *de facto* integration despite the basic fears and prejudices of the Afrikaners. The mines could not exist but for this integration of the races at the point of production. Economic integration would lead gradually to territorial integration and finally to cultural equality, unless some force were exerted to stem the tide.

Challenge of British Philanthropy

Their concept of election caused Afrikaners to react sharply against the basic assumption of British philanthropic thought exemplified especially in the Christian mission to the Africans. By the time the British came to power in South Africa in 1806, certain aspects of the social attitude of the Boers were solidified. The sharp distinction they saw between Europeans and Africans was based on outward differences of cultural development and was visibly written on the hearts of Afrikaners as a sociotheological *a priori*. The African was less than a human being, and it was the Afrikaners' God-given duty to "maintain proper relations between master and servant." Any attempt to induce the Afrikaners to change their preconceived viewpoint was countered by their erecting defensive measures to maintain the "Christian view" (traditional separation). The British government, while not as thoroughly committed to integration as their words might indicate, was nevertheless a threat to the Boers' concept. Missionary influence with government officials on behalf of Africans was suspect. The circuit court that took Khoikhoi testimony seriously was a "Black Circuit" and the leading missionary, the Rev. John Philip, was considered more political than religious. Missionary activities which encouraged the Khoikhoi to take responsibility for their lot were charged with placing Africans "on an equal footing with Christians, contrary to the law of God and the natural distinction of race and religion."[5]

Apartheid the Logical Result of a Long History

The political doctrine of apartheid, developed systematically only in the twentieth century, is the logical outcome of the various challenges and reactions—freedom for Afrikanerdom from domination by the African majority and from white consensus outside the nation. While the doctrine of apartheid was systematized only in this century, many aspects of the idea had a long history. The stronger the Africans challenged the total Afrikaner domination of the culture, the stronger the Afrikaner reaction became. As we have noted, economic integration might have led eventually to cultural integration but for the intervention of an opposing force. Economic pressures in South Africa contributed to the breakdown of traditional tribal organizations, which made the Africans more dependent on the white rules. Consequently, to ensure the continued existence of their ideology, the Afrikaner introduced an artificial boundary, the political and social doctrine of *apartheid*. Economic necessities, however, are opposed to this type of barrier. The pseudotheological ideology of the superiority of one race cannot hope to succeed if the doctrine of absolute segregation is breached at the vital point of economics.

The idea of one elect people, racially speaking, is not possible even when backed by a government advocating apartheid. The society that subverts the meaning of "Christian" and "elect people" to a social category constructs an artificial framework based on faulty presuppositions. Economic necessity and the course of history increasingly will reveal the faults in the system.

AFRIKANER THEOLOGY AND CULTURE
IN FUNCTIONAL RELATIONSHIP

Although the theological development in South Africa was not orthodox in comparison with European interpretations and in spite of the fact that Afrikaner thought was more often implicit than stated, their theological construction served two basic functions in their society.

Unique Afrikaner Theology

First, their own interpretation of theology gave direction to a new society almost without influence from the outside. Although in comparison with the larger context of Western civilization, the end results of the South African development seem questionable, nevertheless the Afrikaner nationalist theology developed within the social milieu and was so thoroughly modified according to unique South African social needs that it formed the normative framework for the developing nation. As we have seen, the theological influence from Europe was sporadic and gave only the minimum of continuing direction to the developing society. Within the context of a broad Reformed methodology, most of the attempts to apply the faith to specific problems were strongly colored by the South African existential situation. The Reformed teaching concerning equality through baptism was gradually modified until the European could continue to hold even baptized Africans in slavery. The Reformed faith that sought to educate all to qualify for church membership was modified because the Europeans came to fear a cultural equality through education. It was assumed, and culturally determined, that the African was capable only of remaining a child and needed constant protection and control. The concepts of Christian and heathen were transferred from the theological to the sociological realm. Severe threats from well-organized Bantu tribes caused the Afrikaners' racist ideology to be stiffened, and their primary concerns—self-preservation—became equated with God's will for His elect people. They chose the ideology of Moses and the Exodus for the national aspirations, the Joshua-heathen-conquest motif for their racial objectives, and the Deuteronomic theology of the Psalms as an expression of the benefits to be derived from continued loyalty to God as they conceived it.

Despite their loyalty to their religious way of life, they were constantly threatened. This led them to an introspective analysis of their society. Perhaps their own faithlessness was being punished by God; hence their constant reference to the concepts of reward and punishment as exemplified in the Psalms. The more their society was threatened, the more their previously concluded theological interpretations were solidified and intensified. Only their confidence in God's gracious intervention in due time kept them seeking new, although increasingly frustrating, solutions to their problems. As long as the Afrikaners could maintain total hegemony in the South African settlement, the theological assumptions, although faulty from an outsider's standpoint, helped to maintain the status of the preferred group—the Afrikaners.

Stability and Hope in Crisis

The second major function of the Afrikaner theology was to provide stability, hope, and encouragement in crisis. In time of extreme crisis and utter defeat in the Boer War, only their faith in God's providence guarded against their complete dejection and dissolution as a people. In many less devastating situations, Afrikaners trusted that their God would bring victory out of chaos. For even minor satisfactions and only slight rays of hope, they gave heartfelt thanks to God. At the end of the Boer War when any outsider might have assumed the Boer nation could not again rise, the Boer nation did indeed rise. Their rebirth after defeat was possible only because they did not interpret their defeat in that way. Their faith in the providence of God was so strong that they could interpret their catastrophe only as a severe trial, and as long as any of them remained alive, God had a plan for them. The Boers' early development of political parties after the war, their domination of the preparations for the Union, and their increasing control of the South African nation since 1910 can be explained only if we recognize the theological dimensions that bound the people to what they interpreted as their God-ordained destiny. The Dutch Reformed churches, the only social organizations not devastated by the war, assumed the responsibility for the theological interpretation of their society and remained strongly associated with nationalist policy a half-century later.

This chapter is a theological analysis as it might be developed from inside the developing nation. As such it provides no objective criterion for judging the theological construction as a whole. From the standpoint of the Afrikaner Christian, all seems extremely logical, biblical, and thoroughly justified. Before completing our study, however, we must step outside South Africa and see their ideology from a larger perspective—from an understanding of Calvinism as it developed in a larger context.

NOTES

1. Bird, *Annals of Natal*, I, 459; Mrs. Steenkamp's notes.

2. van Jaarsveld, *Afrikaner's Interpretation*, p. 19.

3. MacCrone, *Race Attitudes*, p. 71.

4. "There existed amongst the farmer-pioneers an unwritten, common code of behavior toward the non-whites. The development and crystallization of the pioneer's color morality went hand-in-hand with the gradual emergence in the 18th century of the Boer-Afrikaner type." Rhoodie and Venter, *Apartheid*, p. 54.

5. Anna Steenkamp, "Record of Migration," in Bird, *Annals of Natal*, I, 459-468.

X.
Afrikaner Calvinism in
Larger Perspective

Up to this point we have analyzed the theological background of Afrikaner Calvinism within the Afrikaner cultural context. We have shown how each step in its development seemed to be a logical outgrowth of the social and political situation in which Afrikaners were living. Indeed, based on their presuppositions, the cultural construction which they presented to the world was very logical, and each segment was thoroughly interrelated with all other aspects of the culture. For this we give credit to the many thinkers of that country who made their contributions to an extensive interpretation, usually without direct contact with cultural development in either Europe or the United States. For one reared within their intellectual framework, it must have seemed, indeed, that they were God's chosen people in the modern world.

At the present time, however, with technology and travel making the world much smaller and forcing all peoples to live in close proximity to others who share different backgrounds and different cultural assumptions, each culture must be placed in a context larger than itself. Furthermore, since the Afrikaner society is supposedly based on Calvinistic principles, it is necessary to look at its Calvinism from the viewpoint of larger theological concerns as taught by the Genevan Reformer and developed in many other parts of the world. In this last chapter we place certain aspects of the Afrikaner development in a larger context and analyze them from the standpoint of those who were not reared in the unique South African cultural milieu.

GOD'S SOVEREIGNTY, OR PROVIDENCE: HOW CAN GOD'S LEADING IN A CONTEMPORARY SOCIETY BE INTERPRETED?

In the last edition of the *Institutes,* Calvin included his doctrine of the providence (sovereignty) of God as an aspect of God's creation. Here he emphasized two aspects of providence: general providence and special providence. By the former he meant God's over-all control such as His operating under natural law, or common knowledge of God's action, which demanded no special revelation. General providence included those aspects of common sense that Christianity shared with all other religions and even with science and philosophy. Calvin's primary emphasis, however, was on God's special providence. Not only did God create His world, but He was continually involved in maintaining its various actions by His personal direction. All that happened was a fulfillment of God's over-all plan.

> Faith ought to penetrate more deeply [than chance or fate], namely, having found him Creator of all, forthwith to conclude he is also everlasting Governor and Preserver—not only in that he drives the celestial frame as well as its several parts by a universal motion, but also in that he sustains, nourishes, and cares for, everything he has made, even to the least sparrow.[1]
>
> Anyone who has been taught by Christ's lips that all the hairs of his head are numbered will look farther afield for a cause, and will consider that all events are governed by God's secret plan. . . . [Inanimate objects] are, thus, nothing but instruments to which God continually imparts as much effectiveness as he wills, and according to his own purpose bends and turns them to either one action or another.[2]

Calvin found a basis for God's continual concern in the Psalms in a context similar to that used by the Afrikaners. He based one section on Psalm 107.[3] God redeems man from trouble; God saves those in desert wastes; God provides those who are hungry and thirsty with water; God delivers those in prison and in darkness from their gloom; God raises the humble and casts down the proud. The believer has the assurance that he is at the center of God's concern, and God's special care is directed toward his special needs. Not only do the Psalms inform us about the special concerns God has for the human race, but one must have faith that all that happens—salutary as well as devastating—is ordered by God, and all events are part of His total pattern for the believers.

> When dense clouds darken the sky, and a violent tempest arises, because a gloomy mist is cast over our eyes, thunder strikes our ears and all our senses are benumbed with fright, everything seems to us to be confused and mixed up; but all the while a constant quiet and serenity ever remain in heaven. So must we infer that, while the disturbances in the world deprive us of judgment, God out of the pure light of his justice and wisdom tempers and directs these very movements in the best-conceived order to a right end.[4]

This same confidence is expressed in Romans 8:28: "We know that in everything God works for good with those who love him, who are called according to his purpose." In the South African experience, the army that won the battle was blessed by God; those who were not victorious were yet instruments for the larger purposes of God. Hence, one was never left alone. All must have the faith that whatever happens is part of God's over-all plan. We should not concentrate on our own smallness but in faith must see ourselves in God's larger pattern of action. A major question remains, however: How can one recognize God's leading hand in contemporary society? The Afrikaners formed an interesting contrast to what seem to be the main implications in Calvin's thought.

We can have knowledge of God's special care for us only through Christ, Calvin argued. Christology is the only avenue to knowledge of God because our sinful nature has made any direct knowledge impossible. Although the Afrikaner emphasis on Christology was practically nonexistent, they assumed that their faith in God alone made them able to interpret God's special leading on their behalf. They saw themselves not as sinners in need of salvation but rather as chosen people who were even then receiving guidance from God. This misinterpretation led Afrikaners to conclude not only that whatever happened in their society was God's will, but they believed they knew what God's will was for them. Hence, since they were certain of the outcome God had planned for them, they should work on God's behalf as well as their own. God had planned for them a pure Christian civilization on the southern tip of Africa, which implied a rejection of any accommodation with the Africans or the British. With such confidence in their interpretation of the plan of the sovereign God, they were imbued with an almost superhuman determination to carry through God's will in their own society by efforts of their own power. They were confident also that as they committed themselves to the right causes, God would not fail them but would bless their cause, which was His also.

PREDESTINATION

As we begin to use the word *Calvinist* in South Africa, we must define the word and analyze Calvin's approach to the doctrine of the elect people. In the first edition of the *Institutes* (1536) Calvin did not develop the idea of election as a separate doctrine.[5] Rather, it was related to his teachings on the church and played a subordinate role in the larger theological system. In 1543 Calvin was forced to sharpen his concept when he was opposed by the Roman Catholic, Albert Pighius Campenis, arguing for freedom of the will in his book, *De Libero hominis arbitrio et Divina gratia decem libri.* Pighius indicated that the teaching as he understood it—of the bound will including the assumption that God instills evil in the heart of the godless— was a heretical doctrine of the Reformation.[6] Calvin answered him in his work *De aeterna Dei predestinatione* and worked much of the argument into later editions of the *Institutes.* In the last edition in 1559, a large section on providence followed the section on the doctrine of God (I:xvi), and an analysis of election immediately followed the discussion of sanctification and justification (III:xxi-xxiv). The relation between the providence of God and the doctrine of the elect was thus made precise, since they are related through the doctrine of Christ, in whom God in His providence operated to elect those whom He will.

Based on biblical formulation, Calvin drew further implications, all basic to his doctrine of salvation.[7] This was elaborated in opposition to Roman Catholic doctrine in general and to Pighuis in particular. God's election is gratuitous; human beings can do nothing toward salvation on their own, and election is in no way dependent on one's actions, good works, or the possibility that God can foreknow that one will be faithful and hence elect that person accordingly. On the other hand, that certain individuals are not elected is not a negation of God's mercy and kindness but reflects deserved punishment because of their own willful sinning.

God's election, in true Calvinistic sense, is not dependent on culture, education, custom, or skin color, and it is the prerogative of no one to assume that one who now acts as a sinner is truly lost. This is the judgment of God alone. The number determined by God was certain, and they could not be lost. This was the invisible church, the *universus electorum numerus* known only to God. We can have some hint of assurance:

> We have a sufficiently clear and firm testimony that we have been inscribed in the Book of Life if we are in communion with Christ.[8]

> For those whom Christ has illuminated with the knowledge of His Name and has introduced into the bosom of his church, he is said to receive into his care and keeping.[9]

> We teach that the calling of the elect is as a sign and testimony of their election. Similarly, that their justification is another mark and evidence of it.[10]

The Dutch Reformed church, in both the Netherlands and in the far-flung reaches of the Dutch East India Company, based its faith on the Belgic Confession (1561), the Heidelberg Catechism (1563), and the Decrees of the Synod of Dort (1618-1619). Although the doctrine of election was not made as specific in the Heidelberg Catechism as in the Belgic Confession, the theological system that made this a logical implication was there in broad outline.[11] Questions 3 through 11 discuss human misery and the theological idea that all have sinned; they deserve to be condemned because of their own willful sin. They cannot work their own way out of sin but must have divine help. Questions 12 through 17 discuss the place that Jesus Christ plays in this drama, being the channel through which God made possible the restoration of the elect to their justified state. Question 20 allows the implication that the one who has the required faith will be saved. This is not specific, however, so this phase of the doctrine later had to be constructed in more detail. This was accomplished in the Decrees of Dort when eternal election was made the leading part of the creed and the central emphasis of the decrees.

The Synod of Dort was called in November 1618 to formulate a unified Reformed decision concerning the views taught by Jacob Arminius (1560-1609). Because his teaching concerned the possibility of a limited free will, the synod was compelled to single out the doctrine of election more than it had been emphasized in previous affirmations.[12] The decree, however, left a means whereby man could be assured that he was among the elect. This was the intention of the Synod of Dort but not the intention of John Calvin.[13] It is therefore to the decrees of the Synod of Dort and not to Calvin himself that advocates of the most rigid predestination theories appeal.

Afrikaners were among those who held this confessional standard in great esteem and believed that their cultural advantage was one mark of their own election. Their faith, based more on frontier piety and immediate concerns of society than on a theological analysis, gave them assurance that they were central in God's over-all plan. Although small in numbers and militarily weak, they were part of a larger whole, and their sovereign God would not be defeated by any power on earth. The concept of God's sovereignty among Afrikaners was based on Calvinistic terminology, while the content of the ideal society for which they were working was socially and politically conditioned. The Afrikaner cause, which had been transformed into God's cause, was the center of their activity, and all aspects of their culture were conditioned by their prior interpretation. They were sincere in believing that the sovereign God would be able to persevere in all adversities against His ultimate plan. At the same time, however, they did not realize the extent to which they had allowed their own concerns to determine their ideas of God's election. Their prior assumption that they were God's special chosen people, therefore, was decisive for their theological interpretation.

CHRISTIAN FREEDOM IN CALVIN'S THOUGHT AND AFRIKANER PIETY

The concept of Christian freedom assumed such importance that Calvin devoted a section of his *Institutes* to a discussion of the various aspects of the doctrine.[14] "It is a thing of prime necessity, and apart from knowledge of it consciences dare undertake almost nothing without doubting."[15] He was quick to raise certain cautions concerning freedom lest one be led into licentiousness on the one hand or be convinced that there are no differences or choices one must make between greater or lesser actions on the other.

In his positive discussion of freedom, he suggested three levels, or three aspects, to the doctrine. First, believers "should rise above and advance beyond the law, forgetting all lower righteousness."[16] One cannot be saved through the law and thus should not be weighted down with concerns or worries lest one not fulfill the law. The freedom of a Christian is found in another area of concern—when one forgets self and all attempts at works righteousness and relies on the mercy of God alone, through the merits of Christ. This is one aspect of justification by faith and not by works or by the law. So it is that the believer should be completely free from the fears and frustrations of the law. Second, when believers obey the law, they should not observe it "as if constrained by the necessities of the law, but freed from the law's yoke, they willingly obey God's will."[17] One who is concerned about self is concerned about the means of the law and lives each day in the light of certain legalistic requirements. On the other hand, one whose first concern is God sees the law in quite a different light and does the will of God in "joyous obedience" rather than grudgingly. When one has God at the center of his concern, even one's remaining sins cause no concern, for that person has been made free of their influence by the grace of God. Third, Calvin became subjective as he introduced the idea of *adiaphora*, or "things indifferent." Those things indifferent for us are such that "we are not bound before God by any religious obligations preventing us from sometimes using them and at other times not using them, indifferently."[18] Those things which are external (such as eating meat or certain ceremonies) are adiaphora, and we are free to use them or refrain from using them as God intended they be used. If, however, our action causes another to stumble or if our attitude is affected by certain scruples, these are not truly adiaphora for us, and we must act differently.

There are, then, the three aspects of freedom: freedom from the law because our faith has allowed us to forget concerns over the law's impossible requirements; freedom from the law because our concern is on God and not on self; and freedom from rites and ceremonies which are adiaphora as long as these are truly indifferent for us and for those who are influenced by us. "Let them regard this as the law of Christian freedom; to have learned with Paul, in whatever state they are, to be content; to know how to be humble and exalted; to have been taught, in any and all circumstances, to be filled and to hunger and to abound and to suffer want."[19]

This concept of freedom is very much an internalized freedom, an outgrowth of faith. One is free from inner tensions and faulty commitments because one has been made free through the grace of Christ. This is not determined by rules, laws, and commandments or by individual striving, or works, or merits. One is truly free only when united in faith to God. Consequently, Christian freedom is an inward confidence and hope and trust in the God of his faith, the assurance that He has removed the obstacles to one's spiritual pilgrimage, and that He is faithful to fulfill what one cannot do on one's own.

This freedom is not applied to external aspects of life—to one's social position, political status, or economic deprivation. Calvin is at one with Luther in seeing one's relation with external life in terms of Romans 13: "Let every person be subject to the governing authorities, for there is no authority except from God, and those that exist have been instituted by God. Therefore, he who resists the authorities resists whom God has appointed, and those who resist will incur judgment" (Romans 13:1-2). For Calvin, Christian freedom did not mean political freedom or economic freedom. The Western world would have to wait several more decades before the medieval social concepts of Calvin would be expanded to include these commonly accepted modern concepts.

The Afrikaner concept of freedom as a God-given right, however, did include both political and economic freedom from the constituted authority, whether Dutch officials or British leaders. In a sense, Afrikaners were true to the Calvinist spirit but not to the original author of Calvinism. As such, they went beyond the cautions of the Genevan Reformer who allowed resistance to political authority only when the political system would force the believer to deny his God. Just what this implied, Calvin did not specify. Nevertheless, by the time of his death in 1564, several situations in Europe were forcing various groups of Calvin's followers to decide they must go to arms against their unjust political overlords. The French wars of religion began in 1562. The Scottish Covenanters signed their pledge to resist Roman Catholicism in 1557, and their resistance was strengthened during the 1560s. The resistance against tyranny in the Netherlands, the major inspiration for South African nationalism, began in the 1560s but gained strength during the repressions and persecutions of the Spanish duke of Alva beginning in 1567. William of Orange and his associates used Calvinistic terminology as they led the attack on the Roman Catholic "usurpers" of their freedom. Furthermore, the constitution of the United Netherlands of 1581 shows many marks of Calvinistic influence.

It is to the French, the Scottish, and the Dutch freedom fighters that we must contrast the South African emphasis on freedom. The South Africans were not reflecting Calvin's own idea of Christian freedom. Indeed, the Afrikaner nationlists often mentioned the "80-year fight for freedom" among their Dutch forebears, but the South Africans changed the context. The European wars of religion were based on an attempt by Calvinists to extricate themselves from Roman Catholic systems which forced them to deny their God. They had interpreted their freedom in terms of freedom for the true worship according to their interpretation of the Bible. Their faith was not necessarily involved with their total culture, although there were many interrelations.

In South Africa there are several points of contrast. For example, there was never any Roman Catholic threat; the plea for freedom involved two Protestant groups. The British government did not restrict freedom of worship among Dutch Reformed groups in any way. The Afrikaners never-theless interpreted the British repressions in much larger cultural terms. Afrikanerdom was not only a religious faith; it was a total way of life. The British authorities were seen as representing a contradicting way of life. Only in these terms could the Afrikaners assume they were fighting for freedom in a situation comparable with that in Roman Catholic France or Spanish-controlled Netherlands.   Since the Afrikaners had long before equated theological goals with cultural objectives, they could refer to God-given freedom in sociological and political terms without realizing their inconsistencies.

SOUTH AFRICAN CALVINISM INTERPRETED
FROM THE PERSPECTIVE OF SOCIAL PSYCHOLOGY

From the beginning the South African settlement was a venture more eco-nomic than religious and was confronted with unique climactic, racial, and geographic challenges. These factors formed the basis of many of the ten-sions we have observed there, and they must be taken into consideration in understanding the complexity of the Afrikaner mentality. Some of the principles motivating the intellectual developments in South Africa have been suggested earlier. A more systematic analysis of these principles on the basis of social psychology may provide further enlightenment concern-ing the underlying developments in South Africa. These principles are selected from those presented in a standard and widely accepted study of social psychology.[20] They were developed by David Krech and Richard Crutchfield on the basis of a large number of research monographs. General assumptions concerning human perception and attitude formation will be applied to South Africa to provide a possible explanation for many developing attitudes.

General Cultural Developments

As the South African experiment began, there was no group feeling and thus no cultural ideology. All settlers were individuals in a new land, related to the Dutch East India Company, and all were citizens of the Netherlands. There was no thought of reacting against the Company poli-cies and certainly no thought of giving loyalty to any land other than the Netherlands. Within a few years, however, some burghers sought their independence from the Company, and within a half-century enough senti-ment was developed that some referred to themselves as Afrikaners, no longer citizens of Europe.

The psychological principles become evident only after this self-con-sciousness developed. The various activities of the eighteenth century—

eastward migration, extermination of San, confrontation with the Xhosas, attempts to live on the arid lands of the eastern Cape Colony—were outgrowths from and functions of the growing group-consciousness. Krech and Crutchfield state this principle: "Action is not a formless, disembodied and meaningless explosion of energy released by accumulated tension. It has the direction and content, and the direction and content of action are shaped by the individual's conception of his world."[21] The conception of group consciousness developed simultaneously with the opportunities for new experiences on the frontier.

The frontier Boers increasingly sought a central concept around which they could organize their group consciousness. The most common litera- ture of this religious people was the Bible, which became the source of their major organizational framework. The isolated frontier Boer in the year 1750, for example, read the Bible in his family group, and each re- telling of its stories made them more personal. Finally, the Afrikaners equated themselves with God's own people. The earlier groups of God's people were analyzed in the Bible, whereas the later groups were at that moment living through their comparable sacred experiences in South Africa. This factor may be stated: "Functional factors of perceptual organization . . . are those which derive primarily from the needs, moods past experiences and memory of the individual."[22] To be sure, Afrikaners used what experiences and ideas were at hand to construct folk tradition or theological justification. The experiences on the frontier, memory of past glory, and knowledge of history in Europe before their time all functioned to shape their conception of themselves as a special people in God's sight.

As the culture developed into the nineteenth century, the perception became "functionally selective."[23] Not all experiences were used directly to reinforce the self-image. For example, a victory in battle was proof of God's blessing, but a defeat was not really a defeat; it was only God's temporary testing of one's faith. Thus, while the early culture used its past experiences and its only literature to construct its cultural image, as the cultural framework developed selectivity was used. Wish fulfillment was confused with reality. Thereafter interpretations of many experiences were modified or rationalized so as to form meaning in an Afrikaner con- text. Consequently, after the anti-British and anti-African aspects of Afrikaner nationalism developed, they could not be modified without causing tension in the entire closely knit cultural framework. Only those aspects which fit into the previous cultural model were selected—or re- interpreted—for the Afrikaners' purposes. Ultimately the Afrikaners' conception of their culture molded even the interpretations of their experi- ences.

British Challenge

As the Afrikaners were solidifying their cultural image at the end of the eighteenth century, a major tension-producing agent, the British

Empire, entered their experience. The cultural image of the Afrikaner was twisted and strained, and it took well over a century to learn how to deal with this tension. "Instabilities in the psychological field produce 'tensions' whose effects on perception, cognition, and action are such as to tend to change the field in the direction of a more stable structure."[24]   In an attempt to bring their cultural image back to equilibrium, the Afrikaners dealt with the British tension in various ways through the entire nineteenth century. "As long as there is blockage—frustration—to the attainment of a goal, cognitive reorganization tends to take place; the nature of the re-organization is such as to reduce the tension induced by the frustrating situation."[25] The long concern with this British presence usurped the energy of the Afrikaner culture, and they overreacted to such an extent that they neglected to develop other facets of their culture. They failed to keep pace with the thought and the institutional developments of nine-teenth century Europe.

This constant concern with Britain brought forth many attempts to solve their problems. "The frustration of goal achievement and the failure of tension reduction may lead to a variety of adaptive or maladaptive behavior."[26]   These adaptive, or often maladaptive, behaviors among Afrikaners took several forms during the nineteenth century. They at-tempted to ignore the British and to conduct all aspects of their lives as they had before British law came to South Africa. Finding this unworkable, Afrikaners sought to rebel against British authority, as in the Slagters' Nek skirmish. When rebellion proved to be impossible, Afrikaners internalized their frustrations for a number of years until they became convinced that flight was the only solution to the British menace. After the Great Trek, they found that the British tension was not eradicated; it had merely taken a new form and shifted its position. Negotiations in South Africa and in London were tried, with only limited success. Wars for independence were tried both in 1880 and in 1899.

In the twentieth century, the Afrikaners became convinced that the British threat could not be expelled but must be overcome instead. The establishment of Afrikaner political parties in the decade after the Boer War was the beginning of a significant development of an Afrikaner culture to neutralize or even to replace British influence. Shortly after the Union was established in 1910, the more conservative Afrikaner Nationalist party was born under the plea that South Africa must be for Afrikaners only and that there was no place for cooperation with the British. The Afrikaans language movement, finally successful in 1925, was another aspect of their opposition to British influence.

The Afrikaner consciousness was by now coming of age, having its own political parties and its own language. They had learned that "character-istic modes of goal-achievement and tension reduction may be learned and fixated by the individual", or by a society.[27]   Unceasing negotiation and continuing Afrikaner development at the expense of the British seemed to be their most successful method of tension reduction, and they furthered both. The temporary victory of the Nationalist party in the 1930s and the permanent victory in 1948 were major developments for Afrikaner conservatives against British liberals.

The establishment of the Republic of South Africa in 1961, separate from the British Commonwealth, was the last step of their developing cultural ideology. External British political influence is now absent. There remain, however, tensions within South Africa between English-speaking and Afrikaans-speaking portions of the population, and the English influence in economics and finance is as strong as ever. Perhaps there must be even more reinterpretation of the tensions of language and culture among the white population of South Africa.

Development of Racial Ideology in South Africa

At the beginning of the settlement in South Africa, there does not seem to have been an assumption of racial prejudice among the white settlers. They believed that culturally they were so superior to the Khoikhoi and San that any thought of cultural challenge from these people was beyond the Boers' imagination. In such a situation any rationalization of their racial superiority would have been judged superfluous. When they came to know the Xhosas and other Bantu groups, however, Afrikaners realized they had several things in common: both herded cattle, both lived in settlements or towns, and both needed land. Soon the white population began to conceive of the Africans as a threat, and they constructed "beliefs and attitudes of racial prejudice [to] serve in defense of self."[28] Although it was slow in developing, in the eighteenth century they began to use a "belief of racial prejudice to rationalize behavior in the service of a socially approved need."[29] As an aspect of this development, the theology of baptism was changed. Baptism was no longer conceived in universal terms, to bring any individual into the Christian society a free child of God. Now, rather, one could be baptized as a Christian and remain an African slave or servant in the secular world.

Following this defensive use of a developing prejudice, the Afrikaners refined and elaborated their racial attitudes. They found that "man must make sense out of any situation that is close to him and involves his way of life, his circumstances, his daily behavior"[30] and "beliefs and attitudes of prejudice . . . operate in the service of meaning. Man . . . is an organizing animal."[31] They came to believe that the black person was innately inferior to the white person, a condition no educational or social development could change. If this were so, it was assumed, the black person must be low in God's sight also. Consequently the African must always be a "hewer of wood and a drawer of water" or a servant or "child" who needs adult (white) guidance. Only when interpreted in this way could the Afrikaners' predetermined concept of the inferiority of the African be accepted in an

externally Christian society. Afrikaners found meaning in the racial situation by interpreting it in their own way, and the steadily developing prejudice for black skin seemed to be meaningful when compared with everyday
experiences.

Thus far we have analyzed the function of racial attitudes in South
Africa in providing meaning for the Africaner culture. There is another
side to the development, however: "Beliefs and attitudes do something *for*
the person who harbors them, but they also do something *to* the person."[32]
While the ideology functioned to bring meaning to the Afrikaner culture,
the same attitude so molded the cultural image that no more enlightened
analysis of the African culture could have any meaning for the Afrikaner.
This image was constructed in a closed system, and all that did not agree
with this preconception was rejected. After a few generations, the culture
based on a stereotype became a culture on the defensive. It was unable to
meet new ideas or new challenges. The same continuing pride and prejudice that can warp an individual personality in time thwarted the development of a whole culture.

To solidify and institutionalize this twisted and shortsighted racial
ideology, the South Africans, unknowingly, followed yet another principle:

> Before we can have a racial prejudice, then, we must be able
> to perceive the different individuals of the given racial group
> as having certain constant characteristics, as being similar to
> other individuals of the same group, and as being different
> from individuals not of that racial group.[33]

The developments in South Africa with respect to racial questions during
the twentieth century have magnified the differences between races and
ignored their similarities. Afrikaners insist that the African races are
incapable of any social changes comparable with the European development. Consequently, they rationalize their lack of education, health,
political, and economic opportunities for African groups. It is easier to
suggest why there are not or need not be more efforts on behalf of the
Africans than it is to organize and develop these facilities.

Even this ideology was not considered persuasive enough to stand on its
own merit. Increasingly, in the past three decades added legislation under
the apartheid system has been constructed to convince even unbelievers of
the inferiority of one segment of the population. The racial problem in
South Africa presents an interesting irony to the world. Economically the
South African culture cannot ignore Africans, for they are needed to hew
the wood and draw the water, to dig the gold and diamonds, and to do
manual labor for the affluent white population. Ideologically the Africans
occupy quite another status—permanently inferior original settlers on a
rich land where they cannot benefit from its riches. It is not clear whether

economic advance or ideological repression ultimately will win the advantage in South Africa. It is an interesting commentary on one segment of "God's chosen people," sent to South Africa to maintain a "pure" European society. Afrikaners continue to experience many serious tensions as they attempt to follow their culturally determined and theologically justified nationalist goals.

THE AFRIKANER CAUSE

Extrinsic Faith

The Afrikaner faith, election and biblicism, while sincerely held, was basically extrinsic. The severity of the challenges of nature, of the African tribes, and of British imperialism so warped the South African culture that before the Anglo-Boer War, the Afrikaners were never able to turn their attention to broader concerns. They were on the defensive for one reason or another. One partially formulated aspect of their culture was the theological dimension, and those theological concepts they used, when compared with the original, were permutations. In addition to their tendentious appropriation and adaptation of the doctrine, the religious faith for the settler in South Africa was basically "extrinsic."[34] The faith was partial, one-sided, and not of sufficient force to motivate the deepest recesses of the human personality; it was only external. Almost all Afrikaners in the last century would have denied that they were using the form of their faith for preconceived cultural values. Based on their interpretation of the environment in which they were reared and educated, however, a different approach to their faith could hardly have been possible.

Religious faith, to be a motivating force in life—to be intrinsic—must offer ideals and motivations that challenge one's self-centeredness. It must keep certain goals before the faithful and must result in development and change at the center of the culture. The religious faith of South Africa did not do this, and because it was basically extrinsic and formal, it allowed a dichotomy to develop in the thought and action of the individual. The Afrikaner was torn between what his high religious ideals suggested and what his own social and personal situation demanded. Ultimately the latter dominated the former. The Afrikaner dilemma was little different from the *American Dilemma* as studied by Gunnar Myrdal.[35] The formulation of the religious consciousness in South Africa developed as a rationalization of history rather than as a *causa movens*. Although the Afrikaners interpreted it as such, their religious faith was not an ultimate concern. It was only one means to a greater end—Afrikaner religious nationalism.

God-Given Pattern

Afrikaners justified their nationalism and their conservatism by assuming that they were maintaining God-given patterns of life. During the eighteenth century, the Boers in the eastern section of the Cape Colony evolved a self-identity that was basically political and antigovernment, especially anti-British. By the end of the century, they assumed that their way of life was God's way. There was a religious basis to the Patriot movement, and during the insurrection of 1799 one leader suggested that "the Lord is really arrived again at the Cape" embodied in their self-styled opposition. During the first thirty years of British administration, Afrikaners believed their way of life was challenged. One reason for the Great Trek was that in a new area, they could "maintain our doctrines in purity." The reactions against liberal theological influences from European-trained ministers in the nineteenth century and the liberal government of President Burgers were based on the fear of changing from the biblically revealed *status quo*. President Kruger opposed many modifications in his government because he feared the wrath of God; hence logical discussion was to no avail. The moderate Afrikaners whose activities resulted in the Union in 1910 assumed, on the contrary, that their Afrikaner ideals could be achieved through cooperation with Britain. In the next generation, the old fears were born anew, and the moderates were defeated in favor of God's pattern, the Afrikaner nationalism of the late nineteenth century, and of the present day.

Heteronomous Concerns of Afrikanerdom

Afrikaner nationalism became a national self-idolatry. Afrikaner religious nationalism was more subservient to the ultimate concerns of Afrikanerdom than it was obedient to the sovereign God. The religious faith of the Afrikaner, while sincerely believed and devotedly expounded on every occasion, was nevertheless heteronomous. The Afrikaner cause, which they assumed was the ultimate concern for the culture, was itself a construction in a sociohistorical milieu, one set of temporary goals among many. The theological goal, largely constructed on a sociocultural basis, was always subservient to the basic needs of its creating cause. Thus the Afrikaner self-consciousness, supposedly responsive to a theological dimension, heard only a modification of its own self-interest. The Calvinism of South Africa, supposedly subservient to a sovereign God, was really subservient to Afrikanerdom. In this circular system, the religious faith functioned only as a utilitarian aid to further the "Afrikaner Cause."

This utilitarian and heteronomous Calvinism was not consciously recognized as such, and did not spring full blown into history at some decisive point; it progressed through many developing phases. The culture was in turn a migrating cattle-farming society far removed from civilizing influences; a people attempting to maintain their identity in face of an "inferior" and "uncultured" African majority; and a people watching some of the main cultural concerns frustrated and destroyed by "imperialistic" Britain. In the face of so many and varied changes, these people on the defensive used every help at hand. Religion was a strong force in their life. Why should it not be used? Consequently, the theological vocabulary became one means to ensure loyalty to their own glorified tradition, which became more glorious with continued retelling.[36]

An extrinsic use of religious faith allowed the Afrikaners to employ terminology that was both orthodox and Christian, while they used Calvinism to justify conclusions at which they had already arrived. In addition, it fostered a double standard within the culture; one standard for the people on the inside, the family, the church members, the white Afrikaner citizen but quite another for those who by definition were not part of the elect nation, whether British or African.

Circular Reasoning

The religious rationalizations were part of a circular phenomenon. This was a self-sustaining cultural system in which economic self-interest, cultural defensiveness, and theological ideas were delicately integrated. The concept of the elect people was not stable; it fluctuated depending on the situation. The Afrikaner society modified this concept according to the unique context in which the theological justification grew along with it and became more South African and less European—less Calvinistic. Ultimately the cultural situation was clearly reflected in the theological modifications. How could it have been otherwise? Only when a people develop a certain sophistication and true historical consciousness can they look at themselves objectively and compare their basic presuppositions with any objective theological system such as Calvinism. By 1910 the South African people had not sufficiently matured as a society to allow the possibility of such an objective approach. They were never able to relax their defensiveness to consider seriously their own self-image. The word *Calvinism* referred to a specific South African interpretation, which was at variance with the use of the term in other parts of the Christian world. It was not Calvinism that was twisted out of shape such that it lost its meaning. Rather, the theological concerns of South Africa, except for the first few years, had never been true Calvinism. The pious frontiersmen developed a folk theology based on biblical literalism with a thin veneer of Calvinistic terminology and theological content. Some orthodox Calvinistic terms were adopted by, but never assimilated into, the Afrikaner culture. In Afrikaner ideology, theology never held first place in developing and directing the culture; it was always derived from and integrated with more basic conerns.

Although they thought of themselves as elect in the sight of God and while they made much of the doctrine of providence, Afrikaners never

allowed theological judgment on their total culture. Being basically heteronomous in outlook, they could not do so. They used theological concerns
only extinsically. The central concerns of the Afrikaner nation were economic advantage for the in-group, opposition to outsiders, rigid racial
distinctions, and a nationalism based on cultural self-preservation. This
was the heart of Afrikanerdom on the defensive.

The theological concept of God's choosing a specific people for his
cause—the Afrikaner cause—even though extrinsic, was thoroughly intertwined with the total cultural matrix. Afrikaners confused, and even
equated, cultural privilege with theological election and based their assurance of favor in the sight of God upon circular reasoning. The inter-
relatedness of these various aspects may be shown graphically.[37]

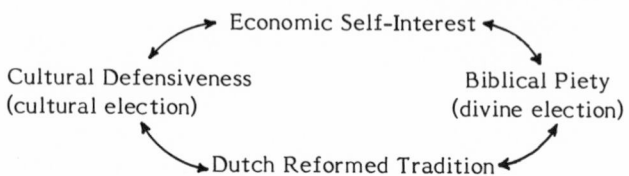

Although theological rationalizations were part of a circular phenomenon, they nevertheless had a deep influence on the culture. Even in this
negative way, we may conclude that this concept of the elect people is a
significant strand of thought woven throughout South African society to
1910. No cultural analysis or attempt to understand this particular nationalism can be complete without an understanding of the crystallization of
imagery around this theological concept. This particular theological motif
added a dimension to the growing culture and gave it stability. Because the
Afrikaners assumed the concept was a true reflection of God's will, it gave
their society a strength and a character it would not otherwise have
possessed.

NOTES

1. *Institutes,* I, xvi, 1.

2. *Ibid.,* I, xvi, 2.

3. *Ibid.,* I, v, 8.

4. *Ibid.,* I, xvii, 1.

5. The literature concerning Calvin's doctrine of election is immense. A comprehensive bibliography of older works can be found in *Library of Christian Classics* (*LCC*), XXI, 920n. A bibliography of more recent studies may be found in François Wendel, *Calvin, Sources et évolution de sa pensée religieuse* (Paris: Presses Universitaires de France, 1950), pp. 200-201, English translation (London: Collins, 1963), pp. 263-264. Only the most significant studies used here are mentioned: five studies from *De l'élection éternelle de Dieu: Actes du Congrès internationale de Théologie Calviniste* (Geneva: 1936); Peter Barth, "Die biblische Grundlage der Prädestinationslehre bei Calvin," pp. 21-49; Donald MacLean, "Predestination in History," pp. 118-126; Stephen Leigh Hunt, "Predestination in *The Institutes of the Christian Religion 1536-1559,*" pp. 131-138; G. Oorthys, "La predestination dans le dogmatique calviniste," pp. 207-235; and Jean Cadier, "Election et Eglise," pp. 269-282. Heinz Otten, *Calvin's theologische Anschauung von der Prädestination* (Munich: Kaiser Verlag, 1938). G. Deluz, *Predestination et liberté* (Neuchatel: 1942).

6. Heinz Otten, *Calvin's theologische Anschauung von der Prädestination,* p. 22.

7. *Institutes,* III, xxi, footnote 1 in *LCC* edition.

8. *Ibid.,* III, xxiv, 3.

9. *Ibid.,* III, xxiv, 6.

10. *Ibid.,* III, xxi, 7.

11. Article XIII (of Divine Providence) of the *Belgic Confession* includes these words: "rien n'avaient en ce mond sans son ordounance" (nothing happens in this world without his appointment).

12. "Election is the unchangeable purpose of God, whereby, before the foundation of the world, he hath, out of mere grace, according to the sovereign good pleasure of his own will, chosen, from the whole human race, which had fallen through their own fault, from their primitive state of rectitude into sin and destruction, a certain number of persons to redemption in Christ, whom he from eternity appointed the Mediator and head of the elect, and the foundation of salvation.

"This elect number, though by nature neither better nor more deserving than others, but with them involved in one common misery, God hath decreed to give to Christ to be saved by him, and effectually to call and draw them to his communion by his Word and Spirit." *Decrees of the Synod of Dort,* Article vii.

13. "The elect, in due time, though in various degrees and in different measures attain the assurance of this their eternal and unchangeable election, not by inquisitively prying into the secret and deep things of God, but by observing in themselves, with a spiritual joy and holy pleasure, the infallible fruits of election pointed out in the Word of God; such as the true faith in Christ, filial fear, and godly sorrow for sin, a hungering and thirsting after righteousness." *Decrees of the Synod of Dort,* Article xii.

14. *Institutes,* III, xix.

15. *Ibid.,* III, xix, 1.

16. *Ibid.,* III. xii, 2.

17. *Ibid.,* III, xix, 4.

18. *Ibid.,* III, xix, 7.

19. *Ibid.,* III, xix, 9. Cf. Phil. 4:11-12.

20. David Krech and Richard S. Crutchfield, *Theory and Problems of Social Psychology* (New York: McGraw-Hill, 1948).

21. *Ibid.,* p. 76.

22. *Ibid.,* p. 82.

23. *Ibid.,* p. 87.

24. *Ibid.,* p. 40.

25. *Ibid.,* p. 112.

26. *Ibid.,* p. 50.

27. *Ibid.,* p. 62.

28. *Ibid.,* p. 456.

29. *Ibid.,* p. 452.

30. *Ibid.,* p. 454.

31. *Ibid.,* p. 455.

32. *Ibid.,* p. 459.

33. *Ibid.,* p. 460.

34. Gordon Allport analyzed the difference between what he calls extrinsic and intrinsic religious experience. Intrinsic sentiment is the more

mature, more satisfying, and more thoroughly related to all aspects of life. It is more apt to take the whole meaning of a set of theological doctrines and to relate them to all of life.

"On the other hand, extrinsic religious sentiment is more apt to be partial, one-sided, and an interpretation of religion for the personal needs of the individual believer." Dr. Allport summarizes the *extrinsic* religious approach in these words: "God is partial to me. Through prayer I can conjure His special favor. Since God is created in my image, His role is to confer security and other benefits upon me. My economy of living is one of exclusion—of barring from my presence out-groups that threaten my comfort. My religion and my prejudice both serve my exclusionist style. They are islands of safety in a frightening world. They are custom-tailored lifejackets to be donned in frightening waters. In such a life religion is not the cause of ethnic prejudice, nor is prejudice the cause of the religion. both strategies are protective; both confer security, a sense of status, and of encapsulation. . . .

"In the case we have described it is clear that religion is not the master-motive in the life. It plays an instrumental role only. It serves and rationalizes assorted forms of self-interest. In such a life the full creed and full teaching of religion are not adopted. The person does not serve his religion; its function is to serve him. The master-motive is always self-interest. In such a life-economy religion has extrinsic value only." Gordon Allport, "Religion and Prejudice," *Crane Review*, II (1959), pp. 8-9.

35. This internal conflict formed the basis for rationalization, as Myrdal summarizes: "The American Dilemma . . . is the ever-raging conflict between, on the one hand, the valuations, preserved on the general plane which we call the 'American Creed,' where the American thinks, talks, and acts under the influence of high national and Christian precepts, and, on the other hand, the valuations on specific planes of individual and group living, where personal and local interests; economic, social, and sexual jealousies; considerations of community prestige and conformity; group prejudice versus particular persons or types of people; and all sorts of miscellaneous wants, impulses, and habits dominate his outlook." Gunnar Myrdal, *An American Dilemma: The Negro Problem and Modern Democracy* (New York: Harper & Bros., 1944), p. xlvii. One major difference, however, is to be seen. American was strongly influenced by pietism, Puritanism, and theological ideas; South Africa was an economic venture, which became a political necessity in face of British imperialism. South Africa was thus never strongly influenced by theological ideas; it was a society long before it developed "Christian precepts."

36. Gordon Allport, *The Nature of Prejudice* (Garden City, NY: Doubleday & Co., 1958). See especially the section in chapter 14 entitled "Cultural Devices to Insure Loyalty," pp. 220-231.

37. I am indebted to the late Professor Gordon Allport for suggesting this graphic and concise formula.

Bibliography

BIBLIOGRAPHICAL RESOURCES

du Preez, A. M. *List of Dissertations and Theses Accepted by the University of South Africa, 1919-1958. Communications,* 1958.

Malan, S. I. *Union Catalogue of Theses and Dissertations of the South African Universities, 1942-1958.* Potchefstroom University, 1959. Supplement No. 1, 1959; No. 2, 1960; No. 3, 1961; No. 4, 1962; No. 5, 1963.

Muller, C. F. J., van Jaarsveld, F. A., and van Wijk, Theo., eds. *A Select Bibliography of South African History: A Guide for Historical Research.* Pretoria: University of South Africa, 1966.

Musiker, Reuben, ed. *Guide to South African Reference Books.* 3d ed. Grahamstown: Rhodes University Library, 1963.

Nienaber, P. J. *Bibliografie van Afrikaanse Boeke, 1691-1948* (Bibliography of South African Books, 1691-1948). Johannesburg, 1943-1958.

Robinson, Antony Meredith Lewin. *Catalog of Theses and Dissertations Accepted for Degrees in South African Universities.* Vol. I, 1918-1941; Vol II, 1942-1958; and supplemented each year since. Cape Town: Library School of the University of Cape Town, 1943--.

PRIMARY SOURCES

Barnard, Lady Anne. *South Africa a Century Ago: Letters from the Cape, 1797-1801.* London: S. Elder & Co., 1910.

Barrow, John. *Travels into the Interior of Southern Africa.* 2 vols. London: T. Cadell and W. Davies, 1806.

Beyers, Coenraad. *Die Kaapse Patriotte, 1779-1791* (The Cape Patriots). Cape Town: Juta & Co., 1929, revised 1966.

Bird, John, ed. *The Annals of Natal, 1495-1845.* 2 vols. Pietermaritzburg: P. Davis & Son, 1888.

The Boer War, miscellaneous pamphlet collection in Widener Library, Harvard. Includes the following, among others:
"Methods of Barbarism" (of British soldiers).
"How not to make peace" (of British burning and looting).
"The Military Leaders of the Boers."
"The Concentration Camps."
"Who Was Right," by C. F. Aked, a pro-Boer sermon by the English minister in Liverpool.
"What We Are Fighting for—High Dividends: Cheap Labor."

Breytenbach, J. H., ed. *S. A. Archival Records, Natal no. 1: Notule van die Natalse Volksrad (volledig met alle bylae daarby), 1838-1845* (Minutes of the Natal Volksraad Complete with All Annexures 1838-1845). Cape Town: South Africa State Archives, 1958.

Breytenbach, J. H., and Pretorius, H. S., eds. *Suid-Afrikaanse Argiefstukke (Transvaal).* (South African Archive Materials) 7 vols. Cape Town: Cape Times Ltd., 1957-1965.

The Cause of the Boer War, an extremist pamphlet collection in Widener Library, Harvard, 1899-1900. Includes:
"Mr. Conwright-Schreiner on Boer and Bond."
"The Witness of the Churches," by leaders of several non-Dutch denominations.
"Boers and Blacks," comments by the Rev. John Moffatt.
"The Last Appeal before the Outbreak of War," by W. P. Schreiner, prime minister of the Cape Colony.
"The Boer Armaments: Were They the Cause of the Jameson Raid or Its Effect?"
"Was There Dutch Conspiracy against British Rule in South Africa, or Is It a Nightmare?"
"The Boer Republics."
"The Raid and the Ultimatum."
"Boer Parson on the War."
"The Efforts of the Colonies of the Cape and Natal to Avert War."
"The Dutch Reformed Church and the Boers."
"British and Dutch in South Africa."
"Capitalism and Imperialism in South Africa."
"The Afrikander Bond and Other Causes of the War," by Theophilus Lyndall Schreiner.

Chase, John Centlivres, ed. *Natal Papers.* 2 vols. Grahamstown: Godlonton, 1843.

Colenso, John Wm., Bishop of Natal. *Colenso Letters from Natal.* Edited by Wyn Rees. Pietermaritzburg: Shuter and Shooter, 1958.

————. *Natal Sermons: A Series of Discourses Preached in the Church of St. Peter, Pietermaritzburg.* London: Trübner, 1867.

Collins, W. W. *Free Statia: Reminiscences of a Lifetime in the Orange Free State.* Bloemfontein: 1907; new ed., Cape Town: C. Struik, 1965.

Dreyer, Andries, ed. *Bouwstowwe vir die Geskiedenis van die Nederduits-Gereformeerde Kerk in Suid-Afrika.* (Source Materials for the History of the Dutch Reformed Chruch in South Africa) Vol. 3. Cape Town and the Netherlands: 1936.

du Plessis, J. S., ed. *President Kruger aan die woord: verkiesingsmanifeste, intreeredes en toesprake van president S. J. P. Kruger.* (President Kruger Speaks: Election Manifestos, Inaugural and Other Speeches of President S. J. P. Kruger). Bloemfontein: Sacum, 1952.

Engelbrecht, S. P., ed. *Paul Kruger's Amptelike Briewe, 1851-1877.* (Paul Kruger's Official Letters, 1851-1877) Pretoria: Volkstem Drukkery, 1925.

————. *Suid Afrikaanse Argiefstukke (Cape Province).* (South African Archive Materials) 4 vols. Cape Town: 1957.

Eybers, G. W., ed. *Select Constitutional Documents Illustrating South African History, 1795-1910.* London: George Routledge & Sons, 1918.

Fouché, Leo, ed. *Het Dagboek van Adam Tas, 1705-1706.* (The Diary of Adam Tas, 1705-1706) London: Longmans, Green & Co., 1914.

Gerdener, Gustav Bernhard August, ed. *Boustowwe vir die geskiedenis van die Nederduits-Gereformeerde Kerk in die Transgariep.* (Sources for the History of the Dutch Reformed Church (N. G. K.) in Trans-Orange) Cape Town: Nasionale Pers, 1930.

Germond, Robert C., ed. and trans. *Chronicles of Basutoland.* Morija, Lesoto: Morija Sesuto Book Dept., 1967.

Godee-Molsbergen, Everhardus Cornelis. *Reizen in Zuid Afrika in de Hollandse Tijd.* (Journeys in South Africa in the Dutch Period) The Hague: M. Nijhoff, 1916-1932.

Great Britain. *Parliamentary Papers* giving the C[ommand] number and the year of the session.

1869	1871	1873	1877	1878	1879
4140	459	732	1776	2100	2220
			1883	2128	2260
1870	1872	1875		2144	2308
99	508	1361	1878	2178	2316
			2079		2367

1879	1881	1884	1890	1896	1899
2454	2892	4194	5892	8063	9707
	2950	4214	5918	8159	
1880	2998		6200		1902
2482		1885	6201	1897	1096
2484	1882	4274	6217	8380	
2505	3098	4290		8404	1906
2584	3219	4432	1894	8423	3250
2655	3381	4587	7554	8474	
2676	3419	4588		8721	1907
			1895		3526
1881	1883	1886	7611	1899	
2783	3486	4643	7633	9345	1909
2794		4645	7780	9404	297
2797	1884	4839	7878	9415	
2837	3947			9507	
2838	4190	1887	1896	9518	
2866	4191	4913	7953	9521	
		5143	7962	9530	

Hattersley, A. F., ed. *More Annals of Natal*. London: Frederick Warner & Co., 1936.

Headlam, Cecil, ed. *The Milner Papers: South Africa, 1897-1899*. London: Cassell & Co., 1931.

Jeffreys, Kathleen M., ed. *Kaapse Archiefstukken*. (Cape Archive Materials) 5 vols. Pretoria: Staatsdrukker, 1926-1935.

Jorissen, E. J. P. *Transvaalsche Herinneringen, 1876-1896*. (Transvaal Reminiscences, 1876-1896) Amsterdam: J. H. de Bussy, 1897.

Keppel-Jones, Arthur, ed. *Phillips—1820 Settler*. Pietermaritzburg: Shuter & Shooter, 1960.

Kestell, J. D., and van Velden, D. E. *The Peace Negotiations between the Governments of the South African Republic and the Orange Free State, and the Representatives of the British Government, Which Terminated in the Peace Concluded at Vereeniging on the 31st May, 1902*. London: Richard Clay, 1912.

Krüger, D. W., ed. *South African Parties and Policies: A Select Source Book*. Cape Town: Human and Rousseau, 1960.

Kruger, Paul. *The Memoirs of Paul Kruger*. New York: Century Co., 1902.

Krynauw, D. W., and Pretorius, H. S., eds. *Transvaalse argiefstukke, 1850-1853*. (Transvaal Archival Records) Pretoria: State Archives, Minerva Press, 1949.

Leibbrandt, H. C. V., ed. *Precis of the Archives of the Cape of Good Hope*. 17 vols. Cape Town: W. A. Richard and Sons, 1898.

————. *Rambles through the Archives of the Cape of Good Hope, 1688-1700.* Cape Town: J. C. Juta and Co., 1887.

————. *The Rebellion of 1815, Generally Known as Slachters' Nek.* Cape Town: J. C. Juta and Co., 1902.

Leonard, Charles, ed. *Papers on the Political Situation in South Africa, 1885-1895.* London: Arthur L. Humphreys, 1903.

LeVaillant, François. *Voyage dans l'interieur de l'Afrique.* (Travels into the Interior Parts of Africa) 3 vols. London: G. G. and J. Robinson, 1796.

London Missionary Society. *Transactions of the London Missionary Society, 1795-.* London: 1804-.

McKinnon, James. *South African Traits: Sketches of His Life at the Cape.* Edinburgh: George Gemmell, 1887.

Mission, Maximilian. *A Cry from the Desert: or Testimonials of the Miraculous Things Lately Come to Pass in the Cévennes or Southern Part of France.* (English trans.) London: G. Terry, 1707.

Moodie, D., ed. *The Record: A Series of Official Papers Relative to the Condition and Treatment of the Native Tribes of South Africa.* Cape Town: Robertson, 1838-1841, reprinted 1960.

Oberholster, J. J., and Van Schoor, M. C. E., eds. *President Steyn aan die woord: openbare geskrifte en toesprake van Marthinus Theunis Steyn, vertaal, byeengebring en van aantekeninge voorsien.* (President Steyn Speaks: Public Writings and Speeches of Marthinus Theunis Steyn, Translated, Collected and Annotated) Bloemfontein: Sacum, 1953.

Preller, Gustav, S. *Dagboek van Louis Trigardt, 1836-1838.* (Diary of Louis Trigardt, 1836-1838) Bloemfontein: "Het Volksblad" Drukkerij, 1917.

————ed. *Voortrekkermense.* (Voortrekker Peoples) 6 vols. Cape Town: Nasionale Pers, 1918-1938.

————. *Voortrekker-Wetgewing: Notule van die Natalse Volksraad, 1839-1845.* (Voortrekker Legislation: Notes from the Natal Volksraad, 1839-1845) Pretoria: Van Schaik, 1924.

Pretorius, H. S., Krüger, D. W., and Beyers, C., eds. *Voortrekker-Argiefstukke, 1829-1849.* (Voortrekker Archive Materials, 1829-1849) Pretoria: Staatsdrukker, 1937.

Reitz, Deneys, *Commando: A Boer Journal of the Boer War.* London: Faber and Faber, 1929.

Report of Speeches on the South African Bill, 16-19 August, 1909. Reprinted from the Official Report: The Parliamentary Debates. London: Truscott and Sons, 1909.

Schikkerling, Roland William. *Commando Courageous (a Boer's Diary)*. Johannesburg: Hugh Keartland, 1964.

Schoon, H. F., ed. *Uit het dagboek van Erasmus Smit, predikant bij de Voortrekkers*. (From the Diary of Erasmus Smit, a Minister of Religion with the Voortrekkers) Cape Town: 1897, reprinted 1967.

Schreiner, Theophilus Lyndall. *The Afrikander Bond and Other Causes of the War*. London: Spottiswoode and Co., 1901.

Shepstone, Sir Theophilus. *The Correspondence and Diaries of Theophilus Shepstone, 1853-1883*. Typed, bound copy at the Library of the University of South Africa (Pretoria).

Sparrman, Andrew. *A Voyage to the Cape of Good Hope*. London: R. Morrison, 1789.

Spoelstra, Coenraad, ed. *Bouwstoffen voor de Geschiedenis der Nederduitsche Gereformeerde Kerk in Zuid-Afrika*. (Sources for the History of the Dutch Reformed Church in South Africa) 2 vols. Amsterdam and Cape Town: 1906-1907.

Theal, George McCall, ed. *Basutoland Records*. 3 vols. Cape Town: W. A. Richards and Sons, 1883.

————. *Records of the Cape Colony, 1793-1831*. 35 vols. London: Clowes and Sons, 1897-1905.

Thompson, Leonard, ed. *Minutes of Proceedings . . . of the South African National Convention*, held at: Durban, Oct 12-Nov. 5, 1908; Cape Town Nov 23-Dec. 18, 1908 and Jan 11-Feb. 3, 1909; and Bloemfontein May 3-11, 1909. Cape Town: Cape Times, 1911.

United Brethren Society. *Periodical Accounts Relating to the Missions of the Church of the United Brethren Established among the Heathen*. London: United Brethren Society, 1790-1796.

van der Vyver, W. B., ed. *Suid-Afrikaanse Argiefstukke (Orange Free State)*. (South African Archive Material) 3 vols. Cape Town: Argiefkommissie, 1952-1960.

van Riebeeck Society Publications. van Riebeeck Society, Cape Town: 1918-1963. Relevant volumes in the series are as follows:
  I. *Reports of de Chavonnes and His Council and of van Imhoff, on the Cape, 1743*. Cape Town: 1918.
  II. Mentzel, O. F. *Life at the Cape in Mid 18th Century: A Biography of Rudolf Siegfried Allemann*. Cape Town: 1919.
  III. Gie, S. F. N., ed. *The Memorandum of Commissary J. A. de Mist, Containing Recommendations for the Form and Administration of Government at the Cape of Good Hope*. Cape Town: 1920.
  IV. Mentzel, O. F. *A Geographical and Topographical Description of the Cape of Good Hope*. Part I. Cape Town: 1921.
  VI. ————. Part II. Cape Town: 1925.

VII. Cory, G. E., ed. *The Diary of the Rev. Francis Owen, M.A., Missionary with Dingaan in 1837-1838.* Cape Town: 1926.

X. Lichtenstein, Henry. *Travels in Southern Africa in the Years 1803-1806.* Vol. I. Cape Town: 1928.

XI. ———. Vol. II. Cape Town: 1930.

XIII. Fouché, Leo, ed. *Louis Trigardt's Trek across the Drakensberg.* Cape Town: 1932.

XIV. Schapera, I., and Farrington, B., trans. *The Early Cape Hottentots Described in the Writings of Olfert Dapper (1688), Willem ten Rhynnes (1685) and Johannes Gulielemus de Grevenbroek (1695).* Cape Town: 1933.

XVIII. Blommaert, W., and Wiid, J. A., eds. *Die Joernaal van Dirk Gysbert van Reenen, 1803.* (The Journal of Dirk Gysbert van Reenen, 1803) Cape Town: 1937.

XXV. Mentzel, O. F. *Geographical and Topographical Description of the Cape of Good Hope.* Part III. Cape Town: 1943.

XXXII. Preller, Johann F., ed. *Die Konvensie Dagboek van sy edelagbare François Stephanus Malan, 1908-1909.* (The Diary of the Convention by the Honorable François Stephanus Malan, 1908-1909) Cape Town: 1951.

XXXVII. Varley, D. H., and Matthew, H. M., eds. *The Cape Journals of Archdeacon N. J. Merriman, 1848-1855.* Cape Town: 1957.

XLI. *Selections from the Correspondence of J. X. Merriman, 1870-1890.*

XLIV. ———, 1890-1898.

War against War in South Africa. Published by Stop the War Committee of London, a collection of weekly publications, 1899-August, 1900.

SECONDARY SOURCES

General Studies of South Africa

Cory, G. E. *The Rise of South Africa.* 5 vols. London: Longmans, 1910-1930.

Davenport, T. R. H. *South Africa: A Modern History.* London and New York: Macmillan, 1977.

de Kiewiet, Cornelis W. *A History of South Africa: Social and Economic.* London: Oxford University Press, 1941, 1960.

Hartz, Louis, ed. *The Founding of New Societies: Studies in the History of the United States, Latin American, South Africa, Canada and Australia.* New York: Harcourt, Brace and World, 1964.

Marquard, Leo. *The People and Policies of South Africa.* 3d ed. London: Oxford University Press, 1962.

Muller, C. F. J. *Five Hundred Years: A History of South Africa* Pretoria and Cape Town: Academia, 1969.

Newton, A. P., and Benians, E. A., eds. *The Cambridge History of the British Empire*. Vol. VIII: South Africa, 1936, revised 1963.
Relevant chapters and their authors are as follows:
II. "The Native Inhabitants," by I. Schapera.
V. "Foundation of the Cape Colony, 1652-1708," by Leo Fouché.
VI. "The Cape Colony under Company Rule, 1708-1795," by S. F. N. Gie.
VII. "The British Occupations, 1795-1806," by Vincent T. Harlow.
VIII. "Cape Colony, 1806-1822," by Vincent T. Harlow.
IX. "The British Settlers of 1820," by George Cory.
X. "Political Development, 1822-1834," by W. M. Macmillan.
XI. "Slavery at the Cape, 1652-1838," by A. F. Hattersley.
XII. "The Problem of the Coloured People, 1792-1842," by W. M. MacMillan.
XIII. "The Frontier and the Kaffir Wars, 1792-1836," by W. M. Macmillan.
XIV. "The Formation of New States, 1835-1854," by Eric A. Walker.
XV. "Constitutional Development, 1834-1858," by H. M. Mandelbrote.
XVI. "The Period of Transition in South African Policy, 1854-1870," by C. W. de Kiewiet.
XVII. "The Establishment of Responsible Government in Cape Colony, 1870-1872," by C. W. de Kiewiet.
XVIII. "The Failure of Confederation, 1871-1881," by Cecil Headlam.
XIX. "Political Development, 1872-1886," by J. H. Hofmeyr.
XX. "The Race for the Interior, 1881-1895," by Cecil Headlam.
XXI. "The Problem of Cooperation, 1886-1895."
   a. "Railways, Customs and the Native Questions," by J. H. Hofmeyr.
   b. "The Jameson Raid," by Cecil Headlam.
   c. "The Results of the Raid," by J. H. Hofmeyr.
XXII. "The Struggle for Supremacy, 1896-1902," by Eric A. Walker.
XXIII. "The Formation of the Union, 1901-1910," by Hugh A. Wyndham.

Oliver, Roland, and Fage, J. D. *A Short History of Africa*. Baltimore: Penguin Books, 1962.

Theal, George McCall. *History and Ethnography of Africa South of the Zambezi, 1505-1795*. 3 vols. London: Swan Sonnenschein, 1927.

————. *History of Africa South of the Zambezi, 1795-1872*. 5 vols. 1926-1927.

————. *History of South Africa from 1873-1884*. 2 vols. London: 1919.

van der Walt, A. J. H., Wiid, J. A., and Geyer, A. L., eds. *Geskiedenis van Suid Africa*. (History of South Africa) 2 vols. Cape Town: Nasionale Boekhandel, 1955.

Walker, Eric A. *Historical Atlas of South Africa*. London and Cape Town: Oxford University Press, 1922.

————. *A History of Southern Africa*. 2d ed. London: Longmans, 1957.

Wiedner, Donald L. *A History of Africa, South of the Sahara.* New York: Random House, 1962.

Wilson, Monica, and Thompson, Leonard, eds. *The Oxford History of South Africa.* New York and Oxford: Oxford University Press, I (1969), II (1971).

Periodical Articles

Allport, Gordon. "Behavioral Science, Religion, and Mental Health." *Journal of Religion and Health,* II, No. 3 (April 1963).

—————. "Religion and Prejudice." *Crane Review,* II (Fall 1959).

Barnard, A. J. "'n Lewensbeskrywing van Majoor Henry Douglas Warden." (A Life Description of Major Henry Douglas Warden) *Argief-Jaarboek vir Suid-Afrikaanse Geskiedenis* [hereafter *A-J v SAG*], XI (1948).

Beyers, Coenraad. "Die Groot Trek met betrekking tot ons Nasiegroei." (The Great Trek and Its Place in the Growth of Our Nation) *A-J v SAG,* IV (1941).

—————. "Laaste Lewensjare en Heengaan van President Kruger." (Last Years of the Life, and the Death, of President Kruger) *A-J v SAG,* IV (1941).

Blommaert, W. "Het invoeren van de slavernij aan de Kaap." (The Introduction of Slavery at the Cape) *A-J v SAG,* I (1938).

Booyens, Bunyan. "Kerk en staat, 1795-1843." (Church and State, 1795-1843) *A-J v SAG,* XXVIII (1965).

Campbell, Waldemar B. "The South African Frontier, 1865-1885: A Study in Expansion." *A-J v SAG,* XXI (1959).

Dicks, B. H. "The Northern Transvaal Voortrekkers." *A-J v SAG,* IV (1941).

Duminy, A. H. "The Role of Sir Andries Stockenstrom in Cape Politics, 1848-1856," *A-J v SAG,* XXII (1960).

du Plessis, A. J. "Die Republiek Natal." (The Republic of Natal) *A-J v SAG,* V (1942).

du Plessis, J. S. "Die onstaan en ontwikkeling van die amp van die staatspresident in die Zuid-Afrikaansche Republiek (1858-1902) (The Origin and Development of the Office of State President in the South African Republic 1858-1902) *A-J v SAG,* XVIII (1955).

du Toit, A. E. "The Cape Frontier, a Study of Native Policy with Special Reference to the Years 1847-1866." *A-J v SAG,* XVII (1954).

du Toit, J. P. "Boomplaats." *Die Huisgenoot.* 27 August 1948.

Duvenage, C. D. J. "Willem Hendrik Jacobsz se rol in die Onafhanklikheid en Eenheidstrewe van die Voortrekkers op de Hoeveld, 1847-1852."

(Willem Hendrik Jacob's Role in the Independence and Unity Movements of the Voortrekkers on the High Plateau, 1847-1852) *A-J v
SAG*, XVIII (1956).

Franken, J. L. M. "Huisonderwys aan die Kaap (1692-1732)." (Private
Education in the Home at the Cape 1692-1732) *Annals of the Union
of South Africa*, XII (July 1934).

Gailey, Harry A., Jr. "John Philip's Role in Hottentot Emancipation."
Journal of African History III (1962).

Geertz, Clifford. "Ideology as a Cultural System." In *Ideology and Discontent*, edited by David E. Apter, New York: Free Press, 1964.

Great Britain. "British Ultimatum, 1899." *Bulletin of the Institute of
Historical Research*, XXVII (1954).

Hattersley, Alan F. "The Annexation of the Transvaal, 1877." *History*
(June 1936).

———. "The Great Trek, 1835-7." *History* (April 1931).

———. "The Zulu Problem of 1878-9." *History* (April 1917).

Hoge, J. "Die Geskiedenis van die Lutherse Kerk aan die Kaap." (The
History of the Lutheran Church at the Cape) *A-J v SAG*, II (1939).

———. "Privaatskoolmeesters aan die Kaap in die 18de eeuw." (Private
Teachers at the Cape in the 18th Century) *Annals of the Union of
South Africa*, XII (July 1934) and XV (June 1937).

Die Huisgenoot. "Die Groot Trek: Gedenkenuitgawe." (Commemorative
issue, the Great Trek). December, 1938.

———. "Uitgawe gewy aan die Groot Trek." (Edition devoted to the Great
Trek) 11 December 1936.

Kistner, W. "The Anti-slavery Agitation against the Transvaal Republic
1852-1868." *A-J v SAG*, II (1952).

Kriel, Johannes David. "Die verhouding tussen kerk en staat in die Republiek van die Oranje-Vrystaat, 1854-1902." (The Relation between
Church and State in the Republic of the Orange Free State, 1854-
1902) *A-J v SAG*, XVI (1953).

Lewson, Phyllis. "The First Crisis in Responsible Government in the Cape
Colony." *A-J v SAG*, V (1942).

MacCrone, I. D. "The Great Trek and Its Centenary Celebration in the
Light of Group Psychology." *Race Relations*, V (1938).

McNeill, John T. "Natural Law in the Teaching of the Reformers." *Journal
of Religion*, XXVI (1946).

Mouton, J. A. "General Joubert in die Geskiedenis van Transvaal." (General Joubert in the History of the Transvaal) *A-J v SAG*, XIX (1957).

Ploeger, J. "Onderwys en Onderwysbeleid in die Suid-Afrikaanse Republiek onder ds. S. J. du Toit en dr. N. Mansvelt, 1881-1900." (Education and Educational Policy in the South African Republic under the Rev. S. J. du Toit and Dr. N. Mansvelt, 1881-1900) *A-J v SAG*, XV (1952).

————. "Ulrich Gerhard Lauts (1787-1865); die skakel tussen Nederland en die Voortrekkers." (Ulrich Gerhard Lauts; the Link between Holland and the Voortrekkers) *Historical Studies*, I (May 1940), II (July-October 1940).

Potgieter, F. J. "Die vestiging van die Blanke in Transvaal (1837-86) met spesiale verwysing na die verhouding tussen die mens en die omgewing." (The Settlement of the Whites in the Transvaal (1837-86) with Special Reference to the Relation between Man and His Environment) *A-J v SAG*, XXI (1958).

Reynecke, G. J. "Utrecht in die Geskiedenis van die Transvaal tot 1877." (Utrecht in the History of the Transvaal to 1877) *A-J v SAG*, XX (1958).

Schutte, C. E. G. "Dr. John Philip's Observations regarding the Hottentots of South Africa." *A-J v SAG*, III (1940).

Spies, F. J. du Toit. "Bloedrivier: 'n ondersoek na die werklike feite." (Blood River: An Investigation into the Actual Facts) *Standpunte*, XVII (October 1963).

————. "Die herinneringe van J. H. Hatting, soos opgeteken deur G. A. Ode." (The Reminiscences of J. H. Hatting, as Recorded by G. A. Ode) *Historia*, IV (September 1959).

————. "Die herinneringe van Voortrekker P. M. Fouche." (The Reminiscences of the Voortrekker, P. M. Fouche) *Historia*, V (June 1960).

————. "Herinneringe van Voortrekkers soos opgeteken deur G. A. Ode." (Reminiscences of Voortrekkers as Recorded by G. A. Ode) *Historia*, IV (December 1959); V (March 1960).

Thompson, Leonard M. "Afrikaner Nationalist Historiography and the Policy of Apartheid." *Journal of African History*, III (1962).

van den Berghe, Pierre L. "Some Trends in Unpublished Social Science Research in South Africa." *International Social Science Journal*, XIV (1962).

van der Poel, Jean. "Basutoland as a Factor in South African Politics, 1858-1870." *A-J v SAG*, IV (1941).

van Jaarsveld, F. A., Van Wijk, T., Muller, C. F. J., and Scholtz, G. D. "Die hervertolking van ons geskiedenis." (The Reinterpretation of Our History) *Communications*, XIX (1963).

————. "Die Afrikaner se Geskiedsbeeld." (The Afrikaner's View of History) *Mededelings van die Universiteit van Suid Africa.* Pretoria, VI (1958).

————. "Die Ontstaansgeskiedenis van van die begrippe Voortrekker en Groot Trek." (The History of the Origin of the Concepts "Voortrekker" and "Great Trek") *Hertzog-Annale Jahrbuch,* II (December 1955).

————. "Ou en nuwe wee in die Suid-Afrikaanse Geskiedskrywing." (Old and New Methods in South Afrikan History Writing) *Mededelings van die Universiteit van Suid Afrika.* Pretoria, Series A, No. 16 (1960).

van Schoor, M. C. E. "Die nasionale en politieke bewuswording van die Afrikaner in migrasie en sy ontluiking in Transgariep tot 1854." (The Growth of the National and Political Consciousness of the Afrikaner in Migration and Its Unfolding in Transorangia to 1854) *A-J v SAG,* XXVI (1963).

van der Vyver, W. B. "Die Geskiedenis van die Stellenbose Gemeente, 1800-1830." (The History of the Stellenbosch Congregation, 1800-1830) *A-J v SAG,* XX (1958).

van Winter, P. J. "Voortrekkers en trekboeren in de geschiedenis van Zuid-Afrika." (Voortrekkers and Trekboers in the History of South Africa) *De Gids,* (1938). Reprinted in *Verkenning en Onderzoek* (Groningen: J. B. Wolters, 1965.

Venter, Willem Adriaan. "Die geskiedenis van die Nederduitse Gereformeerde gemeente, Bloemfontein, gedurende die pioniersjare, 1848-1880." (The History of the Dutch Reformed Congregation (N.G.K.) of Bloemfontein during the Pioneer Years, 1848-1880) *A-J v SAG,* XXV (1962).

Wichmann, F. A. F. "Die wordingsgeskiedenis van die Zuid-Afrikaansche Republiek, 1838-1860." (The Genesis of the South African Republic, 1838-1860) *A-J v SAG,* IV (1941).

Wilson, Monica. "Recent Research on Race Relations." *International Social Science Journal,* XIII (1961).

Yorkshire Post. "England and the Boers." September 18, 19, October 2, 1889.

Published Studies

Adamaster (pseud.). *White Man Boss: Footsteps to the South African Volk Republic.* London: Victor Gollancz, 1950.

Agar-Hamilton, J. A. I. *Native Policy of the Voortrekkers.* Cape Town: Maskew-Miller, 1928.

Allport, Gordon. *The Nature of Prejudice.* Garden City, NY: Doubleday, Anchor Books, 1958.

Amery, Leopold Stennett, ed. *The Times History of the War in South Africa.* 6 vols. London: Sampson, Low, and Co., 1900-1903.

Aylward, A. *The Transvaal of Today.* Edinburgh, London: W. Blackwood and Sons, 1878.

Badenhorst, F. G. *Die Rassevraagstuk, veral betreffende Suid-Afrika, in die lig van die Gereformeerde Ethiek.* (The Race Question, Especially Related to South Africa, in the Light of the Reformed Ethic) Amsterdam: N. V. Noord Hollandsche Uitgewers, 1939.

Baird, Henry. *History of the Rise of Huguenots in France.* 2 vols. New York: Scribner's Sons, 1879.

——. *The Huguenots and Henry of Navarre.* 2 vols. New York: Charles Scribner's Sons, 1886.

——. *The Huguenots and the Revocation of the Edict of Nantes.* 2 vols. New York: Charles Scribner's Sons, 1895.

Benson, Mary. *South Africa, the Struggle for a Birthright.* Baltimore: Penguin, 1966.

Beyers, Coenraad. *Die Kaapse Patriotte, 1779-1791.* (The Cape Patriots, 1779-1791) Cape Town: Juta and Kie, 1929. Revised 1966.

Bezuidenhout, C. P. *Die Geschiedenis van het Afrikaansche Geslacht van 1688 tot 1882.* (The History of the Afrikaner People from 1688 to 1882) Bloemfontein: Borckenhagen, 1883.

Biéler, André. *La pensée économique et sociale de Calvin.* (The Social and Economic Thought of Calvin) Geneva: George and Co., 1961.

Bixler, Raymond Walter. *Anglo-German Imperialism in South Africa, 1880-1900.* Baltimore: Warwick and York, 1932.

Bliss, Edwin Munsell. *A Concise History of Missions.* New York: Revell, 1897.

Bosman, I. D., et al. *Voortrekker-gedenkboek van die Universiteit van Pretoria.* (Voortrekker Commemorative Issue of the University of Pretoria) Pretoria, 1939.

Botha, Colin Graham. *Collected Works.* 3 vols. Cape Town: C. Struik, 1962.

——. *The French Refugees at the Cape.* Cape Town: Cape Times, 1919.

——. *General History and Social Life of the Cape of Good Hope.* 3 vols. Cape Town: C. Struik, 1962.

——. *Social Life in the Cape Colony in the 18th Century.* Cape Town: Juta and Co., 1926.

Botha, P. R. *Die staatkundige ontwikkeling van die S. A. R. onder Kruger en Leyds: Transvaal 1844-1899.* (Constitutional Development of the S. A. R. under Kruger and Leyds: Transvaal 1844-1899) Amsterdam, 1926.

Breytenbach, J. H. *Die Tweede Vryheidsoorlog.* (The Second War for Freedom) 2 vols. Cape Town: Nasionale Pers, 1948.

Brookes, Edgar H. *The City of God and the Politics of Crisis.* London: Oxford University Press, 1960.

————. *The History of Native Policy in South Africa from 1830 to the Present Day.* Cape Town: Nasionale Pers, 1924.

Brookes, Edgar H., and Vandenbosch, Amry. *The City of God and the City of Man in Africa.* Lexington: University of Kentucky Press, 1964.

Brown, Douglas. *Against the World: Attitudes of White South Africa.* Garden City, NY: Doubleday, 1968.

Bunting, Brian. *The Rise of the South African Reich.* Baltimore: Penguin Books, 1964.

Burger, A. J. V., ed. *Worsteljare: herinneringe van ds. A. P. Burger, veldprediker by die republikeinse magte tydens die Tweede Vryheidsoorlog.* (Years of Struggle: Reminiscences of the Rev. A. P. Burger, Chaplain to the Republican Forces during the Anglo-Boer War) Cape Town: Nasionale Pers, 1936.

Cachet, Frans Lion. *De Worstelstrijd der Transvaalers aan het Volk van Nederland Verhaald.* (The Time of Struggle of the Transvaalers as Told to the People of the Netherlands) Amsterdam and Pretoria: Hoveker and Wormser, 1882.

Cachet, J. Lion. *Gedenkboek der Gereformeerde Kerk van Zuid Zfrika.* (Memorial Book of the Reformed Church (G.K.) of South Africa) Potchefstroom: A. H. Koomans, 1909.

Calpin, G. H. *The South African Way of Life.* London: William Heinemann, 1953.

Carter, Gwendolyn M. *The Politics of Inequality: South Africa since 1948.* New York: Praeger, 1958.

Carter, Thomas Fortescue. *A Narrative of the Boer War, Its Causes and Results.* London: John MacQueen, 1896.

Cloete, Henry. *Five Lectures on the Emigration of the Dutch Farmers.* Cape Town: 1856.

Coetzee, Abel. *Die opkoms van die Afrikaanse kultuur-gedagte aan die Rand, 1886-1936.* (The Growth of Afrikaans Culture on the Rand, 1886-1936) Johannesburg: Afrikaans Pers, 1936.

Coetzee, J. Albert. *Dorsland Trekkers (1874-1910)*. Potchefstroom: Dirk Pons and Co., n.d.

————. *Politieke Groepering in de wording van die Afrikanernasie*. (Political Groups in the Origin of the Afrikaner Nation) Johannesburg: Voortrekkerpers, 1941.

Colenbrander, H. T. *De Afkomst der Boeren*. (The Descent of the Boers) Amsterdam: Het Algemeen Nederlandsch Verbond, 1902.

Davenport, Thomas Rodney Hope. *The Afrikaner Bond, 1880-1900*. London: Oxford University Press, 1966.

deGruchy, John W. *The Church Struggle in South Africa*. Grand Rapids, MI: Eerdmans, 1979.

Dehérain, H. *L'Expansion des Boers au XIXe siécle*. (The Expansion of the Boers in the Nineteenth Century) Paris: 1905.

de Kiewiet, Cornelis W. *The Anatomy of South African Misery*. London: Oxford University Press, 1956.

————. *British Colonial Policy and the South African Republics, 1848-1878*. London: 1929.

————. *The Imperial Factor in South Africa*. Cambridge: 1937.

de Klerk, P. J. S. *Kerk en sending in Suid-Afrika*. (Church and Mission in South Africa) Amsterdam: H. A. van Bottenburg, 1923.

deKlerk, William Abraham. *The Puritans in Africa: A Story of Afrikanerdom*. London: R. Collings, 1975.

de Kok, K. J. *Empires of the Veld; Being Fragments of Unwritten History of the Two Late Boer Republics*. Durban: 1904.

Doob, Leonard W. *Patriotism and Nationalism: Their Psychological Foundations*. New Haven: Yale University Press, 1964.

Dowey, Edward A., Jr. *The Knowledge of God in Calvin's Theology*. New York: Columbia University Press, 1952.

Dracopoli, J. L. *Sir Andries Stockenstrom, 1792-1864*. Cape Town: A. A. Balkema, 1969.

Dreyer, Andries. *Die Voortrekkers en hul kerk*. (The Voortrekkers and Their Church) Cape Town: Nasionale Pers, 1932.

————. *Die Kaapse Kerk en die Groot Trek*. (The Cape Church and the Great Trek) Cape Town: Van de Sandt de Villiers, 1929.

————. *De Strijd onzer vaderen tegen het liberalisme*. (The Fight of Our Fathers against Liberalism) Cape Town: Dusseau, 1898.

Ducasse, André. *Guerre des Camisards: Le résistance Huguenote sous Louis XIV.* (The War of the Camisards: The Huguenot Resistance under Louis XIV) Paris: Libraire Hachette, 1946.

du Plessis, C. N. J., and Hofmeyr, N. J. *Uit de geschiedenis van de Zuid-Afrikaansche Republiek en van de Afrikaanders.* (From the History of the South African Republic and of the Afrikaners) Amsterdam: 1898.

du Plessis, J. *A History of Christian Missions in South Africa.* London: Longmans, Green and Co., 1911.

————. *The Life of Andrew Murray of South Africa.* London: Marshall Bros., 1919.

du Preez, A. B. *Inside the South African Crucible.* Cape Town: H.A.U.M., 1959.

du Toit, Jacob Daniel. *Rev. Stephanus Jacobus du Toit.* Paarl: Drukpers Maatschappij, 1917.

du Toit, S. *Die Gereformeerde Kerk in Suid-Afrika, 1859-1959.* (The Reformed Church (G.K.) in South Africa, 1859-1959) General Synod of the Gereformeerde Kerk in South Africa, n.d.

du Toit, S. J. *Die Geskiedenis van ons Land in die Taal van ons Volk.* (The History of Our Land in the Language of Our People) Paarl: 1877.

Edwards, Isobel Eirlys. *The 1820 Settlers in South Africa.* London: Longmans, Green and Co., 1934.

————. *Towards Emancipation: A Study in South African Slavery.* Cardiff: 1942.

Elphick, Richard. *Kraal and Castle: Khoikhoi and the Founding of White South Africa.* New Haven: Yale University Press, 1977.

Elphick, Richard, and Giliomee, Hermann. *The Shaping of South African Society, 1652-1820.* Cape Town: Longmans Penguin Southern Africa, 1979.

Engelbrecht, S. P. *Geskiedenis van die Nederduits en Hervormde Kerk van Afrika, 1842-1942.* (History of the Dutch Reformed Churches (N.G.K. and N.H.K.) of Africa, 1842-1942) Pretoria: J. H. de Bussy, 1936.

————. *Die Kaapse Predikante van die Sewentiende en Agtiende Eeuw.* (The Cape Ministers of the Seventeenth and Eighteen Centuries) Cape Town: H.A.U.M., 1952.

————. *Die Nederduitsch Hervormde Gemeente Potchefstroom, 1842-1942.* (The Dutch Reformed Congregation at Potchefstroom, 1842-1942) Pretoria: J. H. de Bussy, n.d.

————. *Die Nederduitsch Hervormde Kerk van Gemeente Rustenburg, 1850-1950.* (The Dutch Reformed Church of the Community of Rustenburg, 1850-1950) Kerkraad of the South African Republic, n.d.

————. *Thomas François Burgers: 'n Lewenskets.* (Thomas Francis Burgers: A Life Sketch) Pretoria: J. H. de Bussy, 1933.

Fitzpatrick, J. P. *The Transvaal from Within.* New York: Frederick A. Stokes, 1899.

Fouché, Leo. *Die Evolutie van die Trekboer.* (The Evolution of the Trekboer) Pretoria: Volkstem Drukkery, 1909.

Froude, J. A. *"Oceana," or England and Her Colonies.* London: Longmans, Green and Co., 1886.

Galbraith, John. *Reluctant Empire: British Policy on the South African Frontier, 1834-1854.* Berkeley and Los Angeles: University of California Press, 1963.

Garvin, James Louis. *The Life of Joseph Chamberlain.* 4 vols. London: Macmillan, 1932-1934.

Geertz, Clifford. *The Interpretation of Cultures.* New York: Basic Books, 1973.

Gerdener, Gustav Bernhard August. *Ons kerk in die Transgariep: geskiedenis van die Ned. Geref. Kerke in Natal, Vrystaat en Transvaal.* (Our Church in Trans-Orange: History of the Dutch Reformed Church (N.G.K.) in Natal, Free State and Transvaal) Cape Town: Nasionale Pers, 1934.

————. *Sarel Cilliers, die Vader van Dingaansdag: lewenskets van die kerkvader van der Voortrekkers.* (Sarel Cilliers, the Father of Dingaan's Day: A Life Sketch of the Church Leader of the Voortrekkers) Pretoria: J. L. Van Schaik, 1925.

Godée-Molsbergen, Everhardus Cornelis. *Geschiedenis van de Nederlandsch Oost-Indische compagnie en Nederlandsch Indie.* (History of the Dutch East Indian Company and the Dutch East Indies) Weltevreden: 1925.

————. *Tijdens de O. I. Compagnie.* In the Time of the East India Company) Amsterdam and Bandoeng: 1932, 1936.

Goiran, H. *Une Action créative de la mission protestante française au Sud de l'Afrique.* (A Creative Action of the French Protestant Mission in South Africa) Paris: Je Sers, 1931.

Gordon, C. T. *The Growth of Boer Opposition to Kruger, 1890-1895.* Cape Town: Oxford University Press, 1970.

Haarhoff, T. J., and van den Heeber, C. N. *The Achievement of Afrikaanse.* South African News Agency, n.d.

Haggard, H. Rider. *A History of the Transvaal.* New York: New Amsterdam Book Co., 1900.

Hancock, W. K. *Smuts: The Sanguine Years, 1870-1919.* Cambridge: Cambridge University Press, 1962.

Hanekom, T. N. *Helperus Ritzema van Lier: die lewensbeeld van 'n Kaapse Predikant uit die 18de Eeu.* (Helperus Ritzema van Lier: The Life Story of a Cape Minister of the 18th Century) Cape Town: N. G. Kerk Uitgewer, 1959.

————. *Die Liberale Rigting in Suid Afrika: 'n Kerk-historiese studie.* (The Liberal Tendency in South Africa: A Church History Study) Stellenbosch: Die Christen-Studentenvereniging-Maatskappy van Suid-Afrika, 1951.

Hexham, Irving. *The Irony of Apartheid: The Struggle for National Independence of Afrikaner Calvinism against British Imperialism.* New York and Toronto: Edwin Mellen Press, 1981.

Hinchliff, Peter. *The Anglican Church in South Africa.* London: Darton, Longman and Todd, 1963.

Hockly, H. E. *The Story of the British Settlers of 1820 in South Africa.* Cape Town: Juta and Co., 1948.

Hofmeyr, J. H. *The Life of Jan Hendrik Hofmeyr.* Cape Town: van de Sandt de villiers, 1913.

Hofmeyr, N. J. *De Afrikaner-Boer en de Jameson-inval.* (The Afrikaner Boer and the Jameson Raid) Cape Town: 1896.

Hofstede, H. J. *Geschiedenis van den Oranje-Vrystaat.* (The History of the Orange Free State) The Hague: 1876.

en "Hollander" (pseud.). *Toen en Thans: Mededeelingen en Beschouwingen omtrent de twee Republieken in Zuid Afrika.* (This and That: Information and Speculations about the Two Republics in South Africa) Cape Town: Dusseau, 1898.

Hunt, George L., ed. *Calvinism and the Politcal Order.* Philadelphia: Westminster Press, 1965.

Jooste, J. P. *Die Geskiedenis van die Gereformeerde Kerk in Suid-Afrika, 1859-1959.* (The History of the Reformed Church (G.K.) in South Africa, 1859-1959) Potchefstroom: 1958.

Juta, Marjorie. *The Pace of the Ox: The Life of Paul Kruger.* London: Constable and Co., 1937.

Kingsworth, G. W. *Africa South of the Sahara.* Cambridge: Cambridge University Press, 1962.

Knappert, L. *Geschiedenis der Nederlandsche Hervormde Kerk gedurende de 18e en 19e Eeuw.* (History of the Dutch Reformed Church during the Eighteenth and Nineteenth Centuries) Amsterdam: Meulenhoff and Co., 1912.

Koenker, Ernst B. *Secular Salvations: The Rites and Symbols of Political Religions.* Philadelphia: Fortress, 1965.

Kohn, Hans. *The Idea of Nationalism: A Study of its Origin and Background.* New York: Macmillan, 1946.
————. *Zion and the Jewish National Idea.* New York: D. van Nostrand Co., 1946.

Kotze, J. C. G. *Ras, Volk en Nasie, in terme van de Skrif.* (Race, Folk and Nation in Terms of the Scriptures) Stellenbosch: C. S. V. Uitgevers, 1961.

Krech, David, and Crutchfield, Richard S. *Theory and Problems of Social Psychology.* New York: McGraw-Hill, 1948.

Kriel, F. *Die lewe van Frans Lion Cachet met besondere toespitsing op sy betekenis vir die sending.* (The Life of Frans Lion Cachet, with Special Reference to His Significance for Mission Work) Pretoria: n.d.

Kruger, Barend Roedolph. *Die Ontstaan van die Gereformeerde Kerk in Suid-Afrika.* (The Origin of the Gereformeerde Kerk in South Africa) Pretoria: V. en R. Drukkery, 1957.

Krüger, D. W. *Paul Kruger.* 2 vols. Johannesburg: Dagbreek, 1961.

Kruger, Rayne. *Good-bye Dolly Gray: The Story of the Boer War.* London: Cassell, 1959.

Kuyper, Abraham. *Het Calvinisme oorsprong en waarborg onzer constitutionele Vryheden.* (The Calvinistic Origin and Guarantee of Our Constitutional Freedoms) Amsterdam: Höveker, 1873.

Lagdon, Godfrey. *The Basutos.* 2 vols. New York: Appleton, 1909.

Laurence, Perceval. *The Life of John Xavier Merriman.* London: Constable, 1930.

Lauts, Ulrich Gerhard. *De Kaapsche Landverhuizers of Neerlandsche Afstemmelingen in Zuid Afrika.* (The Cape Settlers of Dutch Lineage in South Africa) Leiden: 1842.

Leipoldt, C. Louis. *Jan van Riebeeck.* London: Longmans, Green and Co., 1936.

Le May, G. H. L. *British Supremacy in South Africa, 1899-1907.* Oxford: Oxford University Press, 1965.

Lemon, Anthony. *Apartheid: A Geography of Separation.* Farnborough, Hampshire: Saxon House, 1976.

Leyds, W. J. *The First Annexation of the Transvaal.* London: T. Fisher Unwin, 1906.

————. *Transvaal Surrounded.* London: T. Fisher Unwin, 1919.

Lindley, Augustus F. *Adamantia: The Truth about the South African Diamond Fields, or a Vindication of the Right of the Orange Free State to That Territory, and an Analysis of British Diplomacy.* London: Collingridge, 1873.

Lovell, Reginald, Ian. *The Struggle for South Africa, 1875-1899.* New York: Macmillan, 1934.

Lovett, Richard. *The History of the London Missionary Society.* 2 vols. London: Henry Frowde, 1899.

Luthuli, Albert. *Let My People Go.* New York: McGraw-Hill, 1962.

M'Carter, J. *The Dutch Reformed Church in South Africa.* Edinburgh: Inglis, 1869.

McCracken, J. L. *The Cape Parliament, 1854-1910.* Oxford: The Clarendon Press, 1967.

MacCrone, I. D. *Race Attitudes in South Africa.* London: Oxford University Press, 1937.

MacKenzie, W. Douglas. *John MacKenzie, South African Missionary and Statesman.* New York: A. C. Armstrong, 1902.

MacKeurtan, Graham. *The Cradle Days of Natal.* London: Longmans, Green and Co., 1930.

Macmillan, William Miller. *Bantu, Boer and Briton.* London: Faber and Gwyer, 1929; rev. Oxford: Clarendon, 1963.

————. *The Cape Colour Question.* London: Faber and Gwyer, 1927.

McNeill, John T., ed. *Calvin: Institutes of the Christian Religion.* 2 vols. Philadelphia: Westminster, 1960.

————. "Calvinism and European Politics in Historical Perspective." In George L. Hunt, ed., *Calvinism and the Political Order.* Philadelphia: Westminster, 1965.

————. "John Calvin on Civil Government." In George L. Hunt, ed., *Calvinism and the Political Order.* Philadelphia: Westminster, 1965.

Malherbe, Ernst G. *Education in South Africa, 1652-1922.* Cape Town: Juta and Co., 1925.

Mansergh, N. *South Africa, 1906-1961: The Price of Magnanimity.* London: George Allen and Unwin, 1962.

Marais, Barend Jacobus (Ben). *Colour, Unsolved Problem of the West.* Cape Town: Timmins, 1952.

————. *Two Faces of Africa.* Pietermaritzburg: Shuter and Shooter, 1964.

Marais, J. I. *Geschiedenis der Nederduits Gereformeerde Kerk in Zuid-Afrika tot op de Groote Trek.* (History of the Dutch Reformed Church (N.G.K.) in South Africa to the Great Trek) Stellenbosch: 1919.

Marais, Johannes Stephanus. *The Cape Coloured People, 1652-1937.* London: 1939; Johannesburg: 1957.

————. *The Fall of Kruger's Republic.* Oxford: Clarendon Press, 1961.

————. *Maynier and the First Boer Republic.* Cape Town: Maskew Miller, 1944.

Martineau, John. *Life and Letters of Frere.* 2 vols. London: J. Murray, 1895.

Maylam, Paul. *Rhodes, the Tswana, and the British: Colonialism, Collaboration and Conflict in the Bechuanaland Protectorate 1885-1899.* Westport, CT: Greenwood Press, 1980.

Mitchell, Lewis. *The Life and Times of the Right Honorable Cecil John Rhodes.* 2 vols. London: Mitchell Kennerley, 1910.

Molteno, James Tennant. *The Dominion of Afrikanerdom.* London: Methuen, 1923.

Moodie, T. Dunbar. *The Rise of Afrikanderdom: Power, Apartheid, and the Afrikaner Civil Religion.* Berkeley: University of California Press, 1975.

Moorrees, A. *Die Nederduitse Gereformeerde Kerk in Suid-Afrika, 1652-1873.* (The Dutch Reformed Church (N.G.K.) in South Africa, 1652-1873) Cape Town: S. A. Bybelvereniging, 1937.

Morley, John. *The Life of William Ewart Gladstone.* 3 vols. London: Macmillan, 1903.

Mosse, George L., ed. *Calvinism: Authoritarian or Democratic.* New York: Holt, Rinehart and Winston, 1957.

Muller, Christoffel Frederick Jacobus. *Die Britse owerheid en die Groot Trek.* (British Policy and the Great Trek) 2d ed. rev. Cape Town and Johannesburg: Juta and Kie, 1963.

Müller, Karl. *200 Jahre Brüdermission.* (200 Years of Missions of the Brethren) Herrnhut: Missions-Buchhandlung, 1931.

Munger, Edwin S. *Afrikaner and African Nationalism.* Oxford: Oxford University Press, 1967.

Murray, A. H. *The Political Philosophy of J. A. de Mist: A Study of Political Pluralism.* Cape Town: H.A.U.M., 1963.

Myrdal, Gunnar. *An American Dilemma.* 2 vols. New York: Harper, 1944.

Nathan, Manfred. *The Huguenots in South Africa.* Johannesburg: South Africa Central News Agency, 1939.

————. *The Voortrekkers of South Africa.* London: Gordon and Gotch, 1937.

Neame, L. E. *History of Apartheid.* London: Pall Mall Press, 1962.

Nepgen, C. C. *Die Sosiale gewete van die Afrikaanssprekendes.* (The Social Conscience of the Afrikaners) Stellenbosch: C. S. V., 1938.

Neumark, S. Daniel. *Economic Influences on the South African Frontier, 1652-1836.* Stanford, CA: Stanford University Press, 1957.

Ngubane, Jordan K. *An African Explains Apartheid.* New York: Praeger, 1963.

Niederberger, Oskar. *Kirche-Mission-Rasse, die Missions-auffassung der Niederlandsch-reformierten Kirchen von Sud-Afrika.* (Church-Mission-Race, the Hesitance for Missions in the Dutch Reformed Churches of South Africa) Schöneck-Beckenried, Switzerland: Die Administration der Neuen Zeitschrift für Missions-wissenschaft, 1959.

Oberholster, Jan Andries Stephanus. *Die Gereformeerde kerke onder die kruis in Suid-Afrika: hul ontstaan en ontwikkeling.* (The Reformed Churches under the Cross in South Africa: Their Origin and Development) Cape Town: H.A.U.M., 1956.

Oberholster, J. J., et al. *Die Nederduitse Gereformeerde Kerk in die Oranje Vrystaat.* (The Dutch Reformed Church (N.G.K.) in the Orange Free State) Bloemfontein, 1963.

Odendaal, Bernardus Johannes. *Die kerklike betrekkings tussen Suid-Afrika en Nederland (1652-1952), veral met betrekking tot die Ned. Geref. Kerk.* (Church Relations between South Africa and the Netherlands (1652-1952), with Special Reference to the Dutch Reformed Church (N.G.K.)) Franeker: 1957.

"O'Kulis" (pseud. for Willem Postma). *Doppers.* Bloemfontein: Nasionale Pers, 1918.

Omer-Cooper, J. D. *The Zulu Aftermath: A Nineteenth Century Revolution in Bantu Africa.* London: Longman, 1966, 1980.

Patterson, Sheila. *The Last Trek, A Study of the Boer People and the Afrikaner Nation.* London: Routledge and Kegan Paul, 1957.

Pells, E. G. *300 Years of Education in South Africa.* Cape Town: Juta and Co., 1954.

Pelzer, A. N. *Geskiedenis van die Suid-Afrikaanse Republiek.* Vol. 1. *Wordingsjare.* (The History of the South African Republic. Part I. Formative Years) Cape Town: 1950.

Philip, John. *Researches in South Africa: Illustrating the Civil, Moral, and Religious Condition of the Native Tribes; including Journals of the Author's Travels in the Interior; Together with Detailed Accounts of the Progress of the Christian Mission, Exhibiting the Influence of Christianity in Promoting Civilization.* 2 vols. London: Duncan, 1828.

Pirow, Oswald. *James Barry Munnik Hertzog.* London: George Allen and Unwin, n.d.

Postma, Dirk. *De Geschiedenis van de Stichting en Ontwikkeling der Gereformeerde Kerk in Zuid Afrika.* (The History of the Origin and Development of the Reformed Church (G.K.) in South Africa) Paarl: 1905.

Potgieter, Carel, and Theunissen, N. H. *Kommandant-General Hendrik Potgieter.* Johannesburg: Afrikaanse Pers, 1938.

Preller, Gustav S. *Andries Pretorius: Lewensbeskrywing van die Voortrekker Kommandant-General.* (Andries Pretorius: Life Story of the Voortrekker Commander-General) Johannesburg: Afrikaans Pers, 1940.

———. *Day Dawn in South Africa.* Pretorius: Wallach, 1938.

———. *Piet Retief: Lewensgeskiedenis van die Grote Voortrekker.* (Piet Retief: Life History of the Great Voortrekker) Cape Town: 1906.

Pyrah, G. B. *Imperial Policy and South Africa, 1902-1910.* Oxford: Clarendon Press, 1955.

Reaman, G. Elmore. *The Trail of the Huguenots in Europe, the United States, South Africa and Canada.* London: Frederick Muller, 1964.

Regehr, Ernie. *Perceptions of Apartheid: The Church and Political Change in South Africa.* Scottdale, PA: Herald Press, 1979.

Reitsma, J., and Lindeboom, J. *Geschiedenis van de Hervorming en de Hervormde Kerk der Nederlanden.* (History of the Reformation and the Reformed Churches of the Netherlands) The Hague: Martinus Nijhoff, 1949.

Reitz, F. W., distributor. *A Century of Wrong.* London: "Review of Reviews" Office, 1900.

Rhoodie, N. J., and Venter, Herman J. *Die Apartheidsgedagte: 'n sosio-historiese uiteensetting van sy ontstaan en ontwikkeling.* (Apartheid: A Socio-historical Exposition of the Origin and Development of the Apartheid Idea) Cape Town: H.A.U.M., 1960.

Rivett-Carnac, Dorothy E. *Thus Came the English.* Cape Town: Timmins, 1961.

Roberts, Michael, and Trollip, A. E. G. *The South African Opposition, 1939-1945.* London: Longmans, 1947.

Schapera, I. *The Khoisan Peoples of South Africa: Bushmen and Hottentots.* London: Routledge, 1930.

Schmidt-Pretoria, Werner. *Der Kulturanteil des Deutschtums am Aufbau des Burenvolkes.* (The Cultural Contribution of the Germans on the Development of the Boer People) Hanover: Hahnsche, 1938.

Scholtz, Gert Daniel. *Die Geskiedenis van die Nederduitse Hervormde of Gereformeerde Kerk van Suid-Afrika.* (The History of the Dutch Reformed Church of South Africa) 2 vols. Cape Town: N. G. Kerk-Boekhandel, 1956.

————. *Die Ontwikkeling van die Politieke Denke van Die Afrikaner:* Vol. I, *1652-1806) Johannesburg: Voortrekkerpers, 1967.*

————. *President Johannes Henricus Brand, 1823-1888.* Johannesburg: Voortrekkerpers, 1957.

Schreiner, Theophilus Lyndall. *The Afrikander Bond and Other Causes of the War.* London: Spottiswoode, 1901.

Scobie, John, and Abercrombie, H. R. *The Rise and Fall of Krugerism.* London: William Heinemann, 1900.

Shepherd, George, Jr. *The Politics of African Nationalism.* New York: Praeger, 1962.

Smit, F. P. *Die staatsopvattinge van Paul Kruger.* (Political Conceptions of Paul Kruger) Pretoria: Van Schaik, 1951.

Smith, Edwin W. *The Life and Times of Daniel Lindley.* New York: Library Publishers, 1952.

Spies, F. J. du Toit. *Van ons Land Suid-Afrika.* (About Our Land of South Africa) Brugge: Voorland, 1947.

Spilhaus, M. Whiting. *The First South Africans.* Cape Town: Juta and Co., 1949.

————. *South Africa in the Making.* Wynberg: Juta and Co., 1966.

Spiro, Herbert J. *Politics in Africa: Prospects South of the Sahara.* Englewood Cliffs, NJ: Prentice-Hall, 1962.

Spoelstra, B. *Ons Volkslewe: Kultuur-Historiese Leesboek.* (Our Folk-Life: Cultural and Historical Readings) Pretoria: J. L. van Schaik, 1922.

Spoelstra, Bouke. *Die "Doppers" in Suid-Afrika, 1760-1899.* Cape Town: Nasionale Boekhandel, 1963.

Spoelstra, Coenraad. *Het Kerkelijk en Godsdienstig Leven der Boeren na den Grooten Trek.* (The Church and Religious Life of the Boers after the Great Trek) Kampen: J. H. Kok, 1915.

Stellenbosch. Various authors. Stellenbosch: Horton, 1929.

Stendahl, Krister. "The Called and the Chosen," in Anton Johnson Fridricksen, *et al.* *The Root of the Vine: Essays in Biblical Theology.* Westminster, Dacre Press, 1953.

Stone, John. *Colonist or Uitlander? A Study of the British Immigrant in South Africa.* Oxford: The Clarendon Press, 1973.

Stow, George W. *The Native Races of South Africa.* London: Swan Sonnenschein, 1905.

Thom, Hendrik Bernardus. *Die Geloftekerk en ander studies oor die Groot Trek.* (The Church of the Vow and Other Studies about the Great Trek) Cape Town: Nasionale Pers, 1949.

Thompson, Leonard M. *The Republic of South Africa.* Boston: Little, Brown, 1966.

————. *The Unification of South Africa, 1902-1910.* Oxford: Clarendon Press, 1960.

United Nations. *Report of the United Nations Commission on the Racial Situation in the Union of South Africa.* New York: General Assembly, Official Records: 8th Session, 1953.

Uys, Cornelis Janse. *In the Era of Shepstone, Being a Study of British Expansion in South Africa, 1842-1877.* Lovedale: 1933.

van Broekhuizen, H. D. *Die Wordingsgeskiedenis van die Hollandse Kerk in Suid Afrika, 1652-1804.* (The History of the Development of the Dutch Church in South Africa, 1652-1804) Pretoria: de Bussy, 1922.

van den Berghe, Pierre L. *South Africa: A Study in Conflict.* Middletown, CT: Wesleyan University Press, 1965.

van den Heever, C. M., and Pienaar, P. de V. *Kultuur-geskiedenis van die Afrikaner.* (Cultural History of the Afrikaners) 3 vols. Cape Town: Nasionale Pers, 1945-1947.

van der Merwe, N. J. *Marthinus Theunis Steyn: 'n Lewensbeskrywing.* (Marthinus Theunis Steyn: A Life-Story) 2 vols. Cape Town: Nasionale Pers, 1921.

van der Merwe, P. J. *Die noordwaartse beweging van die boere voor die Groot Trek (1770-1842).* (The Northward Movement of the Boers before the Great Trek 1770-1842) The Hague: Van Slokum, 1937.

————. *Die trekboer in die geskiedenis van die Kaapkolonie (1657-1842).* (The Migrant Farmer in the History of the Cape Colony 1657-1842) Cape Town: Nasionale Pers, 1938.

————. *Trek: studies oor die mobiliteit van die pioniers-bevolking aan die Kaap.* (Trek: Studies on the Mobility of the Pioneer Population at the Cape) Cape Town: Nasionale Pers, 1945.

van der Merwe, W. J. *The Development of Missionary Attitudes in the Dutch Reformed Church in South Africa.* Cape Town: Nasionale Pers, 1936.

van der Poel, Jean. *The Jameson Raid.* London: Oxford University Press, 1951.

————. *Railway and Customs Policies in South Africa, 1885-1910.* London: Longmans, Green and Co., 1933.

van der Vyver, Gert Christoffel Petrus. *Professor Dirk Postma.* Potchefstroom: Pro Rege Pers, 1958.

van der Walt, A. J. H. *Die Ausdehnung der Kolonie am Kap der Guten Hoffnung, 1770-1779: Eine historisch-ökonomische Untersuchung uber das Werden und Wesen des Pionierlebens im 18 Jahrhundert.* (The Expansion of the Colony at the Cape of Good Hope, 1770-1779: A Historical and Economic Study of the Development and Character of Pioneer Life in the Eighteenth Century) Berlin: Ebering, 1928.

van Jaarsveld, Floris Albertus. *Die Afrikaner en sy Geskiedenis.* (The Afrikaner and His History) Cape Town: Nasionale Boekhandel, 1959.

————. *Die Beeld van die Groot Trek in die Suid-Afrikaanse Geskiedskrywing, 1843-1899.* (The Symbol of the Great Trek in South African History Writing, 1843-1899) Pretoria: University of South Africa, 1963.

————. *Die eenheidstrewe van die Republikeinse Afrikaners: I. Pionierhartstogte (1836-1864).* (The Attempts at Union among the Republican Afrikaners: I. Pioneer's Passion 1836-1864) Johannesburg: Impala Opvoedkundige Diens, 1951.

————. *The Afrikaner's Interpretation of South African History.* Cape Town: Simondium, 1964.

————. *The Awakening of Afrikaner Nationalism, 1868-1881.* Cape Town: Human and Rousseau, 1961.

van Oordt, J. F. *Paul Kruger en die Opkomst der Zuid-Afrikaansche Republiek.* (Paul Kruger and the Origin of the South African Republic) Amsterdam: Jacques Dusseau, 1898.

van Oordt, J. W. G. *Slagtersnek: een bladzijde uit de voorgeschiedenis der Zuid Afrikaansche Republiek.* (Slagters Nek: A Page from the Early History of the South African Republic) Amsterdam: de Bussy, 1897.

van Pittius, E. F. W. Gey. *Staatsopvattings van die Voortrekkers en die Boere.* (Constitutional Concepts of the Voortrekkers and the Boers) Pretoria: 1941.

van Rensburg, Patrick. *Guilty Land*. London: Praeger, 1962.

Vatcher, William Henry. *White Laager: The Rise of Afrikaner National-ism*. New York: Praeger, 1965.

Voigt, J. C. *Fifty Years of the History of the Republic in South Africa, 1795-1845*. 2 vols. London: 1899.

Vorster, Jacobus Daniel. *Die kerkregtelike ontwikkeling van die Kaapse Kerk onder die Kompanjie, 1652-1792*. (The Development of Canon Law in the Cape Church under the Company, 1652-1792) Potchef-stroom, 1956.

Walker, Eric A. *The Frontier Tradition in South Africa*. London: Oxford University Press, 1930.

————. *The Great Trek*. London: Adam and Charles Black, 1960.

————. *Lord de Villiers and His Times: South Africa, 1842-1914*. London: Constable and Co., 1925.

Wallace, Ronald S. *Calvin's Doctrine of the Christian Life*. Grand Rapids, MI: Eerdmans, 1961.

Walton, Edgar Harris. *The Inner History of the National Convention of South Africa*. Cape Town: T. M. Maskew Miller, 1912.

Weibach, J. D., and du Plessis, C. J. N. *Geschiedenis van de emigranten-Boeren en van den vrijheidsoorlog*. (History of the Emigrant Boers and of the War of Independence) Cape Town: Saul Soloman and Co., 1882.

Welsh, David. *The Roots of Segregation: Native Policy in Colonial Natal, 1845-1910*. London: Oxford University Press, 1971.

Wieringa, P. A. C. *De Oudste Boeren-Republieken Graaff-Reinet en Zwel-lendam van 1775-1806*. (The Oldest Boer-Republics, Graaff-Reinet and Swellendam, 1775-1806) The Hague: Marthinus Nijhoff, 1921.

William, Gardner Fred. *The Diamond Mines of South Africa*. New York: Macmillan, 1902.

Wolmarans, A. D. W. *Kerkhistoriese Feiten I: Bijdrage tot de Kennis van de Geschiedenis der Ned. Herv. Kerk in Zuid Afrika*. (Church History Facts I: Contributions to the Knowledge of the History of the Dutch Reformed Church in South Africa) Pretoria: J. H. de Bussy, n.d.

————. *Kerkhistoriese Feiten II: Antwoord op "Een Terugblik" van Ds. H. S. Bosman*. (Church History Facts II: Answer to "a Retrospect" of Dr. H. S. Bosman) Pretoria: Commissie de Algemene Kerkvergadering van de Ned. herv. Kerk van Afrika, n.d.

Theses and Dissertations

Badenhorst, W. J. "Die geskiedenis van die Nederduits Gereformeerde Kerk in die Transvaal, 1842-1885." (The History of the Dutch Reformed Church (N.G.K.) in the Transvaal, 1842-1885) D. Litt. thesis, Potchefstroom University, 1951.

Barnard, A. "Die groei en ontwikkeling van plattelandse onderwys in Transvaal, 1836-1934." (The Growth and Development of Rural Education in the Transvaal, 1836-1934) Master's thesis, University of Pretoria, 1935.

Beyers, C. J. "Die Kaapkolonie en die Jameson-inval." (The Cape Colony and the Jameson Raid) Master's thesis, University of Stellenbosch, 1951.

Booyens, Bunyan. "Die Verhouding tussen Kerk en Staat aan die Kaap in die tyd van die Kompanjie, 1652-1795." (The Relation between Church and State at the Cape in the Time of the Company, 1652-1795) Master's thesis, University of Stellenbosch, 1946.

Botha, Gerhardus Petrus. "Enkele Vergestaltinge van die Afrikaanse Lewensopvatting in die Gang van drie Eeuw Geskiedenis." (A Few Impressions of the Afrikaner Conception of Life in the Process of Three Centuries of History) Master's thesis, University of Pretoria, 1958.

Boucher, M. "The Frontier and Religion: A Comparative Study of the United States of America and South Africa in the First Half of the Nineteenth Century." Master's thesis, University of South Africa, 1966.

Butler, Jeffrey. "The Liberal Party and South Africa, 1895-1902." Ph.D. dissertation, Oxford University, 1962.

Buys, M. H. "Vroegste nie-amptelike bronne van die Groot Trek: 'n studie van enkele negentiende-eeuse bronne in die historiografie van die Groot Trek." (The Earliest Nonofficial Sources on the Great Trek: A Study of a Few Nineteenth Century Sources in the Historiography of the Great Trek) Master's thesis, University of Pretoria, 1964.

Coetzee, Andrea Gerardus. "Die beleid van president Kruger, 1897-1899, met betrekking tot die onafhanklikheid van Transvaal." (The Policy of President Kruger, 1897-1899, in relation to the Independence of the Transvaal) Master's thesis, University of South Africa, 1940.

du Plessis, J. H. O. "Die onstaan van politieke partye in die Kaapkolonie tot 1885." (The Rise of Political Parties in the Cape Colony to 1885) Master's thesis, University of South Africa, 1939.

du Toit, Hendrik Daniel Alphonso. "Predikers en hul prediking in die Nederduits Gereformeerde Kerk van Suid-Afrika, 1652-1860." (Preachers and Their Preaching in the Dutch Reformed Church

(N.G.K.) of South Africa, 1652-1860) 3 vols. D.D. thesis, University of Pretoria, 1947.

Goodfellow, C. F. "The Policy of South African Confederation, 1870-81." Ph.D. thesis, Cambridge University, 1961.

Heyneke, C. R. "Boere-reaksie teen die anneksasie van die Transvaal, 1877-1880." (The Reaction of the Boers to the Annexation of the Transvaal, 1877-1880) Master's thesis, University of the Witwatersrand, 1961.

Hooker, M. A. "The Place of Bishop J. W. Colenso in the History of South Africa." 2 vols. Ph.D. thesis, University of the Witwatersrand, 1953.

Jooste, J. P. "Die Verhouding tussen Kerk en Staat aan die Kaap tot die helfte van die 19de eeu." (The Relation between Church and State at the Cape to the Middle of the Nineteenth Century) D.D. thesis, University of South Africa, 1946.

Juta, C. J. "Aspects of Afrikaner Nationalism (1900-1964)" Ph.D. thesis, University of Natal, Pietermaritzburg, 1967.

Kemp, Bernard Harley. "Johan William Colenbrander: A History of His Times and the People and Events with Which He Was Associated, 1879-1896." 2 vols. Ph.D. dissertation, University of Natal, Pietermaritzburg, 1962.

Kotze, C. R. "Die owerheidsbeleid teenoor die Afrikaners (1806-1820)." (Government Policy toward the Afrikaners 1806-1820) D.Phil. thesis, University of Stellenbosch, 1958.

Mulder, Cornelius Petrus. "Die invloed het die Bybel gehad op die ontstaan van die Afrikaanse Volkskarakter." (The Influence of the Bible on the Origin of Afrikaner Folk Character) Ph.D. thesis, University of the Witwatersrand, 1956.

Naudé, Jan Daniel. "Paul Kruger en die eerste anneksasie van die Transvaal, 1877-1881." (Paul Kruger and the First Annexation of the Transvaal) Master's thesis, University of South Africa, 1937.

Nel, J. J. A. "Die verhouding tussen staat en kerk (Kaapkolonie, 1652-1910)." The Relation between Church and State (Cape Colony, 1652-1910) Master's thesis, University of South Africa, 1935.

Raum, J. W. "The Development of the Coloured Community in Genadendal under the Influence of the Missionaries of the Unitas Fratrum, 1792-1892." Master's thesis, University of Cape Town, 1953.

Sass, F. W. "The Influence of the Church of Scotland on the Dutch Reformed Church in South Africa." Ph.D. thesis, Edinburgh, 1956.

Schreuder, J. D. "Die opvoedkundige bedrywighede van die Morawiese Broederkerk onder die Kleurlinge in Suid-Afrika, 1737-1743 (en) 1792-1950; 'n histories-kritiese studie." (The Educational Activities of the

Church of the Moravian Brethren among the Coloureds in South Africa, 1737-1743, 1792-1950; a Historico-critical Study)   Ed.D. thesis, the University of Potchefstroom, 1951.

Schutte, Jan Harm Thomas. "Die kulturele eenwording van die Boere in die republieke, 1854-1877." (The Cultural Union of the Boers in the Republics, 1854-1877) Master's thesis, University of Pretoria, 1944.

Strauss, S. "Beriggewing in *De Volksstem* en *The Star* gedurende die tydperk 1896 tot 1899 oor gebeurteniss wat gelei het tot die Tweede Vryheidsoorlog 1899-1902: 'n kritiese metodologiese analise." (Reporting in *De Volksstem* and *The Star* during the Period 1896-1899 in Connection with Events Which Led to the Anglo-Boer War: A Critical Methodological Analysis)   Master's thesis, University of Pretoria, 1964.

Uys, C. J. "The Life and Letters of Sir Theophilus Shepstone with Special Reference to His Annexation of the South African Republic in 1877." D.Lit. thesis, University of South Africa, 1930.

Vorster, Jacobus Daniel. "Die Kerk en Kerkregering van die Voortrekkers." (The Church and Church Organization of the Voortrekkers) Master's thesis, University of South Africa, 1944.

Index

About the Author

J. ALTON TEMPLIN is Professor of Historical Theology and Church History at the Iliff School of Theology. He is the author of *Methodist and Evangelical United Brethren Churches in the Rockies, 1859-1977*, and numerous articles appearing in the *Iliff Review, Church History, Encyclopedia of World Methodism,* and *Mennonite Quarterly Review*.